THE RESCUE OF STREETCAR 304

THE RESCUE OF
STREETCAR 304

A NAVY PILOT'S FORTY HOURS ON THE RUN IN LAOS

KENNY WAYNE FIELDS

NAVAL INSTITUTE PRESS

Annapolis, Maryland

Naval Institute Press
291 Wood Road
Annapolis, MD 21402

Library of Congress Cataloging-in-Publication Data

Fields, Kenny Wayne, 1940–
The rescue of Streetcar 304 : a Navy pilot's forty hours on the run in
Laos / Kenny Wayne Fields.
    p. cm.
Includes index.
ISBN-13: 978-1-59114-272-0 (alk. paper)
ISBN-10: 1-59114-272-5 (alk. paper)
1. Vietnam War, 1961–1975—Search and rescue operations—Laos.
2. United States. Navy—Search and rescue operations.   3. Vietnam
War, 1961–1975—Aerial operations, American.   4. Vietnam War,
1961–1975—Personal narratives, American.   5. Fields, Kenny
Wayne, 1940–   I. Title.
DS559.8.S4F54 2007
959.704'3092—dc22

2007000508

Printed in the United States of America on acid-free paper ⊗

14 13 12 11 10 09 08 07   9 8 7 6 5 4 3

Dedicated to my heroes,
the pilots and aircrew of the
Jolly, Sandy, Nail, Spad, Sidewinder, and fast-mover
planes, without whose valiant efforts
I would not be alive today.

And to my wonderful wife
for her fortitude during my ordeal
and her unwavering support
throughout the remainder of my naval career
—and beyond.

CONTENTS

ACKNOWLEDGMENTS

Most of the primary participants in my rescue are mentioned throughout the text and identified by name in the epilogue, but the additional men listed below were all involved as "slow movers" in an actual rescue attempt, down low, "in the weeds." I will not list the hundred or so "fast-mover" pilots who, one bomb run after another for hours at a time, pushed the envelope and released their bombs well below the minimum safe release altitude, and well below the norm for weather conditions. They knocked out countless AAA guns and enemy troops to clear the path for the slow movers. Suffice it to say, "Shit hot bombing," fighter pukes! To the Crown crews, thanks for always being there when I needed someone to talk with. And to the four mysterious strafing A-1s on 1 June, thanks for buying me more time.

I also thank George J. Marrett for his persistence that I write this book, and for his advice when I finally did.

NAIL PILOT: Capt. Lee Bergeman.

SPAD PILOTS: Maj. James Reeves, Maj. Don Dineen, Maj. William Constantine, and Capt. John Hayes.

SANDY PILOTS: Maj. D. Brock Foster, Maj. Charley Kuhlman, Maj. Glede Vaughn, Maj. Charles Flynn, Capt. Gene McCormack, and Capt. Ed Conley.

JOLLY CREWS: Maj. Louis Yuhas, SSgt. Coy Calhoun, SSgt. Peter Harding, Capt. Henry Conant, Capt. Glen Lintner, SSgt. Raymond Price, A1C Ember Curry, Maj. Ed Russell, Maj. Milton Washington, SSgt. Bernard Grau, Sgt. J. T. Lombard, Capt. James H. Platt, Maj. Paul Reagan, A1C Narcisco Otero, Maj. Dale Oderman, Maj. Dale Weeden, SSgt. Carl Warmack, Sgt. Jules Smith, Capt. Harry Walker, Maj. Dean Williams, SSgt. Haril Thacker, SSgt. Don Beasley, Capt. James Oliver, Sgt. Kelly Day, and Capt. Edward Heft.

AUTHOR'S NOTE

The American public had a negative opinion about the Vietnam War from its very beginning, and that attitude never wavered. The war never evolved to one wherein soldiers, sailors, and airmen marched off to battle after a rousing parade along Main Street, and those who returned received minuscule "welcome home" celebrations. Nevertheless, as in all wars, heroes abounded. This is a factual account of the harrowing rescue of one pilot by airmen heroes. I don't attempt to persuade the reader about the merits of the war, and I don't try to justify whether we won or lost. I simply tell one remarkable story about heroes—their failed attempts at rescue and one miraculous save. I also pay homage to the secondary story about their wives and families enduring a nervous wait for good news. I believe the reader will come away with what I perceive to be one burning question after reading this story: What is one man's life worth? Is it worth the lives of many to save just one? And, if so, for what future purpose was that one life—mine—saved?

This was a difficult story to write because of the large number of participants, so I have narrowed them to a dozen or so for the sake of readability. Unfortunately, the names and events of many others will be skimmed over. As with any dramatic event wherein many are involved, the after-action accounts vary. I play judge and jury. I've written from the perspective that I gained during interviews of all primary participants, my vivid memories of the action, and Air Force after-action reports. A detailed radio time-log of voice conversations between airborne participants was invaluable in resolving differences of opinion as to what happened, and at what time. The log, a compilation of my memories, and my interviews became the basis for my described conversation between airborne participants. Additionally,

I have invoked an author's privilege and exercised certain liberties to describe some events and conversations in the manner and terminology I experienced as a naval officer and combat pilot.

One's mind can evoke abnormal behavior when under the stress of combat. Even though some events may seem far-fetched, this is a true depiction of the story.

PRELUDE

On 31 May 1968 I was piloting a combat-loaded Navy A-7 Corsair 2 jet near a river in central Laos. It was my first combat sortie off the aircraft carrier USS *America* (CVA-66). It was also the first day of combat operations for the ship since her commissioning.

I was under the control of an airborne forward air controller (FAC), call sign Nail 66, who was in only his fourth week of combat. He designated a target and I attacked it, but was shot down. This is the story about how I was shot down and how, three days later, I was miraculously rescued by heroic Air Force pilots from the midst of overwhelming enemy forces. It's also about how our wives and families dealt with their shock and grief back on the home front. It's a story about good, honorable men and women serving their country.

In late 1967 I was a pilot in a Navy A-7 attack squadron that was "working up" for an April 1968 combat deployment to the war zone in Vietnam, or WestPac as we Navy pilots called it. I and my squadron mates envied those who had already fought and proved their mettle. Navy pilots who had completed a WestPac tour in 1966 and 1967 returned with chests full of medals and spoke in glorified terms about how much good they had accomplished. Those pilots were treated royally by those of us yet to go. During our readiness training, my squadron pilots and I worked overtime to hone our skills because we also wanted to strike a mighty blow on behalf of our country and be known as "tigers."

A bit naïve at the time, I thought Vietnam was a war that the country supported and one in which I was eager to participate. But in January 1968, protest against the war became rampant throughout America. Even Dr. Spock, who had instructed many of us on how to raise our kids, was then advocating draft avoidance. Many young men burned their draft cards or defected. My morale, and that of most of my fellow squadron pilots, was seriously degraded by the perceived lack of support for our cause; so, the attitude of several of my fellow pilots began to change. The situation only worsened. In January 1968, the captain of USS *Pueblo* surrendered his crew and ship, and the North Vietnamese launched the massive Tet Offensive, which the press erroneously labeled a success for the enemy. In February, the news media gave daily accounts of the number of American soldiers killed. In one week alone, a record 543 soldiers were killed in action. In March, the decimation of the My Lai village caused great public consternation. In April, Martin Luther King Jr. was murdered and riots broke out across the land in protest, leaving cities in flames. Later that month, Robert Kennedy was also slain by a bullet. Soon, student protesters took over five buildings at Columbia University until police stormed in seven days later. On 3 May, as my squadron was on its way to Vietnam, the United States and North Vietnam began the Paris peace talks.

Our country was struggling and so indecisive about the war that several of my fellow pilots began to question and doubt the motives of our civilian leaders. And it bothered them that the general population was wavering. Some of the pilots privately decreed the war was not worth getting killed for. They would fight it, but would not press a bomb run if it placed them in serious harm's way. This war wasn't worth dying for, they argued. After listening to all sides, I decided I would follow our commander in chief's decree and fight the war as a just cause. I had no intent to do anything stupid, but I consciously decided that I would fly my missions as trained. I would earn my pay; but my decision and fortitude would soon be sorely tested.

Fifty-one days earlier, USS *America* had departed Norfolk, but our introduction to the war quickened in the last week of the voyage. Only four days before my first combat mission, *America* had been in port at Subic Bay Naval Station in the Philippines, where the air wing pilots attended a local-theater one-day training course named Jungle Escape and Survival Training (JEST). It was a follow-on to the cold weather survival training course we had attended prior to leaving the states. During JEST, we learned how to return in the event we were shot down in the jungles of Vietnam. The carrier then set sail on the 850-mile trip to Yankee Station. On the day before my first combat mission, my wingman and I were the first squadron pilots to actually man planes in a combat scenario when we stood the five-minute alert. We sat in our A-7s ready to launch an armed retaliation within five minutes in the event of an enemy boat attack against the carrier.

Finally, USS *America* reached an "on-line" position in the South China Sea's northern half of the Gulf of Tonkin, just south of the Chinese Hainan Island. The carrier's location was a hypothetical position referred to as Yankee Station, versus Dixie Station—a location off the South Vietnam coast. Yankee Station was approximately fifty miles off the North Vietnam coastline between Danang and Hanoi and situated such that our air wing could strike North Vietnam or provide support in South Vietnam, northern Laos, and northern Cambodia.

My squadron, VA-82 (nicknamed Marauders), was a key member of Carrier Air Wing 6 aboard *America*. The VA stood for "Navy light attack squadron," and our primary mission was to attack enemy ground targets with bombs, guns, and air-to-ground missiles. VA-82 had a complement of twelve A-7As and twenty pilots. The A-7A was then brand new to the fleet, replacing the older A-4 Sky Hawks, and *America* was the second aircraft carrier to deploy with them aboard.

The A-7 is 46 feet long with a wingspan of 38 feet, and gives the impression of a short stovepipe when viewed from the side. It's a shorter but stouter version of the F-8 Crusader fighter. It has a single 11,500-pound-thrust, turbo-fan jet engine capable of powering the plane to a sea-level speed around a maximum of 575 knots. A single pilot sits in a wide, comfortable cockpit at the front of the plane directly over an abnormally large engine intake. The pilot controls the plane with one hand on a control stick for turns, climbs, descents, bomb pickle, and gun trigger; his other hand is used for a push/pull throttle lever on the left console. The Corsair is faster and can carry two to three times more ordnance than the A-4 and for a longer distance or time. It has six pylon wing stations and two fuselage-mounted missile racks, plus two internal fuselage 20mm guns. A normal combat load in Vietnam would consist of twelve general-purpose 500-pound bombs, two AIM-9 Sidewinder air-to-air missiles, and six hundred rounds of 20mm bullets.

I was then a twenty-seven-year-old full lieutenant with six years of naval aviation service. In my first fleet squadron, I was a Bombardier/Navigator (BN) in the A-3B and accumulated eight hundred flight hours and a hundred and fifty landings aboard three different aircraft carriers. After that, I commenced pilot training and there met my future wingman. Iceman was a twenty-three-year-old lieutenant (junior grade) without any aircraft carrier experience.

After fifteen months of training and initial carrier qualification landings aboard USS *Wasp*, we earned our Wings of Gold. Because of our superior flight training grades, we both were rewarded with orders to the first operational east coast A-7 squadron. Once there, our A-7 training culminated with carrier qualification aboard USS *Lexington*.

Iceman and I went on to accumulate six hundred hours of total First Pilot time before our first combat mission, and four hundred hours of those were specifically in the A-7. Our inexperience was not unusual, as normally a squadron like ours would have twenty pilots, and only maybe five of those might have previous carrier experience. In VA-82, the nine most senior pilots had previous operational carrier tours as pilots, and the other eleven pilots—including me—were nuggets, or first-tour pilots.

With twenty pilots, that meant the squadron would pair us up as ten sections of two planes each. A "section" is a two-plane formation and the two pilots train and fly together to become thoroughly familiar with each other's voice, flight tactics, and pilot peculiarities. Since I was number ten in seniority, I would be the lowest-ranked section leader and my section was the only one composed of nuggets. Iceman and I would be under close scrutiny on our first combat flight, so we felt the pressure to "do it right, don't screw up."

On the first day of combat, my section was given the very lowest priority for mission assignment time. Initially we were scheduled to launch at 11 A.M., but we were scratched because of aircraft availability problems. The same thing happened again at 1:30 P.M., but finally we launched on the last cycle of the day at 4 P.M.

The commander of the air group wing (CAG, which rhymes with bag) had deliberately devised a schedule that should've made our first combat day safer. Normally, the Navy carriers had the responsibility to conduct missions solely over North Vietnam. CAG's plan called for the air wing to gain combat experience for a few days over South Vietnam since it was a lower threat area. And, although we'd trained to carry twelve 500-pound bombs on each A-7, CAG's plan dictated on our first combat mission we'd carry only six, plus six hundred rounds of 20mm bullets, and two Sidewinder air-to-air missiles. Six fewer bombs would allow more airspeed and better handling capability.

It was a good plan—except someone forgot to get the word to all the Air Force players.

In addition to my A-7, several Air Force planes played a key role in this story, and I would like to describe them up front.

My initial FAC, Nail 66, piloted an O-2A Skymaster that was a military version of the civilian Cessna 337. It had a high wing and two piston-driven propeller engines. One was forward, on the nose of the plane, and the other was on the rear of the fuselage. One would pull like a tractor while the other pushed. The two engines made it faster and safer than the older single-engine O-1, so it was used for operations over the more hostile areas of Laos. The plane was 38 feet long with a maximum speed of 200 miles per hour, a cruising speed of 145 miles per hour, and a maximum altitude of 19,000 feet. For weapons, it was configured with four wing-pylons and each could hold a single rocket pod which contained seven 2.75-in. diameter white, phosphorous-smoke rockets. The FAC used them to mark targets for bomber attacks, and Nail 66 carried two pods for a total of fourteen rockets.

"Sandy" was the call sign of the U.S. Air Force A-1 plane that escorted and defended the "Jolly" Green HH-3 rescue helicopter. The A-1 Sky Raider was a World War II vintage, single-engine, single-pilot, propeller-driven plane and the only prop fighter then left in the Air Force inventory. It had been chosen for the mission of pilot rescue because it could remain on station for four to five hours. It carried much more ordnance than any jet fighter, and even though slower, it could absorb more gunfire hits and still continue its mission. It might reach 400 knots airspeed in a lengthy vertical dive, but generally all missions were below 240 knots. Flying lower and slower meant the pilot could more easily identify the downed pilot's location and made it compatible to escort the slow-flying rescue Jollys.

The A-1 could carry nearly eight thousand pounds of ordnance plus internal guns, and that was a lot more than any two tactical jets could carry. It had a total of fifteen weapons stations on its wings and belly. On a normal Sandy mission, it would carry two extra external fuel tanks, two pods of LAU-19 rockets, two pods of 2.75-in. "Willy Pete" marker rockets, two white phosphorous bombs, two canisters of anti-personnel cluster bombs (CBUs), and four 20mm guns with two hundred rounds each. It was a dump truck. Its humongous radial engine had a ridiculous number of cylinders—eighteen—requiring gallons and gallons of oil to fill its tank. Then it would promptly leak most of the black stuff away on its next flight. Its two propellers were each a staggering fourteen feet in diameter, so the short, stubby plane was a brute, and everything about it was stout. And it made a lot of noise.

"Jolly" was the call sign of the U.S. Air Force HH-3 rescue helicopter. Each Jolly had a four-man crew which consisted of the pilot rescue crew commander (RCC), co-pilot, flight engineer/door gunner (FE), and a para-rescueman/door gunner (PJ). Each Jolly Green had a long, rescue-hoist cable that could be lowered to a downed pilot, and then motor-driven to lift him to the helo. It had two engines, one forward and one aft, and each rotor blade measured a massive sixty-two feet long. Jolly's normal rescue speed was about a hundred knots and its only armament were two M-60 door guns, fired out of open side doors on each side.

Two Sandy A-1s would always escort one Jolly for a pilot pick-up. Normal procedure was to have a second Jolly in a safe back-up orbit several miles away under the protective wing of two more Sandys in the event the first group encountered any problems. The Jolly crews were very proud and their unit's motto was "So That Others Might Live." Some individual Jolly pilots also carried calling cards that read CALL US IF YOU NEED A PICK-UP. Their creed and pride would be sorely tested while rescuing me.

One further explanation will help ease the reader through the story. The letters "AAA" refer to antiaircraft artillery gunfire and should be read as "triple A" each time the reader sees them. The letters "mm" refer to millimeter, and the larger the number, the larger the gun. Enough pilot talk . . . now, to the story.

Chapter 1

FAREWELL, MY LOVE

Nail 66 was stunned. A Navy A-7 jet, call sign Streetcar 304, had just dropped four 500-pound bombs on top of Nail's target smoke and was now climbing off the target. Suddenly, Nail saw a large section of one of its wings blown off by enemy AAA, and now the A-7 was falling downward at a high rate of speed while tumbling end over end.

Nail realized instantly the A-7 had been hit by at least one of the many firing AAA guns and was severely damaged, out of control, and at such a low altitude that recovery was impossible before it impacted the ground. The jet was dangerously near the minimum altitude for safe ejection.

Nail 66 shouted into his mike, "You're hit, you're hit. Eject, eject."

With those riveting words, the saga of Streetcar 304 began on 31 May 1968. It lasted for forty hours. The valor and skill of many pilots, a few Navy but mostly Air Force, would be given the ultimate test as they tried to rescue me. Seven planes would be lost, or severely damaged. Eight air crewmen would require rescue. One rescue pilot would end up as a prisoner of war (POW) . . . and I was nearly killed by friendly fire time and time again.

I'm Streetcar 304. Fifty-two days ago in Jacksonville, Florida, I was one day away from bidding farewell to my six-weeks'-pregnant wife, Shirley, my five-year-old son, Terry, and three-year-old daughter, Kim. Tomorrow my squadron would depart on a combat deployment scheduled to keep me at sea for the next eight months, my third major cruise since I entered the Navy six years earlier.

We were a seasoned Navy husband and wife team by then, and quite ready for anything. However, at the last moment, we learned Shirley was pregnant with our third child, and now I wasn't sure. But Shirley was content with the news, took it calmly, and thought it no big deal. After all, she'd been pregnant with our second child and gave birth while I was on a previous deployment to the Mediterranean, so she was now an experienced, salty Navy wife. "What better time than an eight-month cruise to carry another child," she said. "And hopefully you'll be home before the baby arrives."

Shirley and I were playful but nervous on my last day home. The day passed too quickly. After dinner I played with the kids, and it was nearly nine before we got them in bed—and I had yet to pack my sea bags.

Shirley helped me; still, it was nearly midnight when we finished. Not much time left. I had a 5 A.M. brief for a twelve-plane flight to join USS *America* at sea, and would have to get up at 4 A.M. in order to make the brief.

After preparing for bed, I placed my sea bags next to the front door, placed my flight suit and boots next to the bed, and then plopped down on it. About then, Shirley turned the bedroom light off and went to disrobe. As I lay there in wild anticipation of her return, I reflected on our life together.

My mind wandered back to the day I first saw her leading cheers at our college, Lincoln Memorial University (LMU). She and another cheerleader bounced out on the stage to teach us freshmen the school fight song. Right away, Cupid pierced my heart with an arrow, and it was love at first sight for me. I couldn't take my eyes off her. She was a five-foot, two-inch cutie with short, dark hair and hazel eyes, and so perky. But it took a long, agonizing year to win her love from other competitors.

We had been married a little over six years now and I'd come to appreciate all her many other attributes. She was intelligent and had been valedictorian of her high school class. During college, she worked to help pay her tuition, but still maintained an impressive work/study ethic and received outstanding grades. She was always quick to point out when I wasn't devoting enough time to my classes, and without that support I might not have qualified for the Navy flight program. We married my senior year, and after college she was a superb teacher until becoming a mother. After I joined the Navy, she worked as a volunteer with the Navy Aid Society helping many sailors and their families when they were in desperate financial need or had other family emergencies. Later, at another air station, she was president of the Officer's Wives' Club. She could've had her own successful career if she'd wanted, but she chose to support my career and our children. She was a dedicated mother and wonderful wife, and never complained about the large load she had to bear when I was at sea. *I'm a lucky man,* I thought.

Suddenly, my chain of thought was broken by the squeaky bathroom door, and its opening cast a narrow beam of light into the room. I peered through the soft glow as Shirley turned and pushed the door to a cracked position. Then, she turned and faced the bed.

Beautiful, I thought. She was draped in my favorite black teddy and with the light behind her, it seemed to make her translucent. For just a moment, I was able to see through the teddy and admire the curves of her vivacious, petite body. The image caused my blood to warm. I hadn't touched her yet, but just the sight of her breasts and thighs, partially covered by the black teddy, made me want to leap from the bed and wrap her in my arms. Her head turned toward the bed and our eyes made contact. Hers sparkled, and then her tiny, shy smile made my blood pressure accelerate even more. Just a tiny smile . . . but it completed the package. I needed her one last time before I risked my life in combat, and hoped she wanted me too. She did, and it was well past midnight when we fell asleep.

Why is the telephone ringing? I glanced at the clock . . . 5 A.M.! Heck, I overslept. I was in a daze, and couldn't comprehend how I'd overslept for one of the biggest days of my life. Had I forgotten to activate the alarm, or did I turn it off and go back to sleep? I couldn't remember, and at this point it didn't matter. I was already late for my brief.

I picked up the phone, knowing it was someone from the squadron. "This is Kenny. I overslept."

The voice on the other end was my wingie, Iceman, who I had intentionally scheduled to be the squadron duty officer (SDO). He hadn't been as fortunate to sleep with his wife on our last night ashore because I, as the senior watch officer, had assigned him to be on duty. I wasn't his favorite person right now.

"Kenny, Skipper (the commanding officer) is starting his brief, so you're late. Is everything okay?"

"I overslept, Fred. Cover for me and I'll be there in twenty minutes."

I was now fully awake. What a knucklehead I was. My ass would be grass if I didn't make it to the squadron ASAP. I didn't know whether to chuckle with delight at the brazenness of my late night fling, or cry in disbelief at my stupidity for not having some type of double alarm.

Shirley was now sitting up in bed, but still too groggy to realize what had happened. I turned and gave her a quick peck on the lips.

"Babe, we overslept. Don't know what happened, but that was Fred, and I'm late for the brief. I've got to haul ass."

Then I noticed how tempting she looked. Last night, she'd been hot and sexy. Right now, she was cute. She was staring through little slits as she tried hard to focus on me. Every hair was out of place from where my hands had stroked it hours earlier. Her black teddy was swooping off one shoulder and one breast was nearly uncovered. I had an insatiable urge to caress her, but darn it, there was no time.

"But I meant to fix you some breakfast before you left," she said. I smiled. Oh, she was so cute. . . . She was barely awake, but looked so ravishing. Resisting the urge to caress her one more time, I quickly sprang to the floor.

In less than a minute I had brushed my teeth, climbed into my flight suit and boots, and had my arm around Shirley leading her to the front door. I grabbed my bags and turned to face her.

"Sorry, Babe, no time to dilly dally. . . . Take care of yourself and the kids, and write me often. Don't worry. I'll make it back okay. Love you, Babe."

Then I noticed she was still half asleep and slightly confused. I wasn't sure she'd heard all I had just said, but I had to go. I dropped the bags, gave her a firm hug, and kissed her gently.

After backing out of the driveway, I turned to look once more. Shirley was still standing in the open doorway, her hand cradled over her mouth as if she was sobbing. A tear formed in one of my eyes. I almost stopped the car, but instead stomped the gas pedal and flew toward the base. As I roared away, a feeling of remorse engulfed me. I was off to fight a frapping war that few civilians cared a rat's ass about, and I might never see Shirley again. Quickly, I uttered a brief prayer out loud.

"God, be with Shirley if I don't return to her embrace." On second thought, "God, please be with me too."

Upon entering the Ready Room, I glanced at the duty clock on the wall and noted I was twenty-five minutes late. Iceman was seated at the SDO's desk in the rear of the room and was taking notes as Skipper briefed the ten other pilots. Iceman glanced toward me with really cold eyes, then gave me a condescending look. I couldn't blame him: I was his section leader and had already let him down before we even cranked our engines. There was a little humor in the situation, but it was obvious that he didn't see it. Must be his Naval Academy training. . . .

"Everyone but you was early, Kenny, so they started without you."

I whispered, "Is Skipper ticked off at me?"

Before Iceman answered, the Skipper's eyes stared at me. "That concludes my brief. Are there any questions?"

Had he intentionally said that for my sake, or was he unaware I had just arrived? Then I noticed the serious looks on the faces of my fellow pilots. No idle chitchat, no barbs being thrown at each other, no bragging about the night before—it was like they had game faces on, and ones I'd never seen on most of them. On second thought, they all appeared really sad. It was a gloomy sight.

I asked Iceman if he had good notes on the brief, hoping he'd give me a quickie brief without my having to beg for it. He said it was a standard carrier landing brief and gave me the radio frequency we'd use with the aircraft carrier.

Subsequent takeoff and flight to USS *America* was made without any further foul-ups, my first combat cruise was now underway, and I'd already screwed up once.

Seven weeks passed between then and today. News to and from home had been slow, and Shirley wasn't sure when our first day of combat would occur. The longer I was gone, the more apprehensive she became. Four days ago, I called her from the Cubi Point Air Station in the Philippines but, due to security reasons, I couldn't give her our schedule. I told her we were finally going on line and shifting into high gear. She understood my code and knew our first day of combat was nigh, and now she'd have to steel herself for a normal thirty-day line period. She knew it was likely that one pilot from our squadron might not be around at the end of this line period. Percentages don't normally lie.

Chapter 2

FIRST DAY OF COMBAT

A catapult fired with a bang on the flight deck above, violently shook my stateroom bunk, and jarred me awake. It was 6 A.M. in the Gulf of Tonkin and planes were launching for the air wing's first strike of the day. After tossing and turning most of the night, the first cat shot of the day was the final straw that made me give up trying to sleep. Who wouldn't have trouble sleeping? For the past six years, I'd trained for combat and now it was here. This was the big day.

My brief was scheduled for 9 A.M. so I put on my flight clothes that today consisted of Marine issue cotton fatigues, green T-shirt, green long-sleeve shirt, and green trousers, versus a standard Navy-issue Nomex flight suit. CAG had contended we couldn't wear the fatigues since they weren't flame retardant like the Nomex, but Skipper stood fast and refused to relent unless CAG gave him a direct order to switch back to the Nomex. He never did, and I'm sure CAG would have Skipper's ass for breakfast if one of us was burned in an accident.

Before leaving my room, I removed my Geneva Convention card and two ten-dollar bills from my billfold and placed them inside my trouser pocket. Later, I would put them in my survival vest, as the money would come in handy if I were diverted to Danang for emergency reasons. I considered taking off my wedding band, but decided that might jinx me. If I were shot down, though, I would need to remove it before I encountered any enemy troops. Some of them were reported to have viciously ripped rings off the fingers of downed American pilots. If your finger was swollen, it might come off before the ring.

The ring reminded me of Shirley, and although I had just written her the night before, I felt an urge to write her again this morning. I wanted to tell her I was going to fly my first combat sortie today, and tell her one more time that I loved her.

"Dear Shirley, Today, we'll fly over the beach for the first time. I'm feeling good physically and mentally and ready to go and I'll do my best to make you proud. You and the kids are on my mind and I love you all very much. Thanks for marrying me and putting up with the separation. I know it's hard on you but I have faith in your ability to keep the family together. Keep the letters coming as I can't wait to hear you're okay. Love you Babe."

I stuffed the letter in an airmail envelope and wrote the word FREE where a stamp was normally placed. In the combat zone we didn't have to buy stamps. I now had about an hour before my first brief, but I wanted to be in the Ready Room to listen to the comments of the first batch of pilots returning from combat.

The air in the Ready Room reeked of cigarette smoke from the pilots who had briefed earlier. Oh, how I hated that stale odor. . . . There were twenty-six brown, leather seats lying back like dental chairs and I plopped down in the one closest to the SDO without thinking about protocol. The SDO quickly reminded me of my mistake. "Not so fast Kenny," he said. "Watch whose seat you're sitting in." I looked back at the blue head-cover on the seat and saw the words "Commanding Officer" emblazoned in gold.

I moved back a row and settled into my private chair, then took a sip of coffee. Crap . . . it was again tainted from when the ship's fresh water supply got an accidental mix of jet fuel. I recalled what our squadron Flight Surgeon had told us after we made a plea for his assistance in getting fresher water for the coffee.

"The little bit of fuel you drink in the coffee won't hurt you and will just ensure your bowels don't get stopped up."

"Right, Quack," joked one of the junior officers (J.O.s). "Your medical specialty was gynecology but now you're our flight surgeon. You're a real expert in the body's plumbing so we should believe you, right?" Laughter erupted.

Right on schedule, Skipper's flight walked in bantering about their first combat sortie, a mud hole for a target and a waste of bombs. Skipper had been the first squadron pilot to fly into combat that morning and he saw that I was listening intently. He smiled at me. "Don't worry Kenny, there's not much going on over the beach today, and your flight should be a piece of cake. Looks like all the good targets today have been grabbed by our Air 'Farce' buddies." He followed that with a folksy looking grin. "You know, I've never heard of a pilot getting shot down on his first mission. Have you, Kenny?"

"No sir." But I felt jinxed. It was like talking about a baseball no hitter before the game was over.

Iceman was a little more laid back, slept a little later, and arrived in the Ready Room just before brief time. That was not uncommon for him and other J.O.s as they always seemed to have a contest going on to determine who could sleep the longest in one stretch. The current squadron record was eighteen hours by a pilot from Arkansas.

A few minutes before 9 A.M., we sauntered down the passageway to Strike Ops and joined twenty-six other pilots and a few backseaters for the general air wing mission brief.

Our squadron Air Intelligence Officer (also called Spook) was the primary briefing officer, and right off the bat he gave the same story I had just heard from the returning pilots. "Gentlemen . . . today should be a piece of cake. Following the president's policy for the previous sixty days, you're still barred from flights over the northern part of Indian Country (North Vietnam)."

Normally, he would have briefed the location of recent enemy MIG fighter sightings, radar-controlled 85mm guns, active surface-to-air missile (SAM) sites, etc. Spook said we shouldn't have to worry about most of that today, as the air wing tasking for our launch called for the bombers to work with FACs in South Vietnam.

The senior Spook briefed that the A-7s should fly to the demilitarized zone (DMZ) and check in with Cricket, the airborne command and control plane for fighter target assignments. No intelligence could be given about the target area because Spook didn't know where we would end up. We were told to expect enemy fire in South Vietnam to mostly include automatic weapons but we would be safe, out of range, if we stayed above three thousand feet. Spooks from squadrons who had completed earlier deployments made it sound simple. "Bombing in South Vietnam is fun. You don't have to worry as much about getting shot down." In general, the brief was a big letdown; I had fully expected to know my exact target so I could brief Iceman on all facets of possible threats before we launched.

The "weather weenie guy" reiterated it was the beginning of monsoon season, so it would be quite warm in the afternoon with probable heavy rains before we returned to the ship. We were told to expect ninety degrees with an overnight low of only eighty, so we should drink plenty of water. Yeah, right, I thought. He was not the one who would be strapped into a seat in a small cockpit for two hours. If the urge to go happened, I would have to extract the family jewel thru two layers of clothing, a G-suit, and then a parachute torso harness just to take a pee through a small vacuum tube. Single-engine attack pilots don't load up on a lot of water before flight.

Then he briefed that the sky over South Vietnam and Laos was currently clear and the visibility was unlimited (CAVU), but he added, "Don't worry, the blue skies of morning will turn to gray stratus followed by certain cumulus with heavy, late afternoon rains. It'll be this way for months."

Then the Spook broke in. "One more thing . . . I've noticed that some of you tigers haven't filled out your personal authenticator cards as directed. Don't leave the room until you've verified we have a damn valid card in case one of you clowns gets shot down. And it wouldn't be a bad idea for everyone to review their individual cards to refresh your memory as to your answers."

I had filled mine out but stopped and asked the junior Spook to pull my card so I could review it. Maybe that was bad timing, as several fighter pilot pukes jeered as they walked by and wanted to know if the Corsair pilots planned on getting shot down.

"Listen, peckerhead. Attack pilots plan for all contingencies." I scanned my five answers but noticed that only one other pilot was doing so. That caused a cowardly blush as I recalled the old military phrase I'd heard so many guys say in war movies: "I have a feeling my number is up." I didn't, but was made to feel that way since the other pilots weren't reviewing their data. They probably thought I was scared. I wasn't, and in fact, felt very cavalier at the moment. My memory was poor so I wanted to review what my answers had been.

While walking back to the Ready Room, Iceman poked fun at my poor memory. I turned my head to confront him but continued to walk. "Iceman, I wish my memory was better so I could remember shit like all you smart-ass Naval Academy guys." Just then I felt a sharp pain and heard a crack as my leg hit a fricking knee-knocker. Damn it . . . now I had a fourth bruise on my shinbone. Get your mind back in the game, I thought.

Casually, the SDO asked what kind of target assignment we received from Strike Ops. Iceman's mouth twisted in a scowl. "Fly over the damn beach at the DMZ and then do whatever the damn Air Force tells us to do. What kind of war is this?" He then plopped in the chair right in front of the SDO—Skipper's chair—and I stood off to the side with my foot on the next pilot chair. What the heck. Every combat pilot deserved to sit in the Skipper's chair once. Then I commenced a cautious and long-winded brief. I rambled on and on.

"Iceman, my tactical call sign will be Streetcar 304 and yours will be Streetcar 307. (Streetcar was the squadron call sign and 304 was my plane.) Today we're loaded with six Mk-82 GPs (general-purpose, high-explosive, 500-pound bombs) that are mechanically fused to explode one delayed split-second after ground impact. Along with the bombs, we'll have our normal two Sidewinders, plus six hundred rounds of high-explosive 20 mike-mike. Make sure the bomb arming wires are attached at both ends. Make sure you set the day's IFF setting into the avionics panel during your walk-around inspection. Make damn sure you hold your hands high and in plain sight of the whole frapping world when the weapon safety pins are being pulled so the ordnance officer doesn't get pissed and so we don't accidentally fire a bullet or missile on the flight deck. Since we have live bombs today, get a positive count of the number of safety pins held up for your count after they are removed by the red-shirts. Count them . . . I don't want either one of us to risk our lives in a bomb run only to have a dud. And make sure you check the damn bomb-rack jettison switch to ensure it's positioned so all racks eject in the event you get a cold cat-shot (insufficient steam pressure) and need more speed to maintain flight."

Together, we computed our gross weight after taking into account the basic weight of the plane plus the ordnance and fuel load. Then I continued my brief.

"Since we have a lighter than normal bomb load today, the ship's captain won't have any problem giving us our necessary wind speed down the flight deck at launch. Be alert to any jet-engine blast on deck in front of your plane when your canopy is open. Close it at the first sign of taxiing planes since it could be blown past the canopy limit, break, and then your damn plane will be grounded. Don't push the limit and leave the canopy open too long just to stay cool. Taxi expeditiously but not over zealously. If you cock a nose wheel during taxi, you *will* suffer the air boss's wrath. And don't forget to put your flaps down prior to crossing the shuttle. Hit your brakes as soon as you feel the plane's nose drop when you ease over the shuttle. Once you're in position on the cat, be damn sure and check your flight control trim settings. After you run the engine to full power on the cat, take the time to really look at your instruments closely to verify all readings are within limits. If they aren't, and the plane is down, no longer safe to fly, do not, I repeated, do not try to give the cat officer a thumb's-down. Instead, nod your head side to side continuously while you transmit on the radio to the tower air boss, 'Suspend Cat Four.' And keep the throttle at military-rated thrust (MRT) until the cat officer steps in front of your wing and signals you to pull it back."

We then argued whether it was safer to apply throttle friction after going to MRT on the cat or to leave the friction off and just trust you could hold the throttle forward with your hand when the cat shot occurred. Afterward, I briefed "bingo" procedures in the event one of us had to divert to the beach at Danang for de-arming a hung bomb.

Next I briefed the landing traffic pattern and flight deck procedures following the arresting "trap" upon our return. "Keep your mask strapped on until the plane has all three tie downs on the wheel struts, and keep your helmet on with visor down until you clear the flight deck."

"Launch procedures will be standard, join-up will be standard. We'll fly at angels two-four till we hit the coastline at the DMZ and then we'll contact Cricket for our target assignments, which will most probably be in South Vietnam. After we're feet dry, Iceman, assume combat cruise position on my signal at six hundred feet in my rear quarter and I'll do some mild jinking at 360 knots airspeed on the way to the target. Don't forget to maintain a little extra speed around the target pattern to compensate for the bomb load. Better to be fast than slow," I reminded him. I could have gone on and on but Iceman stopped me.

"Damn it, Potato, we're ready. We've flown together so much you don't have to tell me all that shit over and over. I'm ready to go."

The SDO laughed and agreed I'd briefed enough. "Relax, Kenny," he said.

"Okay, but one last thing. Help me ensure we get the altitude of any mountains around our target from the FAC before we go hot on the bombs."

Then I had to get one more blurb in. "Iceman, let's be sharp today. Make a snappy clearing turn as soon as you clear the cat, okay?"

Iceman snarled again and gave me his most disgusted look. He took that last remark as an insult because he was a tiger around the boat and no one had to remind him to look sharp.

Just before "man planes" sounded over the ship's intercom (1MC), the maintenance chief walked in with bad news. Wouldn't you know it? The plane captains had grounded two of the scheduled four squadron planes for hydraulic leaks, and the flight deck officer had decreed there was insufficient time to move the bad birds and re-spot two more good birds. My wingie and I were the junior section so we were shoved back to the next launch at 1 P.M.

With time to kill, I scrounged through the side pocket of my chair and found a current copy of the *Stars & Stripes* newspaper. One of the lead stories that week concerned the latest weekly death toll in the Vietnam War. Just two weeks earlier, during the week of 11 May 1968, U.S. military forces lost 562 men killed in action, and the paper said that was the highest single weekly total since the commencement of the war.

"Hey, Iceman, according to *Stars & Bars*, the war is getting hotter over the beach. We're losing more men than ever."

He shot back at me. "You're not going to believe that propaganda, are you?"

He always had the attitude that he was smarter than me. He was, but I didn't like his pointing it out all the time. Iceman wanted to know why I was wasting my time on such inflated and erroneous war stories, and said I should instead study my pilot's bible, the Naval Air Training and Operating Procedures (NATOPS) manual. He had heard a rumor the weapons officer was going to give a pop quiz at the next all pilots meeting (APM). I ignored him, as he usually did me, and continued to read the red and white newspaper.

After a break for lunch, we again listened intently to more mission debriefs by returning squadron pilots. One of them stated bluntly that his flight had been a waste of time and bombs because the FAC had been unable to locate any worthwhile targets for his section. And they encountered no AAA.

We left the Ready Room and trekked again to Strike Ops for a second time, received the same brief as earlier, then returned to the Ready Room and reviewed portions of my earlier brief. We lost our planes for the second time that day, for some reason my wingie and I didn't even care to listen to. It was 2 P.M., the day was dragging on, and we were anxious to get a mission under our belts before the ship stood down for the day. The delay was starting to wear on us as there was only one more launch possibility for us. Soon we received word we were scheduled for the last launch, and that meant a third trip to Strike Ops.

Once back in the Ready Room, I asked if Iceman had checked his pistol to verify it was loaded. "Mine is, but I left one chamber empty for safety purposes," I said.

I got another scowl, and Iceman retorted, "Fiddlesticks, I have no intention of firing my gun at anybody because it'll mean certain death. I'll let them capture me before I fight it out with a pistol."

Finally, we went to the pilot's locker room to suit up. As we "strapped on," we didn't talk and stayed in our own little silent times of reflection. We both had suited up so many times during the past year of training that we didn't have to pay much attention to the process. It was automatic. Zip the green, nylon G-suit on, one leg at a time. Each zipper ran up from the ankle to the crotch and provided a snug fit. The G-suit would allow me to pull maximum G-force without blacking out. Then I placed a leg through the bottom hole of the torso harness, followed by the second. I now had a grayish-green, nylon bodysuit around my body from the waist up to the shoulders that would attach to the parachute once I was seated in the cockpit. It would help to evenly distribute an opening parachute shock in the event of a violent ejection. Next, I picked up the heavy survival vest and placed my right arm through one side. The floatation device was attached to the bottom half and made it quite heavy, so I swung mine around in order to get my left arm comfortably through. The oxygen mask dangled loosely from the front of the vest. Finally, we both were suited up in our forty pounds of flight gear, fully clad in green except for our white helmets.

"It's game time. Let's go wake 'em up, Iceman."

I saw a smirk, or maybe a half-smile, in return. Had Iceman actually smiled at me?

Chapter 3

PILOTS, MAN YOUR PLANES

F inally, it was time to man planes for mine and Iceman's first combat flight over the beach. We had more than proven ourselves during months of training flights and now it was time to prove we could do just as well under enemy fire.

We walked briskly up multiple ladders to the flight deck and passed many white-hats in the narrow passageways of the ship, and some of them offered kind, spirited words of encouragement. I hadn't expected that kind of emotion from the crew and found it exhilarating and proud to be a Navy pilot. It was a little like a football pre-game atmosphere. It had taken months of training to get me to this first combat flight; but, now I sensed that the five-thousand-man crew was rooting for me so I vowed to make the first bomb run a special one for them.

I walked through the last hatch onto a brightly lit flight deck and flinched. It felt like all the rays the sun could muster were spotlighting me. It was blinding because my eyes were adjusted to the ship's weak interior lighting. After lowering my sun visor, I marched toward my steed, as Iceman liked to call our planes. After only a few steps, the intense heat from the flight deck steel felt hot enough to melt the soles of my boots. Only yesterday, a plane captain told me he had lost a bet when an egg actually fried on the wing of a plane. A sweltering, radiating heat was rising from the deck and after only a few steps I had to raise the visor again. The heat vapors under the visor were worse than the sunlight. It was quiet on the deck and twenty pilots like me were parading toward planes amidst a beehive of activity as men in multi-colored shirts moved about preparing our jets for launch. I always liked this time as you could consistently count on hearing some good banter among the flight deck crew, but most of it was not something you could write home about. I tried to listen and take it all in. The atmosphere gave me the same adrenalin surge a player feels right before a big game. So, I stiffened my bearing and walked tall with a deliberate John Wayne swagger toward the gray and white A-7 with 304 painted on the side of the engine intake.

A brown-shirt appeared and my plane captain (PC) greeted me with a big smile before he spoke. "Sir, I gave your bird a special inspection today and it looks in great shape. Are you ready to sock it to 'em today?"

"It's a beautiful day son, and I'm ready to kick some ass. Practice is over. Today is game day. Would you want to go with me?"

Quickly, he turned, spit downwind, and retorted with a serious look. "No, sir. Not for all the tea in China." We both chuckled.

As I inspected the first rack of bombs, an aviation ordnanceman (AO) was there to greet me with a big smile and bulging chest. He reported that the last mechanical nose fuse and arming wire had just been inserted so all bombs were good to go. I had a special fondness for my PC, and for this particular AO. The two were consistently respectful, congenial, and seemed to always have a true concern for my safety. I was glad they were on my team. I asked the AO if anyone on the loading crew had popped a hernia yet from the heavy bombs. He just laughed and raised his arm to show his bulging biceps. "Not with arms like this," he said. Then he asked me to look at some words someone had inscribed in white chalk on one of my bombs. "This one's for you, Fonda!" I was impressed, and dutifully told him I'd find a special target for that one.

My PC followed me up to the cockpit. I leaned in and placed one hand on the ejection seat rocket de-arm handle (head-knocker). The twelve-inch piece of metal was correctly down and steadied me as I climbed in. Once in, I started to fasten my shoulder harness but the PC grabbed the Koch fittings, snapped them in place, and then pulled the two safety pins out of the ejection seat. He made a point to show them to me before he stowed them. "I'm glad I'm not going with you sir." He then stepped smartly to the flight deck and, as an afterthought, cupped his hands around his mouth and yelled, "Good luck, sir."

After placing my helmet on the windshield panel to allow the wind over the flight deck to cool me off, I performed my required sixty-item pre-start checklist. Toward the end, I felt the ship leaning a little to starboard, and felt the vibration as the props began to turn faster. The ship's captain had commenced a slight turn into the wind because he needed a little extra help from surface wind to put thirty knots of wind across the flight deck before the first F-4 fighter could launch. I got a whiff of moisture in the salty breeze, and it smelled fresh and invigorating after the Ready Room smoke and below-deck odors. I paused, and inhaled several large gulps.

Fifteen minutes before my scheduled launch, a voice blared out from the control tower (PriFly) for a standard pre-launch announcement. The same words were used on all aircraft carriers and always put a chill up and down my spine. It meant the game was about to begin.

The air boss gave his play-ball call: "Attention, all personnel on the flight deck. All non-essential personnel should clear the deck immediately. All other personnel should check for proper floatation and protective headgear. Check all chocks, re-check aircraft tie-downs, look for loose gear about the deck, and stand by to start the jets." Then, after a couple of seconds he shouted, "Start the jets."

I put my helmet on and tightened the chinstrap. Off to my left, a yellow-shirted flight deck director was twirling a finger of one raised hand as he pointed one finger of the other hand at me. "Start your engine." Behind me, I heard the increasing whine of the flight deck crew's engine starting unit (huffer) that would assist. I moved the throttle lever around the horn and tapped the ignition switch on the way forward to the start position. Within seconds, I heard the louder whine of my engine blocking out the huffer. I had a positive engine light off, confirmed by a thumb-up from the yellow-shirt. Just then some salt spray smacked me lightly in the face, so I knew the carrier was close to its launch speed.

Caustic fumes and a deafening roar hit me as fifteen other planes roared to life around me. Canopy down . . . now I could hear myself reading my take-off checklist out loud as I moved my hands systematically around the cockpit. After completion, I nodded toward the deck, and quickly a brown-shirt waved at me. My plane captain was standing forty-five degrees off to my left and we made eye contact. He was holding one palm out to indicate he was ready to verify smooth operation of the flight controls. First, he gave me a clenched fist in a circular motion to indicate I should wipe out the controls. I moved the control stick in a full circular motion and noted no binding. Then he raised his left arm parallel to the deck with his elbow at a ninety-degree bent position. He moved his arm to the left, and I moved the stick to the right. He gave a thumb-up to indicate the aileron control had moved the correct direction with full movement. We continued to check the ailerons, rudder, and vertical stabilizer to his satisfaction. He watched as my flaps moved up and down per his command. Finally, he knelt down and ensured no fluid was dripping from the plane. At the end, he gave me a thumb-up, stood erect, and popped me a salute to indicate I was good to go. I briskly nodded my head in return because I didn't salute anyone on the flight deck except the catapult officer (also called the Shooter).

I watched as the PC scurried beneath the nose of the plane to stand by and pull the chock when it was time to taxi. Once they saw my plane was good to go, the AO arming crew went to both wings and pulled the safety wires from my bombs and showed all six to me. I then made my advisory call to the air boss. "Boss, Streetcar 304 is Up. Gross weight is 34.1."

Almost immediately, movement to my right caught my attention and there stood another yellow-shirt director. They didn't take crap from any pilot. I made eye contact, nodded at him, and he returned it with an almost curt, arrogant nod. He had both arms vertical and crossed as a signal to hold my brakes. A chain gang had arrived to remove the heavy chains that were stretched from each of the three tire mounts to the flight deck, so I pushed firmly on the brakes. Then, in one motion, the yellow-shirt swept his hands down close to his body and flung them wide apart. The chains that had been holding the plane tightly were now removed. From now on, it was up to me to ensure the plane didn't move unless directed. My PC scooted out from under the nose and looked back at me as he ran across the deck with shoulders sagging from the weight of forty pounds of tie-down chains. He wasn't smiling.

Five minutes before launch, two fighters were taxied to mid-ship waist cats Three and Four. They would be shot off first so they could relieve the two F-4 fighters currently on barrier patrol (BARCAP) where they protected the fleet of ships at Yankee Station. I was parked with the tail of my plane sticking out over the water on the port side of the flight deck, and about a hundred feet behind the waist cat jet-blast deflector (JBD). As the F-4s increased power to taxi onto the final catapult spot, the huge, flat-walled JBDs had not yet been raised so the exhaust from the F-4 nozzles buffeted my plane. My A-7 started its version of a jitterbug as it tried to bounce down the flight deck.

The damn fighter jock was using way too much power for taxi. Must be a nugget who had little concern for those of us behind him. . . . One of the other planes must have been getting pushed around more than mine, as I heard a pilot key his radio mike button. "F-4 on waist cat, easy on the power or you're going to give some of us behind you a bath over the side."

A second voice chimed in. "Why is it the frapping fighter jocks act like they own the whole damn flight deck when all they do is fly around in circles while we attack studs blast the enemy?"

The buffeting and mention of going into the drink reminded me to arm my ejection seat. I flipped my headknocker up so I could eject at any time, even from the flight deck if it appeared I was being blown overboard. I had both elbows resting on the side rails and my feet clamped on the brakes as hard as I could push before the JBD behind the F-4 finally went up. The wind buffet ceased, only to be followed almost immediately by an instantaneous roar as the first F-4 went to MRT. A second later, a moderate boom occurred as his engine popped into afterburner. Nugget, for sure, I thought. It was daytime, and he was carrying no bombs, but he still lit his burner for launch and wasted fuel.

A yellow-shirt directed me to Cat One on the right side of the bow. The flight deck was a beehive of activity and it was always challenging to taxi a jet quickly and smoothly between all the obstacles on the way to the catapult position. Screw it up, and the air boss was on you in a flash. The process required smooth throttle control and meticulous nose-gear steering in order to align the jet on the shuttle of the cat. If you overshot that position, it was very embarrassing and required many men to push the A-7 backward since we had no reverse. I was proud when I made it to the cat in minimal time.

As I approached the cat shuttle, a green-shirt with white helmet appeared off my left wing carrying a small box with a Plexiglas front panel. I watched as the weight-board guy took his grease pencil and wrote some numbers on it that I could personally verify as my plane's gross weight for the cat settings. This number had to be correct for sufficient steam pressure settings, or I would receive a cold cat-shot, be too slow off the bow, then stall and crash. He walked closer and I looked down at him; his stance confirmed the ship now had a full thirty-knot wind down the deck. He tried once to stand still and hold the weight board so I could read it, but the wind against his back made him lose his footing and he skipped forward a few steps. His pant legs were flapping in the breeze like they would if they were held out the window of a fast moving car, and he again thrust his small Plexiglas board up so I could see the gross weight numbers. The numbers on the board read 34.1, so I gave him a thumb-up and then he turned and flashed the board at Shooter. I made my final taxi forward and felt the nose-gear bar drop into the cat shuttle. This was it . . . I was in position for launch, ready to be "shot."

An F-4 shot by off the waist cat. The plane settled lower off the end of the cat, just off to my left. Whoa, big boy, I thought. Little more back stick there . . . , and then his nose pitched too sharply upward as he over-corrected before finally leveling off. Now I was being directed to ease forward to take final tension on the launch bar, so I inched the throttle forward till I felt the nose slide into final position with a clunk.

A wave from the Shooter got my attention. He was off to my left and just a little forward and facing me. I could see his eyes were watching the men near my nose gear as they checked to ensure my plane was properly attached to the launch bar. Wisps of steam were floating upward from the cat and enveloping them. Then his eyes were looking right into mine, and he was staring as if he was trying to determine if he recognized my face. He didn't normally do that, so he must have realized that today was different from prior days. His arm waved in a circular motion to signal me to wipe out my controls again to be sure no one had left any tools that had jammed them. I moved the control stick left, then right, then up, and then down. His eyes followed and verified they were moving in the appropriate direction. He turned and looked down the catapult path and verified it was clear of men and obstruction. He looked back at me and gave me a raised arm and circular twirling motion signal for full throttle. I instantly jammed the throttle lever forward with my left arm and felt it bang against the forward stop. My left arm was locked into a fully extended position and my right arm was straight and braced with my hand loosely on the control stick. Quickly, I checked each of my instruments to verify I had maximum thrust, and that all system indicators were in the green, with no red lights. I was good to go. At that moment my legs were straining to exert maximum force against the brake pedals, but now I released the brakes. My plane was being held stationary at maximum thrust by only a little six-inch piece of metal called a holdback. Hopefully, it had been manufactured with the right tensile strength, because eleven thousand pounds of engine thrust were trying to shear it apart.

My eyes flicked back to Shooter's and I gave him a short, snappy salute to indicate he could fire when ready. Quickly, I snapped my head back, pressed it firmly against the headrest, and held it there. My head was now angled slightly upward and straight ahead. My eyes were riveted to the left as I watched Shooter. He would launch me as the bow was just beginning to ride an upward wave. His head turned left as he took a second quick look down the cat track to check for the swell of the ship's bow. Now, his right arm swung upward past his head and then downward toward the deck as he stepped forward with one leg toward the bow. His hand touched the deck, and a crewman at another station dropped his hands from the safety position over his head and pressed a button to fire the cat. A compressed steam force was released that exceeded the holdback strength and was calculated to give me the precise speed I needed to fly at the end of the shuttle run. I felt an impact against my back similar to a tackler hitting it firmly from the rear. Immediately, the plane shot forward and my body was thrust so tightly backward against the seat that it felt like I was glued to it, unable to move.

One thousand one, one thousand two, one . . . in less than three seconds I was at the end, had already traveled 120 feet, and my speed was up to 150 knots, but only about ten knots more than needed to keep from stalling. Normal take-off distance at a shore station would be about 5,500 feet versus the 120 feet today.

Near the end of the catapult, there was always one crewman who hunkered down in the catwalk to retrieve the shuttle that was used for the cat shot. Once my plane went by, he would dash out and perform his duty. Since day one aboard *America*, it had been my habit to always glance down at that guy as I shot by. Don't know why, but it was a habit. I usually saw his body from the waist up, with an expressionless face covered by dark goggles.

As I roared by today, I was pleasantly surprised when he gave me a broad smile and a thumbs-up signal. He timed it perfectly because I was by him in a flash.

About 4:10, the shuttle released me with a mild thump as I crossed the bow and I was airborne about seventy feet above the water. My eyes were glued to my instruments. I increased back stick pressure to twelve-degree nose up on the gyro while I reached to raise the landing gear with my left hand. Airspeed was good, and the radar altimeter showed eighty feet above the water. Quickly, I made a snappy fifteen-degree turn to the right to keep my jet wash from affecting other planes that would launch behind me. I felt the gear retracting and then felt a clunk as the doors closed. I glanced at the gauge and saw all three gear indicated up. At a hundred feet above the water and 185 knots, I then retracted my flaps. As they started to come up, the plane began its natural tendency to settle a little. As it did, I didn't try to counter it but instead allowed the plane to settle to fifty feet above the water—today the air boss wouldn't get on me for hot-dogging since I was on a combat flight. The plane was really accelerating fast now, even with four thousand pounds of ordnance.

Three miles ahead of the carrier, I snapped the nose up for a sharp, rapid climb to altitude, but I kept my airspeed at three hundred knots so my playmate, Iceman, could join me quickly. A thought hit me: This is the major league for pilots and I'm one shit-hot aviator. I'm flying a single piloted jet off the deck of a super aircraft carrier on the way to wreck havoc with the enemy. I'm on top of my game and I can make this plane do anything I want.

"Go get 'em, tiger," I yelled in my mask. "Hit a home run today." I was finally airborne and on my way to the beach. I was, at long last, about to realize a dream to support my country in combat. And I wanted to do well. I wanted to help win this frapping war.

Chapter **4**

FEET DRY, HELLO NAIL 66

arlier, at 3 P.M., a young Air Force FAC, call sign Nail 66, was getting ready for another combat mission from the Nakhon Phanom Royal Thailand Air Force Base which the American pilots affectionately called NKP. He'd been in country for about a month, had nineteen missions under his belt, and had received only one minor scare thus far. In fact, his flights had been fun. Just two days ago he had supported the troops at Khe Sanh where he directed an F-4 flight's bomb placement, so he felt his job was very rewarding. The young pilot had dreamed of combat since he was a small child and now he was fully involved and pleasantly surprised at how easy it had been. And for this much fun, they're also paying me extra combat pay, Nail 66 thought.

After suiting up, he grabbed his belted pistol holster and slung the holster strap over one shoulder and across his chest, bandolier style. Then he took off at a brisk walking pace toward the Tactical Unit Operations Center (TUOC) to be briefed on today's mission. It was a beautiful, sunny day, but it was hot and very humid. Within seconds he was sweating, but soon he'd be airborne at five thousand feet, and once there he'd feel a ten-degree cooler breeze through the side window of his plane.

Nail 66 was a short, slender, likeable gent with a constant smile on his round face who loved to talk about airplanes, day or night. He hailed from Stillwater, Oklahoma, and had attended Oklahoma State University on a ROTC scholarship. After pilot training, Nail 66 opted to be an instructor pilot in T-37s versus duty in a combat-ready squadron.

After that tour, he flew photo RF-101s in France and England. After stateside FAC training, he received orders to be a Class C combat FAC in the O-1 Birddog plane with a squadron based in South Vietnam. Class C meant he had no fighter experience, but since he did have jet pilot experience he was transferred immediately to a squadron at Udorn AFB in Thailand to pilot the newer O-2 over more hazardous Laos and North Vietnam. Today, though, Nail 66 would take off from NKP.

Normally, his mission would be to fly to one of four pre-designated air sectors in Laos and conduct a search pattern to find targets of opportunity. Once in his assigned sector, he would spend several hours searching for targets at 100–120 knots between three- and four thousand feet above the ground. Typical targets would include troops, truck parks, supplies, and AAA gun emplacements. Once a target was found he would inform Cricket, and jet fighters would be dispatched to work with him to destroy the target. Cricket was a C-130 plane that served as airborne command and control for the assignment and prioritization of tactical aircraft mission assignments. Cricket told the jets where to take their bombs.

Nail 66 told fighter pilots what and when to bomb, so he was like a little mini-god in his sector of airspace. No one attacked a target within Nail's sector without Nail's permission, and once he gave it, he told them exactly where they should place their bombs by marking the target with one of his Willy Pete smoke rockets.

Today, Nail 66 was briefed to work a sector about seven miles southwest of the village of Tchepone, along the Xe Banghiang River in Laos. The river was a major one, normally about a hundred feet wide but sometimes up to five hundred feet, and was a vital part of the Ho Chi Minh Trail system. Trucks would carry supplies from North Vietnam to the river in Laos, and then sometimes transfer the load to boats that then ferried the supplies into South Vietnam. Nail 66 recognized during the brief that the target area was one he was very familiar with, having flown over it on several previous missions. In fact, it was a key supply route the North Vietnamese used during the Tet Offensive, which had unofficially concluded some forty days earlier.

During his brief, Nail 66 learned that thirty minutes earlier a fellow Nail FAC had spotted an enemy barge offloading supplies. A flight of F-105s (Thuds) had tried to destroy it but failed, so now it was Nail 66's turn. He was briefed that the Thuds hadn't encountered any enemy AAA during their attack. That sounded feasible to Nail 66 since he had personally flown through the same area for each of the previous three days without encountering any AAA. Nail 66 assumed this would be a piece-of-cake mission and all he had to do was find and destroy the barge.

Nail 66 had flown about twenty hours in the past week, but during that time he hadn't found any significant targets and had only been hosed once by enemy AAA. So, he was very hungry for some lucrative targets and excited to have a known barge right off the bat. He was confident that today's target would be a blast since the off-going FAC had briefed, "No AAA."

However, Nail wasn't quite up to speed with the area's past history. The lack of AAA today in the Tchepone area was highly unusual as it was a known hotbed of enemy activity, and one that had recently taken its toll on American pilots. In fact, during one specific thirty-day period, thirty pilots were shot down near Tchepone. Only yesterday, Spad 13, an Air Force pilot, had been shot down nearby. The pilot was rescued within minutes, just before nightfall. Unfortunately, that fact had not yet been provided to my squadron. Most Air Force fighter pilots knew to expect AAA in the area to include multiple quadruple-barreled 14.5mm guns (ZPUs), 23-, 37-, and even 57mm guns. The Tchepone area was bad, and had even been designated a Seventh Air Force 37mm High Threat Area.

Nail 66 took off around 3:45 for a fifty-minute flight to the target area, and he wondered if bad weather might beat him there. It was now late afternoon and the monsoon season had officially begun about two weeks earlier, so there was a distinct possibility late afternoon rains might prevent the fighters from doing their work. But, right now, the weather was absolutely perfect, clear and visibility unlimited (CAVU). Visibility was about fifteen miles and there was no cloud base to interfere with bomb runs. Today, it appeared the rains would hold off and the weather would be perfect for bombing the enemy. But the enemy gunners, if any, would also be able to clearly see the attacking jets. So it was a great day for shooting down American planes as well.

Nail decided to cruise along above the remains of Highway 91 and watch for any targets of opportunity. It ran southeast and would intersect with Route 9 just north of the target, and once there he would follow Route 914 to the river. His target should be just south of that. Once there, he just wanted to break his ineffective string of missions, and today he was pumped and excited to have a known target to blast. He knew the mission's success depended on his ability to find the target and then accurately designate it with one of his smoke rockets.

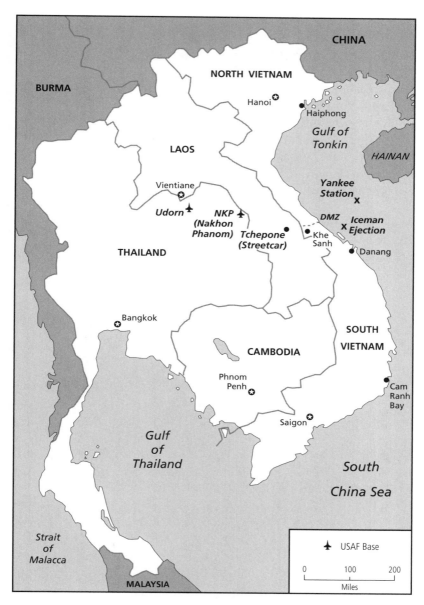

Southeast Asia (Map by Christopher Robinson)

Meanwhile, I'd just launched from the carrier and was now five miles ahead in a shallow climb, waiting for my playmate to join me. Iceman was a great formation pilot and within a minute of my launch, I heard him call. "Lead, Potato Two is joining, over."

I looked down the right wing and there he was, in tight echelon formation, looking sharp. He had already removed one clip of his oxygen mask and it was dangling loosely to the side of his helmet. It was a habit with him that I overlooked. His radio transmissions usually had a little air noise in the background, so I had learned to recognize his radio voice from the hissing sound of oxygen blowing out his mask. All pilots had some quirk that identified them and that one never bothered me. It made him look cool. I nodded my head forward a couple of times to indicate I was adding power and then jammed the throttle against the stop to MRT. Without signaling Iceman, and to hack him off, I then made a sharp turn away from him to head toward the DMZ and damn if he didn't hang right with me.

Passing 10,000 feet, I looked back over my shoulder and saw what we referred to as the Tonkin Gulf Yacht Club in full view. Two destroyers flanked USS *America,* and a third was sliding into her wake to serve as plane guard during the recovery of planes that were now returning from missions over the beach. It was a Kodak moment.

In about ten minutes, we got our first glimpse of Indian country off our right wings. An island appeared about fifteen miles in the distance off my left wing, and I recognized it from briefings as Tiger Island. Unknown to us, an Air Force F-105, call sign Trump O1, had been shot down there only thirty minutes earlier and the rescue forces were still trying to locate the pilot as we flew past. The Sandys were getting hosed badly by AAA as they searched for the pilot. We were too high to observe any action.

In another five minutes we coasted over the beach, going "feet dry" just south of the DMZ near Quang Tri. The weather over Vietnam was sunny and clear, and the visibility was such that I could see about twenty miles in all directions. This was my first sortie over the beach, and I wanted to take it all in at once. I strained to see Danang a little further to the south, but couldn't see the base. I stupidly expected to see all kinds of ordnance being shot in the area of the DMZ, but from my altitude of 24,000 feet it looked just like any other piece of coastal real estate I'd seen from altitude over the United States. I observed no action on the ground, but could see white caps rising from the bright blue water as they billowed in against the coast. It looked like a beautiful sunbathing beach, so I commenced a descent to 16,000 feet for a better view.

"Cricket, Streetcar 304 checking in for target work, over."

"Good afternoon, Streetcar flight. Proceed two-seven-zero degrees for one hundred miles from the channel one-zero-three Tacan (air navigation aid) and make contact with your FAC, Nail 66, on 299.3. Make it fast as he has a good target for you, over."

I rogered his orders.

For some reason, Cricket was more casual than what I had expected for a combat zone. The voice inflection was such that he sounded just like an air traffic controller back in the states.

I looked at my rolling map and plotted the target area. Holy crap . . . it was near some small airfield I'd never heard of named Tchepone, and in Laos. Cricket was sending me to Laos!

I wondered . . . are operations in Laos just as safe as in South Vietnam? We hadn't received much intel on that part of the war zone prior to my launch, and I wondered why Cricket was sending me there. I initiated a heading turn toward the target and hand signaled Iceman to increase speed. I also gave him a push-out signal to assume a combat cruise position which would put him about six hundred feet in trail of me, but at an angle such that I could always see him. I let my speed accelerate to 390 knots to get to Nail 66 more quickly so he wouldn't have to wait and maybe get uptight.

"Streetcar Lead is switching to 299.3, now." After a few seconds, I heard the hiss of Iceman's oxygen. "Streetcar Two is up." I gave him two clicks of my mike button. For now, I would just monitor Nail's frequency.

Meanwhile, Nail 66 was almost to the target area. Directly ahead, he could see the intersection with Route 9. He looked off his left wing, and just north of the road was the old air field near the village of Tchepone so he knew the target area was only seven miles to the south at the end of the valley he was presently flying over. Sure enough, in a minute or so, he saw glittery reflections from the river dead ahead, and he could make out the large bend where the barge was reportedly located. To the right of the target, he could see jungle foliage on the five-hundred-foot-high rolling hills running north and south on his side of the river, and across the river was a 650-foot rocky and forested karst that protruded high above the river.

Nail 66 began a lazy figure eight pattern at three thousand feet above the ground. It's odd, he thought, that there are no large villages

close to the river. He reached the river and began to slowly and meticulously meander downstream. As he looked for targets, he saw a series
of rapids and small waterfalls cascading gradually to the sea, and he
knew that some of the falls were man-made, a residual effect from the
enemy's attempt to build stone bridges for truck crossings. Most likely,
the barge would be just upstream from one of the mini-falls.

"Hallelujah." Sure enough, just where Nail 66 thought it would
be, the barge appeared in view off his right wing. It was tight against
the western shoreline and the enemy was still in the midst of offloading supplies. He saw troops scurrying back into the trees as he flew
overhead, but observed no enemy fire. Quickly, he glanced at his
Tacan, which was providing heading and distance to the base at NKP,
and he made a scribble on his pilot kneeboard. "TGT, 120/103/CH
89." The target was 120 degrees and 103 miles from NKP in the event
any trouble occurred today.

Nail banked the plane sharply left for a 360-degree turn over the
target and looked out his side window to see how many supplies had
been offloaded, but a jungle canopy blocked his view. Sometimes, a
maneuver like he had just performed would draw enemy fire if they
recognized that they had been spotted. Usually that was not the case.
The troops knew that if they fired at the O-2 it would give away their
position, and then the FAC would call in jet fighters and possibly kill
them. The enemy was astute, and well trained to realize that it was better to hold fire until the fighters actually appeared rather than sending
an invitation by firing at the unarmed, inexpensive O-2.

Nail 66 leveled his wings as he passed the target a second time with
the intention of flying further south over the river because he wanted
them to think he had seen nothing and was leaving the area. He had the
target pinpointed, and now he would loiter to the south while he waited
for fighter support before returning to the target site. Perhaps that would
trick any gunners into taking a smoke break after this initial scare.

Well, I'll be a monkey's uncle, Nail thought. Just south of the
barge, he picked up the glitter of small ripples running across the river.
Look closer, he told himself. To his surprise, he saw the dark shadow
of an underwater bridge. "Shit hot!" Nail 66 exclaimed out loud. Two
targets for the price of one today. . . .

The North Vietnamese had built a stone bridge just barely under
the surface of the water to enable supply trucks to drive across the river
during night hours. Usually, it was nearly impossible for the FAC's to
spot them from three thousand feet above. Today, all the conditions

melded so that Nail 66 saw the rectangular shadow image across the river and recognized it as a bridge. That's why the barge was being offloaded—the bridge blocked its path.

Nail 66 was ecstatic, as he now had two great targets in one location. The barge might change location before any fast mover jets arrived with bombs. He made a quick radio transmission to Cricket, briefed him on his targets, and requested immediate fighter support.

Cricket responded that he had two Navy jets inbound to work with Nail, and three more behind the first two. Soon thereafter, I checked in with Nail.

"Nail 66, this is Streetcar 304 with a flight of two checking in for action, over."

"Roger Streetcar, Nail 66. I've got some great targets for you today. How far are you from my position, over?"

"Roger Nail. Streetcar flight is about seventy miles out and will be at your position in ten minutes, over."

"Roger that, Streetcar. Call me when you're overhead, out."

"Nail 66, Streetcar 304. Why don't you go ahead with your target brief so I can home in on your transmission, over?" I then quickly reached for my direction finder (ADF) switch so I could activate it as soon as Nail 66 started to talk, in order to get a heading to his position.

"Roger Streetcar. The weather here is CAVU. Your first target will be a barge that's offloading supplies as we speak, and the target elevation is five hundred feet. Two Thuds attacked it just prior to my arrival and they missed, but didn't encounter any hostile gunfire. I've been working this area for the past three days and haven't seen any AAA myself, although there is a possibility of ZPUs, and 23-, 37-, and 57mm. If you need to eject, then your best escape heading will be two-four-zero degrees. What's your ordnance load, Streetcar?"

Before I answered, my ADF cut indicated he was bearing 273 degrees from my current position so I eased right about 5 degrees.

"Roger Nail. A flight of two A-7s, each packing six 500-pound MK-82s, and six hundred rounds of twenty mike-mike and two Sidewinders."

"Roger Streetcar. Are those 82s Snake-eyes? Over."

"Negative Nail. They're GPs, conical and unretarded, over."

"Roger, Streetcar. I'm in an orbit along the river about three clicks south of the target. Call me when you have a tally-ho, out."

I looked back at Iceman and could tell he was a little more excited than I was because he was jinking excessively and flying from my right side to the left, back and forth. We were high enough to avoid enemy guns unless they were 57mm or larger, but his extra caution was okay with me as long as he stayed in that 600-foot quadrant. I wanted him where he could help me see any threat that might pop up out of North Vietnam just off our right wing. It wasn't inconceivable that a MIG could range this far south for a quick shot since we were near the border. I had confidence my wingie would consistently be where I needed him.

Several minutes later, I was surprised to hear a Sidewinder 406 initiate a radio check with his flight. It was a three-plane flight from a sister squadron aboard *America*, and I assumed they, too, had been tasked to work with Nail 66. Now I knew I had some friendly competition for Nail's services. I recognized the flight leader's voice as that of a lieutenant commander nick-named Spider who was senior to me, and a very aggressive pilot. His wingie was Razor, also known as Lt.(jg) Jack Gillette.

I made an unnecessary call to Nail 66 just to let Spider know I was ahead of him before he checked in, so he wouldn't try to pull rank or anything to get to work with Nail first. "Uh, Nail, this is Streetcar 304 and we're eight minutes out, over."

Just then, I saw the Khe Sanh base area off the left wing. It looked just like any other piece of ground. Nothing significant . . . but, many Navy pilots had participated in the air support just thirty days earlier when it was under siege, and we had been briefed on the intensity of the enemy attack. Today it looked peaceful. The enemy troops had withdrawn and no one knew their current position.

As I closed on Nail, I thought about his comment that he hadn't seen any AAA for the past three days. That thought prompted me to do a mental review of CAG's rules of engagement (ROE) for my target area: "CAG-6 ROE: Over North Vietnam, make one pass and haul ass. Over South Vietnam or Cambodia, multiple runs are permitted. Over Laos, normally make one pass if you encounter AAA. But it's okay to make multiple runs if the FAC considers it warranted."

So if they started shooting at us, I would have to wait and see what Nail 66 said about a second bomb run.

Chapter 5

FIRST BOMB RUN

About five miles from the target, I began a forward scan for Nail's plane. My ADF cut had been perfect and he was right where I anticipated. He was forty-five degrees low at my two o'clock and turning to cross a good-sized river that glistened in the afternoon sun. From my distance, his plane appeared to be the size of a small, remote-controlled model plane.

As I got closer, the O-2 was very visible with its white wing-top standing out in the foreground against the green jungle foliage below. He looked to be about three thousand feet and very slow near a sharp bend in the river which meandered on a southeasterly direction. "Tally ho, Nail 66. Streetcar 304 has you in sight, over."

"Streetcar, this is Nail 66. Let me know when you're ready for me to smoke the target."

"Nail, shoot when ready," I replied. We were still maybe four miles from the target, but I thought it would take him a couple of turns to get ready to shoot.

"Roger, Streetcar. Nail is rolling in to mark, now."

He sharply banked about thirty degrees, quickly dipped his nose a little, and fired a smoke rocket. Astonished at how fast he performed the maneuver, I watched the rocket's trailing plume, and saw it impact on the edge of the riverbank.

I acquired the target and realized I could roll in on my first bomb run as I approached without circling to identify it. That way, the gunners wouldn't know we were in the area until they heard my plane whistling down the chute, and I could be in and off before the gunners knew what was up. I reached up and tightened both shoulder harness fittings, and then gave my lap belt a firm tug. Strangely, my adrenalin flow had not yet begun to increase.

For my bomb run, I wanted to be at 300 knots on a 12,500-foot roll-in perch. During the run, I would accelerate to 450 knots in a forty-five-degree dive, release my bombs at 6,500 feet, and bottom out no lower than 3,500 feet. I was still at 16,000 feet with only a couple of miles to go.

"Iceman, Lead is chopping power." I smoothly eased the throttle back to near idle and pushed the control stick forward and slightly left as I rolled into a left bank for a rapid descent. There wasn't much time to lose 3,500 feet.

"Iceman, speed brake is coming out . . . now!" I pressed a switch on the throttle lever and immediately a metal panel nearly the size of a house door popped out under the center of my fuselage. My body began to float just a little as the plane rapidly decelerated so I pushed forward on the control stick to keep the plane from ballooning upward. I glanced back at Iceman, and he'd matched his speed brake actuation with mine and was hot on my tail.

As I passed 13,000 feet, I initiated level-off and gave Iceman an advisory. "Speed brake in . . . now. Ice, my intent is to roll in hot as I approach the target, without an orbit. I'll make the first run heading east across the river with the sun at my back. Go ahead and start your separation now, over." Two mike clicks in response. . . .

I banked left about thirty degrees and commenced a mild swing for about forty-five degrees of turn so I could set up for a right-hand pull into the target on a west-to-east heading at the attack roll-in point.

"Uh, Nail 66, this is Sidewinder 406 (Spider) and I've got a flight of three, so we'll just sit up here high off to the side until Streetcar finishes, okay?"

Nail rogered.

Mine was the first flight of Navy A-7s that Nail 66 had worked with, so he wondered about our capability. He had no previous knowledge as to our bomb load capacity or accuracy of delivery, and hadn't heard any comments from his fellow Nail's as to our reputation as combat pilots. He only hoped we were as good as most Air Force pilots, or at least better than the Thud pilots who had earlier missed this target. He was very excited about the amount of ordnance the Navy guys were carrying so he thought surely he'd be able to destroy both targets. He would have us attack the barge first, since that was his pre-assigned target, and if successful, he would have us go after the bridge on subsequent runs.

"Streetcar 304, Nail 66. Do you have my smoke?"

"Roger, Nail, I've got it." The white cloud of billowing smoke was standing out so visibly against the jungle canopy that I thought it funny he even asked.

"Roger, Streetcar. My smoke is right on the shoreline of the river bank, so make your first pass with two bombs and put them right on the east edge of the smoke. You're cleared 'hot' for random runs, over."

"Iceman, Lead is selecting stations and setting switches for two bombs on the first run. My master arm is on. Check yours, and don't forget the target is five hundred feet mean sea level (MSL), over."

"Yeah, I got it, Lead." His response sounded casual, as if we were on a training run.

I picked up Nail's plane low, still at my two o'clock position about one mile south of the target near the river, and he was flying from my right to left so he could watch my run. "Nail, Streetcar 304 is in hot now and I have you in sight. Check your eight o'clock high."

I checked my altimeter and was still a little higher than desired so I delayed my roll-in and extended around the circle for a few more seconds. This gave me time to reflect and I was pleasantly surprised that I wasn't the least bit scared. After all, it was my first combat bomb run and I had halfway expected my hands to be shaking and that I'd be dripping in sweat from the excitement. I was neither, but had the same feeling of flowing adrenalin and tremendous excitement I had as a halfback at kick-off time at Big Creek High School in West Virginia. I wanted the ball in my hands. I wanted to hit a real target after six years of bomb practice.

I maneuvered so my roll-in would be out of a setting sun to hopefully blind any AAA gunners. With a west-to-east bomb line, I anticipated seeing my bombs either hit trees if they fell short, or land in the water if my aim was long. Since the barge was tight against the shoreline, a bomb in the trees would not be bad, as it would hit any troops who were offloading supplies. Bombs in the river would not be great. I wanted the first bomb right on the edge of the trees and the next one right on the barge. Years of training took over. I would start my bomb run from 12,500 feet at 300 knots. First, I'd reduce my throttle to eighty percent, then roll into a forty-five-degree dive, and obtain 450 knots indicated speed just before reaching the bomb-release point at 6,500 feet. Once there, I'd depress my bomb pickle switch and pull four G's backstick in a wings-level position and hopefully be out of the dive before 3,000 feet above the ground. The two bombs would eject off the wing bomb racks when my plane's nose was about ten degrees up, as determined by the bomb computer's calculation of speed and distance to the target, etc. Then, during the next ten seconds, the bombs would slingshot for two miles before striking the target. It was time to execute.

I pulled the stick back slightly, snapped it firmly to the right for sixty-degrees bank, and then headed toward Nail's smoke. As the plane rolled right, I relaxed my back pressure on the stick to allow the plane's nose to fall just short of the target.

After rolling wings level in the dive, I was set up perfectly. The gunsight pipper was just short of Nail's smoke and now I could let it track to the target. Through the gunsight view, I could see a large blob of dark green jungle short of the target, and the tree line extended to the south. The thick foliage appeared to merge with the shiny river, and Nail's smoke was just at the merge point. The river was shining back at me like a mirror and to the right I spotted Nail's plane over what looked like a large clearing, devoid of tall trees. With a quick glance, I noted my airspeed was 410 knots and I was in a forty-five-degree nose-down dive. I thought I'd be a little fast at my pickle altitude, but that was fine for my first run and my computer should compensate if it was worth its salt. Better to be fast than slow, so I left the power at eighty percent.

I continued to track the smoke, and soon saw the barge come into view. At sixty-five hundred feet above the target, my speed was 460 knots in a forty-five-degree dive, and the pipper was on the barge. I pressed the bomb pickle switch with my right thumb, smoothly pulled the stick back for a four-G, wings-level climb, and waited for the computer's calibrated release time. After a couple of seconds, my gyro indicated the plane's nose was around ten degrees nose-up, and I felt the thump as the bombs ejected from the bomb rack. I slapped the throttle forward against the stop for MRT and noted I had bottomed out in my dive at thirty-five hundred feet indicated, or about three thousand feet above the ground. Ten seconds until bomb blast . . . at this time I had to make a conscious decision which way I would turn away from the target. I had three options. I could turn left, turn right, or just continue to fly straight ahead as I climbed. During training we always turned left, so I decided to turn right.

Initially I climbed straight ahead as I waited to sense the aircraft unloading from my initial pull-up G's, and now I felt the plane accelerating forward. I pushed the stick hard and rolled into a sharp, climbing turn to the right to clear the target.

"Streetcar Lead is off and clear of the target." I wanted Iceman to get in quickly before any gunners woke up.

At that moment, I was really pumped about my first combat bomb release and my adrenaline was really flowing. Anxious to see where my bombs had hit, I looked back over my shoulder at the target as I turned and climbed. Enemy guns may have been firing at me, but I didn't take the time to scan for them. I was more concerned about the accuracy of my first combat bomb run.

Then, right in the middle of Nail's rocket smoke, I saw a bright flash as my first bomb exploded and obliterated my view of the barge. Then the second bomb exploded in the river, just ahead of the first bomb, causing a giant cannonball splash effect.

"Shit hot!" I screamed in a muffled voice inside my oxygen mask. But no secondary explosion . . . yet! I was still ecstatic, and anxiously awaited Nail's bomb damage assessment (BDA).

"Streetcar Lead, direct hit! Looks like a bull's eye from here. Nice shooting. Two, put your bombs just forward of your Lead's hits. Two is cleared in hot now."

Unknown to me, Nail 66 was now going to have my playmate go after the underwater bridge. My second bomb had impacted in that area but Nail wanted more bombs to ensure complete destruction.

"Bull's eye. . . ." A bull's eye was not an everyday result but I had achieved a few—although not as many as the better pilots in the squadron. I'd had more as a BN in the A-3B. However, had any of those better pilots ever got a bull's eye in combat?

I got really jacked up. It gave me the same feeling as the time when I hit a grand-slam home run for the LMU Railsplitter baseball team against the Vols. I was on cloud nine. On this, my first combat run, I had hit a grand-slam homer. I couldn't wait to step up to the plate and do it again.

I climbed, turned, and looked back at the target while mentally storing the visual picture of my first bomb impact. I had destroyed a barge, and probably killed some troops in the process. Tough shit if I had—I was really pumped. Then the game situation changed in a literal flash.

Suddenly I got my first glimpse of enemy gunfire. Two AAA sites, about fifty yards apart, were now spitting at me from a position four hundred yards right, and short of the target. Both were tracking me and spewing out a high rate of fire as I climbed through eight thousand feet. Each gun was firing so rapidly that it looked like two large blinking spotlights. Our Spook had briefed us about a four-barrel 14.5mm AAA gun that could spit out nearly 2,400 rounds a minute with an effective range of about four thousand feet. Why were these two ZPUs still shooting since I was out of range? Those son-of-a-guns were definitely tracking me.

"Nail 66, they're shooting at me. I've got two guns firing at me from the west side of the river, southwest of the target. Do you see them? Over."

"Roger Streetcar, I've got them, and it looks like you also woke up a 37 across the river."

My head snapped that direction. Oh shit, I hadn't seen that one. So, in my best West Virginia drawl, I answered. "Roger, Nail. Do we need to take out those guns?"

Nail and the four other A-7 pilots listened in disbelief at my question. It had just blurted out of my mouth without any forethought. I don't know why. It was stupid, but not unlike me. I got carried away with impressing the Air Force jock with how cool I could be under fire.

"Hang on just a minute there, Streetcar Lead," he replied. "Let's see what happens in Two's run." Nail's head was still screwed on right.

Spider's ears perked up and he knew he needed to watch things closely now, so he moved his flight closer to the target.

"Iceman, two guns are firing from a position four hundred yards right and short of the target, copy."

"Two has the guns, and is about five seconds from rolling in hot."

I wondered if he was scared now, but he still sounded cool.

Iceman was at my one o'clock high position in wings-level flight, opposite direction and approaching his roll-in point. It was a pretty sight. The backdrop was Carolina Blue sky and in the foreground his gray-and-white plane was rolling in the midst of a very light-white, misty haze. A dream picture. I watched as he performed an aggressive 120-degree descending roll into the target. He snapped his wings level in a forty-five-degree dive, made two quick line-up corrections, and then kept his wings steady during the dive.

Looks like a solid run, I thought. He's not wasting any time and he's about sixty degrees left of where I rolled in, so maybe the guns won't see him since they're still tracking me. I saw him jink slightly and assumed he was evading enemy ground fire. I quickly scanned the target site, but saw no guns firing other than those firing at me.

As I continued to turn and climb, I watched him release his two bombs, pull up, then snap-turn to the left away from me. *Be there baby,* I urged his bombs. The first one made a huge splash in the river just beyond my second bomb and right where Nail wanted it. *Great hit,* I thought. *Probably another bull's eye! My team is shit-hot today.* The second bomb exploded on the far bank, a little long. *Come on Iceman—that's not like you.* He was one of the most accurate bombers in our squadron so he was probably just a little tight, or maybe his damn computer was off. But one bomb creamed his aim-point.

Nail 66 reported Iceman's BDA as a little long, but okay. Mentally he noted that the Navy guys were going lower in their dives than he was accustomed to with Air Force jets (fast-movers), but they had nailed the target. To me, both of our runs were made as we had trained.

I felt the need to atone for Iceman's long hits so this Air Force guy would be left with a good impression of our Navy A-7s. I wasn't ready to depart the target area yet, since we still had four bombs remaining. In my exuberance, I hoped Nail would ask for another run.

I continued to climb and turn toward my next perch but stared at the ZPUs as I did. There were no tracers. That was good. The gunfire from each ZPU gave a visual impression of a circular, revolving pattern of flashes. Although it was daytime, the flashes appeared like ten blinking flashlights at night in a six-foot circle, and they pointed right at me. I knew hundreds of rounds were being fired at me, but I wasn't immediately concerned as I had yet to see a tracer round or flak-burst. I would be testing the ZPU's range at the bottom of my next dive. Was the target worth a second run? Was it worth placing myself in harm's way?

I had a choice to make as flight lead. How did the ROE apply to this situation? Guns were firing. I could follow the rule that allowed one pass when guns were firing in Laos, abort the second run, and put my tail between my legs and run. If I did, we would have to stop and download the rest of the bombs at Danang since bombs couldn't be returned to the carrier once the safety wires had been pulled. My section would then be late for—or even miss—the recovery aboard the boat, and my decision would be questioned. Or I could wait and see what Nail 66 said about another run. Rule Two: If he asked for a second run, I was authorized to do so. If so, I could just release the bombs at a higher and safer altitude. If I did that, it would degrade my bomb accuracy. Or I could just follow the standard forty-five-degree run—the best compromise between safety and BDA effectiveness.

We hadn't been instructed—or trained—to release bombs at a higher altitude when enemy fire was encountered. Some pilots might wimp out when under fire, but I decided not to be one of them. I would pursue the target under the standard trained method even in the face of AAA. Why? I don't know, but it was the macho thing to do. Or was it dedication to duty? Or patriotism . . . or was it maybe just plain stupidity? I really like to think I was just doing the job, in the way I was trained, and paid to do.

Spider, meanwhile, had crept in a little closer so he could see the target, spot the AAA, and listen to our banter. His previous experience in missions over North Vietnam made him feel uneasy right now, but he wasn't about to question a young kid's aggressiveness. Spider thought that was the correct attitude and the best way to stay alive.

My mind was made up. I would take the initiative and question Nail, hoping he would ask us for a second run. If he didn't, I'd have to forget a second run due to the air wing's ROE. I recognized my earlier miscue and wouldn't mention the guns this time around. I rephrased my question.

"Nail, do you want the rest of my bombs in the same place you directed my wingman's bombs?"

Before answering, Nail dipped his little plane's nose and a small puff of smoke formed under one wing. Then, he made a sharp pull-up and turned toward the south. In a couple of seconds, the smoke from another Willy Pete rose through the tree canopy about a hundred feet short of the barge location.

"Streetcar, go ahead. Have at 'em. Hit my smoke, Nail out." Unknown to me, Nail had just placed his smoke where he thought the troops were loading supplies onto trucks.

I was a little confused. Nail's smoke was very close to the two ZPUs. Was that where the troops were, or was that a gun site? Didn't matter . . . Nail had given me my desired second run, so I would just blast the hell out of his smoke and see what happened.

"Ice, this is Lead. The next run will be our final run so select switches to release all bombs on the next pass, over." Two clicks in response . . . Iceman agreed with getting the hell out of there.

Spider really perked up now. ZPUs and 37s were hot stuff, so he was surprised to hear me accept a second run. *This guy has real spunk,* he thought.

During my climb, my head had been mostly out of the cockpit and preoccupied with Iceman's run and Nail's smoke. Now, I glanced at my instruments and discovered woefully that I had climbed too sharply for my bomb load. My altitude was okay, but my airspeed was slower than what I wanted for a proper perch, so I extended away from the target for a minute to allow time for the airspeed to increase, and hopefully cause the gunners to lose sight of my plane. As I extended, I watched over my shoulder and saw that the ZPUs matched my turn and continued to flash. They still had a visual on me and they were still firing.

I didn't yet know how I would feel, looking straight down their gun barrels, so I decided to wimp out just a little. I would pickle five hundred feet higher. And I would turn left off the target or zoom straight ahead, since the AAA was right of the target. I had no trepidation about the second run, but I'd wanted to start it quickly. It was getting hotter, so I needed to get in fast, not go low, and fly straight ahead after release so the big guns wouldn't have time to elevate their barrels as I passed over them. Now, though, I'd given more AAA gunners the opportunity to aim their barrels my direction. I felt a little tentative. Nevertheless, I rolled in.

Chapter 6

EJECT, EJECT

Nail 66, Streetcar 304 is in hot, and I've got you in sight. Out of a bright, fading sunset, I banked hard to the right, pulled the throttle back to eighty-five percent, and dove at Nail's smoke. I took a quick glance and the same AAA site was still firing at me. It didn't faze me.

Amazingly, smoke and debris from my first bomb run was still billowing and Nail's second Willy Pete was about a hundred feet short of that, so the two white puffs gave me a good line-up reference. I rolled wings-level, forty-five degrees nose down, lined up toward the southeast this time, and, dead ahead, about a mile across the river, was a rugged, rocky mountain (karst). It had cliffs, mostly limestone but with some caves and vegetation.

My eyes shot back inside the cockpit. My airspeed was a little slower than I wanted so I shoved the throttle forward hard against the stop for maximum thrust. Then, I looked through my bombsight and my pipper placement was nearly perfect. I had another good run going, maybe another bull's eye. My eyes darted right; the ZPUs were still blistering me with a continuous white sparkle of fire. My eyes returned again to my bombsite pipper and it was slightly short of Nail's smoke, but inching forward. This would be another great hit. But, at that moment, all hell broke loose.

A single line of maybe ten evenly spaced tracers rose from the tree canopy about two hundred yards to the right of my target. It was my first-ever sighting of a large AAA gun's tracers and they looked like brightly shaded red balls, trailing a two-foot flaming plume. At first, they were soaring on an arc straight toward me, but then they ran out of poop and seemingly floated, before falling short. The flaming balls were larger than I'd thought they would be. I had anticipated seeing tracers the size of baseballs, but these looked more like softballs. I knew there were actually four or five more explosive rounds that I couldn't see mixed in with each tracer.

That's probably the 37-gun that Nail saw, I thought. No sweat, I'm out of its range. I checked my gauges. Accelerating through 430 knots and diving past nine thousand feet, I locked my left elbow to make sure the throttle didn't slip back from MRT and looked back at the pipper.

Oh, for Pete's sake . . . directly ahead, from across the river on the karst, a really long string of larger red balls was zooming up at me, but they too petered out below me. I looked back at my bombsight pipper but immediately saw something whiz by off the left wing. My eyes darted that way.

A third gun's tracer pattern was soaring by, about a hundred yards off my left wing, and zeroed in on my altitude. Red softballs were just casually floating by and it seemed I could count their number. I quickly followed the tracer pattern back to the gun and saw that the site was in the trees about a mile left of the target on my side of the river. This one appeared to be a 57, and it was really whacking at me. I could tell the gun barrel was swinging toward me as each successive tracer was getting closer and closer.

Oh, shit . . . the tracers would be zeroed in on me in a few seconds. Quickly, I snapped the control stick for a fifteen-degree bank to the right and turned my head to clear that area. Ah, crap . . . the pattern of fire off the left wing was being replicated off the right wing, and those balls were also quickly sweeping toward me. I snapped back to wings-level position and continued to dive.

"Streetcar, you're *really* getting hosed by multiple guns," Nail casually transmitted. He'd roughly counted about ten different sites that had my plane bracketed with what he described as flaming Budweiser cans.

"Copy," I said quickly. My altimeter was passing 8,000 feet and I made one final pipper adjustment with the intent to release the bombs high. I would wimp out.

Iceman had been busy inside the cockpit verifying wing station selections for a final bomb run and was just hitting the perch when he heard Nail's "hose" call. His head snapped up, and he looked down at the target. He was aghast, shocked by the intensity of roman candles rising from the dark green jungle canopy and seemingly cutting right through my plane.

Two sets of red balls were petering out under the nose of my plane. Scorching tracers were zipping past to my left. And now, flaming balls to my right. After rolling wings-level, I again picked up the target through my bombsight. The pipper wasn't too far off target but it was becoming harder to keep it aimed. Suddenly, a flaming softball was in my bombsight view, coming right at my face and I thought, *Duck!* Before I could, it barely missed the nose cone about six feet in front of me, nearly grazed the front windshield, and zipped over my head less than two feet away. That close, it looked like a flaming volleyball. I looked dead ahead across the river and saw a solid stream of flaming balls from two separate gunsites, and both appeared to have me bore-sighted. Right then, I thought I'd had it.

Crap . . . I'm flying right down the barrels of at least six gun sites. Abort the run, just pickle the damn bombs, and get the hell out of here. Then, in a split second, I changed my mind.

If I'm going to pickle, I might as well try and put 'em on one of the guns. So, I took just an extra two seconds and positioned the pipper on the closest firing AAA site already in my gunsight and held it there for another two seconds. I depressed and held the bomb pickle with my thumb in a death grip, pulled the stick back smoothly for a four-G climb straight ahead, and glanced at the altimeter. Oh, hell, fifty-six hundred feet—you've busted your standard bomb release altitude, you stupid idiot!

Flaming tracers spit past on both sides as my plane's nose started to rise, and my teeth clenched as I waited for my last four bombs to leave the wing racks. It seemed an eternity but finally I felt a solid thump as the first bomb was kicked off one triple ejector rack . . . two, three, four thumps. Bombs away—hope that wipes out at least one of the guns.

Quickly, I gazed inside at the airspeed and altimeter. My bottom out altitude was critical because I feared the ZPUs more than anything else and I was now falling into their range. I stared at the altimeter. 4,000 feet and still descending . . . 3,500, 3,200. . . .

"Come on," I screamed in my mask toward the altimeter. "Climb, you mother—start climbing." Oh, how I wished I had an afterburner! 3,000 feet, 2,800, 3,000, 3,200 . . . all right, I was finally climbing, and I hadn't been hit yet.

I realized my left arm was still pushing hard against the throttle and my right thumb was frozen on the pickle, so I relaxed my grip. Now, for the first time, I felt scared, sweating bullets and bracing myself for what might hit my plane at any moment. There was little I could do until I gained more speed and altitude.

My plane's belly was now in full view and my forward motion along the ground had been slowed by the steep climb, so I was most vulnerable from the AAA gunners right now, for at least another ten seconds. My eyes were glued to the G-meter and airspeed indicator as I worked to ensure a maximum climb profile. I was tempted to yank the stick back to my lap to quickly climb above the effective range of the ZPUs, but at the same time I wanted to unload all Gs and speed zoom out of 37- and 57mm range. Patiently, I struggled to split the difference. I cowered lower in the seat as if I didn't want to see the killer round coming. I cringed, and waited for the probable fatal bullet.

The altimeter said I was in a rapid climb, but it felt like slow motion. I looked over the plane's nose and only saw blue sky. I was hesitant to look left or right. The horizon disappeared from my frontal view so I relaxed backpressure on the stick and deliberately looked inside the cockpit at the vertical gyro instrument (VGI). My nose attitude was ten degrees up and I felt the plane unloading, accelerating quickly. The zoom feeling made me feel comfortable, that I was almost out of harm's way. At five thousand feet, tracers were still chasing me off my left wing, but not as many as before.

Thank heaven, I thought. I've made it clear of the small automatic weapons fire and ZPUs. Now, start turning to avoid the 23s and 37s.

Nail 66 was mesmerized. He had watched as my plane was enveloped in tracers and he was mortified. He couldn't believe I hadn't been hit yet. He says I made a calm, cool-sounding transmission.

"Streetcar Lead is clear of the target."

A miracle, Nail 66 thought.

I felt ecstatic for about five seconds after my clear call and really thought I had climbed high enough and accelerated to a speed where I was safe. I started to breathe again!

Suddenly, I felt a thump against the right wing, and the entire plane seemed to bounce a little left as if someone had pushed me hard. Just a big, quick thump, no explosion. As soon as I felt the thump I knew I'd been hit; but, for just a brief moment, nothing happened and I glanced at the right wing to check for damage. As I did so, my whole world turned upside down.

Nail watched in horror as a large piece of wing seemed to fly from my A-7. In a couple of seconds, the plane yawed back and forth a few times, and then flipped and began to just tumble end over end. Nail realized it was now falling out of the sky rapidly.

While I looked right, the plane suddenly snap-rolled, my body lurched forward, and my head snapped down before the shoulder straps finally restrained me. Centrifugal force seemed to hold me slightly away from the seat cushion. As I struggled to get my head upright, I was in a violent buffet and roll, and in a microsecond the stick was forcefully whipped out of my right hand, nearly breaking my wrist. The rudder pedals chattered loudly as they rocked uncontrollably from top to bottom at lighting speed and with such force my feet were thrown off. I pushed backward with my left hand to get my head up, and saw the plane's nose was dropping quickly below the horizon.

My eyes returned inside to check my altimeter. My head was bouncing so violently, and the instrument panel board was vibrating so much, I couldn't focus on any gauge. I reached for the control stick but it was oscillating wildly and bouncing between my knees. On my second try, I finally collared it in my right hand and tried to apply backstick, but it again forcefully broke loose. Frantically, I collared it again, and this time placed both hands around the neck and hung on for dear life. The nose was up and I couldn't see forward, so I looked left. I saw the ground and recognized a thirty-degree nose-down attitude, so I tried to pull the stick backward. I couldn't. In fact, I couldn't even stop its severe oscillation and my hands were just along for the ride. I have never before, or since, seen such violence in the controls. I had both hands tightly on the stick but didn't have the muscle power to stop it at any one position and my arms felt as useless as rubber bands. They were being stretched from one corner of the cockpit to the other. My feet finally caught the rudder pedals, but were again forcefully thrown away. Then, just for a split second, the VGI was in focus. It was totally erratic, spinning wildly, indicating inverted flight one moment and then quickly, upright. My head was now banging both sides of the canopy, plus bouncing off the headrest pad. Only five seconds, maybe, had elapsed since I took the hit and I knew already I was doomed. But I couldn't force myself to admit defeat and hit the silk.

Nail 66 screamed into his mike, "Eject, eject, you're hit, you're hit!"

Nail didn't have to preface his call with "Streetcar." I knew he meant me, and his voice inflection told me it was time to punch out. His timely call saved my life.

Nail's last "eject" word was no more than out of his mouth before I frantically scooted my butt back in one swift movement to lock the harness and simultaneously raised my hands above my head toward the face curtain (ejection initiation handle). I grasped the bright yellow metal ring tightly and sat as upright as possible.

Suddenly, the nose of the plane dropped and I got my first, full frontal view of the ground, and it was rushing up at me. Oh crap . . . it's too late to eject!

In a panic, I swiftly jerked the ring forward and down till my clenched fists ended up just below my chin, with the face curtain cloth covering my face. One thousand one, one thousand . . . I looked left and saw the plane was inverted now and felt myself floating a little in the seat.

The damn seat didn't fire!

Just for a moment, for just one split second, I thought the ejection seat had malfunctioned. Stark fear hit me. Both forearms flexed and I snap-jerked the handle further down with all the strength I could muster.

Then, *bam, bam,* in quick succession I heard the canopy blow, followed by a short delay. And then I heard a swoosh behind me as the seat rocket lit off. Quickly, the slightly floating seat pan hit my tail hard. As my seat shot up the rail, I looked down and saw the cockpit moving away. I hit the air stream in a flash but felt little wind blast because I had ejected while the plane was inverted and the back of my seat took the brunt of the wind force. Horizon, ground, and sky all passed through my view as I tumbled downward. I was safely out of the plane around two thousand feet, but was rocketing toward the ground at nearly two hundred miles an hour. Oddly, my fists were still locked under my chin, and I was still clutching the face curtain—but it was flapping in the wind. Consciously, I said, "Let go of the damn handle!"

I looked behind me and saw the smaller seat drogue chute fully blossomed, and watched as the larger main chute began to stream. With a pop, it filled with air and abruptly jerked me to an upright position. I looked up, saw a beautifully filled silk canopy against a blue sky, and heard the wind whistling softly as I descended.

I watched in momentary fright as several chute risers entangled; but in a flash, they snapped free and that action spun my head a little toward the right. At that instant, I saw my A-7. Oddly, the jet was slightly higher and spiraling down in about a thirty-degree dive slightly ahead of me, but missing part of its right wing. I didn't watch it impact as I was concerned about my height above the ground. I looked down. . . .

I'm one lucky guy. Unbelievably, I was about three hundred feet above the ground. Thank God for Nail's timely call.

Several hundred feet to my right, between me and my plane, I noticed a helmeted soldier, clad in black, running toward me. He stopped, placed his head against his rifle stock in a firing pose, and hurriedly aimed at me. I heard his rifle pop. He's trying to kill me! Then, several more pops occurred from farther right, and more men were also running toward me.

I'm going to be captured and become a POW, or I'm going to be killed. How will Shirley cope with two young children and a third on the way? The thought must have surfaced from a subconscious worry. Shirley's father was killed in 1944 at age thirty during World War II, and at the time of his death, her mother was twenty-seven, she was five, and her sister and brother ages three and one. There was now a direct correlation. At the time of my ejection I was twenty-eight, Shirley was twenty-nine, and my children were ages five and three with a third on the way. Shirley could now be encountering the same fate as her Gold Star mother, and I couldn't bear the thought of Shirley coming home every day to those gold "war widow" stars in her front window.

About four seconds after the gomers shot at me, I looked straight down. Thus far, my chute had completed only three sideward swings but I was already fifty feet from a rapidly approaching ground. In less than thirty seconds after ejection, I was about to hit the ground in enemy territory and more men with rifles were now running toward my floating chute.

Nail 66 was too far away to actually see my ejection seat soar out of the plane and thought he'd made his ejection call too late. Then he saw my chute blossom. *Oh Lord, it looks like Streetcar has a good chute about four hundred feet above the ground,* he thought.

For a moment, from Nail's angle, it appeared my plane was going to actually fly through my chute. Then Nail saw it floating directly down into the plane's fireball, and he didn't know if I had landed safely or was engulfed by the plane's fire.

Spider, however, saw my chute blossom from a different angle at sixteen thousand feet. He watched as it floated down toward a clearing, but at the last moment drifted and went out of site through some treetops near the edge of the clearing. He saw my plane continue ahead to the forward part of the clearing, impact, and start to burn.

Nail 66 called Iceman. "Streetcar Two, Lead is down. Climb high and contact the Crown bird to activate the rescue force."

Iceman's voice quivered as he rogered Nail.

After that, Nail 66 switched his radio to the emergency guard frequency so he could answer if I came up on my survival radio.

Iceman leveled his plane at 16,000 feet and then fanatically began looking at his pilot kneeboard to find the radio frequency for Crown, an airborne HC-130. The special plane had an extensive long-range communication platform, would activate the search and rescue (SAR), and then strategically coordinate the on-scene rescue effort. Crown could relay messages back to staff, and also re-fuel rescue planes as needed. Finally Iceman raised Crown, who advised he would scramble a Sandy and Jolly rescue team to the scene, and also get some fighters with bombs on the way. Crown then headed toward my location at twenty-four thousand feet.

After calling Crown, Iceman pondered his next move. He had seen my chute blossom and watched it float down so he knew my exact location, but the amount of AAA and my ejection had really rattled him. Iceman was in shock, totally screwed up emotionally, and couldn't think logically. He was trained to fly at five hundred feet over my chute to verify I'd survived the ejection and to mark my exact location. And he knew he should provide immediate covering fire with bombs or guns to slow down the bad guys while I found a hiding spot. But he had just observed the withering AAA and he couldn't make himself dive toward my chute. He stayed at 16,000 feet. It was like his arm was frozen in a level flight position and he couldn't break it loose.

Only one thing kept popping into his mind: *Don't lose sight of where 304's chute went in.*

Nail 66 had been in charge thus far so Iceman deferred to him without a second thought. Nail 66 was trained by Air Force procedures to stay in charge of the scene until the arrival of the Sandy A-1s, and then the Sandy Leader would technically take over as the on-scene commander.

Meanwhile, Crown alerted the TUOC at NKP about a hundred miles away. Immediately, two Air Force Sandy A-1 rescue support planes from the 602nd Fighter Squadron were ordered to my scene. They were already airborne and just returning from an unsuccessful rescue attempt of a Thud pilot. Sandy 5 was the flight leader. Two additional Sandy A-1s, led by Sandy 7, were on alert at NKP, and they too were scrambled. Two Jolly Green HH-3 rescue helicopters were also on alert at NKP for just this type of situation, and within minutes both Jollys were airborne, with Jolly 20 as Lead. Crown estimated it would be about thirty minutes before the first two Sandys reached my area, and about one hour for the Jollys.

Sandy 7's section, on the ground at NKP, was disappointed. They had been only minutes away from standing down after three days of five-minute alert. They were normally stationed at Udorn Air Force Base, but their squadron rotated planes and crews in and out of NKP for alert duty in order to be closer to the action in northern Laos and North Vietnam. Sandy 7 was scheduled for a ten-day R & R break immediately after this alert was over. The past few days had been very boring and he and his wingman hadn't been scrambled once. So, only a few minutes before the scramble was sounded, to save time, Sandy 7 and his wingman had loaded their bags with personal belongings on each plane. In five minutes, they would fly back to Udorn, and once there, Sandy 7 would catch an airlift to Clark AFB in the Philippines.

Sandy 7 tried to save more time so he began to taxi to the end of the runway. With only a few minutes to go on his alert, Sandy 7 was cleared to taxi into take-off position on the runway since his replacement alert pilots had arrived at the alert pad. Suddenly, the tower radioed Sandy 7 that a Navy pilot had just been shot down and his section was needed to support Sandy 5's section. Rescues normally didn't take much time, and Sandy 7 was just going to be a back-up, so there should be no sweat to still make it to Udorn by his appointed airlift take-off time. He led his wingman in a fast taxi to the arming pits where ordnance arming pins were removed. Sandy 7 and his wingman were now hot, so they scrambled to the runway for a rolling take-off.

Chapter **7**

FACE TO FACE WITH THE ENEMY

After my main parachute blossomed, enemy soldiers saw me, popped off a few shots and ran toward me as I floated down. Three sideward swings of the chute didn't give me enough time to prepare myself for landing! I felt the weight of the sea survival seat pan, looked down, and saw it dangling slightly beneath me. I didn't have time to release it because I was heading straight toward a large grove of bamboo trees that were densely clumped and about thirty–forty feet in height. I feared my chute would hang up in them and I'd be suspended above the ground when the troops arrived. I jerked the chute risers powerfully one time with my left arm in an attempt to drift sideways toward a small opening. To my surprise, it happened that way. My corrective jerk caused a fast sideward slip. I crossed my legs to protect the family jewels just before I missed the taller bamboo trees, but fell through several smaller ones about ten–twelve feet tall. I crashed through and heard popping as limbs snapped off. My mind was churning out a multitude of procedures for ground impact.

When my feet touched the ground I attempted to tuck my legs for a forward roll, but the seat pan, for some reason, was directly behind my knees and prevented my effort to bend at the knee and soften the impact. I was able to tumble forward but the rigid seat pan crushed down on the back of one leg and I felt a stab of pain. A greater pain shot through my lower back and immediately I knew I had sustained an injury during the ejection sequence.

Nail 66 logged my ground impact as occurring at 5:45 Hotel time, and about two hours before official sunset. My first combat flight ended up being about thirty-four minutes long.

After tumbling, I quickly tried to stand up before enemy troops arrived. I got halfway up before a surge of pain caused me to collapse. I shifted my weight to the un-injured leg and pushed up again. It was difficult, and felt like I had a large weight on my back. A stabbing pain again hit me in the lower back and caused me to bend forward into a crouched position. My heavy seat pan was still attached so I quickly knelt again and released it. As I rose the third time, I had my hands on the shoulder-mounted parachute Koch fittings, lifted both up in one motion, and released the chute. Next, I popped the bayonet fittings that held the mask to the helmet. It was dangling from the survival vest so I grabbed it, pulled the Velcro apart, and dropped the mask to the ground. As I hurriedly ripped at the mask, I noticed I was about thirty-five feet from the edge of a grove of tightly packed bamboo trees with five-inch-diameter trunks. Before I had time to remove my helmet, I heard a popping sound at the edge of the grove.

Standing fully erect, I stared toward the sound. Then, I saw movement! Less than fifty feet away I saw my first enemy soldier. Black clothes, yellowish skin, dark hair, no helmet . . . both arms were stretched over his head supporting a carbine rifle. One hand was on the trigger. Immediately, I recognized him as a Pathet Lao guerilla. A chill went down my back because the Spooks had briefed how cruelly the guys in black treated captured pilots.

The gomer was struggling amidst the densely packed bamboo stalks and about fifteen feet from clearing them, but it was difficult for him to move and keep his rifle in front of him at the same time. He raised his head and we made contact, eyeball to eyeball. His rifle started to swing upward toward a firing position, but the opening between stalks was too narrow and his rifle banged against one hollow stalk, causing a distinctive *knock*. He made two very quick moves to get the rifle into a firing position and grimaced in frustration at his inability to fire at me. How did I look to him as I stood there in my bulky flight gear and white helmet, with sun visor completely obscuring my face?

I pushed my visor up quickly to see better and then, while still looking at the gomer, reached to draw my lightweight, .38-caliber revolver from its survival vest holster on my chest. My hand touched an empty pocket. Looking down, I was horrified to see the pistol dangling and entangled with several other items at the end of twelve inches of shroud-line cord. Facing the gomer, I grabbed the pistol, snapped it upward toward a firing position, but was stymied about halfway up due to the entangled cord. Mortified, I bent backward from the waist to elevate the short-corded pistol to a firing aim, but was stopped short because of back pain. As the pistol swung toward him, the gomer immediately dove for the ground. I remained erect, facing his location, but he was hidden in tall grass.

One of the tangled cords held my orange shroud-line cutter. I grabbed it, pressed the release button, and the curved-tip blade popped out. With my right hand, I took a slash at the one cord that I hoped held the pistol. Crap . . . my pistol fell to the ground. A sense of doom hit me because I was sure the gomer had seen the pistol fall and would jump up and shoot me before I retrieved it. I had only been on the ground for about twenty seconds and already my heart was trying to beat through my chest. I just knew I was about to be shot.

I lurched down, grabbed the pistol, and rose to a crouched firing position with one knee on the ground, fully expecting to see the gomer about to fire. Amazingly, he didn't get up. I didn't have a shot, so my first reaction was to run before other troops arrived.

The bamboo grove that hid the gomer continued for some distance from my eleven o'clock position to my three o'clock, but the foliage wasn't dense enough to avoid being seen if I ran that direction. *No good,* I thought.

I did an about face and scanned my options. At my ten o'clock, about twenty feet away, was a solid tree line of jungle, and the perimeter density was so thick I couldn't see inside the tree line—so that would be good cover to hide my escape. I began to half-run, half-limp toward it as I watched over my left shoulder. As I closed, I saw a very narrow opening in the thicket. At first glance, it looked like an animal trail. I stopped at the narrow opening, pushed the foliage further apart, and peered in.

Then, it hit me . . . I was scared. My chest was thumping, my breathing was fast, and I sensed I was hyperventilating. I took a deep breath and held it for a few seconds to counter the effect.

The opening was narrow but I saw a large trail on the other side. "Trails are to be avoided," I recalled from my JEST course. Should I take it? Just then, a bamboo knock occurred behind me and I turned and saw the gomer rising to his feet again, raising his rifle toward me. I dropped to my knees. A shot rang out . . . it missed. They're supposed to try and capture me first, I thought. I burst through the opening, not yet knowing what lay beyond, but determined to ignore the pain from my leg and back and just run for my life.

After three or four steps, I forcefully broke clear of a tangle of vines and the view ahead made me stop dead in my tracks. Ahead was a very smooth, ten–twelve-foot-wide packed-dirt trail, or maybe even road. Is this part of the Ho Chi Minh Trail, I wondered. I looked to my right, as that was my intended escape path, and gasped in amazement at the length and beauty of the trail. It stretched in a straight line for a couple of hundred yards before it bent to the left. The view was breathtaking for a man from the hills of West Virginia. Multicolored foliage of every description lined the trail and for two seconds I stood still, in awe of the beauty. I had stepped from outside where it had been bright, sunny, and steamy hot, to inside a jungle where the sunlight was filtered by monstrous trees that shaded the ground. It felt cooler. The dirt was reddish in color and the trail was bracketed on both sides by jungle vegetation with some of it draped over the trail as a trellis. I was now facing west so the fading sun cast a filtered light through the tree canopy, and the trail looked like a park brochure picture. It seemed to glow, inviting me to run. I had found just what I needed for a fast escape; but, dare I take it? The scene was one I'd been trained to avoid. I might rush headlong into more gomers. Reluctantly, I stood frozen for maybe ten seconds and analyzed the situation.

Suddenly, I heard a shout. The gomer was calling his buddies. My decision was easy. I had to put distance between me and the gomer to avoid a gun battle, and this trail was a perfect means to run fast. I had to chance it.

I wasn't a big guy then, only 5' 10" and a lean and mean 140 pounds. Regardless, my forty pounds of flight gear was the same weight a larger guy would carry. So my speed was reduced from a fast run to a quick jog.

I bolted like a frightened deer along the trail. In a matter of seconds I heard little whimpers, and at first I didn't recognize the source. It sounded like soft sobbing. Then it struck me: the sound was coming out of my own mouth. The realization was hard to stomach. I had never experienced such emotions, as I'd been macho all my life. But now, I sounded like a scared, whimpering child. *Buck up, damn it,* I thought. I ran faster. My fear of capture was greater than my leg and back pain, and even greater than death.

Meanwhile, overhead, Nail 66 had seen my plane hit the ground. He watched as it sort of pancaked in, no big explosion, just a burning fireball. Immediately afterward, Nail applied full power, banked his small plane in a sharp left-hand turn, and allowed the nose to drop so he could gain maximum airspeed. He dove from 3,000 feet toward the spot where he had last seen my chute. He would take a big chance and make one quick, low pass over the area to ascertain 304's fate. The plane's airspeed felt excruciatingly slow and this was one time Nail wished he was piloting one of the F-100s he'd previously flown. He leveled his O-2 at 1,500 feet and saw my chute stretched up and over the crown of bamboo trees several hundred yards from the plane's impact point. At that point, Nail 66 showed a lot of moxie. He banked his plane to the left and commenced a circular orbit around the chute in full view of the guns that had fired at me. He stared out the small side window and saw that I was no longer attached to the chute and not visible in the immediate vicinity. Suddenly, he heard the sound of automatic weapon fire, so he banked hard right, headed back south, and climbed to 5,000 feet. Nail had seen enough. 304 made it through the ejection, and was on the ground, somewhere . . . but there wasn't much Nail could do until SAR planes arrived.

I heard Nail's plane as I sprinted along the trail. I thought, *Get some frigging air support in here right now, Nail, to slow the gomers down.* Then, for some inexplicable reason, I actually muttered my next thought, out loud. "Come on guys . . . get down here with 20 mike-mike and save my ass by slowing down the gomers." I wanted an A-7 to scream in with rattling 20mm guns and kill the guys who were chasing me, like they did in the movies. Then I realized my buddies couldn't see me through the tree canopy.

My next thought was, *Call Nail on the radio.* He really needed to hear that I was alive so he would activate SAR immediately, without delay. If he thought I was dead, he might delay.

So as I ran, I held the pistol in one hand and fumbled around with the other to get to my survival radio. Finally, I grasped the 5-inch-long PRC-63 radio, but noticed the 12-inch, flexible, rubber antenna was jiggling wildly as I ran. I tried to steady it and keep it pointed up. The longer I ran, the more I became concerned that I might run upon a gomer so my eyes were roaming the area ahead and behind like a frightened deer. In between, I tried to find the right switch on the radio.

The radio had two switches, side by side. One was a slide switch that was normally OFF but I could slide it to the ON position with a quick movement of my thumb. The second switch was a press-and-hold-down-to-activate, two-position switch. Pressing and holding down one end of the switch would place the radio in a transmit voice mode, while the other end would select receive voice mode. Pressing neither when in the ON position would just emit a beeper signal that would be heard on the military radio guard channel that all pilots monitored.

While still jogging, I slid the first switch to the ON position and then held the radio close to my mouth with the intent of speaking softly. Then I made my first call in a firm, but pleading manner.

"Nail, 304 is on the ground and running from the bad guys. I need air support right now, over." Nail 66 and Spider each only heard what they described as a short, four-second beeper. They heard no voice.

I switched the radio to OFF. After running for another twenty yards or so, it dawned on me I hadn't depressed the transmit side before I made the transmission. I again slid the switch to the ON position and pressed and held what I thought was TRANSMIT. I screwed up again and pressed RECEIVE this time. Almost immediately, a voice boomed out for the entire world to hear. Surely, the enemy had heard it as well. My radio volume was set to maximum and Nail was talking.

"Sidewinder, I just heard a short beeper . . ." and at that instant I released the switch so the voice would stop. The volume of the transmission was like a gunshot. The loud voices scared the hell out of me. Had the bad guys heard Nail's transmission? If so, they now knew the direction I was running and I had no time to talk right then. I turned the radio off. But, at least I now knew the planes overhead had heard my beeper, both the first one and the inadvertent second and third ones. *Settle down 304*, I kept telling myself, *or you're going to screw this up big time.*

As I jogged, it dawned upon me that my radio volume control was set to maximum volume in anticipation of an ejection over water. Aboard a raft, I would need the volume to counter wave noise, etc. The volume control was a very small twist-knob on top of the radio and I couldn't change its setting right now since both hands were full. The volume adjustment would have to wait.

My head was on a swivel. I needed a spot where I could stop and take stock of the situation. After running about 150 yards, I saw a really large, fallen tree that blocked the trail. Its trunk was nearly four feet in diameter and too high for me to hurdle with my flight gear.

I bellied across the left side and slithered down through branches to a fortified hiding spot while I scanned for the gomer who had shot at me. If he had been the only one to see me hit the ground, then wiping him out could buy me more time. If he was still by himself, this was a good spot to take a shot, and a good place to remove some flight gear. I lay down in a prone position to scan forward along the trail, then looked and listened for activity behind me. Suddenly, an explosion occurred in the direction I had just run from. At first, I thought Iceman was bombing the troops I'd seen shooting at me. Then I realized it couldn't have happened that fast. My plane must be burning and one of my plane's Sidewinder missiles had cooked off.

I still couldn't risk talking to Nail, so I again activated the beeper, this time for at least fifteen seconds, and then turned the radio off and stowed it in my vest. I would talk to Nail when I felt my environment was safer.

I noticed that I was sweating profusely from my 150-yard dash. A heavy sweat had soaked through my flight suit and now also permeated my green G-suit, coloring it with white salt marks. It was about 6 P.M., so the sun was still shining brightly and the humidity was stifling. But fear of the gomer caused most of the sweat.

I needed to shed excess flight gear and lighten my pack load while I had the time. But, did I have the time? Could I finish before the gomer came this way? Quickly, I removed my helmet and survival vest, which left me in a precarious position. If I had to run now, I would have to carry the vest in my hand, so I needed to work quickly. While prone on the ground, I unzipped the parachute torso harness, pulled both arms up and out of the top half, and then slid the harness down my legs till they were free. Next, I unzipped the G-suit waist zipper and then dragged both leg zippers down and off. I detached the heavy flotation gear from the survival vest, put the vest back on, and zipped it tight. Frantically, I stuffed the discarded gear under the tree trunk and clawed till I covered it with dirt and foliage. If found, it would verify my escape path direction and also provide useful info which enemy interrogators could use to determine my squadron and plane model. Grisly horror stories about their methods of gaining that info were fresh on my mind and partly responsible for my sweat.

I remained behind the tree trunk for maybe two minutes, fortunately no longer. During that time, I heard neither voices nor foot traffic. I rose and began another dash on the trail. I could consciously feel my eyes darting left and right along the trail's perimeter as they uncontrollably scanned for any sign of trouble. I had never before been conscious of such rapid eye movement and it was as if I didn't have to think about it. Someone else seemed to have control of my eyes. My brain was churning out thoughts faster than I could process all of them. Should I get off the trail now, or continue? Should I run fast, or slowly? Should I call Nail 66 now, or later? I decided to run cautiously till I saw a good hiding spot.

Meanwhile, overhead, Nail 66 was now in a tight orbit at 5,000 feet, just close enough to keep a visual on the scene but still well south to steer clear of the guns. I couldn't see or hear his plane. The image of my tumbling A-7 was vividly engrained in Nail's mind, but he had experienced a wave of relief when he realized I had made it safely to the ground and was free of the chute. Now he assumed I was either running, hiding, or at worst, already captured. Nail, again, transmitted on guard but got no answer from me and heard no beeper in direct response.

Nail thought, *304 is dead and it's all my fault. I should have squelched that second run and I should've put the target smoke some other place.*

Nail was in agony. He wanted to immediately get a fast mover down low over the crash site, but was reluctant to ask Iceman to fly down in the weeds until he knew my precise location. Plus, what would he do if my wingie were also shot down? In his excitement and shock, Nail 66 had totally forgotten about the Sidewinder flight of three A-7s also orbiting overhead at 16,000 feet.

The flight leader, Sidewinder 406, was a thirty-four-year-old experienced combat pilot who, during a previous deployment, had flown the smaller A-4 Skyhawk during fifty-three missions over North Vietnam. He called himself Spider. I knew him fairly well and enjoyed his pleasing, humorous disposition. He was unpretentious, would tell you exactly what was on his mind, and would hold no punches if he thought something needed to be said, even if he was talking to the CAG. Plus, he was well respected for his ability as a bomber pilot. He and I both shared one trait: we were both loose cannons. We would charge ahead, sometimes to the chagrin of our CO's. But Spider had one trait I loved. He was fearless, and right now, I needed a tiger pilot to charge ahead at full speed, regardless of ramifications, and save my butt. Spider was no conservative, candy-assed pilot. He had steel balls.

Spider saw my chute blossom for just a few brief seconds, but long enough to get a spot on its location. He watched as Nail's plane drifted around the scene and heard him report no body was attached to the chute. From experience, Spider knew I was now evading, and he also knew Nail couldn't provide any immediate gun support. Spider had thirty minutes or less to help rescue me because, according to the Spook's statistics, I would be captured if I were on the ground any longer in Laos or North Vietnam. So he didn't hesitate. Spider armed two bombs.

"Nail 66, this is Sidewinder 406. I'm assuming On Scene Commander and I'm coming into the target area to support 304, over." He waited for a reply. Nothing. He called again. Nothing, for a second time. Nail 66 didn't respond as he was on Crown's frequency at the time. Spider was not about to wait any longer.

He directed his wingie, Razor, to stay high with the section leader in the third plane, and orbit at 12,000 feet to provide cover for him. "Arm your switches for two bombs," he directed. "But don't drop any bomb without my approval because we don't want to hit 304 by mistake."

Then, about four minutes after I hit the ground, Spider fearlessly entered the fight. He dove from his high, perch position and soared down through arcing tracers toward my chute. At 15,000 feet he rammed his throttle forward to the stop, and started a mild roll toward the crash site. Then he pulled back on the stick until the plane was lined up with my burning A-7. He leveled his wings in a thirty-degree dive and let the speed accelerate to the maximum. Soon he relaxed the stick and increased his dive to forty-five degrees. As he spotted my chute, he was still diving and accelerating through 490 knots airspeed so he hauled back on the stick to level off at five hundred feet.

Meanwhile, on the ground, I had just left the fallen tree and was again running along the trail. In the distance, I first heard a single pop, then another. Many rifles began to fire, followed by a whistling sound, and then a quick passing roar as an A-7 sped past.

Spider zoomed overhead of my chute at 480 knots in level flight at five hundred feet. In a quick scan, he saw a dozen or so black-clad soldiers running in a clearing between the burning plane and my chute. They quickly shouldered their rifles toward him as he zoomed overhead. Instantly, he knew they were after me and recognized I didn't have much of a head start so he had to slow them down to give me time to escape. At the same moment, tracers were now spitting past him as the AAA gunners tried to catch up to his speeding plane.

"304, this is Sidewinder. Do you read, buddy?"

No reply—because I didn't have the radio on. Fearlessly, Spider snapped the stick left for a sixty-degree bank to remain near the chute as he looked for me. While pulling four Gs, he decided he had to try and take out the troops.

Oh shit, he thought. *I'm set up for a forty-five-degree manual bomb run. What gunsite mils do I use for a five-hundred-foot, level-release run at 480 knots?* He couldn't recall, and wasn't in a very good position to check his kneeboard card. Hell, he would just pickle the bombs manually when he thought it looked like the right time. Spider was confident in his ability to place his bombs amidst the troops, and had no thought that an errant bomb might also take me out. So he pickled two 750-pounders, not realizing I was then less than a hundred yards from his target.

I had trotted fifty yards or so from the fallen tree by then and was still running. Suddenly, and totally out of the blue, a bomb exploded just off to my left. The concussion was so close that the ground vibrated and the explosive shock wave sent dirt and wood fragments flying, both against and past me. Small, shattered tree limbs landed around me and dirt splattered my face.

Finally . . . I thought. *Iceman* (I assumed) *is laying down support fire with his four remaining bombs.* On second thought, *He almost killed me because he didn't know my exact position.* But I didn't give a shit about the debris; I was just happy he was now protecting my rear.

Spider's two bombs wiped out most of the troops who were in the open, and the rest dived for cover. That bought me some valuable time and most likely saved my life.

Enemy AAA fire was now chasing Spider around in a tight circle near my chute, and it would only be a matter of time before it caught up. He'd already seen what happened to me on a second run so he hauled back on the stick to climb. Red, flaming AAA balls zoomed past his cockpit the entire way. At 12,000 feet, he switched to Crown's frequency and heard him telling Nail he was estimating arrival at the scene in fifteen minutes, and that rescue forces had been scrambled and were enroute. Spider quickly butted into the conversation.

"I saw a good chute and heard a short beeper which I assumed to be 304. The AAA is particularly hot on the north side, and my flight was fired at each time we flew over it. Also, black-clad enemy troops were in the immediate vicinity near the plane wreckage, but I either eliminated or scattered most of them. I can remain overhead for another hour, or at least till relieved by an Air Force On Scene Commander. I've got two Navy A-7s with four bombs remaining, and two others with six remaining. We'll orbit overhead, but do nothing until we make contact with 304."

My wingie and Spider's wingie were both on their first combat mission, but the fourth remaining A-7 pilot, Spider's section leader, was combat experienced.

While running through Spider's bomb debris, I shuttered momentarily. The bomb blast had been so close, but it was odd how certain things gave you a thrill. As a bomber pilot, I recognized how close I had come to being killed by one of my own shipmates—but I was still exuberant. *Way to go Iceman, shit-hot bombing . . . keep it coming buddy.* I ran more confidently now, pumped up that my buddies above were now covering me.

After Spider's bomb debris, I ran another hundred yards and suddenly heard two or three loud, excited voices approaching fast from my rear, no more than thirty yards behind me. Their volume and tone was such that I could tell they were running in my direction, and that they were very excited. I thought, *Now, the first gomer has reinforcements and he's briefing them about me.*

My blood pressure increased a little when I ejected, and maybe another fifteen percent when I saw the first gomer and then maybe another twenty percent when he shot at me. But, now, my heartbeat shifted into afterburner mode and I went from a jog to a full, all-out sprint. The voices sounded so close that I looked over my shoulder, fully expecting to see them, but a slight bend in the trail was between us and protected me. I could actually hear the huff and puff sound of their voices and knew they were running hard, and after another ten yards, could tell they were faster and gaining on me quickly. The damn gomers were outrunning me because of the bulky survival vest.

At any moment, they were going to see me and shoot. They had no fear of a lone American with a small pistol. Then the voices stopped.

I rounded another bend and twenty feet ahead to the left was a thicket of vegetation with foliage like a blackberry briar patch in full leaf. Instinct from childhood war games told me it was a good hiding spot, and the best available right now. I had run about three hundred yards on the trail and I needed to get off, *now!*

The voices suddenly re-appeared, seemingly right behind my shoulder. *Holy cow, they're almost on top of me.* Momentary fright . . . they now seemed to be just a few feet behind me, and instantly my heartbeat went to a level I never knew existed. But a quick glance to the rear showed their view of me was still temporarily blocked by the previous bend in the trail. Could I get off the trail before they rounded the bend and saw me? With everything I could muster, I accelerated toward the thicket.

At the edge of the trail, I jumped with every ounce of strength I could muster into the thicket, and then attempted a slide so I would face the trail. Instead, the first foot to touch the ground snagged on a root, and I stumbled and rolled forward as thorns ripped my shirt and slashed my skin. I rose to one knee, gasped for air, and deftly scrambled another four feet to the center of the thicket. Once there, I lay flat on the ground amidst heavy vines and positioned myself toward the trail. About eight feet of dense foliage now blocked most of my view of the trail, and hopefully the view of anyone looking my way. Frantically, I snapped the stems of several large fronds and placed the foliage to camouflage my prone body as I nestled the ground. I felt like a scared rabbit must feel as he hears an armed hunter approach.

Damn, too close for comfort! Within seconds, and I literally mean like five to six seconds, three bad guys ran into view. Quickly, I aimed my pistol toward the leader and nervously drew the hammer back. They were running fast, clad in black, rifles raised, and talking excitedly as they passed single file about ten feet away. Two guys passed by without looking my way, but the third turned his head directly toward my position. I saw his eyes clearly, and for one very brief moment I quivered, thinking he had seen me. Had he? Should I shoot first? But he kept running.

They were there, and then gone in a flash. Their voices slowly faded down the trail.

Chapter **8**

CHATTERING TEETH

few seconds after the three gomers passed, I rose to my knees to
monitor their fading voices for distance and direction because I
needed an accurate fix in the event I changed my hiding position. I
also listened for any more suspicious sounds from the direction I had
run. After maybe thirty seconds I could still hear the voices of the three
gomers in the distance, but otherwise it was eerily quiet. In a matter of
moments though, I began to hear a strange noise and it seemed to be
next to me. At first, I didn't realize what was happening and thought the
noise signaled danger. Maybe an animal or a snake? I was hearing an
unfamiliar sound and it was loud enough to cause me to tremble
slightly. *What's that clicking noise?* I strained my ears to listen and
scanned the area.

Suddenly, it hit me. My teeth were chattering. No shit. No way, no
frapping way . . . but it was true. My jaw was moving up and down
uncontrollably as if a tiny motor was driving it. I could feel, and hear,
the light impact as my upper and lower teeth collided. I held out my
hands for inspection, expecting them to be trembling, but they
weren't. I listened to my breathing rate. It sounded okay. I appeared
under control except for the damn clicking teeth and it wasn't just in
my head. The sound was so loud I actually feared the enemy would
hear it. *Listen closely . . . the sound can't be that loud,* I thought. I did, and
it was. My teeth were making a heck of a lot of noise and it was loud
enough to be heard by anyone within ten feet. What if another bad
guy came along the trail before I settled down?

What a hell of a mess. Shot down, chased by bad guys—and now,
runaway jaws and clicking teeth! What's the decibel rating of clicking

teeth? It sounded like it must be up there at a level with a woodpecker tapping on a metal house gutter.

My first attempt at an immediate solution was to use my hands to physically restrain my jaws in a closed position. Unbelievably, that didn't work. It would slightly muffle the sound but it was physically impossible to prevent the jaws from moving up and down. Next, I tried holding my breath but that didn't work either. *Think, Fields, think.*

After a few seconds, I realized I had somewhat planned for this, and had placed an item in my survival vest that had a triple purpose. It would protect against the known leeches in the waters of Laos and Vietnam; it would provide some quick energy from its sugar content; and, it often had a drug-like calming effect. I pulled out my magic potion, a red and green bag of Redman Chewing Tobacco. I sank to a seated position and tried to cram a big wad into my mouth, but the interval between clicks was much too fast for an opening. That was down right ridiculous, weird, and almost funny—but I didn't know whether to laugh or cry. My mind seemed to be functioning fine, but why wouldn't my teeth stop clicking? After some effort I crammed three fingers of one hand into my mouth, and while my teeth nibbled at my fingers, finally got the tobacco in place. The wad muffled the clicking sound, and within a minute my jaws ceased their movement, and my teeth ceased their scary clicking. The Redman served its purpose well.

The close call with the three gomers caused a pinnacle of fear I had never experienced before. I had been in several near-death situations earlier in my life, but had never encountered a feeling of this magnitude. I could feel it curdling and swelling inside my gut and jumbling my mind. It was a feeling of fear that I never, ever want to experience again, but one that I now know does exist in the far fringe of my mind.

I instantly felt as if my manhood had been robbed, in one swell swoop. It was a huge letdown for a twenty-eight-year-old macho pilot from Bartley, West Virginia, and later, "Bloody Breathitt" County, Kentucky. In those mountains, real men weren't frightened by anyone, or anything. But my fellow squadron pilots had spent considerable time in discussion about the horrific torture of American pilots in the Hanoi prisons, and obviously, the horror stories had affected me; I had an inner fear of capture that was much higher than I had ever imagined. I was totally demoralized as I lay on the ground. Was I a wimp? I began to talk to myself in an attempt to thwart the feeling.

What should I do first, I wondered. Get some help! No one but me was responsible for my predicament, but shame wouldn't keep me from asking for help now. And I wanted all the help I could get. An inner feeling told me I needed big time help to stay alive, so my first action would be to seek help from the one I had the most confidence in. I would ask God for his help—but for a brief moment, the thought occurred that God wouldn't listen. After all, I had just dropped six bombs and probably killed a few of his children, so why should God have mercy on me now? And I wasn't real sure I was right with God.

I didn't consider myself the most righteous of individuals, but did believe strongly in the principle of God, country, and family, in that order. God should come first in your life, but I hadn't consistently practiced that principle even though I was saved and baptized as a youngster. I sometimes read the Bible, said a prayer on most days, and tried to live by the Ten Commandments. Now, I wished I had consistently lived by the Golden Rule, and adhered to all the Commandments, but I had not. Regardless, I would make a conscious, sincere request for his assistance. There was no need to get into detail as I was confident God knew the particulars already. So I bowed my head and softly uttered a short prayer, out loud.

"God, I need your help. If you get me out of this situation I will—" *what would I do?* "God, help me and I will try extra hard to live a better life in your name. Amen."

Would God help me, or let me languish? I didn't know. I had total confidence that he heard the prayer, would consider my request, and grant it if that was his plan for me. I had erred often in my faith, and perhaps my prayer would just be considered another broken promise. I did have confidence, though, that it would be given a fair review.

I also knew that God expected me to do most of the work. I'd been taught that prayer was a wonderful thing and not to be abused, nor was it the only answer to a problem. You have to put out maximum effort to help yourself and now it was time for me to do so if I was to survive. God would watch over me and maybe assist, maybe not. Most of the work would be up to me.

In a few seconds, I felt a calmness that hadn't been there since the flak enveloped me during my second bomb run. I reached the pinnacle of fear when the three bad guys ran past, but now I seemed fortified. My fear, which had quickly soared to momentous height and subsided so very slowly, was now gone. God might not save me from eventual capture, but he lifted my morale and gave me courage to buck up to my enemy.

The time was about 6 P.M. I'd been on the ground for about fifteen minutes, and now realized that the rescue forces had less than two hours to pick me up before darkness set in. But would the Air Force even attempt it after dark? And how long would it take them to reach my position? I pondered my next move.

Meanwhile, the rescue force was slowly beginning to take shape. Crown had earlier directed Spider to squawk 77 on his friend or foe identifier (IFF) so Crown could get a quick fix for heading purpose. As Crown sped to the scene, four F-4s were diverted to rendezvous with Nail 66. Now, Crown was in a high orbit near the scene and he informed Spider, the on-scene commander, and Nail 66, that once the F-4s arrived, the four Sandy A-1s and two Jolly HH-3s would remain well clear of the area until it was softened up. Additionally, Crown had requested a Blind Bat night-flare plane, and one had been ordered to the scene.

Back aboard USS *America*, many of my fellow squadron pilots were gathered in the pilot's Ready Room for a daily ritual before dinner bull session. In a few minutes, they would mosey down to the Officers' Wardroom for dinner. The first day of combat was nearly over and all squadron pilots had flown and returned safely from their first mission except for me, Iceman, and the SDO.

Many of the pilots were comparing notes about their individual first combat missions. Some were realistic, many were bragging in loud and boastful voices. None had seen any AAA to speak of, and all of them thought it was going to be a piece of cake for the next few days over South Vietnam. Suddenly, the SDO's squawk box (inter-department intercom) blared out with a call from the combat information center, and the room went silent.

"Ready Room Six, go ahead C.I.C."

"Ready Six, we just got word that 304 was shot down. Pilot ejected. No word on status yet. Send a rep to C.I.C. to assist, out."

The pilots were literally stunned, but one of them eased toward the posted flight schedule grease board to verify the pilot of 304. The first day of combat ops was not yet complete and one of them had been shot down already! How? No one got shot down unless they flew over North Vietnam. That was the consensus they had learned from Navy pilots who had made earlier deployments to the war zone. We had been told that targets, anywhere other than over Indian country, were only protected by light automatic weapons that couldn't harm you above three thousand feet.

All eyes turned toward the Old Man, who hadn't moved a muscle, and was still slouched in his chair. Skipper was much older than most of the pilots, and looked it. He had flown in the Korean War and was an old hand at this game. He had warned his nuggets that one bullet could bring you down, and it could happen any time you were over the beach. Without rising out of his slouch, he turned his head toward the SDO. "Who was in 304?"

"Kenny was the section leader, and Fred was his wingman," the SDO replied.

From the rear, a callous retort came from one of the senior prima donna pilots who thought he was infallible and could do no personal wrong. "Damn it, I knew that pair was too inexperienced to fly as a section."

Skipper's lips immediately curled a little to show his anger before he turned to his second in command. "XO, send someone to C.I.C. to see what they know, and you go talk to the Spooks."

The two pilots left the room without a word while Skipper sank back into his leather chair. He reclined and closed his eyes. He had hoped to make it through the entire cruise without losing a pilot, but he hadn't even made it through day one.

Then he thought of the wives. He hated that his wife would have to inform Kenny's wife of her loss. How many kids did Kenny have? He couldn't remember. The SDO's telephone rang and interrupted his thought.

The SDO said "Yes, Sir," a couple of times to the caller, and then turned to Skipper. "Sir, the CAG wants to see you right away in his stateroom."

I'm not looking forward to this, Skipper thought. While hurdling one knee-knocker after another, he wondered why his least experienced pilots had taken the only real AAA of the day. *What damn rotten luck for them and me*, he thought.

He knocked on CAG's door and a single word, "Enter," came booming through the door. He walked into the room and saw that CAG was seated and writing at his desk. Without turning, CAG said, "Take a seat." Skipper started to take the chair beside CAG, and his knees were already buckled when he was jolted by CAG's words.

"Skipper, initial reports indicate your boy was knocked down during a second bomb run in Laos. To me, it doesn't appear he followed my Rules of Engagement, since it prohibits two bomb runs. Maybe your squadron's training has been inadequate? Do you agree?

Skipper stood erect, and his temple bulged from the instant rise in blood pressure.

"Damn it CAG . . . my boy has a name, and he's been humping it for the Navy now for about six years, and he has a wife and two kids. Right now, I'm more concerned whether he's dead or alive than whether he violated our air wing policy. Secondly, if he was bombing in Laos with a FAC, I'm not sure he violated any policy. I recommend we hold our criticism till we get more facts, sir."

CAG held his ground. "Okay, Skipper. For now, we'll give him that benefit of doubt. However, if he didn't, there will be serious repercussion.

Skipper stood stoic, and his face expressed surprise at the CAG's comments. "First we have to get him back, CAG, hopefully in one piece. Will that be all, sir?"

"Commander, make sure your boys know my ROE, and keep me informed about the SAR. That will be all."

Skipper walked stoop-shouldered back to the Ready Room, and sagged into his chair. The SDO saw his pained expression and had the balls to ask him if everything was okay. "Nothing I can't handle, son," came the reply. Within a few minutes, the XO returned from his visit with the Spooks and slid in his chair beside Skipper to brief him privately.

"Basically, Kenny went down in an area called Tchepone, where it's wall-to-wall with AAA, and he's surrounded by enemy troops. The Spooks have since learned this Tchepone area is a known hotbed of enemy activity, and one where many pilots have recently been shot down. In fact, one was rescued just yesterday within several miles of where Kenny went down. We weren't told of this because the Spooks didn't know we would be striking in Laos today."

Skipper responded. "Why the hell are we just now hearing about this? Why weren't we briefed before now? Kenny shouldn't have been in that area on his first day of combat."

Meanwhile, Spider became concerned I'd be captured or killed before the Jollys arrived. During the past twenty-five minutes, he first tried to raise me on the radio but had no joy. Next, he made multiple circular orbits of the area, and each time around he received heavy flak from a 37 on the north side. So each time around, he plotted the AAA sites for

Nail's use when the rescue force arrived. After one orbit, he informed Crown that my chute had disappeared.

Nail 66 was dubious and made a low pass over the area. He verified that the chute was in fact still in the same location but no longer lying across the trees. It was now stretched out fully in a clearing and a smoke flare was billowing on the ground nearby. He concluded it was an enemy trick to entice him to fly lower, but Nail didn't bite.

Iceman flew alone and confused at 16,000 feet during the first ten to fifteen minutes after I was shot down. He followed Nail's instruction to call Crown, but then he didn't know what to do next other than keep an eye on the exact spot I went in so he could tell others. Spider had jumped in and declared himself On Scene Commander but didn't provide Iceman with any instructions, and Iceman didn't ask for any. He still had four bombs, but he was waiting for direction from Spider as to what, and when, he should attack. In his mind, he could still see the many guns firing at me and now firing sporadically at the Sidewinder flight. The scene scared him. Even at 16,000 feet he still felt vulnerable to the ground fire, so he kept his throttle setting at high power as he orbited. He felt the need for speed—to remain safe. His plane was going fast, his mind was racing, and he didn't know what to do. His four remaining bombs were causing additional drag, and his high speed was just gobbling up his fuel. He was nearing "bingo" state, the level of fuel required for the return trip to the boat, but he knew he shouldn't leave me. However, he also knew it would do no good to run out of fuel and lose another A-7. Reluctantly, he called Spider.

"Sidewinder 406, this is Streetcar 307. I'm nearing bingo and need to return to base [RTB], over."

"Negative 307. You can't proceed feet wet as a single plane for safety reasons and we may still need your bombs. Maintain your orbit till the Jolly arrives and then join with my flight for the return leg to the ship, out." Spider then re-considered and gave an order to his number three plane. "Break off, go hold hands with Streetcar for safety's sake."

Iceman hung tight, stiff-lipped, but still maintained a high rate of speed, wasting fuel. Neither he, nor his combat-experienced Sidewinder wingman, took the initiative to slow down and conserve fuel because they were in the midst of sporadic AAA.

Spider was now in a dilemma. Forty minutes had passed since I hit the ground and the Sandys weren't yet at the scene. He had made up his mind that he wouldn't leave the area before the Sandys arrived while his flight still had bombs. There was no way he would bail out on Streetcar and leave him unprotected. However, he recognized that Iceman had low fuel problems and all the A-7's had a recovery land time in thirty minutes aboard USS *America*. They were about two hundred miles from the boat, it would take about thirty-five minutes to reach it, and it was a big deal in carrier aviation if a flight was late for a scheduled recovery time. If late, it would normally delay the carrier's entire schedule as it waited for planes to land before it could commence launching the next wave of planes. Fortunately though, Spider's flight was the last one scheduled for recovery before the carrier ceased ops for the day, so he had a little time to play with. The ship's captain wouldn't be happy steaming into the wind as the ship wasted fuel to wait on Spider's flight, but it would be no big problem, and Spider would get a "Charley on arrival" (a ready deck for landing).

About fifteen minutes after Iceman asked for permission to return to the ship, the first two Sandys checked in with Crown and solved the dilemma. Since the Sandys were now in the area, Spider thought it was a good time to turn On Scene Commander over to them and head back to the boat. And frankly, he hadn't heard my voice yet, nor a recent beeper, so he wasn't very confident I was still alive. Crown informed him that the Sandys were just a few minutes away so Spider cleared Iceman and his Sidewinder wingman to head back to home plate.

Before leaving, Spider asked Nail 66 to smoke one of the AAA guns that was raising so much hell on the north side of the perimeter so he and Razor could have a go at them before they too RTB'ed. Spider had four 750-pounders remaining, and Razor had six.

Nail 66 was a little dubious about dropping more bombs before he knew my status and location; but he didn't want to waste any available ones because he knew he had to knock out a bunch of guns before the Sandys could pinpoint my location. Nail already had some Air Force F-4s checking in for flak suppression. He already had the gun sites in mind that he wanted to kill, so he marked one particularly troublesome 37 and told Spider, "Have at it." Spider then told Razor they would make simultaneous runs against the gun, but each would roll in from different angles. Spider then headed for what he thought would be the safest perch. I was unaware any of this was going on.

About thirty-five minutes had elapsed since I hit the ground and I was sitting, just unwinding in my thicket, and simply taking in the sights and sounds of the jungle. I had heard no enemy sound for several minutes so my brain had returned to sanity. *I might just make it out of this mess yet,* I thought. Maybe the guys on the ship will be so impressed with my survival skills that they won't give me too much crap about my shoot down. "Yeah, right. Big fat chance of that happening," I muttered under my breath.

The drone of Nail's small engine broke my daydream and reminded me that he was still nearby, but I couldn't hear any jet noise. A massive tree canopy blocked most of the sky, but if I looked straight up, I could see a small patch of sky. No plane had flown through it yet. If I stood up I'd have a better view, but I wasn't yet ready to take that chance. I hadn't yet talked with Nail 66 since hitting the ground and knew he was uncertain whether I was dead or alive. *Rescue forces should be arriving in a few minutes,* I thought. I decided there was no need to talk to anyone until I heard the sound of a Sandy plane. There was no reason to chance a radio transmission being heard by the gomers before the rescue forces were in place. That was my plan two minutes after hitting the ground, and after pondering, it was still my plan. My radio would remain off till I heard a Sandy.

At that moment, I heard the whine of jet engines and it sounded like A-7s. I rolled toward the sound and looked straight up through the one small opening. There, I saw an A-7 on its perch as it banked left toward me in an apparent bomb run dive. It was about time my buddies got in the fight again. Nearly twenty minutes had gone by since I last heard bombs. The A-7 was diving in from my right to my left and heading toward the river. My spirits rose as I assumed this signified the start of the rescue attempt.

I stared at the plane and was pretty sure I saw orange color on the tail, so that meant the Sidewinders were attacking. Spider's still around. Then I lost sight as he descended below my viewable horizon, but immediately the sound of heavy guns erupted with a steady stream of tracers soaring upward. He was really getting hosed. I heard the engine sound change as he started his pull off and I knew his bombs were on the way. A few seconds later, I heard the distant rolling thunder of each boom, boom, boom, boom—and felt the rumbling reverberation as the ground shock wave reached me. I heard one secondary explosion from the first two bombs, then several smaller ones after the third and fourth bombs, and I assumed some ammo had been destroyed. Way to go Spider! I heard a second jet so I looked up toward the same previous perch position. Everything looked pretty much the same except that this A-7 was heading almost directly toward me. *That's got to be Razor rolling in,* I thought. It was his first combat bomb run so I wondered if he was scared.

He rolled toward me, disappeared from sight behind the trees, pulled off the target and in a few seconds I braced for the impact. What the hell? The first of six bombs exploded nearby with a loud, thunderous BOOM and the second was even closer, and then the rest began closing on me in quick successive booms. They were going to hit me! I flung myself flat on the ground, covered my head with my hands, and cringed as I heard the bomb explosions walking toward me. For a split second, I thought I'd be in the bomb pattern. The ground shook below me! Then the last bomb exploded, and dirt, stones, and wood splinters flew over me just as the ground again reverberated, this time more severely. If Razor had dropped two more bombs, he would have killed me. If the gomers didn't get me, my buddies would, eventually.

"Nail 66, Sidewinder 406 is turning On Scene Commander over to Sandy 5 and my flight's now bugging out for home plate. Be advised that the area to the north is really hot. I tried to cool it off but there're lots of guns near 304 so it's going to require a lot more bombs to knock them all out." Fifty minutes after my ejection, Spider and Razor left the fight. Iceman and his Sidewinder playmate had bugged out thirteen minutes before them. All my Navy buddies were now gone. . . .

After Razor's bombs nearly wiped me out, I thought about my situation for several minutes. I needed to talk with Nail now, before someone else put another bomb on me. Then, in the next second, I changed my mind and decided to chance more bombs rather than chance voice conversations being heard by the gomers. My recent jungle survival training course in the Philippines was the main reason. During JEST, we were shown an old training movie that depicted enemy troops walking through the jungle with a backpack containing directional finding equipment that homed in on radio transmissions. The movie stressed that the enemy had the capability to home on your survival radio transmission to find your hiding location. It cautioned against excess radio transmissions when one was evading. It was an old movie, and I was sure the enemy had refined the technique so I wasn't about to test its effectiveness. I decided to stick to the plan wherein I waited until I heard either a Sandy or Jolly plane before I made any type of voice transmission. But Nail needed to know I was still alive and another beeper transmission should suffice for that. First though, I removed my right glove and twisted the small, circular black volume control knob to a medium volume position. Then I slid the switch to the ON position and left it there for fifteen seconds of beeper to allow for an ADF cut by Nail. That should have been enough time if he was sharp.

"Nail, this is Sidewinder. Did you get that beeper on guard channel, over?"

"Roger, Sidewinder, I got a good bearing. It appears to be coming from an area west of the crash site but I have no idea how far. It could be 304 on the run, or it could be an enemy trap. I'll try again to get him up on the radio, out." Nail tried to contact me over the next twenty minutes while he received sporadic pot shots from enemy rifles.

I, meanwhile, spent that same agonizing twenty minutes in my clump. No planes, no bombs, but I was somewhat familiar with the routine and knew Nail was waiting for the Jollys to arrive, and that it should only be a short lull before that happened. After all, I had read a quote from a Jolly pilot; "Fighter pilots have no fear, Jolly Green Giants are always near." Being my first combat mission, I was naïve enough to actually believe they were hovering on airborne alert somewhere close by and would get to me in a matter of a few minutes.

Any second now, I thought, I should hear the *whop whop* of the Jolly Green Giant's massive rotor blades. I sat on pins and needles as I waited for the sound of a helo. Time dragged by as I watched the sky. Then a thought occurred: what if the Jolly rushed in before the AAA was suppressed? A helicopter, even at treetop level, wouldn't be able to withstand the amount of AAA I had encountered. It would be blasted out of the sky! I felt sorry for the poor Jolly who was sent my way. Upon reflection, though, I wasn't going to worry about an Air Force helo pilot whose job was to rescue me. Jolly knew the mission and it was his call as to whether he tried. Maybe he had already made the call and that was why I was still waiting.

I was self-centered and more concerned about my own safety than that of others. The feeling was not right. Yes, I wanted to be rescued, but I was the one who got shot down trying to be a hero. If Jolly deemed it too risky for a pick-up here, then I understood. Back and forth, back and forth went my mind. Finally, I decided the Jolly should at least try to reach me. But would he be able to see me in my current position?

I studied my surroundings. The foliage in the thicket was about five feet high, and I sat in a four-foot section that was smooth and open, almost like a deer bed; but the perimeter was dense with heavily foliated vines and plants. I couldn't see much laterally but there was a small opening in the tree canopy above. I rose to a crouched position, but even then, I couldn't see much of the peripheral area around me. I could, though, make out the edge of the trail. Had I left a trail of broken twigs or pressed foliage when I first jumped in the thicket? I crawled toward the trail through vines to the perimeter of the thicket. Then I wiggled backward toward the center and tried to arrange the foliage so it looked natural. No one could detect I had entered the thicket. It was a good spot to sit tight till rescued.

About forty minutes had gone by since I hit the ground. Rescue planes should have arrived by now. I went to the receive mode of my radio and listened for the next few minutes. Nothing, no one was talking on Guard channel.

Unknown to me, Sandy 5 (the A-1 Leader) and his wingie had flown into the area about five minutes earlier. Within minutes of that, the first Air Force fast movers, as Nail called them, also arrived. In another five minutes the first two Jollys arrived. Crown advised the Sandys and Jollys that the area was too hostile and instructed them to remain well clear until it was safe enough to affect a rescue. The Jollys replied they would hold over the "Rooster Tail," an area about twenty miles away that was normally safe from AAA. The Sandys would provide air cover for the two Jollys until Nail deemed it safe for them to pinpoint my position. Nail 66 then began to work the fighters to suppress the AAA.

"Nail 66, Silver is ten miles out with two F-4s, each carrying 500-pound GPs and ready to work, over."

Nail 66 then briefed there were ten active AAA sites near my position to include ZPU, 23, 37, and 57s, plus lots of small arms fire. Next, he shot a smoke rocket at the AAA site that was closest to my plane's still-smoking wreckage. "Silver flight, have at 'em."

Suddenly, I heard jet engines whine as fast movers entered my area, and I immediately sprang into action on my radio. The engine sound was different from the A-7 whine so I knew Air Force fighters would be dropping bombs, and I wasn't certain the Air Force jocks would be any more careful with their bombs than the Sidewinders. And, they might not be as accurate as the Sidewinders, so I needed to remind them I was still around, and to be cautious.

I activated the beeper for another fifteen-second burst, still refusing to talk. Crown heard it, and informed Nail 66 who had missed it because he was talking on another frequency with the fighters. Nail then tried again to make voice contact with me but couldn't, so he decided to go ahead and start the flak suppression. He thought I would call if they got too close with the bombs; but he still wasn't sure whether I had been captured, or if the beeper was an enemy trap.

Silver flight then made their bomb runs, got hosed, but caused a few more secondary explosions. Next, a Banyon flight was told by Nail to pickle on the closest active firing gun. One of the bombs exploded close by and dirt and stone again rained down upon me. Tree trunks made a sharp, cracking pop as they splintered and crashed to the ground nearby. I didn't move an inch as I was impervious to more bomb blast. It no longer fazed me. I had learned that it was too late to dive for cover once the explosion started so I just sat and listened as the trees fell a couple of hundred feet away. *Must be my guardian angels at work,* I thought. Just then, a very large group of monkeys began to squeal loudly in unison amidst all the fallen trees. The bomb must have detonated right in their midst and they were cutting a real monkeyshine.

The bombs lifted my morale, as I knew the Air Force was now starting its rescue attempt. No further panic, as now I had reached a casual, but alert, mental mode. The last bomb did convince me that it was time to talk to Nail and let him know how close the bombs were, before they killed me.

My plan was to use the beeper as a heads up-alert to ensure someone was geared to listen to my transmission. Quickly, I put out another beeper signal of two-seconds duration. Then I pressed the receive side of the slide switch, held the radio tightly against my ear, and listened for five seconds. No one was talking at the time. I moved my thumb to the transmit side, pressed it down, and spoke in a calm, but hushed mode.

"Nail 66, this is Streetcar 304 on the ground, over."

Five long seconds passed before I heard him scream. "Streetcar 304, this is Nail 66, great to hear you buddy."

Nail was excited and probably spoke in a louder than normal tone and shocked the living daylight out of me. I had reset my radio volume to medium strength, but the volume was still so loud that any gomer within fifty yards would have turned his head toward the sound. Nail was still talking but I wasn't listening. Oh, shit. I instantly thrust the radio under my armpit to muffle his words. This was why I was reluctant to use the radio. Surely the enemy had heard his loud voice.

Quickly, I turned the volume all the way to minimum setting and again pressed the receive switch. Nail was still talking, and the volume seemed about right; but, I released the switch to listen closely for the sound of any foot noise which might indicate gomers walking toward my position. I heard none and felt lucky, again.

I went back to receive mode. Nail 66 was still talking. I liked his attitude.

"All aircraft, cease transmissions! Streetcar 304 just came up on his radio so stay off the air while I re-attempt contact with him. Nail out."

"Nail 66, this is Streetcar 304, over."

"Roger, Streetcar, I'd just about given you up for dead. How do you copy, over?"

"Got you loud and clear, Nail."

"304, what's your status and location? Over."

"Nail, I'm in good shape but the bad guys are nearby. I think I'm hiding about three football fields northwest of my chute, over."

"Roger 304. I've got a spot on your chute and know your approximate position. Don't worry. The Sandys and Jollys are here now and you'll be outta there in a few minutes. Continue to monitor your radio and dig yourself a deep hole while we take out the AAA. Keep your head down, Streetcar, and we'll have you outta there in no time, over."

"Roger Nail. I'm not going anywhere, out." I actually believed him. . . .

Nail's voice was calm. His voice inflection was even-keeled as if he'd just met an old friend. Like, "What's up, Joe?" He didn't sound excited, but did sound happy to hear my voice. His radio manner was reassuring and gave me confidence he'd soon extract me from this terrible mess I'd gotten myself in. My morale soared, but then I began to really reflect on what might happen when the Jolly arrived overhead.

How could a Jolly hover and hoist me up with gomers so close? I knew I had big problems even if they killed all the AAA guns. One lone gomer could be hidden nearby, just waiting for me to break cover, and then he would rush in and either capture—or kill—me. Would the Jolly be shot down as it hovered, or would I be shot on the way up the hoist? I was beginning to have serious doubts about an immediate rescue.

Nail then went back to work. Within the first hour after I punched out, nearly twenty bomb runs were made against the AAA sites but the enemy fire was still as intense, and probably more so. At that point I began to think the enemy AAA sites might just physically run out of ammo due to the number of bomb runs and subsequent secondary explosions caused by the bombs. As I watched and listened, I learned a valuable lesson that would help me a great deal, later on.

When each fighter dove in from a high perch and rolled his wings level, the AAA gunners around me would commence firing and would continue to do so until the nose of the plane started to rise out of the dive. As soon as the pilot released his bombs, pulled back on his stick, and commenced his climb, the enemy knew bombs were on the way and all firing would cease. The gunners would take cover. Immediately after the bombs exploded, the AAA would again commence firing at the jet as it climbed out. The enemy's pattern was simple. They fired at the jet during its dive, ran for cover when the nose of the jet pitched up, and quickly got back on the guns after the bombs exploded. That partially explained why I thought I had made it safely through my bomb run only to be hit as I was climbing. An attacking jet was most vulnerable as it pulled off the target. From the ground, it appeared the jet was almost stationary at that time. It had little forward motion, was at its lowest altitude, and had its belly in full view of any forward gun. I would store that fact for my own bomb runs later, if I got to make any more than the two today.

Sandy 5 and his wingie were holding ten to twelve miles away at 12,000 feet, and had been joined by Sandy 7 and his wingie. The four of them were in a protective orbit over two Jollys at the Rooster Tail location, and a third Jolly was enroute as a back-up. The rescue force was now in place awaiting Sandy 5's decision to deem it safe enough to try an ID pass. He had been monitoring the aircraft radio chatter between Nail and the fighters so he already had a pretty good mental picture of AAA location and intensity, and to him it seemed to have diminished somewhat. Sandy 5 and his wingie flew closer to the scene to verify same and determine the safest approach corridor for a low-level pass to pinpoint my exact location.

Sandy 5 made his first look-see pass at 12,000 feet and observed the last bomb run by one of the Gunfighter F-4s. He was astonished by the amount of 37-flak rising from multiple gun sites near the pick-up area. There was no way he was going to fly at five hundred feet for an ID pass with that amount of enemy opposition. He immediately requested Crown to have the fast movers drop some CBUs to kill the gunners, while the Sandys continued to orbit, high. CBUs would quickly kill the gunners, but thus far, none of the available fighters were loaded with any. Crown told Sandy 5 that it didn't look like they would be able to get any before dark.

Sandy 5 pondered his options. He knew it would be impossible to wipe out all the AAA before nightfall without CBUs, and he knew I didn't have much of a chance to survive if I remained on the ground overnight. He knew he would risk his life if he flew into the teeth of the huge amount of enemy fire he had just witnessed. What should he do? A pussy would turn tail, run, and come back tomorrow after the fighters wiped out the AAA. *304 might not survive if I turn tail*, he thought.

Sandy 5 was no pussy. He would perform his duty and ignore the obvious hazards. He told Crown to have Nail 66 put the fast movers on hold. Brazenly, he started a turn to the south to set up for his first ID pass so he could approach on a northerly heading to avoid the heavier guns to the north and east of my location. Sandy 5 descended to 1,000 feet above the ground.

Nail 66 was still receiving occasional pot shots at his plane, so to avoid being hit, he had flown continually at maximum speed. That consumed more fuel, and now he was dangerously low, and well past his normal RTB amount. Another Nail FAC had arrived to relieve him. As Nail 66 marked targets for the jets, he also briefed his relief Nail pilot on the situation so he was busy, scared, and sweating. He was briefing the new Nail on one frequency, directing the attacking jets on another frequency, and checking in additional fighters on another frequency. It became a challenge to just maintain order at the scene and simultaneously keep track of all the players. Now he was told to stand by while Sandy 5 checked the area. The prudent thing was to RTB and let the new Nail take over, but he couldn't make himself leave me, unrescued. "Damn it," Nail uttered, "I'm responsible for 304 being on the ground and I'm getting him out before I leave. But, how?" As he wiped sweat off his brow, Sandy 5 called.

"Nail, Sandy 5 is descending to the south and then I'm going to fly north to get the survivor's exact location, over."

"Roger, Sandy. Be aware the area is still hot with guns. Lots of automatic weapons, ZPU's, 23s, and even 37s, over."

"Nail, roger that. Contact the survivor. Tell him to be on the lookout for me and to have a smoke flare ready. I'm switching to Guard channel at this time, out."

Things didn't look good to me. During the last fast mover's bomb run, I had heard a steady *boom, boom, boom* when 37s opened up on him. As the jet dove lower, a faster series of booms announced that the smaller 23s were firing. Next, I heard a deafening roar of bass hissing as the ZPUs opened up at him. The hissing was the sound of hundreds of shells per minute leaving the gun barrel. The finale terminated with automatic weapon fire, and the last to fire were the individual soldiers who took crazy pot shots with rifles. *Pop, pop, pop.* It was a waste of ammo to fire at the jet but a problem for any helo, I thought. Was it this way every time the Sandys and Jollys made a rescue? Maybe so. And maybe they were just good enough to pull it off. What a hell of a mission, though.

Chapter 9

FIRST RESCUE ATTEMPT

nknown to me or Nail 66, the enemy force surrounding me was
stiffer than normal with a mixture of North Vietnamese regulars
and Phatet Lao guerrillas. Why were so many in Laos?

For several weeks, the Seventh Air Force staff in Saigon had tried to
locate the remnants of the North Vietnamese Army Division that was
defeated at Khe Sanh. Finding that division had been a high-priority
task. Once found, waves of B-52s would wipe them out with a high-
altitude bombing mission, code name Arc Light.

The Seventh Air Force (7AF) staff now had a solid indication I might
be in the midst of that division, and staff personnel were already arguing
whether the life of one American pilot was worth losing the opportunity
to decimate an entire enemy division. "Send the B-52s in and hope the
Navy guy survives," some of the staff argued. But the commanding general directed that I be rescued before ordering the B-52 blitz, and the rescue units would learn over the next thirty-eight hours just how badly the
general wanted that.

While bombs continued to fall around me, I had nothing to do
but wait so I prepared for Jolly's arrival. First, I checked my pistol. For
safety purposes, I had only loaded five bullets prior to flight, and it was
not until after the three bad guys ran past that I had time to load the
sixth. I now counted eight additional bullets in my survival vest.

Next, I removed my one smoke flare from my vest and decided
which end I would use. The day end, when popped, would emit a
highly visible orange smoke, and the night end would emit a bright,
burning-white light. Small nipples were on the night end so I ran my

fingers over them to verify that end, then flipped the flare in my hand so I would have the day end up, ready to pop first. Jolly would get the orange smoke first, and then the night end as it got darker. I placed the smoke flare on the ground beside me, but had no intention of using it until a Jolly was in sight.

I removed my pencil-shaped pen flare-gun to be a back-up to the smoke flare. At five inches long, it looks like a pencil laser pointer. The top was open so a two-inch-long, metallic-cased flare could be screwed into it. There was a small lever on the side of the pen gun that could be drawn downward to compress a high-energy spring, and then the lever could be rotated into a ready firing position. To fire, you only had to rotate the lever out of the ready position, release it, and then it would spring forward. A sharp point in front of the spring served as a firing pin that caused a pistol-like pop and detonation, which launched the flare. One red tracer would be fired and it would look similar to a roman candle in flight, except the pen flare flew a longer distance. It also would look similar to one tracer round from a small AAA gun! If I used it, the enemy would probably hear it pop and learn my approximate hiding location. I considered the pen gun as a last ditch effort to pinpoint my location, but knew it would also come in handy as a defensive weapon. If I ran out of pistol bullets, I could use the pen gun as a weapon since it had kill potential. I loaded one round but didn't retract the spring to the arm position.

At that moment, I was ready to be rescued. Surely it would happen soon, but I was dubious as to how we'd fare against the small arms fire that was all around me. What if I made it to the helo hoist and got shot on the way up? I had heard stories of pilots being shot at when they were on the hoist and knew this was a distinct possibility for me also.

Sandy 5 was diving in for his first ID pass so a rescue attempt was very close to fruition, and Nail 66 needed to hang in just a little longer to fulfill his perceived moral obligation to get me out before he left. He was critically low on fuel, but he'd chance it just a little longer before RTB.

Nail 66 called me. "Streetcar 304, we're coming to get you outta' there. Get your smoke flare out and watch for Sandy 5, over."

No way, I thought. *What's he thinking? I can't risk a smoke flare for Sandy. The enemy will also see it and it'll give away my position. No frapping way.*

"Negative on the smoke, Nail, too risky, over."

"Roger, Streetcar. Sandy is inbound."

Sandy was inbound. That meant the Jolly wouldn't be far behind, and the statement caused euphoria. I was ecstatic. Visions of a welcome back party on USS *America* immediately raced through my mind, and I could feel the pats on the back and accolades that I might receive for my survival skills. I wouldn't be a frapping hero because I had lost a new A-7, but at least I would be given credit for my evasion skills. I stared up and over the treetops in anticipation of an A-1's thundering roar, but another selfish thought popped out. *Come on, damn it Sandy, hurry up! Get in the fight and get me out of here. Do your job and do it now.*

Immediately, the thought made me feel bad. Sandy 5 was about to risk his life for mine after I had caused the predicament. Had I been seeking glory, a pat on the back, instant hero status, and was that why I was shot down today? And now, someone else was bailing me out. *Quit thinking only of yourself,* I thought. But I couldn't. I rationalized that my mission was to attack, and Sandy's mission was to rescue.

Hang on for fifteen more minutes, I thought. In fifteen minutes, I'll be safe aboard the Jolly and on my way home. At that moment, I noticed the sun had set while I was engrossed in thought. There wasn't much time left before darkness would hamper the rescue attempt, so I needed to be ready, and it was important I did my part right, on the first attempt. Otherwise, any pats on the back would be coming from the Pathet Lao.

Sandy 5 was not your ordinary Vietnam War pilot. To begin with, he was the squadron's "Old Man" at age 44. But he wasn't an old fuddy-dud. He had piloted A-26s in the Korean War, and first fought in Vietnam in 1961 as an air commando pilot in the T-28. In 1964, he piloted A-26s in the Congo, assisting Cuban mercenaries. In 1965, he returned to Vietnam for a second tour as an A-1 pilot, and then piloted F-84Gs in Europe. Now, he was back for a third tour flying the Sandy mission. He was probably one of the most experienced combat pilots in the Vietnam War arena, with over nineteen hundred hours of combat time in various wars. On an earlier Sandy rescue mission he had received a Silver Star medal for bravery under fire, so he had already proven his mettle. He could get the job done.

"Streetcar 304, this is Sandy 5, over."

Anxiously, I rose to a seated position. "This is 304. Man, am I glad to hear you, Sandy. Go ahead."

"Roger, Streetcar. I'm heading in from the south for an ID pass. Pop a smoke when you see my plane, over." Sandy 5 then pickled his three-hundred-gallon centerline fuel tank to rid the plane of its weight and drag because he wanted maximum airspeed.

No way, I thought. If I pop a smoke, the bad guys will see it and come running to my hiding spot. A smoke would make it easy for Sandy 5 to find me but I couldn't take the chance. Plus, I only had one smoke and Jolly would need it to find me and determine the wind direction when he hovered over me. I would wait till he got real close so the bad guys wouldn't have time to see the smoke and get to my position before I was hoisted aboard. *We'll have to do this another way, and it's going be my way,* I thought.

"Sandy 5, negative on the smoke. Too many bad guys around. I'll give you a 'hack' call and bearing direction when you fly past, over."

His mike keyed and I heard a pissed-off grunt, or snarl. "Copy, Streetcar, Sandy is on final leg."

I listened for the roar of Sandy 5's engine and dredged up its sound from memory gained during my first cruise aboard an aircraft carrier. Navy A-1s were then part of the air wing, so I was familiar with them. They made a very distinct noise.

Within a minute of Sandy's call I heard his engine, so I rose to a position with both knees on the ground and my face toward the bass roar. I positioned for the best possible view, but Sandy's pass would have to be very close to my position or I wouldn't see him. Fortune smiled on me again, as there was a narrow opening in the tree line to the south, toward the sound. I could see about a half mile in that direction and would have about ten seconds to point out my bearing once his plane appeared. Gunfire began in the direction of the engine sound. I placed my finger on my radio's TRANSMIT switch, ready to press it and talk.

I heard Sandy's engine, but also heard scattered rifle shots. The number intensified, indicating to me a large number of troops. Automatic weapons were soon fired in rapid burst and I determined Sandy's position and bearing from the firing gun sites. Suddenly, I heard the frightening sound of a ZPU less than a hundred yards away. It was spitting out rounds so fast it made a hissing sound, and was so close and loud that it blocked out Sandy's engine noise. The hissing was so dramatic and scary that I immediately thought Sandy 5 would surely be blown out of the sky. The closer he got, the more intense the gunfire became around me, and I feared he wouldn't even make it into sight. Now I fully understood the magnitude of what we were up against. I had to warn Sandy!

"Sandy, this is Streetcar. You're getting hosed pretty good. There's a hot ZPU firing close by. Maybe you ought to abort your run, over."

A buddy (Lieutenant Brown) back on the boat in C.I.C. heard that call and cringed. *They'll never get him out alive,* he thought.

Sandy didn't reply but pressed on, and by some miracle made it through the hail of fire. I saw him heading directly toward me about three hundred feet above the treetops. He looked mighty slow and low at about 230 knots, and it appeared even I could shoot him down. Where's his wingman? I was unaware the Sandy leaders left their wingmen up high at five thousand feet. Sandy 5 was less than a half mile away and I estimated he'd pass within fifty to a hundred yards in a couple of seconds. I spit out my words quickly.

"Sandy 5, got you in sight, turn five degrees starboard. I'm off your right wing tip." His left wing banked just a little in the wrong direction and in another split second he was abeam my position, but seventy-five yards away. I spoke in a loud voice. "I'm off your starboard wing . . . hack, hack, hack . . . now you're past me. Did you copy?"

He was in view for about ten seconds and then he was out of sight, but I continued to hear guns firing at him. How the hell did that ZPU miss him?

"Streetcar, I think I have your location but I'm going to make one more pass for positive ID, over."

No, that didn't make sense. "Sandy, you took a lot of ground fire on that pass. Are you sure you need to make another one?"

"Roger. I need to get an exact tree location, out."

Sandy 5's wingman was overhead, monitoring his leader's progress and talking to Crown at the same time. Crown relayed that some Yellowbird, Hot Rod, and Spitfire fighters were on the way with CBUs, but no one discussed waiting for them as darkness was nigh.

Did Sandy 5 understand the intensity of ground fire? I never saw any jinking, but then I only saw his plane for about ten seconds. Sandy probably never saw the ZPU muzzle flash because of the thick jungle canopy, and wouldn't unless he flew directly over the gun site. By then, it would be too late to avoid the gun's rapid fire. But it was puzzling how the ZPU gunners missed at such close range.

In a couple of minutes, Sandy was inbound for the second time. He again wanted a smoke flare, but again I declined. He was in danger of being shot down—but I was certain I'd be captured if I popped a smoke. It was a tough decision for both of us.

Sandy 5 came into view and this time it appeared his flight path would be even closer to my position. Unfortunately, his second pass was almost identical to the first in speed and heading but he was a little lower, maybe two hundred feet above the treetops. I was surprised he had come in from the same direction as before because the enemy gun barrels were probably still bore-sighted in that direction.

The enemy gunfire became even more intense. Suddenly, a tracer round arched right to left over his plane and left a beautiful, red, flowing trail against the fading sunset. The area around me erupted in a crescendo of musical gunfire sounds. Guns began to fire from all directions. First, I heard a single pop from a rifle in front of me, followed by the hiss of the ZPU off to my right. It stopped firing and an AK-47 began burping from an area under the approaching plane. The enemy gunfire was deafening; it sounded like the ending to a fireworks show with a continuous and unrelenting, popping, rattling, and hissing of guns. Sandy was really getting hosed so I had to help him more this run than the last. Quickly, I rose to a standing position to give him a better chance to see me below. Now exposed for all to see, my eyes briefly darted among the many trees in search of gomers. Then I stared upward at his cockpit.

I panicked! He was about to whiz by me.

"Hack, hack, hack," I screamed. His head then turned my direction, and his starboard wing dipped down. For a brief moment he looked down at me, so I waved my extended right arm twice. Then he was out of sight.

"Streetcar, I've got a good lock on you, out."

I was duly impressed and softly mumbled out loud. "Shit-hot, way to go, tiger. You've got nerves of steel."

Sandy 5's courage in the face of such enemy fire was overwhelming. *His plane must be riddled with bullet holes,* I thought. Could I have mustered the same courage he had just shown?

Then I got real excited. Sandy was probably flying to the Jolly holding pattern to escort the helos to my position. But, again, I thought a helo wouldn't make it through the wall of enemy ground fire. Someone would have to take out the ZPU or Jolly would be dead. *It's Sandy's call,* I thought callously.

The time was about 7 P.M. During Sandy 5's second pass, his plane appeared darker and no sunlight reflected from his canopy. The enemy tracers had been more brilliant. I noticed the sun had faded beyond my view and it was actually getting dark under the tree canopy. I began to get nervous about the amount of remaining daylight.

For five or so minutes, I reflected on Sandy's action. Selfishly, I didn't believe Sandy should have made a second pass and waste daylight time. Why hadn't he brought the Jolly in with him on that pass? And certain combat statistics kept popping to mind. "The longer a pilot is on the ground, the less chance he has for survival. Any pilot who is not rescued in the first hour is most likely captured." And, "Only five percent of the pilots survive when shot down in Laos." Those chilling thoughts made me shutter.

But I knew in my gut that no helo could have made it to my position through the fire that Sandy 5 took. Now, he was most likely rendezvousing with the Jollys before escorting them to my position, and again, I was torn between my emotional desire to be rescued and a concern for a fellow pilot's safety. It was beginning to bug me that I was letting pilots make a rescue attempt when I knew they might be blown out of the sky. Could I let another pilot die trying to rescue me?

I debated and struggled with my conscience. Hey, they're the experts and know their limitations better than I. And more importantly, they have more combat experience, or so I thought. The aviator in me kept saying, "Be a man and tell Sandy to abort his rescue attempt due to the heavy enemy gunfire and try again tomorrow." But I again made a selfish decision. My mission as an A-7 pilot was to attack targets and I had pursued my bomb run in the face of enemy fire. The mission of the Sandy and Jolly pilots was to rescue me, and I wasn't there to tell them how—or when—to do it; but it was their job to do it. It was Sandy's call about the feasibility of a rescue now. I felt pity for the poor guy. I couldn't convince myself I would've tried the same rescue if I were the Sandy pilot. My situation was putting the lives of many others in peril, and that thought weighed on me then, and for the next thirty-eight hours.

The jungle became eerily quiet. Five long minutes passed without a radio call. The wait was excruciating. What the heck was taking so long?

Unknown to me, after Sandy 5 passed overhead, he encountered big trouble and then made a radio call which I didn't hear. But Nail 66 heard him loud and clear.

"Sandy 5 has taken a hit, and I'm streaming oil, over." Nail was surprised how calm the voice was. Sandy 5 had taken a ZPU slug in his engine rocker arm, and another had exploded in one wing after he passed out of my sight.

His wingie, 6, responded to Sandy 5's call. "Sandy 5, this is 6. I've got you in sight. Take up a heading of three-zero-zero degrees for home base, and I'll join on you. Any problems with your controls? Over."

"Negative, controls are working for now, but the engine is running rough and the oil pressure is starting to fluctuate. I'm RTB."

The Jolly leader immediately broke his orbit and asked Sandy 5 to give him a short count for a bearing. Sandy depressed and held his transmit button and Jolly's ADF needle swung wildly a couple of times before stopping. After the count, Jolly gave Sandy 5 the heading that would place the two of them on the most expeditious path for rendezvous. Soon, they were within sight of each other and Jolly then followed Sandy 5 and 6 toward NKP.

Sandy 7 and his wingie, Sandy 8, were in orbit at the Rooster Tail as the two protected the lone remaining Jolly. Sandy 8 had a visual on Sandy 5 when he made his distress call, and watched as Sandy 5's plane headed west, and to him it looked just like a scene from a World War II movie. Sandy 5's A-1 was climbing slightly and beautifully silhouetted in the western sky against a pink sunset as a long trail of oil smoke billowed in a curling trail. Sandy 8 said it would have made a pretty picture if not so real. He watched till it disappeared as a small dot.

Nail 66 had also heard Sandy 5's calm distress call and quickly scanned the sky for his A-1. He saw it in the distance, trailing oil smoke. The sight of a second plane in trouble was enough for Nail. *This situation is a bad one, getting worse,* Nail 66 thought. *We shouldn't be trying for a pick-up yet as there's still too much ground fire. And I don't have enough fuel to wait anymore.* He made the decision to RTB, turned the scene over to his relief Nail, and immediately took up a heading to try and catch Sandy 5.

Then it hit him. Streetcar 304 was his responsibility and he couldn't abandon him. Not yet. Nail thought it imperative he remain overhead as he knew best where I was hiding, so he quickly changed his mind. He commenced a turn back toward the scene and reached for the front engine throttle. Without hesitation, he pulled it back toward him and shut down his front engine. Flying on one engine would save him some gas and buy him a few more minutes overhead 304, but he would be slower and more vulnerable to the guns.

Nail 66 was quickly back in the fight. He had seen the ZPU that fired at Sandy 5 on the second pass so he smoked it with a Willy Pete for a flight of fast-movers whose call sign was Vampire. Nail was amazed at the intensity of gunfire as the Vampire leader dropped his bombs. As the fast-mover pulled off the target, a different AAA site opened up just a few hundred feet away from the one he had just bombed. Nail now had a sinking feeling. There were too many guns to risk the Jollys, and he needed a whole lot of CBUs to kill the AAA gunners. But there was insufficient daylight left to wait for their arrival. Nail made a very painful decision, his second in just a matter of minutes.

He called Crown. "Recommend we abort the rescue attempt because the guns are still too hot, and it's getting too dark for the fast-movers. I'll follow Sandy 5 back to NKP, but would like to have a second Jolly join me in case I run dry on the way." Crown concurred.

The second Jolly then broke orbit and joined Nail 66. Now, two Sandys, one Nail, and two Jollys were out of the fight. It would take nearly an hour for them to fly back to NKP, and most would land after dark. That left one Jolly and two Sandys in orbit, with another scrambling Jolly enroute.

Sandy 7 was the leader of the back-up section of A-1s, and had been in a holding pattern at 8,000 feet about ten to twelve miles southwest with the Jolly. He had listened intently during Sandy 5's two ID runs and could hear Sandy 5's words, but couldn't hear my low-powered transmissions, so he only got half the conversation. Just prior to Sandy 5's second pass, Sandy 7 had moved his orbit position to a point where he could observe Sandy 5's track. Sandy 7 wanted to verify my location and that of the firing AAA sites.

Sandy 7 heard Nail 66 and Crown discuss the rescue abort but the two didn't ask for his input. *How come?* he thought. He was now the Sandy leader and it was his responsibility to carry out the rescue. From what he had personally seen thus far, he thought he could dash in, get a visual on me during his first pass, and then return with the Jolly for a quick pick-up under the cover of twilight. Then he could hustle back to his base and maybe still make his airlift flight to Clark AFB for his hot date and ten days of R & R.

Sandy 7 was a thirty-one-year-old Air Force Academy graduate from the very small town of Winlock, Washington, population 1,300. Prior to his Sandy A-1 tour, he had piloted the multi-engine C-130 (Ski & Skyhook test bed version), and had also flown a reconnaissance version in a tour where he routinely flew missions along the Soviet border. Sandy 7 was slim and tall, handsome, outgoing, and quite a ladies' man. Among his squadron pilots, he had a reputation as being highly intelligent with an unlimited vocabulary, but also an incessant talker and teller of jokes. He was in his thirteenth consecutive month of Southeast Asia combat and one month into a six-month extension, which he had requested.

Most importantly to me, he was the most experienced rescue pilot in the squadron. He was on his 257th combat mission in A-1s, had assisted in the rescue of seventeen pilots, had been awarded three Silver Stars, and was at the point in his tour where he considered himself infallible. He described himself as invincible; he was immortal, or so he thought. In pilot terms, he thought he was shit-hot.

Sandy 7 knew he was a terrific, fearless combat pilot. The enemy guns didn't scare him any more because his pilot skill and technique always kept him safe. He was cocky, but had recently recognized he'd been pushing the rescues to limits beyond that of normal safety. An inner feeling told him he was cheating death, more and more each mission.

But at that moment, there were no second thoughts. Sandy 7 had never left a live pilot on the ground, and he wouldn't leave Streetcar in the jungle overnight. His mission was to get the pilot out, and he would do whatever it took, even at his own peril. That was the type of man he was, and he felt it was ingrained in him while he attended the academy. Morally, he couldn't desert a downed pilot even if it meant giving his own life since his primary goal was to live an honorable life, above all else. So, on his own initiative, he sprang into action.

Nail 66 was well out of the area and just starting to relax when he heard a transmission by Sandy 7. Nail was flabbergasted.

"Sandy 7 is assuming on-scene commander. I think I can pull this thing off."

I didn't hear his transmission, but Crown did, and liked what he heard. Without hesitation, Crown made an interrogatory call to the 7AF rescue command center (Blue Chip). "Where are the frapping flare planes and CBUs?"

Sandy 7 dove for his first pass. As he did, he directed Sandy 8 to remain 5,000 feet above him in close contact with Crown, to remain alert for enemy AAA, and to keep a visual sighting of Sandy 7 at all times.

His wingman, Sandy 8, was your stereotypical good-looking, young fighter jock. He hailed from Grand Island, Nebraska, and had attended Iowa State College where he prepped himself for his lifelong dream of becoming a pilot. Flying was his love, that was all he wanted to do—he took his job very seriously and consistently did things by the book. He had previous jet fighter experience flying F-101 jets in the Air Defense Command. After that, he had been a jet test pilot at Edwards AFB for four years before his tour with the Sandys. He was

new to the squadron and had only been flying combat missions in the
A-1 for three weeks, but had already proven himself. He had pro-
gressed rapidly through the various stages of checkout and had already
flown eighteen missions as a Firefly strike pilot against ground targets.
But the Sandy mission was an advanced stage of qualification. One
had to prove he had the skills to handle the extreme low-altitude flying, the precise delivery of ordnance, and the headwork attributes to
handle the complex rescue scenario.

Sandy 8 proved adept and qualified quickly, and now was on his
very first Sandy mission. He would have his hands full. It would be difficult to keep an eye on his leader at all times because he'd have to
avoid enemy fire while talking to numerous fighters waiting to provide
bomb support, in addition to talking to the Crown plane on UHF,
monitoring Streetcar, etc., etc., etc. He would be switching back and
forth between three radios just to talk to everyone. Only a special aviator could handle that load, but as instructed, he followed his leader,
Sandy 7, toward the scene.

As Sandy 7 leveled off for his first ID run, Sandy 8 saw flames from
my A-7's wreckage glowing brightly in the fading twilight. The jungle
around the burning hulk looked dark and foreboding, and he was glad
he hadn't yet qualified to be the "Low Sandy," the one who flew low in
the trees.

Suddenly, in the midst of everything else, Crown couldn't believe
his ears. Streetcar 307 (Iceman) was now screaming "Mayday," and it
had only been twenty minutes or so since he had left the rescue scene.
Someone in the back of the Crown plane made a half-joking call over
the intercom. "Looks like the Streetcar flight is having a really bad day."

Meanwhile, I'd been waiting patiently for a Jolly, unaware that Sandy 5
had been hit and replaced by Sandy 7. Six long minutes had passed
since Sandy 5's second pass and I had heard nothing. I was concerned.
I put out another short beeper message on my radio to alert them I
wanted to talk.

Then I called Nail 66, not knowing he'd left the area. Crown
answered, then advised "they had a little trouble," and asked me to
verify my position again. Verify my position?

"Roger, Crown, I'm still in the same area as when Sandy made his
first two passes, about three hundred yards diagonal from my chute's
location." Crown then advised I should watch for Sandy.

Suddenly, my radio crackled. "Streetcar 304, this is Sandy and I'm inbound for an ID run. Get your smoke out, and pop it when I call for it, over."

I was dumbfounded and didn't answer immediately. *What the hell was wrong with this plumber?* He will most likely get shot down on a third ID pass, and then it will be too dark to rescue either one of us.

"Sandy, you've flown over me twice, and dipped your wing at me for positive ID. You're taking a lot of enemy fire on each pass so I don't recommend another one, over."

"Roger, Streetcar. Sandy is inbound anyway, over."

"Roger, Sandy. I won't give you a smoke. Too dangerous, over." At that point, I thought Sandy was a looney. I had told this guy twice already that there would be no smoke. Why did he keep asking for one?

"Roger, Streetcar, Sandy out." Quickly, Sandy 7 pickled his empty centerline fuel tank and then, his still-full right wing fuel tank. He felt the need for speed, and that might give him another twenty knots.

Right after that, Crown requested two more Alert Sandys at NKP be scrambled to the scene. But it would take them at least thirty-five minutes to get to the fight arena.

This is stupid, I thought. A third run? (I still thought it was Sandy 5 who was making another pass.)

My no-smoke edict started to weigh on me again. I knew troops and AAA were extremely close to me because their noise made it hard for me to hear anything else when they fired. And the gomers who went by on the trail could have stopped a short distance away. I didn't know how many others might have rushed to their aid. No, I couldn't afford to pop smoke, but I had to show some balls.

With all the gun noise, would one more bullet sound be noticed? I would shoot one pen gun flare in front of Sandy's nose to help him fix my position. The timing would be important though. I would only have about three to four seconds to see Sandy's plane and then get the shot off. Reluctantly, I placed my pistol in its holster and put the pen gun in my right hand.

In the distance, I heard a reverberating sound followed by the pop of a rifle. I went to one knee and stared in the direction of the first two runs. Sandy's plane was now in earshot and closing on me. Then the enemy AAA barrage began, much heavier this time than during the first two runs. My heart sank in fear that Sandy wouldn't make it through. But amazingly, the AAA stopped, and I could hear Sandy's engine. Had the twilight saved Sandy? Could the gunners not see his plane? Then, just as suddenly, I heard several AK-47s firing, and Sandy appeared in view as if he were riding a wave on top of the trees. He seemed to be about the same speed as during the first two runs, but at a lower altitude, and no more than fifty feet above the treetops.

I stood up and aimed the pen gun, waiting for the right moment to fire. Don't forget to lead him, I thought. AK-47s were still firing sporadically, but then the same ZPU as before opened up! It fired one long, hissing burst at close range, but evidently missed. Almost simultaneously, I heard a *boom, boom* noise in the distance off to the left of Sandy's flight path, followed by two flaming balls whose red plume trailed across the sunless sky. I watched in fright as they arched right to left over the cockpit of Sandy's plane. They seemed to merge with his cockpit, then miss.

"Sandy, you're taking tracers from your port side. I've got you in sight and I'm off your starboard. Look starboard, I'm firing a pen flare—NOW."

I released the firing pin and it sprang forward and the sharp point pierced the back of the flare. It popped like a .38 pistol retort and the tracer went zooming out of my hand. It stood out like a sore thumb as it shot upward, leaving a pretty, bright red trail. But I hadn't led the plane enough and it looked like the flare was going to hit him right smack dab in the cockpit area. For a split second, I cringed in fear that the tracer would hit Sandy. I sighed in relief as it passed directly in front of his cockpit, a little to the starboard as I intended, and then up and over his head. A frapping lucky shot. But his head was turned away from me.

I waved my extended arm for maybe two or three seconds as I looked at the broadside of Sandy's plane, hoping he would look my way. The stubby A-1 was only a few feet above the treetops and clearly silhouetted in dark form against a fading, blue backdrop. The engine was roaring but the props were invisible due to the revolution speed.

Sandy said nothing. Suddenly, the ZPU fired again, a really short burst. It sounded like a short *zit* followed by a small thud sound.

It became very quiet; the engine roar was gone, and no guns were firing. It was eerie for about a second before I realized I could count four motionless prop-blade tips. In less than two seconds, I had watched a rapid, instantaneous engine seizure. Damn, did I do that? Did I knock out Sandy's engine? No, I positively saw the flare fly up and over his cockpit. Sandy was hit by the ZPU.

Amazingly, I could easily hear the air whistling past his frozen prop and up and over his cambered wing. It was a bit similar to the flapping wing-noise of a flight of geese flying low overhead. I took a few steps forward in a crouched position and strained to maintain visual contact with his plane, but in less than four seconds it was out of view, obliterated by the tall trees. During those four seconds, the enemy guns had ceased firing and the jungle was eerily quiet. I actually heard his plane biting through the air as it glided out of sight, still wings-level.

About ten seconds after losing sight of him, I heard an explosion and recognized immediately his escape-system rocket had fired to extract him from the aircraft. I guessed he was punching out no more than a half-mile north of my position.

Sandy 7 had heard me make my starboard call and panicked as he mistakenly looked first left, then right. Suddenly, a tracer zoomed past the cockpit and his head turned to the left, in the direction the tracer had come from, and he almost immediately felt a solid blow to his plane. It shuddered just briefly, like a small earthquake tremor under one's feet. The plane's instantaneous loss of power caused a forward momentum of his body and he felt himself sliding forward in his seat. He now saw his frozen prop, so Sandy pulled back slightly on the stick to climb. *Oh shit,* he thought, *I'm not infallible.*

His plane began to roll and Sandy saw his right wing folding slowly up toward him. He had no time for a Mayday call. Without hesitation, and in a near-panic, he reached and fired the A-1's unique extraction system with one hand as he struggled to maintain level flight with the other on the control stick. Fortunately, the plane had climbed some and hadn't rolled much before the seat was jerked upward out of the plane for about a hundred feet. Sandy felt as if he was falling toward the ground and thought he had a bad chute. Just then, he popped upright with a jerk by a fully blossomed chute. He had made it out alive when he thought he wouldn't.

He looked down and saw the tree canopy about two hundred feet below. The jungle looked dark and foreboding in the twilight, but fortunately the darkness was helping hide his descent. He saw no gun flashes. He could see the treetops but the darkness below made it seem they would catch him like a glove. He crossed his legs as he prepared to enter the trees in order to protect the family jewels. Before he could pick out an opening, the tree trunks were rushing by as he crashed down through the foliage. Miraculously, he hit nothing on the way down and his chute didn't snag high in a tree. As he sank deeper into the jungle, it was too dim to judge his distance above the ground. He recoiled, steeled his body for impact, and felt one foot hit the ground causing a stabbing pain up his leg. Instead of rolling to cushion his fall, he froze, locked his body and hit like a steel spring, staying erect after a few hops forward. A sharp pain in one leg made him wince.

Quickly, he released his chute and then slowly swiveled his head to scan for enemy troops. It was slow and scary work, as every small tree trunk appeared as a human figure in the dim and faint afterglow of the sunset. Once he felt secure, he turned toward the area that offered the least resistance for running and bolted like a rabbit. His one and only thought was to place lots of distance between himself and his chute before the bad guys arrived.

After running several hundred yards, he calmed down enough to realize he was running out of control. He forced himself to stop and get his bearings. He crouched to one knee and grabbed his pistol from its vest pocket, and rose to his feet. Again, he listened for any noise of approaching troops but heard none, so he took off running in the southwesterly direction where he knew I was holed up. He wanted to team up with me.

In the sky above, Sandy 8 had been trying to observe his leader's ID run while talking to the next batch of incoming fighters. At the precise moment Sandy 7 was hit by AAA, Sandy 8 was writing notes on his pilot kneeboard about fighter ordnance loads. He finished and looked down at the ground, and his eyes focused first on the burning hulk of my A-7 as it still cast a red glow in the twilight. For some reason, it appeared pretty in the foreground of the river ahead. Suddenly, off to the left of that scene, a white explosion caught his eye. At first, he thought one of the fighters had just dropped a bomb. Then, at the last moment, he saw a white parachute canopy make its final descent through the crown of massive trees. It was in view for just a few seconds and then it was gone, sucked up by the dark jungle. He called Sandy 7 several times but received no reply.

"Crown, this is Sandy 8. I've lost contact with Sandy 7 and think he may have been shot down. I saw a chute but it blossomed awful low, over."

"Wait one, Sandy," replied Crown.

Sandy 8, on his first rescue mission, was now the on-scene commander by default with only one Jolly for support. His brain wouldn't compute. He was flying around, knowing he had to make a decision on the next step, but found himself unable to concentrate clearly enough for any decision. He made a second call to Crown and told him the enemy gunfire was intense and he could barely see the ground due to darkness. "It's too risky for a pick-up attempt," he told Crown. Sandy 8 wondered whether he was making the right call.

Crown couldn't believe the magnitude of what had just happened. The rescue crew commander (RCC) was a major, and experienced enough to know he was involved in a mess. A Navy pilot had started the whole affair and was now evading on the ground. A Sandy had been hit and might not make it back to base, and his wingman was escorting him home. Nail 66 was returning to base and might run out of fuel before he got there. Two of the three available Jollys had flown home with the Sandy and Nail pilots. Now a Sandy was down, so there were two pilots on the ground awaiting rescue, and there was only one Sandy and one Jolly to assist.

Crown had earlier requested two more Sandys but it would be several minutes before they arrived, and by then it would be too dark for the Jolly. This was all too big for Crown to handle so he relayed the same facts to Blue Chip.

Crown received his marching orders quite fast, and relayed them to Sandy 8.

"Sandy 8, Blue Chip directs you to get all aircraft, including the fighters, out of the area now, and stay clear of all enemy guns until further notice. Do not, I repeat, do not make any low passes, out." It was around 7:15 P.M.

Damn it, damn it, damn it. A Sandy had been hit and was in the same situation as me—if he was lucky. My heart sank. I didn't know if Sandy had survived his low-altitude escape from his plane. Thus far, I had heard no emergency beeper to indicate he was on the ground, and alive. I felt terrible, I was disheartened. I sagged back to my prone position on the ground. I felt like hitting someone, or something, so I hammered the ground with my fist. Another pilot may have just lost his life in an effort to save mine.

A feeling of doom enveloped my body and made me suddenly feel tired. I now feared the worst as I had just witnessed the magnitude of the enemy opposition in my area. *I'm never going to get out of this situation. I'll be captured, or killed.*

I pressed the TRANSMIT button and called very softly. "Sandy pilot on the ground, this is Streetcar. Do you copy? Over."

Nothing. I tried again, louder and more firm. Nothing again. Maybe he's running, so I'll wait and try him again in a few minutes.

While returning to base, Nail 66 heard the advisory about Sandy 7's chute. Nail was mortified. He was nearly in tears, feeling he had somehow helped cause all of this mess.

While returning to base, Sandy 5's engine was gradually losing power and making it difficult to maintain altitude. The engine was running rough but still chugging when he finally sighted the base ten miles ahead. At that time, knowing that Sandy 7 had gone down, he released the Jolly so it could return to the rescue scene.

Jolly 9 and his crew were standing rescue alert when the firetrucks rolled to their runway crash position for the inbound Sandy 5. From his position, Jolly had a vultures-row-view of the probable pending crash. When Sandy 5 came into view, Jolly heard the A-1's engine begin to sputter, and then saw it belch short bursts of white smoke out of the engine cowling. Then he saw a streaming trail of black oil. At first, Jolly didn't think the A-1 would make it to the runway, but after a couple of pops and one final surge of power, the plane skimmed across the airfield fence and slammed the runway. Sandy 5's engine then finally seized and quit during rollout.

The Jolly 9 crew discussed how lucky the Sandy pilot had been, but they didn't know the full extent of his luck until later. And the crew of Jolly 9 had no idea then how involved they would become with the enemy gunners who had caused the A-1's engine damage.

Nail 66 landed in the dark shortly thereafter, without incident. Nail 66 and Sandy 5 had made it home safely on day one and would now have the entire night to think about tomorrow. Both had escaped a harrowing experience and each felt very fortunate to be alive, but their exuberance was tempered by the fact that I hadn't been rescued and they had left me and Sandy 7 behind. It was difficult for either to accept that fact.

Immediately after their arrival, they both rushed to provide the intelligence weenies with their description of the day's events. "Streetcar 304 clobbered the target with his bombs," Nail 66 reported. "In fact, his bomb accuracy was the best I've seen as a Nail controller. But a lot of guns opened up and now need to be knocked out before another rescue can be attempted."

Sandy 5's report echoed the same. "I took fire each time I got within five miles of the survivors. It's going to take a mess of fighters with CBUs to suppress the guns before we can get in there to get 'em out." Sandy and Nail helped the Intel folks make an accurate plot of the known AAA sites and the exact location of Sandy 7 and me. Then they were dismissed for the evening.

Nail 66 returned to his quarters, took a shower, and walked to the O' Club for dinner. While there, he became very distraught. His pride was wounded, and he couldn't get the vision of 304's tumbling plane out of his mind. *Somehow,* he thought, *I was responsible for the shoot down of Streetcar 304. What mistake did I make that caused this whole ball-buster scenario? Will I get a chance to redeem myself tomorrow?* As Nail pondered that, a guilt complex began to build. He began to drown his moroseness in alcohol.

Nail 66 finished dinner and was sitting at the bar, recanting the day's events with the barkeep, when another squadron pilot walked up. The ops plan was posted: Nail 66 was scheduled to brief at 3:30 A.M. and be over Streetcar 304's position at sunrise. Holy Toledo—he would, after all, be the primary Nail for the second day of the rescue attempt.

Nail 66 was stunned. He hadn't really expected to be thrust into such a dangerous situation two days in a row. He desperately wanted to get Sandy and me out of our predicament, but felt he'd be pushing his luck. At the same time, he was eager to make up for what he perceived to be his mistake. He left his half-empty glass on the bar and departed the club, returned to his room, and tried to sleep. It was impossible. He tossed and turned and sweated. Over and over, he jerked awake from a dream wherein a single A-7 was tumbling end over end. Finally, he gave up and got out of bed.

Sandy 5 was handling the day's situation with a different attitude. He seemed to take the severity of the mission in stride and was more comfortable with the current status of the survivors than the younger, less-experienced Nail 66. But then, he didn't consider himself responsible for the Streetcar guy being on the ground, and he could just as easily be on the ground instead of Sandy 7. That was the risk and luck of war, he thought. He felt loose and relaxed and thought he'd just received a lucky enemy shot when his engine was hit. The whole thing didn't appear to be a big deal with him. So, when informed he would again be leading the Sandy flight on the next day's rescue attempt, he readily accepted his fate. He quickly finished his dinner, had a drink, and returned to his room for a shortened night of solid sleep.

Chapter 10

SANDY 7'S RUNNING GUN BATTLE

andy 7 had been shot down. Now, he was running as fast as he could for high ground. He spent several minutes busting wildly through foliage and ripping the limbs aside to make his way forward. But, now he slowed to a cautious jog as his mind began to return to a little more normal and cautious state. He grabbed his next handful of jungle foliage, pushed it aside, and brought his foot forward for the next step. Abruptly, he halted in mid-stride, one foot still in midair as he noticed he was about to step out into the open onto a wide dirt road. He eased back into the foliage of an elephant ear plant and sank to a knee. Pistol in hand, he eased his head forward and looked left, then right along the road. The lighting condition was not as dim on the road as under the jungle foliage, so he would be visible if he crossed the road. He saw no movement and eased back inside his cover to consider his next move. He knew he couldn't re-trace his steps as his burning plane and open chute were behind him and the enemy would be rushing toward the area. Streetcar should be maybe half a mile south, and the protective cover of the karst is due west, he thought. He pulled his survival radio from its vest pocket.

"Streetcar, this is Sandy 7, I'm on the ground, over." There was no immediate answer so he transmitted a second time.

Nine long minutes had elapsed since the Sandy pilot who I assumed to be Sandy 5 punched out of his A-1, and I'd just about written him off. At first, I was caught off guard by the call. Why was Sandy 7 on the ground? I was mystified. I thought Sandy 5 made all three ID passes over me.

Sandy 7 spoke in a hushed tone. I had to strain to hear his words. He sounded very cautious but I detected no fear in his voice. He wasn't panting, didn't sound nervous, and appeared cooler under fire than I felt.

"Roger, Sandy, this is Streetcar. What's your status, over?"

"Streetcar, I'm okay. I know your position and will make it there for join-up. You stay put till then. I'm getting ready to cross a road and will call you again once I make it to the other side, out."

"Good luck, Sandy, 304 out."

His call lifted a big weight from my shoulders and I actually gained some comfort knowing that I might have another pilot as reinforcement against the enemy troops. Two of us should be able to hold them at bay better than one. I began to theorize how I could help him make the rendezvous. I looked at my small wrist compass and took a bearing on the direction where I thought his chute would have landed. I was now prepared to give him a heading to me once we talked again.

Slowly, Sandy 7 rose from his kneeling position. As he did, the canteen strapped to his side made a sloshing sound, so quickly he placed his left hand over it to muffle its sound. Instead of bolting, he decided to walk slowly across the dirt road as if he were a soldier. Maybe he could get away with it in the dim light? But halfway across, a series of loud words pierced his heart like an arrow. He heard an unintelligible shout, and from the tone he knew it was directed at him. He jerked his head to his left toward the sound. Three human shadows were about seventy-five feet down the road, side by side, and each was just raising their weapon into a firing position. One shouted a command. Sandy 7 froze, hoping they couldn't recognize he was American. He was nearly a foot taller, so who was he kidding? All three were in uniform and in the dim light he couldn't quite make out the color, but it definitely wasn't black. One of them clutched an automatic rifle in his right arm, finger on the trigger, and with his left arm beckoned him to come to them. The guy took a couple of steps toward Sandy 7, and without hesitation Sandy 7 raised his pistol, shot once, and the head honcho in front appeared to fall as the other two sprang off to the side for cover. Sandy 7 sprinted across the road and fired two more quick blind shots over his shoulder before crashing into the darker jungle. Then he began to run for his life.

In the past year, Sandy 7 had seen several pilots survive after being shot down because they were able to hide in the protective cover of the dense karst. The closest one was due west about one click. So he aborted his plan to reach me. *I've got to make it to the karst or I'm dead,* he thought.

From the direction where I thought Sandy 7 should be crossing the road, I heard three small *pop, pop, pop* sounds, followed by a louder burst of automatic rifle fire. A vision of the scene hit me like a hammer, and many years later I can still recall the sound of the rifle as it fired at Sandy 7. Sandy tried to cross the road, was seen, and killed on the spot, I instantly assumed. I waited and keyed my ears in that direction for any other sounds. After thirty seconds, I had heard nothing.

"Sandy 7, this is Streetcar, over." Nothing. I tried again, in a louder tone. "Sandy, this is Streetcar, over." Nothing again.

Suddenly, sporadic, single rifle shots began popping in the distance. Was Sandy being chased like I had been, or was this a search party firing rifles as they had done to intimidate me? He's either running or hiding, I thought. I'll give him a minute before trying again.

"Nail 66, this is Streetcar. Sandy 7 is alive on the ground and he and I just made radio contact. Did you copy our conversation, over?"

Crown answered. "Roger, Streetcar. Stand-by, out."

Sandy 7 was running pell mell when an automatic rifle fired from the direction of the three soldiers. To Sandy, it seemed the gun would never stop firing. Bullets sprayed all around him, snapping branches from trees and impacting tree trunks, but they missed him. Instantly, one thought entered his mind. *Run. Run for your life.* First he ran, not conscious of the crashing sound he was making as he snapped one after another of the small, dead tree branches lying along his path. Then a white, blinding muzzle flash occurred off to his left and he returned the fire with another hurried pull of the trigger. Sandy 7 was shooting as he ran and he was shooting wildly in retaliation at any sign of a muzzle flash from the rear. *Click.* Then, he heard another audible click. His pistol was out of bullets. Run—run and reload. He fumbled to reload as he ran in pitch-black darkness. In the process, he dropped his bullets one and two at a time as he ran in panic, running for his life. "Come on. Come on legs, keep running," he said to himself. The gunfire behind him was sounding closer. He was on his last batch of bullets, having lost many, but finally the pistol was reloaded. He stopped, turned, and fired at the approaching sounds behind him. Once, twice, bullets flew out with a blinding white flash at the end of his hand, and then the third round spit out into the darkness with a

red flaming trail as evidence of its source. "Holy rat's ass—I'm shooting tracer rounds. Stop firing," he commanded himself. But his finger
seemed frozen on the trigger and he couldn't let go. He couldn't stop
his firing action and three more tracers went racing through the darkness at the enemy's gunfire flashes. *Click. Click.* His pistol was again
empty. In a panic, he thought, *Run—run like a scared rabbit.* He ran
and, after a short spell, realized he was carrying the empty pistol and
had no more bullets in his vest. He was out of ammo. *If they catch me
with a pistol, they'll know I was the one who shot their buddy.* He dropped
the pistol. It was no longer of any use to him.

What's that sound? The small chain attached to his canteen's top
was making a jingling sound as it bobbled against the canteen's metal
neck, so he held it with one hand as he ran. He ran until the firing
ceased behind him and the initial adrenalin wore off. He continued to
run until he physically could run no more. He had no idea how long
he had run, but he did so until he felt he was getting away and his
lungs burned so badly he could no longer stand the searing pain.
Eventually, he could no longer make his legs move forward under the
weight of his survival gear. He was still wearing the parachute torso
harness and it was making him sweat like a pig. Sandy 7 flopped down
against a tree to catch his breath. He took a second radio from his vest,
having lost the first during his running gun battle.

Panting heavily, he pressed the TRANSMIT switch. "Sandy 8, this is
Sandy 7, over." Sandy 8 and Crown both heard the transmission, but
I didn't.

Sandy 7 got his words out between giant gasps for air. "I'm running, and heading to the top of a ridge and will hide there. The gomers
are hot on my trail."

He then rose to his feet and took off into the near darkness at a
slow jog. He hadn't removed any excess flight gear because he was
reluctant to take the time.

After a minute, I again tried to contact Sandy, but to no avail. In my
heart, I felt he'd been killed. Realization struck. This is a deadly game
and the only way I'm going to win is to use my experience gained as a
kid in the mountains of West Virginia, where I excelled at the Hide and
Seek game. This won't be a quick rescue, and I'll have to find a better
rescue spot. Am I worth the effort and possible loss of more life,
or should the Air Force sit tight and let me walk to a safer location
for pick-up?

One minute later, unknown to me, Sandy 7 answered a call from Crown. "I'm still running and can't talk now, out." Sandy 7 was running in a direction that was actually placing him further from my location, but he was trying to place distance between himself and his pursuers before he took the time to find a hiding spot.

Another minute later, Crown asked Sandy 7 if he could be left on the ground overnight, and if he could make it to my position. Sandy replied, "Wait one—" Sandy 7 wanted to talk to Crown but he was gasping for air, physically unable to reply. He wanted to put all his energy into his run and was not about to waste time talking while pursuers were hot on his trail.

Meanwhile, Cricket dispatched a steady stream of fighters to the scene but all Crown could do was stack 'em high and keep 'em topped off with fuel. Blue Chip was adamant: no fighters were allowed to strike any AAA till he decided what the next course of action would be.

Seven minutes later, and thirty-three minutes after he hit the ground, Sandy 7 answered another call from Crown. "Sandy 7 is at the top of a ridge and I think I can make it through the night, but I don't know if I can make it to Streetcar's location."

It was now nearly dark and Sandy 7 could barely see the shapes and forms of the trees surrounding him. He had lost all his directional bearings and was on the verge of hyperventilating and physical exhaustion. *I'm barely hanging in there,* he thought. It was 7:45 P.M., and in just a few minutes it would be totally dark in the jungle. He needed to find a good hiding spot before it became too dark to determine a good one versus a bad one. How do you hide in the jungle? How did he hide in the woods as a kid in Washington? *Think, damn it, think.* Then he remembered. *Climb a tree, you idiot!*

As a kid, he learned that the other kids would keep their eyes glued to the ground so they wouldn't trip and fall in the woods. The American kids never looked up when they were hunting others. Maybe the enemy did the same? He needed a tall tree to climb, so he groped around and found one with thick vines twined and spiraling upward on the trunk. He couldn't see beyond its lower branches but the trunk was huge. *Perfect,* he thought.

He stored his radio and started a laborious climb, using the vines to pull himself higher up the tree until he reached a point where the trunk was only a foot or so in diameter. Then, he braced himself on a limb while he pulled the letdown line out of his parachute torso harness and tied his body to the main trunk. He leaned his head against the trunk and now felt the extent of his tiredness. His body sagged and settled around the limb as every muscle in his body seemed to collapse at once, and if not for the tie down, he would have fallen from the tree. He had run and climbed to total exhaustion, and slowly his heartbeat stopped its pounding, and his heavy breathing subsided. How high was he? He looked down at the base of the tree and was surprised at the difference in light conditions. Sandy 7 was high enough in the tree that a waning moon was providing some moonlight between a thin layer of drifting stratus clouds and he could still see his boots. Further down, it was totally dark near the base. He hoped he was high enough to avoid detection in the morning. Very carefully, he removed his canteen from its belt position and took a long drink of water. Then, Sandy 7 leaned against the trunk and tried to piece together why he was about to spend a night lashed to a tree trunk well above the ground. *I was long overdue to be shot down,* he thought.

Meanwhile, I had heard none of the conversation between Crown and Sandy 7, but I knew a rescue attempt today was most likely a thing of the past. Official sunset was 8 P.M. and it was now 7:50. Under the tall tree canopy, it was dark already. I wondered whether the Jollys made night pickups. My question was soon answered by a call from Crown.

A crusty-sounding voice started talking to me in a very low-key tone as if he was casually leaving his office at the end of the workday. It appeared I was most likely talking to an older pilot, and from his tone it sounded like this was something he did every day.

"Uh, Streetcar, it looks like it's getting too dark for another rescue attempt, so all planes are returning to base. They'll return at first light in the morning. Uh, sunrise is 5:58 A.M., so stay off your radio to conserve your battery till then." He switched to a real firm, positive, and reassuring voice inflection. "A Spectre AC-130 gunship will be orbiting your vicinity all night and if you need any help, just call. Otherwise, if you want to improve your chances, you might try to move to a location that would be better for rescue attempt. Do you think you can make it through the night okay? Over."

I need help right now, I thought. *I don't think I can make it through the night.* But I maintained my cool, Navy pilot image.

"Streetcar copies, no problem. See you in the morning, out."

I knew it was coming but I was still a little shocked that they were leaving me overnight. His BS about the rescue being terminated by darkness didn't slip by. I knew that the area was just too hot for the rescue forces, and the enemy was presently winning this fricking battle.

Back aboard *America*, several of my fellow squadron pilots were in CIC listening to a relay from Crown of the radio chatter at the rescue scene. After they heard that Crown was aborting the SAR attempt for the day, one pilot said he would not bet ten cents I would still be around in the morning. He just knew I would be captured—or killed—by then.

I'd been on the ground for only two hours, but it seemed longer than that, or it seemed shorter than that. I couldn't decide. It was now time to sit down, relax a little, and reflect on my next play. I removed one of my two water bottles and took my first drink since hitting the ground. As I did, I reflected about the day's events and wondered what Iceman was telling the brass back on the ship. I could imagine CAG and Skipper were grilling him. And I wondered about the Air Force guy who'd been shot down trying to rescue me. Did he have a family also?

Meanwhile, things weren't going real smooth for Spider and Iceman either. As soon as Spider started back to the boat, about thirteen minutes behind Iceman, he requested in-flight refueling support from Crown. He and Razor were switched to a frequency for a KC-135 that was tracking south over the Gulf, just north of Danang. A rendezvous was made just after it turned and passed the DMZ, heading on his northerly track. At first, there was a minor disagreement about how the refueling would be conducted. The KC-135 crew wanted the A-7s to comply with Air Force procedures wherein the A-7 would stabilize in formation behind the KC-135 with the A-7's refueling probe extended. The KC-135 crew would then maneuver their refueling basket and fly it into place on the A-7's probe. Sidewinder argued, "No." He wanted to do it the Navy way, wherein the KC-135 would extend his basket, and Spider would then fly and ram his probe into the basket. They ended up doing it the Navy way, and the refueling was accomplished without incident. Spider had plenty of fuel now.

Iceman's return flight to the boat was iffy from the time he left my scene. Right off the bat, he didn't believe he had enough fuel to make it back even if he followed the standard altitude and airspeed for maximum range. As he and his Sidewinder playmate approached the coastline at Danang, his fuel state confirmed his fear. He desperately needed fuel, so Iceman checked in with *America* and asked for permission to re-fuel at Danang. After a brief discussion, the request was denied, and he was instructed to continue toward home plate to rendezvous and re-fuel from the Whale, an A-3 Skywarrior tanker plane, at 15,000 feet.

"I don't believe I have enough fuel to do that with any reserve left over," responded Iceman.

"Take it to the tanker," came the reply.

Iceman snorted some words out of the corner of his mouth as he switched his Tacan to *America*. *This is a bad plan*, he thought. As he coasted out feet wet just north of Danang, he switched radio frequency for the rendezvous.

The A-3 is the Navy equivalent of the Air Force B-66, except it was converted from a bomber to a refueling plane. It's a very maneuverable plane, and the Navy pilots were very proficient in formation flying. They could always be counted on to help a needy pilot affect a quick rendezvous, and in this case, they understood the urgency of Iceman's fuel needs.

Fairly soon, Iceman got an advisory from *America* that the tanker was in his six o'clock position at three miles. He couldn't spot the plane, but was told by the Whale pilot to maintain level flight and constant heading. His Sidewinder playmate eased under Iceman's plane to a cruise position on the port side. The Whale pilot proceeded to fly past Iceman's starboard wing and slowed to 250 knots about a hundred feet in front of the A-7. Immediately, Iceman saw a fifty-foot refueling hose snake backward toward him from the underbelly of the A-3.

Soon, the Whale pilot reported, "My package is fully extended and appears sweet. Stick it in me, Corsair."

Iceman stared at the bobbling, thirty-inch-diameter basket at the end of the hose. Then he checked his fuel gauge for the umpteenth time in the past fifteen minutes. He had less than ten minutes to get plugged in and receive more fuel, or he'd flame out. Sweat beads dribbled past his eyes. He raised his visor, swiped at the sweat, and then moved the switch to deploy his refueling probe. Once extended, it looked like a large, man's arm sticking out of the plane. The front tip of the probe was at his one o'clock, five feet from his head and about three feet from his cockpit canopy. Now, all he had to do was drive it into the basket.

Iceman would have to smoothly match the altitude and speed of the A-3 because once the probe was inside the basket, the nose of his A-7 would only be about fifteen feet below the tail of the A-3. If he got slower, the probe would slide out. If he got too fast, he would fly farther under the A-3 and possibly impact his A-7's tail against the underbelly of the A-3. There would be no excess room to bounce around chasing the basket.

Pilots excel at different things. Iceman excelled at control stick smoothness and had proven many times he could usually plug in on his first attempt. But this time was different. He had just seen his flight leader shot down, and he was dangerously low on fuel. He had to suck it up and get the probe inserted on the first attempt.

Iceman quickly matched the altitude and speed of the A-3 and aimed his plane's nose at the basket. He gently pushed his throttle forward and began a smooth closure rate toward it. As he closed on the basket, he experienced the normal wing turbulence caused by the A-3 that required quick and smooth applications of control stick and throttle. About ten feet away, he had good depth perception to the closing rate. His head was cocked to the right at a forty-five-degree angle, and his eyes darted back and forth from probe tip to basket. From ten feet in, he barely moved the throttle as he crept toward the basket. About three feet out, he felt the normal turbulence caused by the airflow change over the nose of the A-7. The basket began to bounce around. If he hesitated, it would be out of control and he'd have to back away and start the process over again. Iceman pushed the throttle and forcefully drove the probe into the basket with a solid clunk, and the hose began to whip and recoil from the impact. It was whipping like a snake so he quickly sucked some power off. He finally stabilized at the same airspeed as the A-3 and the hose steadied out. Then, he scanned his fuel gauge. *Maybe five minutes of flight left, at best,* he thought. *Come on Whale, please expedite.*

His eyes shot to the row of lights where the hose exited the A-3. What the heck, he exclaimed. The damn hose light is indicating red. I forgot to push the hose back into the belly of the A-3 the required six feet to start the fuel transfer.

Quickly, he added power, but cringed when it thrust him forward until his cockpit was well under the A-3's belly. The hose was again snaking dangerously close to the A-3's bottom antennas. Too far, he thought. He pulled back on the throttle just a tad and the plane began to coast backward. The hose again began to straighten. Then, he saw a yellow light, followed by a green light. "Green light," he excitedly announced. His fuel gauge indicated 150 pounds remaining!

Iceman's eyes darted between the fuel gauge and the A-3 hose. After what seemed an eternity, the fuel indicator finally started to increase.

"I'm getting fuel," he reported. Then he let out a growl that only some-one inside the cockpit could hear. Iceman was good at that. He could lower his head, twist it slightly to one side, and then, almost under his breath, mouth his displeasure. *I've had enough of this blooming war today,* he thought. *After I land this bird, I may just turn my wings in.*

It looked like the decision-makers on *America* had lucked out. Ice-man was topping off, and would make it safely back to the carrier. At that point, his Sidewinder playmate assumed Iceman was in good hands, kissed off, and sped toward *America* to make his scheduled Charley time.

Iceman looked back inside and saw he now had fifteen hundred pounds of fuel. But, after a minute or so, the green refueling light on the A-3 disappeared, replaced by a yellow one meaning the flow of fuel had stopped. Iceman quickly assumed he needed to move the hose back in a few feet, so he pushed the throttle forward. Nothing happened! Instead, he was slipping further backward from the tanker and now saw the A-3's red light. At that instant, his refueling probe snapped out of the basket. Coincidently, red warning lights illumi-nated his cockpit. He heard a pilot's worst, nightmarish sound. His engine was unwinding. He jammed the throttle forward. No response! His eyes darted to the RPM gauge. It was falling below fifty percent, and his engine temp was also decreasing. *Why? I've got plenty of fuel.* Then, it hit him. *Flameout. What the hell? Just when I thought I was home free. I've got to re-light this sucker!*

From memory, he quickly executed the emergency procedures for an abbreviated air start. He pulled the throttle back to idle, moved a toggle switch to manual fuel control, and pressed and held his air igni-tion switch. Nothing—no re-light!

The Whale pilot felt the A-7 pop out of his drogue and realized something was wrong. "You got a problem back there, Streetcar?"

No response.

The A-3 flight engineer was facing aft in his normal seated posi-tion right behind the pilot and came up on the ICS. "I've got him, boss. He's just off the left side and appears to be dropping quickly. You're clear for a left turn to get a visual on him."

Iceman wasn't quite ready to panic yet. Maybe his airspeed was too slow on the first attempt? He dumped his nose and waited for the airspeed to increase another fifty knots, and then tried a second start using the same procedures as before. Still, no re-light. He reached down to the pocket on the right leg of his G-suit and pulled out the

4×9 inch "Pilot's Emergency Pocket Checklist." He had time for one full air-start attempt and he wasn't going to take any chance he might forget a step and screw it up. He flipped to the Air Start page.

Step 1: Extend the EPP. It popped out of the left side of the fuselage and the wind stream revved up the small generator for the emergency power package. Now he had power for the radio and primary instruments. Meticulously, he then read and performed each of the next fifteen steps. Still, no re-light. Now frantic, he switched to guard channel on his radio and broadcast in the blind to anyone, and everyone.

"May Day, May Day! Streetcar 307 has an engine failure. Unable to re-light. Squawking emergency."

He switched his IFF to 77, the emergency position code, so Red Crown and *America* would receive a blip on their radar to show his exact position.

"Streetcar, this is Red Crown and we have a positive lock on your position. Steer zero-four-five degrees for home plate. A Big Mother helo and frigate are on the way. Keep us advised, out."

"Streetcar, this is the tanker. I've got you in sight and will follow you down, over." The Whale pilot's calm voice was comforting. At least Iceman had a security blanket nearby if he had to eject.

When Iceman made his Mayday call, Spider was flying at 1,000 feet and 360 knots abeam the starboard side of the boat, and only moments from kissing off his wingman before breaking for the downwind landing pattern. "How the hell did I get back to the boat before him, and what the hell is happening to Streetcar now?" he blurted inside his oxygen mask.

Spider quickly checked his fuel state and extended upwind. "Boss, Sidewinder 406 has two thousand pounds fuel remaining. Should I break it off and scatter to help Streetcar?" There was a thirty-second pause and he knew the air boss was conferring with CIC and the squadron rep in the tower.

"Negative, Sidewinder. Red Crown has Streetcar under his control. You're a Charlie on arrival so we can get your flight on board before the Whale arrives. Expedite please."

Spider promptly blew a kiss toward Razor. Then, he broke hard left in a four-G, ninety-degree bank, inducing a stream of white vapor mist from each wing tip. He felt the G-suit inflating and pressing hard against his stomach and legs. After flying a three-mile downwind leg, he was again abeam the carrier at the one-eighty position. By then, he had slowed to his final landing speed of 135 knots and had descended to six hundred feet above the water.

"Sidewinder 406, one-eighty, gear down, flaps down, hook down," he reported. As he passed the fantail, he rolled into a 30-degree bank for the final 180-degree turn, reduced his power and commenced a descent. After 90 degrees of turn, he saw the plane guard destroyer at its normal position bouncing in the white, foamy, and churning wake of the carrier. For some reason, he wondered how many pilots it would have to fish out of the water this combat cruise because of a ramp strike or cold cat shot. Just then, the destroyer disappeared from view under his high right wing. He added a little power as he crossed the carrier's wake and rolled wings-level three-quarters of a mile aft at 150 feet in a 600-feet-per-minute descent. He spotted the landing mirror on the port side of the flight deck and its small, circular, amber "meatball"—all eighteen square inches of it—was centered between the green datum lights on either side. *Perfect,* he thought. Quickly, Spider made the required call to the landing signal officer (LSO) to let him know he could see the ball, and to give his fuel state so the arresting gear could be set to properly handle his plane's landing weight.

"406, Corsair Ball, 2 point 0."

The meatball began to glow a little red. This meant he was a little low on the glide slope, so he added power to climb—but added too much and the ball shot to the top of the mirror.

The LSO calmly advised, "You're going high, ease it off a little."

Spider sucked a little power off for just a second and quickly squeezed it back on. About then, he felt the burble of turbulence immediately aft of the fantail, so he squeezed the throttle forward just slightly before quickly retarding it again. By then, his gear (wheels) crashed into the deck. Immediately, Spider rammed the throttle to full power just before his tailhook grabbed the "four wire," the last of the four arresting-gear cables. His head snapped violently down as his upper body uncontrollably lurched forward, straining against the shoulder harness straps. After a short, 250-foot roll-out, his plane came to an abrupt halt and sprang backward a few feet.

Spider straightened up in the seat and looked to his right. There, a yellow-shirt signaled him to snap the throttle back to idle and raise the tailhook to disengage from the cable. As Spider began to taxi clear of the landing area, the LSO turned to his assistant and yelled, "Fair, little low start, little high at ramp, 4-Wire." The assistant LSO wrote in the book: F, LLS, LHR, 4. That ended Spider's string of solid green blocks for OK traps on the ready-room "greenie board."

After engine shutdown, Spider waited for Razor near the deck-edge hatch. The young, inexperienced pilot approached him with a quizzical look. "Hey, Spider, are all combat flights as hot as this one?"

Meanwhile, deeper in the bowels of the ship, our squadron rep, Chaser, was in CIC monitoring my situation. A junior lieutenant standing nearby suddenly shouted over the chatter. "Hey, Chaser, your Streetcar 307 is declaring a Mayday. He just incurred an engine flame-out and is ejecting."

Chaser was devastated. In the desire to debrief Iceman about my shoot down, and to have his plane aboard for tomorrow's combat sorties, the squadron had now lost a second A-7 on the first day of combat. How could this be? The tanker got to him in time, and he had fifteen hundred pounds of fuel at last report.

Reluctantly, Chaser bent over the Squawk Box and held the TALK button down. "Ready Room Six, CIC. Inform the Skipper that Fred just flamed out near Tiger Island."

Skipper was still in his Ready Room chair and heard the call. This time he said nothing to anyone but laid his head back, closed his eyes, and wondered why this was happening to him. His career had been going well, but now he'd probably get passed over for captain. He dreaded the next call from CAG.

Iceman flamed out one hour and fifteen minutes after I ejected. He had maybe four minutes of glide time before he'd have to eject over water. Enough time for several more re-light attempts. But, if he didn't get the engine restarted, he'd be facing a parachute landing at sea, near hostile forces, with darkness approaching.

As the jet glided ever downward, Iceman continually tried numerous relight attempts. Finally, ejection became inevitable and he made up his mind to do so at 8,000 feet. He stowed all of his cockpit gear and then stared at the altimeter. It was unwinding more quickly now.

Approaching 8,000 feet, he was near hyperventilation but he checked off his emergency procedures flawlessly. He removed his pilot kneeboard, and stowed it and the rest of his loose gear so it wouldn't fly and hit him during the ejection. Next, he pulled back on the control stick until the airspeed slowed to 200 knots. At that point, he tapped a couple of clicks of nose-down trim so the plane would glide downward and not flop around and fly through his chute after it blossomed. He pushed himself tightly against the seat back, and then tugged his lap belt and both shoulder harnesses as tightly as possible. He didn't want a broken back during the ejection sequence. Time to go. He reached over his head and yanked the face curtain down.

The ejection seemed soft, with a very smooth upward ascent and chute deployment. As he floated downward, he watched his A-7 spiral gradually into the water. It hit with a small splash, literally drove through the water, and rapidly disappeared from sight. No break up, no fireball, just one big belly flop and it was gone. The A-3 then circled by and Iceman extended a thumb-up sign.

Fortunately, the lighting conditions during descent were excellent for judging his height above water, so as he closed, he started his pre-water entry procedures. First, he inflated his floatation pouch, and then reached down and released his seat pan. It separated, and out tumbled his life raft and sea survival pack, attached to a long tether. They now dangled below him, and once they hit the water, would signal the time to pop his shoulder harness fittings to detach himself from his parachute so he wouldn't be pulled under and entangled with his chute. He performed the water entry as trained and was uninjured on impact. The URT-33 inside the life raft began to beep on guard frequency.

After landing, he easily shimmied into his raft and waited for what he thought would be a quick rescue. But Iceman was demoralized. His icy steeliness was gone. As he waited, he pondered all that had happened during the past hour and a half. Then he made up his mind: this war wasn't worth getting killed, and he definitely would turn in his wings when he got back to the boat.

Since Red Crown was involved, the Whale was told to return to the ship. The Whale driver passed the Tacan bearing and distance of Iceman's raft to Red Crown, and then headed for home plate. Now, no one was overhead Iceman to vector the helos to his raft.

But, it got even worse! The Air Force had been trying to home in on a beeper that appeared to be floating in the sea and assumed to be that of Trump 01, the pilot who was shot down shortly after my flight coasted in past Tiger Island. Now Iceman's beeper was intermingling with the one from Trump 01 and causing confusion. It would be fourteen minutes before the planes searching for Trump 01 were aware that Iceman was also down near Tiger Island.

Back on the boat, CAG was waiting when Spider entered the Ready Room. He then proceeded to question why Spider was late for his recovery time. Spider waited patiently for his squadron commanding officer to intercede, and for the questioning to cease. It was taking too long, so he looked CAG directly in the eye: "This is war, CAG, and events don't always go the way CAG plans them. I just left a buddy over the beach, and his wingie is floating in the water out there somewhere, so with your permission, sir, I'm going to Strike Ops to see if I can add anything that might help this situation." CAG seemed to understand.

Spider then turned and ambled toward the back of the Ready Room to drop his flight gear in the locker room. He hadn't noticed that a flight surgeon had been listening during his meeting with CAG. As Spider approached him, the doc smiled, and then a cupped hand eased out of a pocket and moved toward Spider's hand. "It appears to me you might need some night rations." Spider took the small bottle of medicinal bourbon, gave a smile of thanks, and deftly stuffed it in his pocket.

After thirty minutes of floating in his raft, Iceman began to get very concerned. It was twilight and if the helo didn't arrive soon, it would be hard for them to spot him. He certainly didn't want to spend the night on the water. He noticed that his raft was slowly drifting toward a large island to the South. That might be Tiger Island, and if so, an enemy boat might capture him before the rescue forces arrived.

Sixty fearful minutes after splashdown, he finally heard the *whop-whop* of a helo. His raft was between it and Tiger Island, which was to Iceman's back. Iceman decided to make sure the helo knew his location, so he fired two pen-gun flares. It was twilight and the tracers left a bright red trail as they sped at the helo. The helo pilot assumed the tracer was enemy gunfire from Tiger Island, so he turned tail. But, after discussion, the crew convinced the pilot he was too far from the island to be shot down. So, he turned toward Iceman again.

Eventually, the helo hovered nearby. It was only then that Iceman realized it was an Air Force Jolly Green and not a Navy Big Mother helo. Suddenly, Jolly landed in the water, and at first Iceman thought the helo had also incurred an engine failure. He swam toward the helo, but a rescue swimmer met him part way and then helped him board the helo. Once aboard, the Jolly took Iceman to Danang, where he received an unexpected hero's welcome.

Chapter 11

FIRST NIGHT ON
THE GROUND

Around 8 P.M., it was really, really dark for my first night on the ground in Laos. The canopy of tall trees obscured any view of the sky and I felt like I was inside a closet, without light. I placed my hand in front of my face, almost touching it, and still was unable to see my fingers. It was pitch black.

I'd been on the ground for two hours and fifteen minutes, and as far as I knew, a Sandy pilot had probably been killed, and Iceman had returned to the carrier. Crown had said "good night," and I was now all alone in my clump of jungle vegetation.

But, unknown to me, Sandy 5 had been hit and made it back to base, and Sandy 7 was in a tree somewhere nearby. Iceman had ejected but was rescued from the sea. Two A-7s and one A-1 had been lost, and another A-1 was seriously damaged. One pilot had been rescued, while two more awaited their fate. It was good that I didn't know all the facts then, because I felt bad enough with what I did know.

Around 8:20, I took a couple of small drinks from my water bottle that I had filled on the boat. It didn't quite taste like Perrier. It was very soft, seemed to be very salty, and left an aftertaste of jet engine fuel. It even smelled like gas and caused a momentary fear of dysentery, which I couldn't afford.

The distinct odor of jet fuel reminded me of the boat, and I wondered how my squadron mates were reacting to my situation. Were they disappointed in me, or did they agree I just encountered too much enemy opposition today?

I then noticed just how small my water bottles were. They each held only twelve ounces of water, and I knew that wouldn't be enough for more than a day in the hot jungle environment. I had already sweated that much liquid and should be replacing it, but I'd have to ration my water until I found another source. For planning purpose, I had to assume I might be on the ground for several days, and I would need water to survive. I stifled the desire to gulp the water and placed the bottles in my survival vest. It was now time to devise my plan of action.

It was a scary thought, but I knew I had to move from my current hiding place. It had served me well and obviously was a good spot since the enemy had bypassed it on several occasions. However, I knew it was difficult to see from the air, and too many gunners were nearby for a safe Jolly pick-up. I faced reality and accepted the fact that a Jolly would be decimated if one tried to hover over my current position. I needed to suck it up and move to a different spot, clear of AAA and troops. After several minutes of thought, I finally had a plan of action.

Nail 66 gave me an escape heading of 240 degrees during his target brief, so I placed my faith in him. I decided to wait till midnight, when hopefully all the enemy troops would be bedded down for the night, and then hike cautiously on Nail's recommended escape path from midnight until daylight in hopes of getting clear of the troops. I had about three hours to steel myself for the effort and get my gear ready.

Meanwhile, Sandy 7 sat in his tree, still unwinding from his running gun battle with the bad guys and still unsure whether they had lost his trail. He lowered his chin to rest it on his chest, stared down the tree, and listened intently for any sound, but the darkness was so rich he couldn't even see what angle his eyes were actually scanning. *Crack.* He heard a noise, and it was followed by several more crackling sounds. *Snap, crack.* It sounded like footsteps breaking small twigs on the jungle floor. Was it animal or man? Then, in the distance he saw a line of multiple lights in a spread about fifty feet long, and they bobbled up and down as the line moved toward him. The enemy was in a line-abreast formation and beating the bushes for him, Sandy concluded.

Over the next few minutes, he watched as the line of lights began to separate into single forms and get closer. Eventually, he heard the murmur of Asian voices and soon several lights were directly below him. A dark form stopped briefly at the base of his tree, but fortunately its light didn't shine upward and in the next instant it was again rolling and bobbing forward with the line of other lights. The lights began to meander in all directions under and around the tree, accompanied by the constant murmuring of voices. Sandy's tail puckered before the small lights began to disappear one by one as several small fires began to flicker and glow, encasing the area in reddish light. *Ah, shit,* he thought. Campfires. What rotten luck! The damn gomers were making camp within two hundred feet of his tree. The murmuring continued inside the perimeter of the fires for about forty-five minutes, and then slowly, one by one, all murmuring ceased and it was quiet except for the night sounds of the jungle.

Sandy 7 knew he was in deep trouble because he was certain the troops would still be there when the sun came up. He was afraid to make any sound for fear it would be heard. They might run to his tree like a bunch of coon hunters in the south, throw their flashlight beams up at him and then he'd be treed, and maybe shot. Suddenly, he remembered his radio. *What if Crown called me now and the bad guys heard his voice?* Quickly, he removed it from his vest, made sure it was off, and decided he wouldn't chance its use until he was out of the tree. He would wait the bad guys out and wait till they moved before using the radio.

Was he hungry? No. Was he thirsty? Yes. But, he wasn't going to pull any water bottles out in the dark for fear of dropping one from the tree and risk it being heard or found by a gomer. He pledged to stay awake all night and then hope for the best in the morning.

Meanwhile, I prepared to move out at midnight. I grabbed a handful of dirt and rubbed it over my hands, face, and balding head. I took a branch of shrub foliage and stuck its stem down the back of my neck inside my shirt. That, along with my drab green shirt and trousers, should make me blend into the jungle.

I then took off my survival vest to take inventory of what I had available for my hike. After fumbling in the dark, I found my larger, Boy Scout-style flashlight and the smaller penlight. The larger one fit in its own pocket on the front of the vest with a ninety-degree neck at the top to shine forward, leaving my hands free. I placed one hand over the lens to dampen the light while I tested its brightness level. The batteries appeared strong but I doubted if I'd ever use it other than as a back-up. The pen flashlight also tested well, so its smaller light would be my primary, and I used it during my slow and tedious inventory.

Its beam highlighted salt stains on my green, nylon vest, so obviously I had already sweated through my tee shirt, flight suit, and vest. The survival vest fit snugly and was no burden to wear, but I wanted to ensure I didn't carry any extra weight that might cause fatigue so I took everything out to see what might not be needed for my trek. As I removed each item, I reviewed its value to my current situation, and also reviewed in my mind when, and if, I might use the item.

My vest contained one extra battery for the radio, a serrated six-inch-blade knife, and a ballpoint pen-size flare gun with a supply of six three-inch-long flares. Next out was a general-purpose survival kit about 4×5×6 inches, with small specialty items. Inside was one pack of hard Charms candy, a pack of high-energy caffeine hard candy, fish hooks, sewing kit, mosquito netting, fire starter, etc. Small items. Then, I removed a similar sized medical "Seek" kit but didn't open it. In addition, the vest contained a flasher strobe light, a whistle, one day/night smoke flare, a signal mirror, two water bottles, and a wrist compass which I placed on my left wrist. The vest had everything I would need for twenty-four hours, maybe longer. I kept everything except the mosquito netting.

After that, I rechecked my lightweight Smith & Wesson .38-caliber pistol to ensure all six chambers were loaded. While doing that, I noted that I was still wearing my wedding band. That wasn't good. I was optimistic about rescue so instead of discarding the ring, I placed it inside my right boot.

I inspected my one and only spare radio battery. It had a little corrosion on it so I scraped it off with the knife. By this time, I knew how important the radio would be to my survival and now wished my squadron had argued harder for more batteries. The theory was the same old ageless one. A Navy pilot would most likely eject over water, be rescued immediately, and not have to face a long duration period on the ground. That was generally true, I thought. Most Navy pilots were either captured quickly over North Vietnam or rescued soon after an ejection at sea. Who had planned for a war in Laos?

The corrosion on the backup battery prompted me to remove the active battery from the radio. Crap—it also showed some corrosion and that really torqued me off. The two batteries might be the difference between life and death for me.

With time to burn, I reviewed the contents of the medical kit. It contained all of the normal bandages, sterilizing ointment, etc., but I had added some Darvon tablets, which the flight surgeon had provided on the sly. Doc had told us the Darvon would be good for pain or stress reduction, so I sat and pondered taking one now but decided against that as I was leery of losing my edge or dulling my senses.

I'd now gone without dinner and wasn't hungry yet, but was really glad I'd eaten lunch before take-off because my only food supply would be the one pack of sugar candy and one pack of caffeine candy. I needed to keep my energy level up, but also knew the candy would have to sustain me for at least another day. I ate two of the ten Charms and vowed to only eat two at each following mealtime to make them last. That would provide me a little nourishment for a probable two days. The caffeine candy would be saved to rejuvenate me if I physically wore down and needed a quick pick-me-up. Of course, the sugar from my Redman would also help sustain me, but at the rate I had been popping a replenishment wad in my mouth, it wouldn't last through the next day so I vowed to use it sparingly also. Inventory complete.

About then, a positive surge swelled inside me and I gloated. *I can survive*. Unknowingly, I had trained for this moment much of my life during war games as a kid, followed by years of experience while hunting for squirrels and rabbits. *If anyone can make it out, I can*. My fear was gone and I was now upbeat and positive.

It was around 9 P.M. and I was ready to hike to another, safer area. But, for now, I would sit tight for the next three hours. During the wait, my mind roamed.

At one point, the guys back on the carrier bounced into my thoughts. The ship had completed its day's ops, and by now the squadron pilots would be gathered in the ready room to watch the evening movie. I couldn't help but wonder if they would have one tonight or if they'd just sit and discuss my situation.

I didn't have full confidence that the majority of the pilots would understand the magnitude of the enemy gunfire I had faced. Some were probably saying I must've screwed up. Hopefully, Iceman and Spider had told the others how many guns I had faced because I was concerned about my pride and reputation as a pilot. Every kid who dreams about flying in combat has an image that he'll strike the enemy with a magnificent blow and return as a conquering hero. I didn't want to return as a "dumb ass."

Where were the night noises of the jungle that I'd always heard about? It was completely dark, but I heard no animal or insect noise, nor felt any bugs or snakes. It was totally quiet around me and I hadn't heard a gunshot for over thirty minutes.

That thought made me think of Sandy 7. The time was around 10 P.M. and it had been nearly two hours since we last talked. Had he been killed by small arms fire? I couldn't let it go without trying to contact him one more time.

I called Sandy 7. No reply. I tried a second time with the same result. He was either dead, captured, or hiding just like me and had his radio off. I decided to try again in the morning.

Suddenly, I was jolted by rifle fire nearby. I bounced to a kneeling position and craned toward the sound. Almost immediately, I heard shouts. Several seconds later, I clearly heard words in both English and Vietnamese maybe a hundred feet away, but I couldn't discern what they were saying. I dropped to the ground and stretched out facing the voices. A tiny tremor rocketed through my body. Soon, I was able to discern multiple human voices spaced some distance apart and interspersed with sporadic, single rifle shots. To hear better, I cupped one ear toward the voices and listened carefully. They were coming toward me along the same trail I had traveled.

Then, it dawned upon me. Troops were conducting a search pattern to find me and they were spread out on both sides of the trail, and getting closer. They're either firing rifles at possible hiding spots or trying to scare me into bolting from my cover. From the pattern of voices, the troops were spread out in a line-abreast formation and shouting to each other to maintain positioning as they walked in the darkness. The voices were clearly audible at the moment I saw flashlights probing the darkness about fifty feet away, shining left then right, bobbing up and down with the bad guy's gait. Would they be able to see me through the thicket cover when they arrived in a minute or so?

Holy cow! I was caught off guard when a voice boomed out in clear English from my left, no more than fifteen feet away on the trail. "Hey, G.I. Joe, come on out, give yourself up, and we won't hurt you."

My head snapped toward the voice but I saw only a flashlight beaming straight down. He repeated the same phrase, but more softly, as if he knew I was only a few feet away.

The speaker spoke in an authoritative tone and his words were clear but with a slight accent. I stared but couldn't make out his form, and sensed he was facing me. Slowly, I moved my right arm so my pistol was aimed just above his flashlight. Seconds passed and I neither saw nor heard any movement. The guy stood perfectly still. Suddenly, his flashlight swung upward and beamed directly at me, fanning slowly side to side as if he was scanning my thicket. Could he see me? Was he alone, with one rifle pointed at me, or were there others with him? As if reading my thought, a second flashlight then appeared behind the first, but its beam searched down the trail.

Thoughts raced through my mind. *Damn it, how many are there? This is like a frapping movie. They don't say stuff like that in real life, do they? Do they know I'm actually here, or are they hoping I'll bolt?*

My belly hugged the ground, my pistol aimed toward the voice. Oh, no, the English speaker took two cautious steps toward me. Gently, I eased the pistol hammer back to a cocked position. Decision . . . I'll shoot if he starts moving any of the foliage on the outer perimeter of my clump of vegetation.

At that moment, he moved backward a few steps. Had he seen me or was he afraid to penetrate the clump? Several males chatted back and forth in what I assumed to be Vietnamese. Again, the English speaker spoke, this time in a really slow and pleading manner, as if he didn't want to kill me.

"Come on G.I. Joe, come on out, and give yourself up so we don't hurt you."

It was scary that his English was so good. And, for some reason, I imagined a smile on his face as he spoke.

Heck, he must have seen me and told the others, I thought, because a second set of voices and lights was now approaching from my right and walking directly toward me. It appeared they would walk right through my clump. Again, I couldn't see any human forms but could track their progress by their bobbing flashlight beams. I was contending with two groups, one in front on the trail and the other off my right shoulder. My eyes darted back and forth. Finally, I was able to see two human forms on the trail when each shined his beam at the other as they talked and gestured. Is one directing the other to move in on me?

Don't walk off the trail, I silently implored. *Don't make me shoot and give away my position.* I noticed a third man had joined the first two on the trail. Their lights were bouncing around but seemed to mostly illuminate the ground. Each flashlight's beam was shielded somehow so that the glow of the flashlight only illuminated the ground in a half-moon shape and didn't cast an upward beam. They were casually talking with no apparent fear of action by me.

Was it bravado, or stupidity? Were they not afraid I'd shoot one of them since the glowing flashlight certainly gave away their position?

I made a firm decision based on their tentativeness. I'll shoot the first guy who tries to enter the thicket and while the others dive for cover, I'll run like hell to the rear. I won't let them just walk in and grab me.

Cautiously, I eased up to a crouched, ready-to-fire-and-run position. Just then, voices from the second group caused me to glance off my right shoulder. Three or four flashlights were there, too, about twenty feet from my clump. Oh crap, I was being surrounded. I was staring at them when suddenly, off my left shoulder on the trail, a rifle shot rang out and I nearly crapped in my pants as its bright muzzle-flash temporarily degraded my night vision. As I whirled toward the muzzle light, I expected to see or hear a gomer charging toward me. I heard no foot noise. No one was advancing.

Had they seen me and tried to kill me, or were they just trying to jolt me into bolting to give away my location? My thoughts whirled: just remain calm, don't make a sound, and shoot the lead guy if he makes a move off the trail.

A flashlight beam sliced through the thicket but I didn't move a muscle as it panned past. Now, it dawned on me: the bad guys were rabbit hunting. In West Virginia, I always hunted for rabbits without a dog so I'd look for brush piles or any likely hiding spot, then walk up to it and give it several good kicks to scare the rabbit into bolting. If it remained still when I kicked at the clump of brush, I most often would walk by, never knowing it was there.

I remained immobile in my crouch. After a minute of anguish for me, a commanding voice gave a loud order and the gomers began to mosey farther down the trail. Off to my right, that group of flashlights also began to move, but they were heading straight toward me. Would they enter the thicket? I shifted my crouch toward them and watched as they got within fifteen feet before finally skirting around my perimeter. When they were forty or so feet away, I stood up. For the next twenty minutes or so, I stood erect, frozen on alert, and scanned back and forth as the two groups slowly, very slowly, plodded farther and farther from me. Several times, I heard them stop and repeat the same tactic they had used when near me. Shouts in English, "Hey Joe . . ." Then a rifle shot, then they would walk a little farther away and try it again. First, their flashlights disappeared from view and then slowly they gained distance till I could no longer hear their voices. After a while I sagged, totally depleted, to the soft, moist ground in a prone position and rested on one elbow.

During the next thirty minutes, I listened as several more search parties passed right to left through my area, but none as close as the first. I evaded the initial sweep and my teeth hadn't clicked once during the encounter, nor had my hand shook as I aimed the pistol. I'd been very apprehensive but felt cool during their intimidating scare tactics. A surge of pride occurred as I'd now successfully evaded the enemy during three close encounters.

But, now, I really understood the gravity of my planned midnight hike. There were a lot of troops in my area and some had walked past me heading in the direction Nail 66 had told me to use as my escape path. If I followed his advice, I would have to walk through them again to reach Nail's safe area.

I had several hours to reconsider my decision. Was there really a safe area 240 degrees from my location that would place me out of harm's way, or had Nail just thrown that direction out as one to fulfill his requirement to advise me of such? I had about two hours to decide which direction to travel when I moved out. This was a very big decision and could determine whether I made it out alive, so I was very careful in my deliberations.

Option One: I could try and make it on the heading that Nail 66 had given me. I had to assume that better cover was available along his suggested route and that probably meant mountainous terrain, maybe a karst. There would be more cover for protection and I'd feel at home in that environment.

The river where I had just bombed was behind me. It was option two. If I made it to the river, I could possibly float down river away from the troops I'd seen. But I also knew there were a large number of AAA sites around the river, and that probably meant even more troops. That didn't sound real attractive since the enemy gun crews would love to get a piece of me after I'd killed a few of them.

Option Three: I could just remain where I was since it was obviously a good hiding spot. Yes, it was a good place to hide, but it appeared I had zero chance of being picked up there because of all the AAA.

I carefully weighed the three options and decided to proceed along the route given by Nail 66. It scared the hell out of me to know I'd have to walk through an area with known bad guys, but after an hour of debate, I convinced myself to take the risk in order to avoid anyone else getting shot down. I needed to find a pick-up site free of troops and guns. Trust Nail 66.

Not long afterward, the success of my decision seemed a little more likely due to something I heard. I'd seen movies and heard conversation about the loud and sometimes frightening jungle sounds at night. So, I expected to hear wild animal calls, tigers roaring, etc. But the first significant sound I heard was quite different from that.

I heard the banging and rattling noise of metal and instantly recognized the source. The damn gomers had quit for the day and were
preparing dinner. As they did, it seemed nearly a hundred voices were
carrying on loud conversation. I rose to a standing position and faced
the sound. My view was pretty, yet discouraging.

Maybe a half mile away, and slightly to the right of my planned escape path, I saw the eerily reddish, burning glow of what I initially thought was a single large fire. At first, I assumed the fire to
be a secondary effect from the day's bombing. But soon I saw that the
perceived one fire was actually ten to twelve smaller ones scattered around. It was an enemy base camp, and a good-sized one, I
theorized.

You'd think the enemy would be concerned about detection in the
midst of a war zone. Not so—they were shouting and carrying on like
they were in a Saigon bar.

As an aviator, it was difficult to comprehend the scenario. I had
read stories about how frustrating and difficult it was for our troops to
find the elusive North Vietnamese and Pathet Lao troops. Well, it
appeared to me that our troops were simply not looking in the right
place. I had found a whole passel of them and they obviously had no
fear of detection by American ground troops.

If Sandy 7 was alive, could he see the fires also? There was no need
to try and ask him, though, because I was sure he, like me, had his
radio off to conserve batteries.

As I listened and watched the scene, I realized the campfires could
work to my advantage because they vividly highlighted the area to
avoid. They enabled me to easily see an exact camp perimeter and all I
had to do was get to the other side and put some distance between it
and my next hiding spot. I stared at the fires and estimated I needed to
hike a couple of miles before dawn to reach a safe, distant point on the
other side. However, the thought of walking close to the camp scared
me. But I had to do it, and steeled myself for a midnight attempt. Until
then, I would lie down.

While I rested, the rescue forces made plans for the next day's operation. At 10:54, Crown 3 was directed to be in the area of the survivors
at 5:45 A.M. Then Blue Chip established a five-mile "bomb line" around
my location. That meant that no planes could attack any targets or drop
any bombs within five miles of my position unless they were a part of
the specific rescue effort. The restrictive bomb line would apply to all
forces, including Navy, Marine, Army, and Air Force.

Meanwhile, the Sandy pilots at NKP were all huddled in their famous drinking room, "The Sandy Box." Tonight, there was zero idle chatter or bravado boasts. All conversation was serious business and centered on how to get their buddy and the "Streetcar Guy" out without losing anyone else. They wanted a united approach. After much discussion, many drinks, and a little argument, a consensus of opinion was finally formed and passed up the chain of command: "The road to the north of the two survivors is wall to wall with 37s and 57s out to ten miles from them, and there are also deadly ZPUs and other automatic weapon fire in all directions capable of taking out any Sandy or Jolly. The Sandys recommend massive CBU and napalm strikes by the fast-movers before attempting a Jolly pick-up." That said, the Sandy pilots then got down to serious drinking and bragging.

Sandy 8, the surviving wingie of the downed Sandy 7, was one of the Sandy Box participants but stood mostly on the sideline sipping a beer. *I'm just a junior pilot,* he thought. *No one will listen to me.* He didn't think there was a ghost of a chance he'd be sent back out the next day since he'd lost his leader today. So, after the more experienced Sandys began to drink, he decided to get drunk to block out Sandy 7's loss. He took a few quick gulps from his bottle of green beer. Just then, one of the senior squadron pilots sidled over to him.

"George, you're going back again tomorrow because you know the area."

Shocked, Sandy 8 nearly fell over in disbelief when he was further told he'd again be flying wing on the "Low Sandy." And, the Low Sandy would be none other than Sandy 5, who'd been hit and barely made it back to NKP today. The thought of going back to the scene where Sandy 7 had been lost, and Sandy 5 nearly so, scared the bedoozle out of Sandy 8.

Later, the recommendation of the Sandys was taken to heart and eighteen F-105s and fourteen F-4s were scheduled for sunrise alerts. Fourteen of the thirty-two would carry CBUs and GP bombs; fourteen would carry rockets and GPs; and four would be loaded with napalm. In addition, eight Sandys were scheduled to support the effort with maximum weapon loads. Six would be airborne at first light and two would be on standby alert status. And three Jollys were fragged for the morning mission.

Meanwhile, the noise I heard from the enemy base camp slowly diminished and the fires no longer illuminated the horizon. Around

10:30 P.M., the jungle was completely quiet. The enemy was asleep. It was an eerie, black silence. The day's bombing activity must have scattered or killed all the animals around me because I couldn't hear a peep from anything.

I lay on my back with my arms behind my head and stared upward. I saw nothing. It was as if my eyelids were closed. No stars, no moonlight, and no campfires were visible from my prone position. I stuck a finger across my nose and couldn't see it either. I had never seen it so dark. For several minutes, I fought the urge to nap.

Suddenly, multiple small lights appeared straight ahead in the darkness near the trail, about twenty feet from my position. Alarmed, I sprang to a crouch and aimed my pistol.

What now? Troops with small pen flashlights? How did they get so close without my hearing them? In total disbelief, I counted more then ten lights moving erratically in a circular pattern. It appeared enemy troops had returned in force and were probing my thicket and methodically working their way toward me.

During the next agonizing minute or so, they moved closer, but amazingly I still couldn't hear foot noise nor pick out any human forms. I was totally confused, but decided to sit frozen in hope they would bypass my exact spot. Soon, several light beams were only a few feet away! What do I do? Do I shoot, or run? Just then, I recognized the individual lights were blinking and moving in a fluttering manner. Quickly, one moved right over me and I got an up-close view. I let out a sigh of relief and chuckled at my stupidity.

My enemy was a large flying insect. This one was much larger than a West Virginia lightning bug and its illumination candlepower was at least ten times more. During its illumination period, it emitted a bright, white glow more brilliant than I'd ever seen from a flying bug. I concluded they were some variety of a Southeast Asia lightning bug that was feeding on other insects, or mating.

After the initial scare, my nerves returned to a normal state and I lay down on my side and watched the miraculous show. It was beautiful and peaceful. During one moment, the entire group fluttered to a point directly over me, danced around for about thirty seconds, and then fluttered twenty feet away. For several more minutes the bugs danced around me like a troupe of miniature angels. Then, they departed in the direction I had decided to hike. Was that a good sign? Was a "higher authority" guiding me?

The bugs were intriguing, but I was glad when they finally flew away because I wanted nothing to call attention to my location. Total darkness was my giant security blanket. I had another hour or so till my vowed midnight hike time, so I kept repeating to myself: *Keep your eyes open, don't fall asleep.* . . .

Chapter **12**

MIDNIGHT HIKE

Midnight arrived, and it was time to depart the thicket of briars where I'd hidden for the past six hours. With trepidation, I slowly rose from my furrowed, ground position. My back was stiff and aching from the ejection and my leg was sore from the bruise caused by the seat pan on ground impact. For several minutes I stood immobile as I slowly turned my head and listened intently for any foot traffic or voice noise. I heard none.

The lighting condition was unchanged. No moon had risen; I couldn't see any stars and it was difficult to tell up from down. It was so dark I couldn't see my feet, couldn't see what was in front of me, and knew I would be walking blindly. I would have to rely on my one-inch-diameter wrist compass to maintain my escape heading, but that would be impossible unless I used a flashlight. If I did, it would have to be the small penlight and, even then, I couldn't take a chance to use its beam all the time. In fact, there was no way in hell I was going to use a flashlight to walk by and give myself away. I clinched my survival vest tightly one more time and then removed the penlight from my pocket. Using my body as a shield, I placed my wrist against my chest to steady the compass and pushed the little button to activate the penlight for one quick heading check. I stared at the compass. The damn thing was spinning wildly, but steadied itself in about twenty seconds. Finally, I had my body positioned to hike in a southwesterly direction, but I felt as if I was glued to the ground. My feet didn't want to move.

Suck it up and move out, Fields, I commanded myself. I turned the light off, listened another moment for any noise ahead, and then took my first blind step out of the thicket. I raised my left leg, thrust it slowly forward about eighteen inches, and very cautiously placed it on the jungle floor. I heard a very soft *crack* as my foot broke the first of many twigs that night.

I was a six-year-old kid in West Virginia when World War II ended, and my friends and I often played war games wherein we tried to creep up on each other without detection. In daylight conditions, I had been very good at the game. This time was different. I was walking in absolute darkness on unfamiliar terrain while trying to maintain a constant 240-degree path. The jungle floor was laden with brittle wood and each touch down of my boot caused a *snap* or *crack,* and my anxiety seemed to amplify the decibel level. I soon found that it would be impossible to walk faster than a snail's pace without making a sound.

At first, I exercised a great deal of patience and made my steps slow and cautious. The routine was simple. Place one foot forward. Drop it, slowly. Pause, check to see if anyone else reacted to the noise. Then, place the other foot forward. It was slow going at first because I kept my hands in front and felt my way along. Initially, I pushed through small trees and limbs, but soon I began to bump against larger trunks, which meant walking around them. That caused me to get disoriented and necessitated another compass check. After thirty minutes, I realized I wasn't getting anywhere fast and only had four hours left before sunrise.

Fortunately, I had one thing going in my favor. The closer I got to the base campfires, the more they cast a reddish glow that illuminated the camp perimeter and placed me in the shadows. The glow could provide enough light for me to quicken my pace. I thought, *why not just take it right to 'em and maybe they'll think I'm one of them? In the dark, who will know I'm an American?*

So, after only thirty minutes of walking, my long-debated plan was scrapped. I decided to assume the bad guys were all asleep, forgo my compass, and just walk right to left around the outer perimeter of the camp. My plan then became a simpler one.

I walked cautiously but directly toward the campfires until their glow provided just enough luminance to make out the tree trunks around me. At that point, I stopped briefly and checked for movement or sound by any sentries between me and the camp. No activity, but, I could hear the fires popping and crackling. That noise should blend in with my footsteps, I thought, so while staying in the shadows I began to walk at a brisk pace to get around the camp before daylight. I walked without pausing. I kept the camp just off my right shoulder and stayed on the outer edge of the glow so it illuminated the ground for me. I worried about being spotted by sentries on the perimeter. Hopefully, my swagger might convince them I was a "friendly," and hopefully again, my bold decision wouldn't come back to bite me.

Meanwhile, the Air Force rescue force staff continued to work through the night to finalize the details of the next day's attempt to rescue Sandy 7 and me.

At 1 A.M., Crown requested the Seventh Air Force liaison officer provide him with the authentication data for Streetcar 304. All combat pilots were required to have answers to specific questions on file so that an airborne command plane could use them to authenticate the identity of a downed pilot. If a rescue force entered a target area for a second attempted rescue, the downed pilot would be asked to authenticate before a Sandy or Jolly approached the scene. If the pilot was captured, and forced to talk on the radio at gunpoint, he could then provide false answers so the rescue forces wouldn't be lured into a trap. Also, this data would prevent an English-speaking enemy soldier from using the radio to lure rescue planes into a trap. USS *America* provided my data from my squadron's Spook, the same one who had smartly reminded us to review the data as we left his mission briefing.

At 3 A.M., 7AF received an inquiry from the task force commander aboard USS *America*. The Navy, somewhat sarcastically, wanted to know if the Air Force required its assistance in the rescue attempt. The commanding general declined the offer and reiterated the Air Force could complete the mission without Navy assistance. The general diplomatically asked the admiral to have his Navy planes support the active rescue attempt then ongoing near Tiger Island.

Meanwhile, I steadily crept around the camp's perimeter for nearly four hours until the fires were just embers and no longer any use to help see the terrain. At 4 A.M., I had traveled maybe three hundred yards, and most of the camp was behind me in my five o'clock position. I had another hour before sunrise to place some additional distance between me and the camp.

Walking confidently, I placed my left foot out for the next step and let it descend to the ground. But the ground wasn't there, and all at once, I had a falling sensation. Oh shit—the ground wasn't where it should've been, and my foot was dropping lower than a normal step. It felt like I was stepping off the end of a cliff. Immediately, I pushed firmly backward with my right foot to do a sloppy version of a backward pike dive to the ground. In a panic, I thrust my hands out to the side and clawed the dirt to retard my descent.

My quick response saved me. I lay on my back for a couple of seconds to stabilize myself as one foot hung over the side of a drop-off. Then I rolled to my belly and inched forward, feeling the ground. A damn hole was right in front of me.

What was the depth and diameter? I considered using my penlight but the camp was still too close to risk it. A sentry might see the beam. Cautiously, I scooted to my left about two feet, felt with my hands, and the hole was still in front. Slowly, I moved to the right and also felt a drop-off there. After scooping around, I found a decent sized stone, dropped it in the hole and listened for impact. One thousand one, one thousand two, *clunk*, impact. "It's deep," I muttered. "Over my head, probably."

Before the last word was out of my mouth, a very loud, piercing, and ferocious sound broke the jungle silence only a few feet in front of me. I visualized a wild boar, and for a few terrifying seconds, I assumed it was charging toward me. In a panic, my eyes searched the darkness. Then I realized the boar was in the hole. Would it climb out and attack, forcing me to fire my pistol? But, it was too dark to aim. So, for several seconds, I was in a high state of alert, i.e., my blood pressure really shot up.

The rock had abruptly awakened the boar, and it was startled, frightened, or angry. Its continuous squealing noise was definitely an alert to anyone else who might hear it and that concerned me greatly. I didn't know how far the hole stretched in front or to the sides of me, so, I didn't know where to run for safety if he charged me in the dark. I sat immobile while considering my options, and slowly the boar stopped its clamor. How could I continue to walk if there were holes around me? I finally decided to risk the penlight to see my opponent. Carefully, I placed it in my left hand, held the pistol in my right, and then stuck both arms into the hole. I pressed the small button. An animal appeared dead center in the flashlight beam, standing still, and then its head jerked up. It stared at the light. "It's a frapping yellow pig," I uttered out loud. I chuckled at my fright. Hearing my voice, it started to squeal even louder and run around the hole like a chicken with its head chopped off. I jerked backward and turned the light off, hoping that would make it stop squealing. In that quick glance, the hole appeared to be about ten to twelve feet deep so the pig couldn't get out. He ran in a circle and cut a shine for another thirty seconds, and then slowly paced and snorted for another minute. Then the pig was quiet, and I suppose just as confused as I.

I hadn't taken time to check the width of the hole but didn't want to get the pig riled up again by using the flashlight. I was afraid one of the gomers had already heard the pig squealing and would come running at any moment to shoot it for a meal. While lying flat on my stomach with my right hand on the lip of the hole, I scooted to the left, and after maybe five feet, the hole ended. I crawled slowly forward with my arms stretched out in front. After maybe two to three feet, I came to another hole, so I crawled back to my original position and scooted toward the right side of the pig hole and also found another hole in front of it. The frapping area was full of holes. I sat up to a seated position. Another decision was required before I moved an inch.

Reluctantly, I decided to wait till first light and then hopefully negotiate the holes and move farther away from the camp before the bad guys awoke. I scooted back about six feet from the hole so I wouldn't inadvertently fall in, and vowed to remain there for the rest of the night. That position protected any frontal advance by troops who would have to avoid the holes.

It was four o'clock in the morning, and I hadn't slept or even closed my eyes for a brief moment in the previous twenty-two hours. I didn't feel tired but knew my body was running on adrenalin and Redman tobacco. I was susceptible to falling asleep if I unwound too much, and sunrise was another hour and half away. *Keep your eyes open . . . keep 'em open . . . don't tempt sleep.*

Meanwhile, at NKP, Nail 66 had tossed and turned in his bunk all night. Each time he fell asleep, he'd break out in a sweat and soon awake from a horrific nightmare. Over and over again, he saw an A-7 tumbling through the sky. Sleep was impossible for him. So, he eventually stopped trying, got up, took another shower, and then suited up.

Sandy 5, who had been hit by AAA and barely made it back to NKP, slept well even though he'd been informed that he would again be flying Low Sandy on day two. Sandy 5 wasn't overly excited and actually considered it an opportunity to atone for his previous day's mishap.

Sandy 8, like Nail 66, couldn't sleep. He was scared and apprehensive. He had been the wingman of Sandy 7 when he was shot down just eight hours earlier, and would be the wingman of Sandy 5 the second day. He had an ominous feeling about his fate. Two Sandy pilots had already been hit by enemy gunfire during the Streetcar rescue attempt, and his gut swelled with a feeling that he would be the next. The same premonition recurred over and over. He wouldn't make it back from his next mission. He would be killed or captured, and then be a prisoner of war for a very, very long time.

As he tossed around in his bunk, Sandy 8 thought of his wife and family and how devastated they would be if he were shot down. Perhaps he should write them one last letter.

Sandy 8 got up and carefully composed his "last" words to his wife. It was a short, but difficult, letter, and he dwelled on it for over an hour before he was satisfied. He tried to explain the value of the mission, and why he thought it important that he not take himself out of the game. He said he would never be able to live with himself if he weren't a participant in the rescue attempt of his section leader.

He wrote, "I've just got to do it, Jan. Leonard would do the same for me if the situation were reversed."

At the end, he expressed his love for his wife and family and told them how important their love was to him. They were on his mind and he hoped they would forgive him in the event he didn't make it back. After finishing, he placed the addressed envelope on his desk and again tried to sleep. He tossed and turned, got a little sleep, and was up and dressed in time for the 3:30 A.M. brief.

Nail 66 was demoralized, tired, and nervous when he arrived at the TUOC for the brief. There was an unusual presence of senior squadron officers and this was the first time he had been briefed in the presence of so many. Nail 66 saw this as an amplification of the danger and significance of the morning rescue attempt. Were they sending him back because no one else wanted to do it? He didn't dare ask the question.

First, he was informed that he was selected for the mission because only he and Sandy 5 knew the precise location of Streetcar 304. The briefing officer told him to time his take-off to be over the survivors thirty minutes before sunrise. Once contact was made with either pilot, he was to notify Crown. And, once he advised the weather was good enough for a rescue attempt, the major portion of the rescue force would scramble. The briefer then stated an obvious fact to those who had been there the day before. "Intelligence has confirmed that numerous enemy troops and at least a dozen AAA gun sites are ringed around Streetcar 304."

Nail 66 was told to take his oxygen mask in the event a special incapacitating chemical gas agent (Juicy Fruit) was dropped over the rescue scene. When released, it would incapacitate all persons on the ground in the vicinity of the gas cloud for at least fifteen minutes. Nail interrupted, and bluntly told the briefer that a 0-2 plane didn't have an oxygen system, thus no mask.

One of the senior officers shot back at him. "Just stay upwind if we use the damn gas. Okay?"

"Yes sir," Nail 66 replied.

The final portion of the brief focused on fighter support. As soon as Nail 66 reported the weather was suitable for strikes, thirty-two jets would scramble at staggered takeoff times and additional ones would be available all day if needed. Nail was directed to attack until every last AAA gun site was destroyed.

Nail 66 would have a Nail wingman to assist him on the second day. The second Nail pilot would fly at a higher and safer altitude and be the initial contact for the incoming fighters. He would note the ordnance load of each fighter, provide them with the general target scenario, and give them their escape heading in the event they were hit by enemy fire. When Nail 66 needed a specific ordnance load, the second Nail would switch the fighters with that load over to the control of Nail 66.

Sandy 5, the low lead Sandy, listened and began to grasp the magnitude of the enemy opposition he had encountered the previous day. The first inkling of concern for his personal safety began to float through his mind. He had encountered lots of enemy fire throughout his career and was confident he could handle one more mission, but he wasn't as confident now as he was the night before. Sandy 5 carefully marked his map with the location of the known enemy AAA sites. It would be his decision about the flight path of the rescue force during the pick-up attempt, and he definitely wanted to avoid the guns since the lives of the Jolly crews would be in his hands.

Nail 66 and Sandys 5 and 8 briefed while I was handling my pig situation. Shortly thereafter, they were airborne while I sat and waited for sunrise. Two Sandys took off from Udorn AFB around 4:45 A.M., and Nail 66 lifted off from NKP at five. Fifteen minutes later, four more Sandys were airborne at NKP along with three Jollys. All would arrive overhead my position around sunrise. The fighters sat tight on scramble alert.

Between 4 A.M. and first light, I remained back from the holes, fearful to move an inch in the dark, and fought the urge to sleep. It was an agonizing ninety or so minutes. The enemy camp was totally quiet, and the fires had dimmed to just occasional flickers in the midst of a black hole. Even the pig was asleep. For over an hour, I sat hunched over and became more apprehensive with each passing minute as I contemplated my plight.

Since the pig episode, the jungle had been eerily quiet, almost totally devoid of noise. Suddenly though, I heard the roar of a tiger or lion in a hunting or fighting mode. The roar echoed toward me. Initially, the intimidating sound was far enough away that I wasn't too concerned. But, gradually, I recognized the animal was working its way toward me, and its curdling roar now sounded more frightening. It was getting closer and closer and I assumed it was night-stalking a prey. Would it get a whiff of my scent, and would I then have to use my pistol in self-defense? That would certainly alert any enemy sentry. I knew my small pistol wouldn't stop a tiger. In just a few minutes, though, my fear was alleviated. I listened to a fierce fight between the tiger and some other animal—and, after that, all was quite again. Something was now dead.

Toward dawn, my morale began to sag a little due to the failure of my plan. I had hoped to be a mile away from the camp by then, but I was still dangerously close. I really, really needed to place distance between myself and the camped-out gomers, but I couldn't safely move because of the damn holes. I would have to sit tight till daylight, and I was very leery about what might happen then. Morning patrols from the camp might be on top of me in a flash.

Chapter **13**

MYSTERIOUS TEEPEES
AND VOICES

O fficial sunrise was 5:58 A.M. Around five-thirty the initial stage of daybreak was beginning to take effect, so my first night on the ground was almost over. I could just make out the edge of the hole beside me, and then a few minutes later, the tree trunks around me began to sprout out of thin air. Just dark forms, but visible enough to tell it was a tree and not a human. I cringed because I saw only short vegetation around me, and the trees were too widely spaced for optimum cover. But, as it got a little brighter, I noticed the ground around me was one hundred percent covered in a fern type plant that rose about eighteen inches high. After lying down, I found I'd be nearly invisible unless someone walked within twenty feet of me.

I saw what I thought was campfire smoke drifting my way before realizing it was a bank of wispy, smoky-colored mist instead. I watched the bank float toward me till I was completely enshrouded in a light blanket of morning fog and mist. That's good, I thought. More protection, but it was eerie. I could see it drifting but couldn't sense any wind; the air was completely still. In another few minutes, I looked up at the tree canopy which completely covered me like an umbrella. There, the treetops were basking in the morning sunlight, but it was still foggy down below at ground level. Before long, the sun filtered through the upper branches, and random sunbeams caused quick and drastic changes around me. I felt a little chilled from the moisture, so I scooted over a few feet and actually sat in one of them. During the next few minutes, I watched the sun's rays slowly work down the trunks, painting each in a lighter color. Finally, it was bright enough to see that multiple trees surrounded me but not tight enough for protection. And, I saw the magnitude of the holes in front of me. There was enough daylight to see by so it was time to move out.

I tried to rise to my knees but sank down immediately from a sharp pain in my leg and stiffness in my lower back. Then, I remembered my injury from the ejection. My condition had worsened after sitting on the ground for the last few hours. Pistol ready, I gritted my teeth, rose to a standing position, and began a slow scan of 360 degrees, looking for danger. My eyes had just commenced their second orbit of the area when, without thinking, "Well, I'll be damn," popped out of my mouth loud enough for anyone close by to hear. How the heck how had I missed an object that large when I looked in that direction just a few seconds ago? Frantically, I did a quick belly flop to the ground, rolled facing the object, and aimed my pistol as I rapidly scanned for any human movement.

I couldn't believe my eyes. The fog had lifted enough so that I could see a big problem at the nine o'clock position from the pig hole. I hadn't seen it the first time I scanned that direction, but now it loomed very large, less than seventy-five feet away.

Through a foggy mist, I stared at two conical Indian-type teepees approximately twenty feet tall, and spaced twenty-five feet apart. It was obvious they'd been constructed with the nylon parachutes of some earlier downed American pilots. I wondered about the fate of the pilots. It occurred to me that the teepees might be used as sleeping quarters for enemy troops, and they hadn't arisen yet. What was that sticking out of the top of each teepee? I stared, and what I initially thought was a wooden pole was actually a metal gun barrel. I could see now that the teepees covered two enemy AAA guns, and I estimated them to be at least 37mm.

I surmised there'd be three to four men inside each teepee, and I'd be in a lot of trouble if they arose and came outside while I was still around. The base camp was only two hundred yards off to my right, and the nearest teepee was less than twenty-five yards away to my left. If the gunners had instead slept in the base camp during the night, that meant they would be walking past my current position on their way to man the gun. Could I, or should I, risk moving my position now?

Make up your mind fast, Streetcar. My escape path was straight ahead, over the pig hole, so all I had to do was get up and run straight ahead to place distance between both threats. It sounded simple.

Crap. I couldn't make myself do it as the trees were too widely spaced without much foliage between so I'd be running naked, without sufficient cover. I didn't want to run helter skelter, as that was a good way to run smack dab into the arms of any gomers, so I moved back from the pig hole to consider my options. I lay flat, resting on my elbows, with only my head above the eighteen-inch-high ground foliage while I pondered this latest dilemma. Maybe the teepee gun crew had slept late today. Time would tell.

Shortly after 6 A.M., the light drone of a plane's prop made me look skyward. I turned toward the teepees to check for activity, but saw none. The sound didn't have enough bass for a Sandy's A-1 so I assumed Nail 66 was arriving for work. I removed my precious radio from the tight pocket on the front of my survival vest, went to the receive position, and held the radio to my ear for nearly five minutes. Nail didn't make a transmission or fly directly overhead, so I assumed he was just doing a weather recon and waiting on the rescue armada. It was too early to waste my battery before the rescue force was in place, so I turned the radio off. During the next thirty minutes, I listened as Nail's plane droned near the river to the north of my position, and I assumed he was trying to locate Sandy 7.

Unknown to me, Nail's first task was to check the weather. He reported the weather in the area was good; there was only a thin stratus layer of clouds at ten thousand feet which appeared to be clearing. Eight fighters scrambled immediately. Nail 66 then tried to contact Sandy 7 and me, to no avail.

Meanwhile, Sandy 7 had spent the night very high in a tree, lashed to the trunk. It was a long, painful night, but now sunrays were highlighting the very top foliage of the tree. Sandy knew he'd soon be in a very tenuous position. Was he high enough to avoid detection from the ground when daylight fully arrived? Plus, his right foot had hurt like hell all night long, and it appeared he might have broken it during his parachute landing. *I must have been pretty scared to run on it so long last night,* he thought. It was now light enough for him to get some Darvon pain pills out of his survival vest, but he was afraid to try for fear of dropping them. A gomer might be sleeping at the base of the tree and hear it fall. He bit his lip and grimaced. His day was not starting out very well.

Sandy 7 watched as the sun finally burst through the upper foliage and now slowly inched its way down the trunk toward him. Dawn was looking beautiful, but Sandy wasn't sure he actually looked forward to its full glow. He was now getting very apprehensive about what he might see once the sun illuminated the jungle floor beneath him. The sun was strong enough to filter its warm glow through the heavy tree canopy and promptly encased Sandy 7 in a sunbeam. He could easily make out his hands, yet the jungle floor below was still encased in black. Minute by minute though, the light inched further down the trunk, and Sandy's fear heightened. He hadn't yet heard any movement or voices below, and was still hoping his eyes had been playing games the night before. *Lordy, Lordy, I hope the gomers are far gone from the base of my tree,* he sort of half-prayed.

Then he heard a small plane and knew the Nail FAC was coming into the area to search for him and Streetcar. Should he dare risk talking to Nail? No, there was a good chance he would be heard, or he might drop something from the tree if he tried to remove anything from his vest. He would stick to his original plan and wait for the troops to leave the area before contacting the rescue planes. But the sound of the plane made his spirits rise. Help was close by when and if Sandy 7 was ready to talk.

Soon, the jungle floor below Sandy sparkled from the glow of sun hitting water crystals on leaves. Shortly thereafter his heart sank. Major fear again reared its ugly sense within his head. Soldiers, clad in khaki—North Vietnamese Regular uniforms—were slowly arising from their beds among the leaves and wandering in and out of the bushes as they emptied their bladders. Then, each moved toward a central gathering spot several hundred feet away, but out of Sandy's view. There, a faint trail of smoke rose up through the jungle canopy. *They're cooking—I'll remember that,* he thought, *and on my next Firefly recon mission, I'll watch for the early morning trail of smoke to rise out of the tree canopy. Then, I'll plaster that area with bombs. That is, if I ever get out of this mess I've placed myself in.*

Sandy's view of the breakfast mess area was blocked by foliage so he couldn't confirm or deny it, but the sound of voices gradually increased and he heard the metal clanging of pots and pans. A pungent smell of fish and oil wafted toward him, but the smell of that type of food didn't appeal to him for breakfast and in fact drove any hunger away. As the minutes wore on, Sandy lost count of the number of troops within view, and he now realized he was in a tree, smack dab in the center of a base camp for at least a company of North Vietnamese Regulars. No wonder Streetcar and I encountered so much enemy fire, he thought. Normally, Sandy 7 would have expected to only see Pathet Lao guerillas in this part of Laos, but it was also swarming with North Vietnamese Regulars. *Will they spot me before they break camp,* he wondered.

Soon, soldiers began to form up into platoons and depart the area heading in different directions. Sandy recognized they were heading out on patrol, probably to search for him and Streetcar. But to his dismay, some soldiers stayed within sight of his tree and remained there all day. Sandy 7, unlike me, had no options.

At sunrise, I heard different noises than what Sandy 7 heard. Soon after my sighting of the teepees, I was shocked by the blaring sound of a bugle from the direction of the base camp. Stupidly, I thought it was a "charge" signal and meant someone had seen me, and troops were rushing toward me. The bugle sound was that close and that was just what popped into my mind. But after that, I heard the sound of pots and pans banging against each other and concluded the gomers were being rousted for their morning chow. Unbelievably, in the midst of war, the base camp had been awakened with the sound of a bugle sounding *Reveille.*

Soon, many voices echoed from the camp. The clarity made me realize I was actually closer to it than I had previously thought when I walked past during the night. The troops seemed happy this morning as a lot of cheery laughter intermingled with their words as they ate. The thought of breakfast didn't bother me; I wasn't hungry even though I should've been. My dinner the night before had consisted only of two pieces of candy, but I still wasn't feeling any hunger pain or reduced energy level. In anticipation of a hot day, I broke out a water bottle and took my one rationed morning drink while I sat and marveled at the commotion in the base camp. Next, I stuffed a wad of Redman in my jaw. I was good to go.

Breakfast in the enemy camp occurred quickly, and suddenly the camp noise began to subside. Shortly thereafter, I heard the tinkling sound of several bells, and loud prayer chants then echoed in unison toward me. The magnitude was such that I surmised there must be a hundred or more men chanting their morning prayer simultaneously. All other sounds of the jungle were drowned out as a loud, bass hum rolled and reverberated around me. Being so close was intimidating, but it also made an indelible imprint in my mind of their dedication to their religious faith.

The prayer chants lasted for maybe one minute before the hum ceased, followed by very loud authoritative orders that seemed to come from a bullhorn. The orders were given, and then the camp erupted in a loud sound of movement and voices, and I surmised they were getting up from the prayer position and breaking camp. I imagined their Plan of the Day was quite simple. Spread out, and capture the two American pilots. The thought of hundreds of troops searching for me was nerve racking. Frankly, my current hiding spot wasn't going to hack it, and I knew I didn't have much time to improve upon it.

About that time, I heard a snort. I'd forgotten about the pig because he had slept peacefully for the last hour or so. He was now awake, and I scooted forward and leaned over the edge of the hole to get a look at him in daylight.

Man, was I lucky, or what? My angel must have been working overtime last night. A miracle had stopped me one step short of falling into a hole at least five feet in diameter and ten feet deep. The walls of the hole were too smooth to climb up if I'd fallen in. And there was the pig. . . .

From my perch he didn't look that big, and he wasn't the intimidating boar I'd first envisioned. In fact, I could have handled him with ease. As if he felt my eyes staring at him, he looked up, squealed real loud, and began to run in a tight circle to find an escape route. Suddenly he stopped, cocked his head at a forty-five-degree angle, looked up at me, bared his teeth and snorted in his most fierce manner. I chuckled. *I feel sorry for you little buddy, but better you than me.*

It was now fully daylight, and I could see another obstacle that I'd luckily avoided during my night hike. A seventy-five foot long trench line ran from the teepees toward me, and it was about three feet wide and maybe four feet deep. If I had walked a little left during my hike, I would've stumbled into the trench and possibly have broken a leg. I surmised the trench line was used as a safety position for the enemy gun crews. If American bombs became a danger, the crews could hastily leave the gun, dive into the trench, and thereby avoid any above-ground bomb blast near their gun site. That explained why it was so difficult to knock out some enemy guns even when your bomb appeared to be a direct hit. Even CBUs, with their hundreds of anti-personnel bomblets, wouldn't kill the gun crews unless one bomblet luckily landed and exploded inside the ditch. The gun crew could fire at the plane during its dive, jump in the trench for cover after bomb release, and then quickly re-man the gun after the bombs exploded. They could then fire at the American pilot as he pulled off the target. Learning that proved to be a very helpful tool for my survival.

A noise in the distance broke my chain of thought. This plane had a gutsier, more bass noise, and I knew the Sandys were now arriving for work. I looked up and realized I'd be unable to see any plane overhead because the trees around me were at least 150 feet tall with very dense crowns. It didn't matter as the Sandy flew north of me, and again I assumed they were checking on Sandy 7 first, hopefully even talking to him. I surmised that Nail 66 would soon arrive in the area to check on my status and talk since the Sandys were now here. I just knew Nail wouldn't do anything until the fighters were overhead, so I stayed off the radio.

Unknown to me, six Sandy A-1s and three Jolly HH-3s arrived around 6:15 in a holding area about twenty miles to the southwest. It had been a tortuous flight for the Sandys as the weather was really crappy between me and NKP. The Sandys had flown through considerable rain to the west of my position, and had narrowly avoided a mid-air collision. None of the Sandy pilots thought there was a ghost of a chance to rescue me this morning unless the weather improved dramatically.

Intermittently during the next thirty minutes, I heard the sound of Nail's plane as he droned in the distance, but I still heard no jet sound. But, about 6:25, I heard Nail's plane flying toward me, and I couldn't stand to wait any longer to make today's first contact. I sat up and pulled my radio out of the vest.

Before I could turn it on, I heard voices behind me in the direction I had walked during the night, and they were on the move. Immediately, I flopped back to the ground toward them in a defensive gun position. Slowly, I inched my eyes above the fern tops and stared toward the sound. The voices were close enough to distinguish words but no one was in visual range. Which way are the voices moving? Toward me! It's time to talk to Nail right now.

I scooted back to my previous furrowed spot and dug in again, in a flat, prone position on my belly. I anchored myself on my elbows and gave Nail a short beeper burst over the radio. He quickly took the bait, and a wonderful, motivating transmission blared out amidst static and crackling.

"Streetcar 304, this is Nail 66. Do you copy? Over."

A feeling of calmness came over me as if the very presence of Nail made me feel safer. The sound of his plane now seemed directly overhead my position. Quickly, I replied in a low murmur so as not to be heard more than a few feet away.

"Roger, Nail. This is Streetcar 304, and it's great to hear your voice, over."

Nothing. I heard no reply.

Again, I transmitted to Nail and again received no acknowledgement. Come on Nail, answer, damn it. I need some help before the voices get any closer.

I waited a minute in hope Nail would call me, but no joy. For the third time, I transmitted to Nail but received no response. Instead, the sound of his plane was moving farther away, and I began to sweat bullets. Is he going to fly out of my radio's range before we make contact? In a near panic, I reached inside my survival vest, took out my only other battery and quickly exchanged it with the one in the radio. Did this one have any juice left? In a louder voice, I again transmitted.

"Nail 66. This is Streetcar 304, do you copy? Over." The wait for the answer seemed longer than it actually was, Nail's voice was much more dynamic this time, and I could sense the excitement through his inflection.

"Roger, Streetcar. You had me worried there for a moment as I thought we'd lost you. How're you doing today, buddy?"

My response was short, quick, and to the point. "Roger, Nail. I'm okay but ready to go home, over."

Nail replied in a very calm, reassuring voice. "Roger, Streetcar. Don't worry. I'll get you out. You'll be outta there in a few minutes! What's your condition, 304, and what's your position in relation to where I left you last night? Over."

"Roger, Nail. Both available radio batteries are low juice, but otherwise I'm okay, no major physical problems. I estimate I moved a quarter to a half click from last night's position on the escape heading you gave me yesterday. There's a AAA gun site within seventy-five feet of my location, and a gomer patrol is close by, over."

"Roger, Streetcar. I copy and understand your location. Have you had any contact with Sandy 7? Over."

I then proceeded to give Nail 66 a quick description of my radio conversation the previous evening with Sandy 7, and told him about the gunshots I'd heard from the area where Sandy 7 ejected. Since then, I had no other contact with Sandy 7. Had he?

"Negative Streetcar, but I'm going to try and make contact with Sandy 7 this morning. Then I have a gaggle of fighters lined up for AAA suppression, so find a hole and keep your head down while we work the guns. Let me know if the bombs get too close for comfort. You'll be outta there in a few minutes, Streetcar. Just hang in there, and stand by for fifteen minutes, out."

I smirked. "You'll be outta there in a few minutes. . . ." The Nail pilots must be trained to keep the morale of the survivor up by repeating the same phrase, over and over. I recognized his caring ploy, but knew he had a big problem with the guns that wouldn't allow him to follow through on his promise. After all, I could see the guns in the teepee and knew they were big. But why wasn't Nail concerned about the voices near me?

After Nail left, I positioned myself on the ground to be in a defensive position to watch the area around the teepees on my left, the random voices to my right, and the base camp directly in front. The trees around me weren't very tightly spaced, and the ground cover was mostly low-lying ferns so I had a decent view in most directions. Hopefully, I would be able to see an enemy advancement before they picked me out of the jungle floor. I knew I had to place some distance between myself, my neighbor AAA gun site, and the voices, or there would be no rescue today.

As I was checking in with Nail, a squadron buddy, Lieutenant Brown (the one who wouldn't bet a dime on my surviving the night), was shot off Cat One aboard *America* for a mission in South Vietnam. He says, "I got the shock of my life just as I raised my gear and flaps. Someone announced over the radio that Streetcar had survived the night. Immediately, I burst into tears of happiness for him. I couldn't believe he was still alive, free, and working hard at getting out." Later, Brown told me he was also shocked when he learned I had bombed in Laos on my first mission.

Soon thereafter, Nail 66 tried one more time to raise Sandy 7 on the radio, but had no joy. He and Crown decided to have Sandy 5 break orbit and join with Nail 66 in order to provide air cover as Nail tried to pinpoint my new position. Sandy 5 was the low lead Sandy, and thereby on-scene commander for any morning rescue attempt. He and his wingie, Sandy 8, left four other Sandys in orbit with the three Jollys and rendezvoused with Nail 66. Once he had a tally-ho on Nail 66, Sandy 5 eagerly expressed his concern about enemy guns to Nail. He empathetically stated that he wasn't real keen about flying over my location until all guns had been suppressed. But, by the time they had hashed it all out, rain began to fall. The weather deteriorated so much Nail recommended to Crown that the fast-movers be placed on hold until it improved. Nail reported scattered, occasional rain showers with ceilings that were intermittently two- to three-hundred-feet overcast.

A light drizzle began to gently spray the ferns around me, and the smoky-colored bank of mist floated in again. All enemy activity ceased. The jungle got quiet. It was a good time to try Sandy 7 one more time. Again, I got no response. I didn't know the man, but he was a fellow pilot who had risked his life to save mine. The thought made me feel crappy.

I reflected about Sandy 7 for a few minutes before I again heard the voices off to my right. They had been quiet when Nail and I talked. Now, though, several different voices were casually chatting less than a hundred feet away, and I wondered if they had heard my conversation with Nail 66. They were coming from the direction I'd hiked during the night, and I surmised some gomers were tracking me from where I'd left the trail the night before. They appeared to be spread out and methodically searching, beating the bushes, and I didn't know how long it would take them to expand their pattern and find me. If something positive didn't happen soon, I'd be boxed in. I waited on pins and needles.

Reluctantly, at 6:40, or about ten minutes after we first talked, I told Nail 66 that enemy troops were approaching and now were within a hundred feet. I asked for help. "Can you put a few bombs down here?" I didn't feel comfortable that he knew my exact position for targeting purpose, but was willing to chance friendly fire so the bad guys would bury their heads in the sand for a while. It was raining and therefore unsuitable for fighters, but I was desperate. I thought I was in a real pickle.

Nail promptly asked how many smoke flares I had, hoping I'd pop one to use as a spot for bomb reference. I replied, "Only one." He rogered that, but then said my radio transmission was breaking up and advised me again to standby but keep my head down. His request for a smoke confirmed for me that he didn't know my exact position. The Air Force guys thought it stupid I only had one smoke. If only our Navy budget was as large as theirs.

Nevertheless, Nail 66 understood my dilemma and made another pass over my area, but the weather was just too crappy to work the fighters and he didn't have the heart to tell me. For the next twenty minutes, Nail frantically attempted to find a weather hole to get fighters down through to help me, but was unable. Finally, he reluctantly told Crown the fighters might as well hold on the tankers for now as the weather was too bad for flak suppression. Nail 66 prayed that I'd survive till the weather broke. He felt useless at that point.

Meanwhile, I was shocked by Nail's comment that my radio was breaking up. I had a serious problem. The little radio was my lifeline for rescue, and I'd be in deep trouble if both batteries died. My primary radio battery had no juice, and now my one and only spare also appeared too weak to power a decent transmission. Quickly, I again removed the battery from the radio and scraped the ends with my survival knife before re-inserting it.

In no time, the light drizzle turned to a steady, light rain, and I hunkered on my stomach for thirty minutes or so in a bed of ferns as the rain fed them and soaked me. The cool rain hit the hot humus soil of the jungle floor, and a foggy cloud, almost like cigarette smoke, slowly rose, floating upward until I was completely enshrouded in a protective vapor. It was nigh impossible to see inside the jungle and that apparently stymied the bad guys since their voices became more subdued. I didn't get the bombs I requested, but I got a godsend vapor that gave me temporary respite from the bad guys. They were now silent. Did they get disoriented in the fog and go in a different direction? Or were they just sitting tight while it rained? Were they still nearby? I didn't know, but my respite was short.

Shortly after 7 A.M., the rain stopped and wisps of vapors made a quick, spiraling exit through the treetops. Just as quickly, the voices became loud again. Then, it hit me: maybe the voices belonged to a gun crew. That made sense, since they seemed to be hanging around the same spot. Either way, they were too close for comfort. I initiated another call to Nail 66. Fortunately, my minor repair on the battery had done some good and the radio seemed to be working okay.

I told Nail I was in a precarious position with troops nearby. "The rain has stopped around me so can you expedite rescue?" Nail again advised me to keep my head down, and again promised that bombs would be falling very soon.

I was losing patience. Since sunrise, I'd been all keyed up for a quick morning rescue and it wasn't happening. It wasn't entirely the Air Force's fault. I recognized that the weather was shitty. Nevertheless, I still had a selfish urge to tell Nail 66 to cut the BS and to get on with it. I didn't. But I muttered to myself. "Damn it Nail, for Pete's sake, give me a few bombs this morning. Put some fear in the heart of the bad guys around me."

Fifteen minutes went by, and sure enough, Nail had blown smoke at me again, and the bombing didn't start. Nail 66 was just as discouraged as I was. He wanted to kill the damn enemy AAA sites, but the weather wouldn't allow him to put the fighters in, and he was getting hassled by the staffers because of that. At least sixteen fighters, six Sandys, and three Jollys had been orbiting for over an hour, and Nail had not yet been able to put a single bomb run against the AAA sites. The six Sandy planes had been cycling back and forth in pairs to NKP for refueling, and the fighters and Jollys had been hitting the tanker to stay topped off on fuel. Now, the tanker was saying that he could only give fuel for maybe another hour. A call was placed for additional tankers, but none were available. It looked as if many of the fighters might have to RTB for fuel if Nail 66 couldn't put them against the AAA sites soon.

Another thirty minutes passed. At 7:30, still no bombs, but no rain either. In fact, it looked like the clouds were clearing a little. The teepees were still quiet, the pig was asleep, but I steadily heard the sound of voices and movement to my right. It's got to be a AAA gun site crew preparing for the Sandys to come into the area, I thought. Still not sure, I continually scanned for the enemy troops I expected to see at any second. I'd been lying prone, in a ready, alert position for one and a half hours, and the suspense was killing me. I needed a bomb run to serve as a diversion while I moved away from the voices, but it didn't appear forthcoming any time soon.

I queried Nail for the fourth time since 6:30.

"No shit, Streetcar—this time is for real. The fighters will start smacking the AAA gun sites in the next few minutes."

Right, I thought. *I'll believe it when it happens.*

About then, the voices grew loud enough to make out words so I became very engrossed in an attempt to spot the gomers. I rose to my knees, determined to find out what was going on. I stared through a mixture of trees and plants toward the voices for several minutes, but though they seemed close enough, I couldn't spot a body. Suddenly, I was caught off-guard when for the first time today, I heard the sound of a jet. Hallelujah! This time Nail's words held true, and his flak suppression commenced around 7:35, nearly two hours after he had arrived overhead. A flight of four F-4 Phantoms was the first to bomb.

I heard a jet in a dive. At first, it seemed to be whistling, and then I heard the engine increase to full power, followed by a small boom when the pilot popped the afterburner for climb-out. I was familiar with the routine, and knew the first bomb of the day had been released. An explosion would occur in about seven seconds.

To my left, I saw a bright, white flash followed immediately by a large *boom*. Instantly, I slammed my forehead into the soft humus for protection and felt the vibration as the shock wave waffled by. I heard a sharp, cracking noise as tree trunks shattered and debris rained down on me. I was thrilled. The bombing had finally gotten underway, and, as I had wished for, the explosions were close. I had hoped the first bomb would hit behind me near the voices, but it had exploded about a hundred yards past the teepees and on my projected escape path. I didn't believe Nail knew my exact location so he must have spotted an active AAA there, unaware how close it was to me. Then, a second plane made a run, and this time the bomb blast was a little farther away and reverberated as if I was in a valley between mountains. Was I? Did I walk farther during the night than I thought? I didn't know. About then, Nail asked if I'd seen or heard the bombs explode and if so, my relative position.

"Roger, Nail. I'm about a hundred yards north of the last bomb."

Nail told me again to keep my head down while he worked over the guns. About a minute later, the next section of F-4s dropped several CBUs about a half-click north of my position, and minor explosions rolled like thunder as three- to four hundred bomblets exploded one after another. Right afterward, Nail 66 called to confirm my position relative to the CBUs. After my description, he said he had a pretty good fix on my location.

The time was approaching 7:50, and Nail 66 had been airborne for nearly three hours so he was close to bingo fuel. He had almost run out of fuel the night before and had no intent to push the limit again today. His plane didn't have in-flight refueling capability so a replacement, Nail 40, had been scrambled from NKP and was due to arrive within a few minutes.

Shortly, Crown told Nail that four A-1s, loaded with Juicy Fruit, were on ready alert at Pleiku Air Base in South Vietnam, and once scrambled, could be at the scene in ninety minutes. However, Blue Chip (7AF) was reluctant to give final authorization for the mission for some unstated reason. If used, the gas agent would drift over the battlefield and temporarily incapacitate all those exposed to the gas, including me. Maybe Blue Chip was smart enough to realize the rescue force didn't yet know my exact position to be able to rush in, find me on the ground, and hoist me up if I were totally incapacitated.

Chapter **14**

THE MONKEY TREE

etween sunrise and 8 A.M., I lay prone on the ground near the
teepees, just a few steps back from the pig hole. Bombs had
rained in a steady downpour during the past thirty tedious, harrowing minutes. Several exploded too close for comfort. How long
could I maintain my luck and not be hit by one? I was still fearful that
if I stood up, a gunner would throw open a flap, burst from a teepee,
and catch me in the open. They could be there, manning the guns and
just waiting for a plane to fly over. None had flown directly overhead
my position yet, so there had been no opportunity for the teepee guns
to fire. Or the voices to my rear might walk in my direction any
moment. Their sound remained loud and clear, and I was totally confused by their presence. I had heard them close by all morning and I
couldn't decide what the hell the troops were doing back there. It
made me uncomfortable being close enough to hear them talk. I
wanted distance between me and them, but the time was not yet right
to run. Maybe the guns in the teepees are just backups for a site to my
immediate rear, where the voices are, I thought. Would the gunners
change position from one gun site to the next by running inside the
trench line, and did the trench in front of me weave to a gun site
behind me? The whole scenario was unexplainable, and I felt the need
to separate myself from it but hadn't seen the right opportunity yet.

At 8 A.M., clouds started to drift in tightly around the little weather
hole Nail had been working for the past thirty minutes. He informed
Crown the area was socked in again. Confusion reigned for several
minutes. First, Crown transmitted that all forces were to RTB until the
weather cleared except for Nail 66, his relief Nail, two Sandys, two
Jollys, and one flight of fighters. More than a dozen fighters, four

Sandys, and one Jolly left the scene. Then, in less than five minutes, the clouds moved away as if blown by a giant wind, so Nail frantically asked Crown for the return of all planes. Nail then quickly smoked one AAA site that had been the last he'd seen firing before the weather hold, and his one flight of available fighters began to pound it. They knocked it out, and during the last plane's bomb run, a surprised Nail saw no enemy AAA fire for the first time of the day. It looks like all of the AAA sites may have been killed, he thought, so he told Sandy 5 the enemy guns were silent.

"Sandy, do you think the area is safe enough to check things out?"

Sandy 5 was not new to this fight. He was the same pilot who had been hit on his second ID pass the evening before, and had just barely made it back to NKP before his engine quit—for good. If you recall, he was older, and more combat-experienced than most of the Sandy pilots. Nevertheless, he'd almost been killed the day before, and he'd decided he wasn't going to take as many risks today. Sandy 5 cautiously flew toward my location.

Nail 66 called me around 8:10 and told me to be alert for Sandy 5's entry into the area. Nail said Sandy knew my location but needed to verify that the guns around me had been silenced before he could bring the Jolly in. Sandy knew my location? I wondered how, since I had moved during the night and he had yet to fly over today.

Things were quiet for several minutes before all hell broke loose. "Holy Toledo," I uttered. In the distance, I heard a steady crescendo of AAA fire, more than any time this morning, and I knew they were firing at the approaching Sandy. I didn't need a call from Sandy or Nail to inform me it was still too hot to attempt a pick-up.

Sandy 5 quickly aborted his ID pass, and told Nail 66 to resume flak suppression. He then sternly informed Crown that the area was still too hot to risk sending the Jolly in, and that the guns would have to be suppressed completely before he'd agree to a pick-up attempt.

Shortly after that, Sandy called me. First, he casually asked if I was okay. Then he wanted to know exactly what kind of enemy gunfire I was hearing. After my response, he calmly spelled it out.

"I'm sorry 304, but it's just too hot to send a Jolly in right now, and we won't come in till all AAA is killed. More ordnance is on the way, so keep your head down. Hang in there, buddy."

Man, I thought, *Sandy sure seemed casual in the face of death.* He and his cohorts are doing a job that few men would take on, even for higher pay. But Sandy had laid it out clear and simple. It was going to be a while before I saw a Jolly, so I turned my radio off to conserve my precious battery.

Nail 66 was debriefing his replacement Nail when Sandy 5 started his ID pass. Nail thought he'd killed all the guns, and I'd be rescued soon. Maximum flight time for his O-2 was four and a half hours, and if he RTB'ed right now, he'd be in those time limits when he landed. Once he saw the magnitude of new AAA, he knew he had to stay in the fight since he knew the area best.

More fast-movers were hustling in for flak suppression, so Nail 66 again smoked some AAA sites as aim points. Once the bombs began to fall, I noted they just happened to be in the path of my escape heading. I had danger to my left in the form of teepees, greater danger to my right in the form of the base camp, and the voices to my rear. I needed to run forward to find a more secure pickup spot and get myself out of this pinched position.

The nearby voices finally got to me. Sometimes, one can make a rapid decision, and if done in haste and without forethought, it can turn out to be disastrous. In this case, I made an agonizing, prolonged decision. It was formed around what I had observed earlier in regard to the trench lines and my theory about the gun crews jumping in them just before the bombs exploded. I made up my mind to run to a more secure hiding spot and use the bomb blast as a diversion. I projected that the gunners would dive into holes just after a fighter released bombs and stay there till the explosions ceased. Hopefully, they wouldn't see me running during those few seconds. I decided to run forward at full gallop for twenty seconds after bombs were released. Nail 66 had a whole gaggle of planes lined up so I should be able to run for a considerable distance, twenty seconds at a time, before they all expended their bombs. Of course, I'd be exposing myself to the bombs, but I had to bite the bullet and do it. I made up my mind to break cover when the next section of planes rolled in close to me.

Several minutes passed without any jet noise. Wouldn't you know it? I had made up my mind to move, and now there was no air support. Then I heard them, across the river, maybe a mile or so away. Nail had a flight of four Marine F-4s dropping napalm along the karst where several pesky 37s and 57s had fired at Sandy 5 during his last foray into the area. A few more minutes elapsed before I heard the whine of a jet, and he seemed to be diving right at me.

For the first time today, a jet was directly overhead. As if by signal, multiple AAA sites began firing from all quadrants around me, including the area of the voices. That pacified me somewhat. The voices didn't belong to a search party after all. Then, just as I projected, the firing stopped when the pilot started to climb, and within seconds bombs exploded no more than one hundred yards dead ahead of me. I assumed his wingman would place his bombs near that bomb. I waited for his roll in, and sure 'nuff, it sounded as if he was whistling down the pike right toward me.

AAA started firing. I stood up, hunched over. Ouch. My back was really stiff now and my leg was still sore, but I shuffled several feet to my right and stood in tight formation with a tree trunk for camouflage as I got my legs under me. There, I waited for an engine noise change to indicate "bombs away." This was my first chance since daylight to get a full 360-degree scan from a standing position, so I first looked left at the teepees. No movement there. My head swiveled right and I saw no visible danger toward the camp. My scan continued farther right where the voices were now excitedly shouting over the thumping, firing noise of their AAA gun, but I still couldn't make out the gunners through the trees. Just then, the jet's engine sound changed, and I knew the pilot had pickled his bombs. The gunners stopped firing. One thousand one, one thousand two . . . they should be in their holes. Take off, run.

I bolted around the right side of the pig hole, paused to look down, and uttered a short, sincere Thank-you to the pig. He was standing, and looked up at me with a frightened stare, but didn't make a peep as I ran past. I turned my head back and aimed myself in the direction where the first plane's bombs had exploded. I jumped the three-foot-wide trench and then paused to look down its length, toward the teepees, fully expecting to see men inside. I saw nothing but a long, empty hole. Quickly, I accelerated to a full-speed sprint, and as I did, I placed my radio mike next to my lips and spoke in a firm tone at medium volume between huffs and puffs.

"Streetcar 304 is running on the ground. I say again, Streetcar 304 is running for new cover. Keep the bombs coming." I didn't wait for a reply.

I ran toward the probable bomb blast site at full speed, grabbing tree trunks and jerking myself past them, running right through the smaller saplings just like one would do if he wanted to run over a tackler. I burst through anything in my way in order to maintain a straight path.

During my baseball days with the Railsplitters I'd shown excellent speed on the base paths. I had quick forty-yard speed, but was not exceptional at one hundred yards. Forty-yard quickness was all I needed now. I had wanted to move about forty yards forward in the twenty or so seconds that the gunners would probably have their heads in a hole, but trees, holes, and survival gear slowed me down.

Just then, the first bomb exploded at my eleven o'clock position. A monstrous white light was followed by a thunderous boom. The shock wave rocked me and debris peppered me in the face, but I kept running straight at the blast site. Lucky me, no shrapnel damage—for just a split second, I felt a tinge of relief that I was still alive, but wondered where the second bomb would hit. Flash, *boom*—there it was, and fortunately it exploded a little farther away.

"I'm still alive, you frapping mothers," I mumbled out loud. I felt macho, but thought, *this is not real. It's too much like a frapping movie. Keep'em coming Nail; I wish you could see me running down here.* I was proud of myself right then. I was finally helping my rescuers.

Two bombs had exploded so it was time to hit the deck. I picked a spot with vegetation a foot or so tall, did a baseball slide on a soft mattress of plant humus, rolled flat on my stomach, and rested on my elbows as I rapidly scanned for troops. A pleasant odor drifted up. The soil was a really dark color, very wet and loamy and smelled just like a bag of garden humus. It was a nice spot to catch my breath while I waited for the next bomb run and reflected on my first sprint. I had encountered multiple holes and trenches that either required me to run around or jump over 'em. If that continued, it would reduce the distance I could cover each sprint.

Within seconds of the wingman's second bomb explosion, the gunners again fired viciously as the plane climbed back to altitude toward the south. The number of nearby active AAA guns was staggering, and the noise of their fire was thunderous. I wondered how any pilot could survive such a barrage, and how I could be rescued with so many active guns almost on top of me. It was evident I had to put lots of distance between the guns and me so I vowed to be ready for the next fast-mover's bomb-run and press forward immediately.

"Nail, this is Streetcar 304. Place your next set of bombs due south about fifty yards from your last impact. Do you copy, Nail?" He rogered, without questioning why. Now, if the next Air Force puke wasn't good at his job, my ass would be grass.

Within minutes, another flight of fighters was pounding the area ahead and I was up and running pell mell again. My plan was simple. Run when the guns cease their fire. Sprint forward while the bombs explode and while the gunners are busy firing at the jet as he climbs out. Stop running and dive for cover when the guns stop firing. I just had to watch for gunners as they exited their holes.

Each time I slid to a halt, the ground felt soft and spongy from the earlier rain, making it easier to burrow into the moss and loam to hide and wait for the next set of bombs to fall. The running and hiding made me feel exuberant, and I loved this part of the "game." *I'm good at this,* I thought. My confidence was growing in leaps and bounds, and I didn't mind the smell of muck or the grime of dirt. I kept giving Nail instructions to move the bombs ahead of my path, and I steadily gained more distance, maybe three hundred yards from my boxed-in situation near the teepees.

Nail had commenced his bomb runs at 7:30 A.M., and at 8:45, one fighter after another was still pounding the AAA sites. Nail 66 was doing it very diligently and systematically and currently had a Pistol flight hitting the guns. A Metric flight would be next to come down the chute.

Meanwhile, unknown to me, the two A-1 Spads loaded with Juicy Fruit were scrambled at Pleiku but wouldn't arrive for ninety minutes. The three Jollys were queried about the number of gas masks on board; two of the three had sufficient masks but one crew had none. The third set of masks was on the Alert Jolly back at NKP. This now placed a clinker into the plans of Blue Chip to possibly use the gas agent to get me out. Plans had called for all the Jollys to have the masks, but the planning had fallen through a crack somewhere along the chain of command.

I lost track of the number of sprints I had made but finally saw brightness ahead. Around 9 A.M., I made one final dash through the forested jungle area I'd been in since last night and made it to the edge of the tree line. Once there, it was open, bright, and sunlit, and the ground was thick with tall grass. I stopped running, knelt down, scanned ahead for any problems and considered my options.

I could continue walking left or right and stay under the jungle canopy, but then I basically would be staying in the same area I'd been in for the past fifteen hours. No, I needed a better view of the sky. I saw several medium-sized trees rising out of tall grass slightly up a rise to my right, about 150 feet away. That looked like a good spot to hide, but to get there I'd have to cross an area where I'd be totally exposed unless I crawled the entire way. Come on, Nail 66, I pleaded. Give me just one closer bomb blast. Magically, I heard a jet engine whistling in.

Thus far, I hadn't seen many planes in their actual run and had timed most of my sprinting based on engine noise changes. This time, I had a beautiful view of a Thud's broadside flying from my right to left in about a 120-degree left bank. The Thud driver rolled wings-level in about a forty-five-degree dive, and his nose slowly settled in on the target. I could tell instantly he'd be pickling off a few bombs directly ahead of my position. Suddenly, it dawned on me that I was sitting in the middle of a tiny weather hole. Gray clouds were all around except directly overhead where there was a small cone of blue sky; the Thud was perched in the middle and the sun reflected off his airframe. A steady crescendo of thumps erupted as the AAA gunners commenced their fire at the now-glistening, green Thud. Immediately, a steady stream of red tracers rose from the ground toward the Thud driver, perfectly matching his forty-five-degree dive. The plane appeared to be just a few feet above the tracer pattern, skimming downward, and seemingly riding a wave of rising red balls. The Thud's wing bobbled a few times as the pilot made pipper adjustments to stay bore-sighted on the target, but he pressed on. More guns began firing just before the plane's nose began to pitch upward. Bombs away! All guns stopped firing. I rose, positioned myself toward the tree on the right on the higher ground just past the tall, grassed, open area, and sprinted in a hunched-over position through the open terrain.

"Please, please let all the gomers be in a hole," I pleaded, "so they won't see me."

I made it safely to the tree. Once there, I sat down with the trunk to my back and faced forward in the direction I'd been running and gasped for air. I was puffing hard. After regaining my composure, I looked around and noted that a large, level, open field was just off my right shoulder. There was no way I could risk crossing that much open distance in the daylight.

I had four options. I could change my direction of escape slightly left of my previous path and continue to hide in the cover of the larger trees. That would mean walking in a direction that would put me closer to my original crash site. I wanted to get farther away from the crash site, so option one wouldn't work.

The second option was to bear right to stay inside the tree line, but that heading would take me back toward the base camp. That thought scared the pee-doodle out of me. I scratched option two, fast.

Option three was to brazenly continue straight ahead on my original escape heading, without deviation, and crawl through the open field directly ahead. I studied that option for a minute or so. The plant foliage appeared to be waist high, but there were no trees of any significance. The distance across the open field appeared to be about a hundred yards, so I could do it if I crawled and stayed below the tops of the grass.

I decided to exercise option four. Wait for darkness to cross the field—if this spot protects me until then.

I looked around at my surroundings and immediately liked what I saw. I hadn't noticed during my sprints, but now I could see that I'd been running slightly uphill, so in this spot I had a commanding view in all directions. My tree was on a slight knoll and around it was a mixture of heavy plant foliage and tall, sage-type grass, so I'd be well hidden but still able to see any approach by gomers if they came within seventy-five feet. I commenced a slow 360-degree scan.

To my front, I saw waist-high foliage for fifty to seventy-five feet, and past that point were thick trees and jungle. I felt comfortable that no one could approach from the front without my detection.

Scanning right, I saw I was only about ten feet from the edge of the field. In a seated position from my slightly higher elevation, I could see most of the field, and my view was such that I would have a clear, unobstructed view of any approaching enemy threat along the right side of my perimeter.

To my rear was the jungle of trees where I'd just spent the past fifteen or so hours. I knew my most probable threat would be from that direction, but also knew that many enemy troops had either been killed or wounded by the constant bomb barrage. Those left would hopefully be leery of moving in my direction since so many bombs had fallen between us.

On my left perimeter, about thirty-five feet away, was another mid-sized tree about forty feet in height. Till now, I had paid little attention to it. It was similar in structure to an average-sized sweet gum tree and had a similar, rounded canopy. Just as I scanned past the tree, I saw movement out of the corner of my eye. I flicked back toward the tree and now saw it was inhabited. The recent bombing and my sprint past it must have frightened the occupants so much that they had remained motionless and totally quiet until now. The tree was absolutely full of small monkeys, and it appeared they considered me a threat. I found it puzzling that at least a dozen were sitting quietly, facing directly toward me, and staring. I was fascinated and found myself staring back at them. My stare must have blown their minds, as one of the occupants let out one little squeal. Inadvertently, I made eye contact with the largest, meanest-looking monkey. He bared his teeth and let out a fierce scream directed toward me. All the rest then simultaneously began jumping around the tree while squealing. It appeared to be a deliberate scare tactic by the monkeys. And it did scare me, because the noise would certainly draw attention to my position. The gomers behind me would know that something had upset the monkeys and come to investigate.

I went into a prone position and pointed my pistol in the direction from which I had just run, expecting to see gomers running out of the trees at any moment to check out the clamor. How long would this incessant monkeyshine last? They jumped around and hollered for at least a minute before they finally quieted down and took up stationary positions in the tree, while the big, ugly one continued to glare at me. I moved so he couldn't see my face, in hope he'd contain any further outburst.

Enough about the monkeys. My new hiding spot was in the middle of a weather hole near an excellent spot for a helo pick-up so I really anticipated a rescue within the hour. I sat with my back against the tree and faced south, with the open field running parallel off my right shoulder. The monkey tree was off my left shoulder, the base camp was to my right rear quadrant, and the area I had just run from was to my left rear quadrant. Dead ahead was the area I would next travel, or use for the helo pick-up. The trunk of the tree serving as a backrest was large enough to shield my body from view in the direction from which I had just run, and the monkeys would serve as sentries for danger from all directions. I really felt that I was in an optimum position.

But at about 9:05, the sun's rays disappeared. I looked skyward and saw dark, ominous-looking cumulus clouds thickening overhead and knew my hole of good weather was about to disappear. Since sunrise, I had experienced intermittent mist, sprinkles, rain, and partial sunshine. In the last thirty minutes, the temperature had soared and had already dried my clothes, wet by the morning rain. I was sitting against a tree that didn't provide much shade, so it was getting hot. A cooling rain would feel good, but again hamper my rescue. I wanted the sun to shine brightly. The hotter, the better, and, I wanted Nail to expedite.

Speaking of Nail . . . unknown to me, Nail 66 took some small arms fire from visible troops, so four Thuds made several strafing passes and decimated the troops who had the balls to fire at a Nail. I was unaware of Nail's problem but did hear the hissing of the Thud cannons as they made multiple gun-runs. I couldn't hear any enemy AAA fire in return, so hopefully that meant all the guns had been killed by the sixteen fighters who had pounded them for the past hour and a half.

I sat and reflected on my situation. Nail really needed to pinpoint my new position so he didn't inadvertently bomb me, and so he could promptly vector the Jolly to me. I thought it would be easy as I was sitting next to the large, open field that should stand out like a sore thumb from above. All I had to do was describe my location to Nail. Then, he would find it immediately, as would Sandy, and the Jolly would dash in and pick me up. I called Nail.

"Nail, I'm in a new location in the middle of a small weather hole and it sounds like all of the guns in my vicinity have been silenced. It looks good for rescue. Do you concur? Over."

"Roger, Streetcar. Concur. Stand by, over."

My wife says I'm easily confused. But, "Stand by?" What the frap was that all about? I thought the rescue team would be all set to go on a moment's notice once the AAA was suppressed. Come on Nail, send Sandy in now!

Unknown to me, Crown called Nail on another frequency as he and I talked. Nail was also in the process of being relieved by another FAC, so he had his hands full and I had interrupted things.

Crown told Nail that bad weather was developing in the nearby valleys, and that the weather hole over me was filling up quickly with multi-layered clouds topping at ten thousand feet. He reported the weather between the orbit point of the Jollys and my location was deteriorating quickly and it would impede the flight of the Jollys, so he was recommending a weather hold.

During the next fifteen minutes, there was much discussion between Nail, Sandy, and the Jollys about the weather. Finally, around 9:20 A.M., the rescue was again officially placed on hold. The recent scramble by the Juicy Fruit birds at Pleiku was canceled just as they were rolling for take-off. Nail, two Sandys, and two Jollys were told to remain in the area but to remain well clear of the scene until the weather cleared. The third Jolly was told to refuel from Crown and then return to NKP. The two Jollys who remained at the scene were then topped off by Crown. All other forces were directed to RTB and refuel during the weather hold. I didn't yet know any of this.

Nail 66 was reluctant to make the call and tell me for the second time that he was RTB'ing and leaving me behind. He turned his plane, flew toward my position, and stared down at the dark tree canopy wondering what it must be like down here, with bad guys chasing you. Oh, how he hated to make the call, but he winced and pressed his guard transmitter to inform me that the rescue was being placed on hold pending an improvement in the weather. I was totally surprised by the action, but tried to be the coolest jet jock in the world.

"No problem, Nail 66. I'm in a good spot for rescue so get me out as soon as you can, out."

But, to myself I said, "I'll probably be captured before they return." I felt my luck was due to run out unless I had a very, very good angel.

Unknown to me, Crown was just now picking up word that an F-4, call sign Hammer 72, had just been shot down near the coastline, and the crew was in the water. His wingman was overhead awaiting the Jollys. I wasn't the only fish in the pond as far as Crown was concerned.

I looked up, directly overhead, and could still see blue sky but recognized there was less now than a few minutes earlier. I was mildly shocked to hear the mighty Air Force was delaying the pick-up due to bad weather. It appeared to me that the hole was big enough to work in, and I had to assume that I was in a small hole of good weather with lots of bad weather nearby. I was on higher ground than before and could see several miles in all directions, and the sun was again shining as far as I could see. I hadn't moved far enough to have any significant difference in weather between the pig hole and here, but it did appear weird that my perception of the weather was "good" and theirs was "bad." Maybe they had a wrong perception of my actual hiding spot? I'd bet my last dollar on it.

At that moment, I had a really bad premonition I would be captured before the rescue forces came back. I fought my glumness, before saying out loud, "I can hack this. I can evade."

I was completely comfortable with my new hiding spot, and it was a perfect place to observe the jungle environment while waiting. Then my mind did a flip-flop. I no longer wanted to wait, and didn't feel I should have to. I needed to get out of this mess now and something was screwed up and preventing that from happening. At that point, I momentarily lost a little faith in the Air Force. The rescue attempt was on hold because of bad weather, but I was getting sunburned.

Navy Lt. Kenny W. Fields (Streetcar 304) manning his A-7A Corsair II cockpit for a mission after his rescue. (Courtesy Kenny W. Fields)

An A-7 from VA-82 (Streetcar Squadron) attaching to the catapult shuttle on the flight deck of the USS America *(CV-66).* (Official U.S. Navy photograph)

A Streetcar A-7 with 500-pound bombs on mission over North Vietnam. (Official U.S. Navy photograph)

View from above of target area for Streetcar 304, the crash site, and Sandy 7's parachute (small circle above A-7 crash site). (Official U.S. Air Force photograph)

VA-82 A-7s and VF-102 F-4J Phantoms over North Vietnam during a mini-alpha strike. (Official U.S. Navy photograph)

An A-3 Skywarrior (Whale) refuels an F-4 Phantom. (Official U.S. Navy photograph)

VA-82 commanding officer Cdr. Jack Jones, USN, and his wife Doris at a squadron "Mess Dress" social function just before the squadron deployed to WestPac in 1968. (Courtesy Doris Jones)

Cdr. Jack Jones (Skipper), USN, preflighting his A-7 on the USS America *flight deck.* (Courtesy Glenn Jones)

Air Force Capt. Pete Lappin (Nail 69) on the ramp in front of his 0-2A Skymaster after a hot mission. (Courtesy Jon McMurtry)

An 0-2A, loaded with white phosphorous (Willy Pete) munitions, similar to the one flown by Nail pilots during the Streetcar mission. (Courtesy of Jon McMurtry)

Air Force Capt. Jon McMurtry (Nail 66) posing at NKP. (Courtesy Jon McMurtry)

A view from above of the base at NKP in 1968. (Courtesy David Richardson)

Air Force Capt. Ed Leonard (Sandy 7) beside his A-1E Skyraider after a Sandy mission in 1968. (Courtesy Ed Leonard)

Air Force Maj. Thomas Campbell (Sandy 9) beside his A-1E before a mission. (Courtesy Thomas Campbell)

Air Force Maj. Bill Palank (Sandy 5) in front of an A-1E prior to a mission in 1968. (Courtesy Bill Palank)

"Sock it to'em," the A1-E flown by Air Force Capt. George J. Marrett (Sandy 8). (Courtesy George J. Marrett)

An Air Force F-105 Thunderchief (Thud) fighter-bomber, like the one flown during the rescue of Streetcar 304. (Courtesy Pete Lappin)

Navy Cdr. Ken (Spider) Webb. In 1968 he was attached to VA-86 aboard the USS America. (Official U.S. Navy photograph)

An Air Force HH-3 Jolly Green Giant similar to the one flown by the Jollys during the rescue of Streetcar 304, refueling from an HC-130 Hercules (Crown) bird. (Courtesy David Richardson)

A Jolly lifting a downed pilot from the jungle. (Courtesy David Richardson)

Streetcar 304 rescue crew in front Jolly 9's HH-3. Front, L-R: *Maj. Brock Foster (Sandy 2), Maj. Louis Yuhas (Jolly co-pilot), Capt. David Richardson (Jolly 9), Maj. Thomas Campbell (Sandy 9).* Rear, L-R: *SSgt. Coy Calhoun (Jolly flight engineer), Sgt. Peter Harding (Jolly para-rescueman).* (Courtesy David Richardson)

Air Force Capt. David Richardson (Jolly 9), inspecting an M-60 door gun aboard his HH-3 Jolly helicopter. (Courtesy David Richardson)

Navy Lt. Kenny Fields being littered across ramp at Nakhon Phanom (NKP), Thailand, air base after rescue by the Jolly Green crew. (Official U.S. Air Force photograph)

Navy Lt. Fred Lentz (Iceman) on the flight deck of USS America, *toting what's left of his flight gear following his ejection during Streetcar 304 mission.* (Official U.S. Navy photograph)

Navy Lt. Kenny Fields on flight deck of USS America, *surrounded by squadron mates upon his return to the ship.* (Official U.S. Navy photograph)

Air Force Capt. Jon McMurtry (Nail 66) on the ramp at NKP toasting his last mission in March 1969. (Courtesy Jon McMurtry)

Air Force Capt. George J. Marrett (Sandy 8) is awarded a Distinguished Flying Cross by Col. Edwin White, USAF. (Courtesy George J. Marrett)

Streetcar 304 family portrait taken one year after his rescue. Left to Right: *Terry Fields, Lt. Kenny W. Fields, Shirley Fields, Todd Fields, Kimberly Fields.* (Copyright provided to Kenny W. Fields, courtesy Olan Mills)

Air Force Maj. Ed Leonard (Sandy 7) receives a welcome-home handshake at Clark Air Force Base in the Philippines after five years as a POW in North Vietnam. (Courtesy Suzanne Leonard)

Air Force Maj. Ed Leonard (Sandy 7) enjoys his welcome home parade down Main Street in Winlock, Washington. Left to Right: *Ed Leonard, Don Foreman (Karen's son), Karen Raye (Ed's sister).* (Courtesy Suzanne Leonard)

Chapter 15

SANDY TAKES A HIT

Crown had placed the rescue on weather hold, and the more I thought about it, the more confused I became because the sky above me was now clear and sunny. Admittedly a small hole, but clear.

"Nail 66, Streetcar 304. Can you verify you know my exact position after my morning move? Over."

Pause . . . still no answer . . . finally Nail responded. "Streetcar, understand you're in a new location since this morning? Over."

"Nail, that's a Charlie. I'm next to an open field maybe three hundred yards south of my morning location. Suggest you fly over the area and I'll hit you with my—" I stopped in mid-sentence as I suddenly heard men in the field, and they weren't speaking English.

"Stand by, Nail, I've got a problem down here." I couldn't see anyone from my seated position so I reluctantly forced myself to rise up to a crouch to peer across the tall grass.

"Aw, crap, here they come again," I muttered out loud. In the middle of the field, I saw a squad of ten or so Pathet Lao guerillas from the waist up, clad in solid black uniforms, and they weren't farming. I was sure they were coming to capture me. They were sauntering across the field toward me in single file formation, gesturing and talking loudly. On their present heading, I projected they'd exit the field within twenty-five to fifty feet of me. Suddenly, the radio crackled. Nail 66 was calling me, but I turned the radio off.

My first thought was that the enemy had listened to the radio talk between Nail and me and must have taken a radio bearing on my position. They were sending troops to capture me. If that were the case, why were these troops making so much noise instead of quietly surrounding me? This was a crazy war. The enemy was all around me, talking and walking without fear of detection.

Quietly, I crept to the edge of the field in order to have a better view of the troops. I settled in some deep grass and pulled more of it over me for camouflage purpose. Now, I could see the squad clearly. Their rifles were shouldered so they probably didn't know my exact position, but could be on patrol looking for me. They were bantering and smiling as they walked, and at their current pace would be on top of me in about five minutes. I felt secure in my hiding place, though, and amazingly wasn't even experiencing a rise in blood pressure. *Cool,* I thought. *I'm into the game now and can handle the pressure. I'm not going to let these guys scare me and blow my cover. In fact, I'm going to wipe them out!*

Nail 66 was confused. I had abruptly stopped talking to him, and he'd been unable to re-establish contact. He breathed a sign of relief when he heard my voice again.

"Nail 66. Streetcar has a big problem, over."

"Go ahead Streetcar, what's up? Over."

"Roger, Nail. I've got a visual on ten or so gomers heading toward me from the middle of a field, and I estimate they'll be on top of me in five minutes. They're sitting ducks right now for the fast-movers, over."

"Roger, copy Streetcar. Stand by and let me see what I can do, out."

Unknown to me, the only planes over me at the time were Nail 66, his incoming relief Nail, their two protecting Sandys, and an unarmed Crown plane. Nail fully understood the gravity of the situation but didn't think he could help me since all the fast-movers had just bingoed back to base. And, Nail was nearly out of fuel and again pushing his plane to its absolute limit for fuel endurance.

But damn it, I've got to do something right now or I'll lose 304, Nail thought.

He had a quick discussion with Sandy 5 about my situation. It was a real gut-check time. Sandy 5 could have had plenty of excuses to use as a reason to delay action: the weather was coming in fast, such that he'd have to dive through clouds to reach my position; he didn't yet know if all the AAA had been killed, and he'd already been nearly shot down the night before; it was only a Navy pilot on the ground; Sandy had been airborne for over four hours, etc. But Sandy 5 knew if he didn't act quickly, I might be captured in broad daylight.

Sandy 5 weighed his options and then made a courageous decision: he would go down for a quick look. He asked Nail 66 to find him a weather hole for descent. Nail offered to lead him down through the hole to my position, but was told by Sandy to remain high, as he didn't think Nail could survive the withering fire he expected once under the clouds. Nail 66 then vectored Sandy 5 to a point over the river several clicks south of me and advised Sandy to dive through the hole, fly north over the river until he saw the sharp bend in the river, and then turn due west to fly over me and the field. That was Nail's best guess as to my current position.

In reality, I was sitting in the middle of a weather hole, and Sandy 5 could have spiraled down through that hole. However, Nail and Sandy were unaware that the clear hole was available right over my new position.

Around 9:45, Sandy 5 left the safety of his high orbit, followed in loose trail by his wingie, Sandy 8. Sandy 5 nosed his bird downward in a spiraling dive until he reached 290 knots, the max he could get. While in and out of clouds and still in the dive, he picked up the river and the sharp bend that pointed toward me. Once there, he leveled at five hundred feet above the river in point-blank range of the enemy AAA. Sandy 8 stayed higher, just below the cloud base, but in a position to monitor his lead's flight path. He, too, was perilously close to the enemy guns. Sandy 5 then added full throttle, turned toward my position and roared across the treetops with as much speed as his A-1 could muster.

Within seconds, a ZPU opened up on him and Sandy 5 banked hard right. *Thunk.* Sandy 5 felt a solid hit. An enemy round had found his plane, and he knew immediately it had been larger than small arms fire. Almost immediately, he had visual indications that he had taken a damaging hit in the plane's engine. Engine instruments began to fluctuate, and then pressures began to fall. He realized the finality. Frantically, he keyed his mike.

"Sandy 5's been hit, and I won't get this one back." Short and sweet, no further explanation was required.

Sandy 8 was just flying through a cloud when he heard his leader's call, and he was shocked. This was the second time in a little over fourteen hours that his section leader had taken a hit. The first one, Sandy 7, had been shot down. He rolled out of the cloud and scanned below. Where is Sandy 5?

Suddenly, Sandy 8 saw an A-1 straight ahead, slightly low, trailing a misty vapor of some type fluid. He rammed the throttle against the stop and pushed the stick forward to help gain speed. In less than a minute, Sandy 8 was flying fifteen feet under his leader's belly at 1,000 feet and

160 knots, about five miles west of me. During a quick inspection, he noted Sandy 5 had already jettisoned his extra fuel tanks and all of his ordnance to get rid of the drag. There was a steady stream of fluid pouring from the belly of the plane, but Sandy 8 couldn't make out the color. It's black, he decided.

Just then, Sandy 5 screamed, "Hot engine oil is blowing into the cockpit, burning my face and making it hard to see the instruments."

Sandy 5 didn't need anyone to verify he'd been hit hard. He knew it, and also knew it would just be a matter of minutes before the engine quit. He didn't need instruments to tell him he was about to lose his bird. It was something a pilot with his years of combat experience could tell. Today's hit was different from the one he'd taken yesterday. The engine was running much rougher, and the hot, oily smoke was indicative of a serious leak. It was only a matter of time before he lost all engine oil, and then the engine would seize.

Sandy 8 knew it was time to clear the underbelly so he eased his plane to the right parade formation slot. It was fortunate he slid over when he did because, almost immediately after settling in, he heard Sandy 5 say, almost casually, "I'm getting out."

"Crown, this is Sandy 8. Did you copy Sandy 5 has been hit? Notify the Jollys we need help ASAP, over."

On the ground, I heard none of the preceding. I had made my call to Nail for help and was told to stand by. I never heard Sandy's plane get close to me, or knew that Sandy 5 took a hit and left the area. This was the second time it had happened to Sandy 5, unknown to me both times.

The timing of Sandy 5's hit was just after the first two of three Jollys had finished their in-flight refueling. The first Jolly to finish was already some thirty miles away when Sandy 5 took the hit. The second one, Jolly 9, had just finished and was off to the side when Sandy 5 made his call.

Crown informed the Jollys of Sandy 5's problem, and Jolly 9 acknowledged he'd heard the Mayday call and would take up a heading to join on Sandy 5. Jolly 9 had already taken a directional cut during Sandy 5's radio chatter, so he was ahead of the game. He could rendezvous with Sandy 5 in just a few minutes, if Sandy could hold on until then.

Jolly 9 was topped-off on fuel. As soon as he heard Sandy 5 say he was getting out, Jolly 9 pickled his F-100 external fuel tanks and their two hours of fuel. Now, he would have more speed and maneuverability for the pick-up. Less fuel meant less weight, and that meant more speed to reach Sandy quicker and less power required to hover. All good stuff for the pilot.

Just prior to punching out, Sandy 5 made a final advisory call. "I won't get this one back. I'm getting out." So, six minutes after the enemy gunfire hit his plane, Sandy 5 leveled his wings and initiated the extraction sequence. The A-1 did not have an ejection seat.

Two rockets behind Sandy 5's seat fired upward, and a long, trailing cord jerked him out of the plane like a puppet. Then his chute blossomed fifty feet above Sandy 8 and just off his left wing. Sandy 8 then spiraled around the floating chute and watched as it landed in a mostly dead, 150-foot-tall tree that was fairly devoid of foliage but in a heavily forested area.

As he floated down in his chute, Sandy 5 saw his wingie off to the side so he was confident he'd be rescued within minutes. He felt good about a quick pick-up. Suddenly, that thought was shattered by the popping sound of pistols and rifles. Someone on the ground was taking a pot shot at him which meant the enemy was not far away from his projected ground impact point. Fortunately, they were either bad shots or out of range. Sandy's blood pressure shot way up, and now he was scared for his safety, whereas just a few seconds ago he had thought he was fearless.

Then, his bad luck continued. His chute abruptly grabbed one of the higher limbs of a tree and partially collapsed. Sandy felt like he was on a bungee jump for several seconds as he bobbed up and down, and then side to side a few times. He dangled precariously in mid-air and felt like a piñata that was about to be struck. *No problem,* he thought. *I'll just wait for the Jolly to pluck me out with his hoist.*

But that thought was shattered when he looked down and saw a helmeted, black-clad soldier with a rifle run by the base of his tree. The bad guy didn't look up. Sandy 5 removed his pistol and wondered if the Jolly would reach him before he was shot or forced to surrender. He was in no position to even surrender, though, unless he could extract himself from the tree. Just then, several more troops rushed by. Sandy's jaw dropped! How many could run by without looking up? In a couple of minutes though, Jolly 9 hovered over Sandy 5. The FE reported that the chute was snagged on a tree limb, partially deflated, and Sandy was about fifty to sixty feet above the ground. Then the FE looked out the side door of the Jolly and guided the pilot to a hover position over Sandy. Once there, he made eye contact with Sandy and received a thumb-up from him indicating he was okay. The FE started to lower the jungle penetrator hoist for Sandy 5 to grab, attach himself to, and ride back up to the Jolly.

As the penetrator began to fall toward him, Sandy 5 flinched when he again heard the popping of rifle fire, not knowing whether it was directed at him or the Jolly. The penetrator seemed to be settling toward him in slow motion.

When the penetrator was about halfway down, the FE informed his pilot that the helo's rotor wash was causing Sandy's chute to bounce and it might deflate at any moment. Before Jolly 9 could react, the FE reported the bubbled chute had slipped off the limb and was dropping through the tree limbs. It would catch a limb briefly, then detach, and drop a little more before grabbing another tree limb. It looked like, at any moment, Sandy 5 would possibly fall a great distance to the ground.

Before that happened, the penetrator arrived at a position reachable by Sandy 5. The FE watched as Sandy, while holding the pistol in his right hand, used his left hand to detach his right shoulder fitting from the chute. He then wrapped his left arm around the penetrator, but didn't lower the seat portion. Then, he reached up with his right arm to detach his left shoulder fitting while still holding his pistol in the same hand. Sandy released the final fitting but couldn't maintain his one-armed grip on the penetrator. He slipped off before he got the second arm around it. Tumbling, he plummeted through one tree limb after another, and the FE watched in horror as Sandy 5's head violently struck the ground on impact. Sandy lay immobile in a prone position next to the base of the tree. The FE immediately began to retract the penetrator and informed Jolly 9 they would have to lower the PJ to the ground to retrieve Sandy.

The penetrator had retracted to about ten feet from the belly of the helo when the FE heard Sandy on the radio. "Jolly, I'm okay." He then saw Sandy 5 move, rise to a sitting position and look up at him, and give another thumb-up. The penetrator was immediately lowered again, and this time Sandy attached himself to it without incident and was hoisted aboard the helo in a successful rescue, eight minutes after he left his plane.

After Jolly 9 cleared the danger area, Sandy 5 was examined and decreed in good condition except for a broken tooth and a bruised leg. Sandy 8 then escorted Jolly 9 back to NKP. Sandy 5 was mighty fortunate. In the past fourteen hours, he had been hit by enemy gunfire twice and shot down once.

The enemy was doing quite well against us. In fact, right now they were ahead in score and winning the game. Three A-1s and two A-7s were now out of service, four pilots had ejected from their planes, and two pilots were still on the ground either evading or captured.

I, again, knew nothing about what had just happened to Sandy 5 and was still patiently waiting for planes to wipe out the gomers who now had taken a break in the middle of the field. This was a great chance to take out an entire enemy platoon, but we were going to lose it, I thought, if Nail didn't get a plane down here immediately.

But Nail 66 had an even bigger problem now. He and his relief Nail, plus two Jollys, were the only planes left near the scene. Nail couldn't risk the slow-flying Jollys to support me, and the two Nails only carried smoke rockets. Nail 66 screamed for fighter support.

I waited patiently, unaware of Nail's problem but totally mystified by his inaction. FACs worked their butts off on every mission to find worthy targets for pilots such as myself. For once, we had uncovered a huge enemy force around me, and you'd think Nail would have had fast-movers in quickly to bomb the shit out of the troops since that was what the war was about. "Find the enemy and destroy him," or so I thought. But what did I know? I was on only my first combat mission.

Ten minutes dragged by as I waited for a fast-mover to appear. About then, the enemy squad rose again and started to meander around in the field as if they were diligently searching for me. I could count their rifles. They seemed to think I was hiding in the field. Had they heard my radio conversation with Nail about the field? Minute by minute, they checked every possible hiding spot as they closed on me. I was torn with indecision. I felt the need to change my location for personal safety, but I also wanted to be in position to pinpoint the squad for an attack plane. So I radioed Nail again. He replied, "Stand by," in such a hyper voice that I perceived he had his hands full with something, but I wasn't sure it was with my problem. I was really getting pissed off about the inaction because this was the second time today I had informed Nail about nearby troops, and nothing had been done to help me. I didn't know all fighters had RTB'ed. Nail 66 was quite upset also!

After a few minutes, an amazing scene unfolded. I heard the heavy bass drone of multiple planes nearby so I looked up and saw a flight of A-1s that I assumed to be Sandys. Nail 66 must have fragged them in response to my plea for help, I thought. I was now duly impressed and regretted my earlier sarcastic thoughts about the Air Force.

Then, I glanced back at the last location of the enemy squad. They were out of sight and must've dove for cover as soon as the planes appeared. Four A-1s were visible against a clear, blue-sky backdrop at what I estimated to be five thousand feet. As I watched, the flight leader peeled off from his perch, dropped his nose at the area where I had last seen the bad guys, and commenced a forty-five-degree attack run. As he passed about three thousand feet, I saw a small puff of smoke under one wing and heard a *rat-a-tat-tat* sound. He was strafing with his left-wing stub mini-gun. He kept doing so down to about fifteen hundred feet before he sharply broke off left, toward me. Quickly, I sprang to a crouch only a few hundred feet away from the A-1's target as his bullets ripped apart the middle of the field. Even though I strained, I couldn't confirm whether the squad had been hit. No one cried out in pain.

Rifles began to pop as the A-1 leader climbed back to altitude. A second A-1 started a similar attack, from the same perch. He rolled in, and I heard the steady hum and rattling of his guns as he fired. The noise of his guns was nothing compared to that which soon erupted from enemy AAA sites in the forested area across the field from me. I could no longer discern the A-1's gunfire as it was overwhelmed in magnitude by the enemy's return fire. It didn't seem to frighten the A-1 flight; number three rolled in from his perch as soon as number two pulled off. Again, the AAA fire was intense, and they weren't using tracers. This is stupid, I thought. The A-1s probably don't see the AAA and are too slow to be dueling against a AAA gun, even a smaller caliber one. Another plane was about to be shot down. I'd seen this scenario before with an A-1 getting hit within eyeshot, and I couldn't believe it was going to happen again. I had to stop it.

"Nail 66, this is Streetcar 304. The four A-1s that are strafing now are really getting hosed by ground fire. Recommend they abort and be replaced by fast-movers, over."

"Roger 304. I'm unaware of any planes in your area, but I'll check it out."

After several more runs by the A-1s, Nail had still not gotten back to me. I tried several times to make direct contact with the A-1 flight leader on guard channel, but got no response. Finally, I made a transmission "in the blind," meaning I was making it but didn't know if anyone was listening.

"This is Streetcar 304 calling a flight of four A-1s strafing an open field just west of a river. You're receiving tremendous enemy ground fire without tracers each time you make a run. Suggest you abort your gun runs, over." Nothing. I said it one more time in a loud, firm voice but again, no response. Obviously, the A-1s weren't monitoring guard frequency.

Oh well, I tried. After that, I scooted back to the tree, rested my back against it, and watched in anxious admiration as the A-1s made a total of eight strafing runs against the field and the base camp area across the field. The scene was like a frapping training movie that an instructor might use to train student pilots on the proper way to conduct a four-plane strafing pattern. The four pilots flew each gun pass like they were on a stateside training mission, oblivious to the enemy gunfire. The flight leader established a high perch, and the rest of the flight took turns rolling in off that same perch for a total of eight times in a daisy chain formation.

I grabbed a long stick lying nearby and pretended I was aiming a rifle as an A-1 dove. It appeared that it would be so easy to shoot them down, and I could only conclude that the enemy gunners were really lousy shots. The planes were in sight continuously for at least fifteen minutes, and the enemy gunfire was extremely heavy each time an A-1 attacked. But the enemy gunners missed, and missed, and missed with thousands of rounds. I don't know how, or why, the A-1s survived. The guys in black just weren't very good shots and only appeared to be able to shoot planes down by the sheer number of bullets they sent skyward.

Who were those masked guys? They weren't Sandys or Nail 66 would have known about their presence. I couldn't make out any markings on the planes, but I suspected it was a Spad flight of A-1s from Danang that simply happened to be on a strike mission looking for targets of opportunity and saw the squad walking across the field. The flight leader probably knew nothing about downed pilots in the area, and was totally unaware of the restrictive no-bomb line around Sandy 7 and me. Nevertheless, those guys flew through hell many times that day and probably never knew how much peril they'd been in. But, on 1 June 1968, around 10 A.M., four angelic A-1 pilots put on quite an air show and helped save my life. I saw it up close. I heard the actual sounds. It was dramatic, spine-chilling, and a hoot to watch. It took guts. But, had they wiped out the squad?

After the A-1s left, I rested my head against the tree and closed my eyes for a moment. I could still vividly see them diving out of a bright blue sky, hear their guns spewing out the bullets, and hear a hiss as the enemy guns spit back larger rounds. "Those jocks are fearless, real tigers," I muttered out loud. They apparently had no fear of getting shot down, killed, or captured. Their apparent attitude inspired me to be a tiger too.

Nail 66 hadn't seen nor heard the A-1s in my area during the past twenty minutes, and had instead been monitoring the rescue of Sandy 5 while at the same time attempting to brief his relief Nail. We hadn't talked since he told me to stand by, but now Nail 66 called me. He stated he was at bingo fuel and was returning to base, but wanted to assure me, "The rescue forces will get you outta there soon." I didn't want to bust his bubble, but after all, I'd heard that before. I knew Nail 66 had good intentions and wanted to keep my morale up, but I knew the reality of the situation. The four A-1s had taken a hell of a lot of fire—which a Jolly could never survive—so the Nails had a lot more work to do before a Jolly could get close to my location. Before he departed, I questioned Nail again about the four strafing A-1s, but he still was unaware of who they were.

Nail 66 and his back-up then returned to NKP, replaced by two new Nail pilots. For the second day in a row, Nail 66 sucked fumes on the way home and nearly ran out of gas. He and I had been talking to each other for nine out of the last seventeen hours, so he kept wondering how he could've done things differently. Nail 66 had given his all, but things were beyond his control, and he wasn't a very happy camper because he'd left me behind for a second time. By the time he landed he'd been airborne for five hours, well beyond the normal range of his little O-2. But I'd now become an obsession with him, and he couldn't wait to refuel and try again.

I still didn't know Sandy 5 had been shot down and that the rescue forces were in utter chaos at the moment. I was very confused myself. Nail had informed me the rescue was on hold for bad weather, but a flight of four A-1s had just made eight gun runs in clear view from my location. What was going on? It didn't take a rocket scientist to realize the rescue forces didn't know my exact hiding spot, and that they weren't about to try and pinpoint me until the weather cleared.

Reacting to Sandy 5's shoot down, Blue Chip issued new orders straight from Saigon. He was alarmed about how many planes had been lost and issued an order to prevent the loss of any more until his staff came up with a better plan. Nail heard it and thought it was a stupid order, and undoubtedly made by some staff weenie unfamiliar with the way the rescue coordination was done. The order stated that only fast-mover fighters were now allowed in the area, and they were to bomb the AAA gun sites until all were silenced. The new Nail FAC was to stand off to the side as a weather bird only, well clear of enemy fire, and await the arrival of a new batch of Sandy and Jolly pilots. That meant the fighters would be trolling for gunfire in order to spot the gun site locations. It also meant the fighter pilots would have no one to accurately describe my location, and that placed me in direct peril from friendly fire. The fighters would now be dropping bombs around me without any knowledge as to my exact location, and I was now fair game for an errant bomb.

So was Sandy 7. He was still hiding in his tree, lashed to the trunk. Since dawn, he'd been listening to the distant, reverberating boom of bomb explosions. From that, he knew I must still be alive, and the enemy resistance remained stiff. He knew he was a considerable distance from my location because the explosive booms were far away. He decided he wouldn't chance using his radio since soldiers had been within fifty feet of his tree most of the time since dawn. As long as Streetcar was still evading on the ground, he knew the Sandys would be overhead, and he could call them in later. *He was content to let me be the focus for the enemy, wait until I was rescued, and then let the Sandys or Crown know he, too, was still alive.* Then it would be his turn for rescue, and maybe all the enemy gunners would be dead, and a considerable number of the bad guys might have withdrawn. That was his plan.

Sandy 7 had a total of three survival radios and five batteries. Months earlier, he'd been involved on a rescue where the survivor's radio battery went dead, and he had vowed it would never happen to him. He also had four baby bottles of water along with a side canteen, so he wouldn't run out of water, but for now he would save it for later. He wouldn't take a chance to look at the contents inside his vest as that meant taking it off, and he still feared dropping an item that might give away his position. His food snacks were also inside the vest, but he wouldn't chance dropping something to the ground, even for food. I can go a day without food, he surmised. The sight of men going in and out of the bushes below to relieve themselves did make him feel a similar urge. That would have to wait, too, but when he did go, he made up his mind he would hit the trunk with his stream so it didn't mist out of the tree. His plan was to sit quietly and wait until the soldiers left and I was rescued. He would know that when he no longer heard the sound of bombs.

After Nail 66 left, I was confused for the rest of the day as to which Nail pilot I was talking to at any one time. At least eight different Nail pilots, call signs 35, 13, 56, 24, 28, 40, 58, and 15, rotated in pairs between 10 A.M. and nightfall. It was very difficult for me to know when one Nail left, and his relief arrived. Some checked in with me, some didn't. Some of the new Nails tried to pinpoint my position, but most didn't due to the Blue Chip directive to stay clear of my area.

Around 10:30 the weather cleared sufficiently, and the fast-movers again swarmed in and tried to silence the AAA guns without the Nail's help. They did their own spotting. They trolled for active AAA gun sites, then attacked the first one to fire and continued to hammer it until they killed it. By then, many AAA guns were returning fire so the fighters simply rolled in on the next closest firing one. For forty-five minutes the noise from gun sites around me was awesome, but gradually quieted. The suppressive bombing moved farther and farther away, until finally it was concentrated on the numerous 37s and 57s on the karst across the river, and others ringed along the highway north of me. I patiently sat against my tree as the fast-movers worked. Eventually they were so far away I only heard a faint roar from their engines when they pulled off the target, but heard a rolling thunder as their bombs impacted on the karst and echoed across the valley toward me.

At 11 A.M., an F-105 took a hit in the nose of his plane, but was able to return to base. The current Nail reported the enemy ground fire was so intense that he estimated it would take the fighters another two hours to kill all the active firing 37 and 57 guns. That advisory by Nail prompted Blue Chip to again issue another directive.

"The Crown plane and Nail are to remain in the area, but the Sandys and Jollys are directed to return to base while the fighters continue to kill the guns."

Unknown to me, Blue Chip was starting the rescue over again. They were sending all other rescue forces home to regroup while the fighters tried to neutralize the area. It wasn't a bad idea, except there was little coordination to actually define the exact area that needed to be sanitized, i.e., the fighters didn't know my location. It turned out to be a moot point because within minutes, shortly after 11, the fighters again ceased their gun suppression due to bad weather.

What? I didn't understand. The weather around me at the time was still just fine, sunny and clear. It seemed I was sitting in a small hole of good weather that the rescue forces were unaware of.

During the bombing lull, it was obvious what the enemy was doing to fill the time. I heard lots of people talking, and I heard lots of equipment motors running. The enemy was clearing fallen trees from around its gun site revetments and re-supplying ammo to the gunners before another air attack began. I heard a constant barrage of orders being barked. All the voices and ground activity really emphasized the magnitude of troops surrounding me, and I thought we should be bombing more right around me and not somewhere across the river two miles away, so I called Nail.

No response. I waited thirty seconds and called again.

"Come on Nail, this is Streetcar, over."

A booming, authoritative-sounding voice barked back. "Streetcar, this is Crown 3. Do you have a problem? Over."

Ouch, that hurt. The tone of his voice and the stupid question really hit me hard. I really needed a little more tender loving right then than I perceived I was getting. I thought, *No, I've got no problem. I'm just sitting here in the middle of a frapping jungle full of gomers, tigers, and leopards waiting for the next Jolly helo to come along this route so I can get back to the security of my aircraft carrier. And lately no one seems to be talking to me, and the bombs are falling at least a mile from my location. No, I've got no problem.* Having rid myself of my anger, I then depressed the transmit button.

"Roger, Crown. I'm fine, but haven't heard any status lately. What's up? Over." He gave me a really short re-cap. He basically said the weather was too bad in my area, and the fighters hadn't yet been able to suppress the enemy guns around me.

"Streetcar, just lay low and stay off the radio, except to check in every hour, on the hour, out."

I was experienced by then with the rescue scenario, and thought I'd been very patient during times when it appeared to me that the rescue effort was discombobulated. I had suppressed most negative thoughts about the rescue force and told myself they knew how to do it, and I had to stay cool and not get involved with telling them how to do their job. I was just along for the ride. But frankly, Crown's answer to my simple question was too brief and didn't jive with what I was seeing from the ground. I took great exception to the weather statement as it was then sunny over my position. The fighters weren't bombing close to me, and I really thought they had no awareness of my hiding spot, give or take a few miles. But, I didn't tell Crown that.

My morale took a nosedive. The SAR was too complicated and dangerous for the rescue force. I would never be rescued, at least not today. And, with the number of troops and AAA, I most probably would be captured. So, I went into a pout mode and vowed I wouldn't call for help ever again. I would stay off the radio, but if I did have something to say to the rescue forces, I would say it anytime I wanted to. I would stay well hidden and provide no more idle chitchat, no more advisories to them. They all seemed to be lost, working some other area of the jungle, and not too concerned how I was getting along. The time was around 11:30, and I vowed to be hard-headed and not talk to any of the airborne forces until I knew it looked good for rescue.

As time went by, my good-sized hole of good weather got smaller and smaller until the blue sky was gone, replaced by puffy, popcorn clouds, and then it began to drizzle again. Well, Crown is right about the weather now, I conceded.

At noon, I didn't make my first hourly call to Crown. Screw him! I heard no plane noise and knew the weather was too bad for rescue, so there was no need to waste my battery. I relaxed with my back against the tree, my face upward, and embraced the steady, cooling, light rain. I extended my tongue to quench my thirst, and the water tasted pure. I then tried to catch some rain water by letting it dribble from a piece of plastic into one of my water bottles, but the rain wasn't coming down fast enough so I gave up and just enjoyed the moment.

The monkey tree had become my own little Laotian zoo, so now I focused on it again. I turned to my left, and the scene made me smile. All the monkeys were sleeping, motionless on their individual limbs, but turned so that each was facing me. Those with babies had them curled under an arm for protection. Man, it looked like there were more monkeys in the tree now. I counted about twenty-eight monkeys of various sizes in the one tree.

In a few minutes, the majority awoke and then began to playfully swing and chase each other around the tree in a game of tag for twenty minutes or longer. Then, just like a bunch of kids, one of them pulled another's tail too hard, and a small fight broke out between the two. All the others immediately stopped playing and quietly took up positions and glared at the two until one stopped fighting and left the tree. He bounded down the trunk and squealed back over his shoulder as he left, and I never knew if he came back as I couldn't tell them apart. After that, they seemed to pair up for a short respite and just sat and scratched each other for a goodly amount of time. While all that was going on, the mothers with small babies just calmly sat off to the side and simply fed and nurtured their babies, ignoring the playful ones. Then, one by one, they started to have a midday snack.

I envied their ability to find bananas. Monkeys would leave the tree on the side opposite from me, and then each would return shortly thereafter with a banana about six inches long. The source of their fruit was a different tree, but I couldn't see its location or how close it was because the monkey tree blocked that side from my view. Since my last meal aboard ship twenty-four hours earlier, I had eaten only two small, hard, rock-candy pieces, and I was beginning to feel a little hunger pain. I wanted a banana but was afraid to move since it would scare the monkeys, and the tree might again erupt in noise. I couldn't chance that. But it began to really torque me off that those little jerks seemed to deliberately sit on a limb facing me while they enjoyed lunch. And they seemed to have little smiles on their faces. It began to bother me a lot, but I knew the monkeys were my watchdog angels. I felt certain they would squeal to alert each other of any troop movement toward their tree and, thereby, also alert me. I needed their watchful eyes more than a banana.

Shortly thereafter, I heard what sounded like an O-2 engine so I turned my radio on. A Nail pilot soon called and said he was entering my area and to watch for him when he descended below the cloud base. He wanted me to tell him when he was overhead so he could get a fix on my location. I liked this guy immediately. I heard his plane faintly, but it sounded a few miles away. It never got close enough for a visual sighting before Nail broke off his brazen attempt to fly beneath the clouds at fifteen hundred feet in full view of the enemy gunners. Reluctantly, he climbed back up through the clouds and told Crown the weather was still too bad for fighter operations.

The time was around 12:30, and most of the planes left to take advantage of the weather to refuel and take a lunch break. I'd now been on the ground for eighteen hours and hadn't slept any the previous night. I wasn't sleepy or hungry, but had to keep my energy up. I feasted on two more of the orange-flavored, sugar Charms for lunch.

To make it last, I sucked on the candy as I watched the monkeys. It was midday and past their playtime I suppose, as they were now mostly sitting quietly and napping. Some were paired off, cleaning and inspecting each other. Others were just lying on limbs as they slept. They all appeared content to just be in the tree. All was quiet and peaceful around me. It had been some time since I'd heard any voices or the sound of enemy gunfire, and it appeared the whole jungle had settled down for a noon siesta. I felt secure in my hiding spot, but no nap for me. The second piece of candy was now gone, so I stuffed another wad of Redman tobacco into my cheek. This wad was smaller because now I had to conserve all assets. All chance for a quick rescue was gone.

My thoughts suddenly focused on Shirley. Casually, I leaned back and nestled softly against the tree bark and daydreamed about her. I loved Shirley. I loved the way she pampered me and the kids. I had to survive for her sake. Had the Navy informed her of my predicament yet?

Chapter **16**

SAD NEWS FOR
THE WIFE

I t was 31 May 1968 in Jacksonville, Florida, around 9 P.M., and
Shirley thought she'd made it through one more day without me.
She had just sat down on the couch to relax after putting the kids to
bed. For an hour or so, she'd have some private downtime to relax
before going to bed. She needed the respite because she had been
experiencing morning sickness due to the pregnancy, and that, plus
caring for two kids, exhausted her by the end of the day.

She channel-hopped through TV programs. Although it wasn't her
normal preference, a war movie love scene between a pilot and his
wife caught her attention. She noticed a similarity between the movie
and what was going on in her life. The movie reminded Shirley that
other wives had gone through a similar military separation. She also
found that the war scenes actually gave her a better grasp of what I
might be encountering in day-to-day combat ops. She'd never before
enjoyed war movies, but found that she was actually becoming
absorbed by this one. It was enlightening, and a good love story.

She'd been watching the movie for about twenty minutes when
the doorbell rang. It was about 9:30 and dark outside, so it initially
frightened her. She sat upright on the couch and tried to recall who
might be coming to the door at such a late hour. Perhaps Edna needed
to borrow something?

Tentatively, Shirley went to the door, flipped on the outside light
switch, and glanced through the security peephole. She saw a man in
Navy uniform standing next to Skipper's wife. The uniform insignia

was that of a chaplain; her heartbeat began to accelerate wildly. Shirley clutched her chest. Panic. She couldn't make her hand reach for the door lock. She was frozen in disbelief, and unable to function. *No— this can't be happening to me like it happened to Mother.*

Her first inclination was to bolt and run for the bedroom and pretend it wasn't happening. But Shirley wanted to know the details. As she fumbled with the door lock, she felt a massive welling of tears. Finally, she managed to open the door and then look pathetically at Skipper's wife.

"What's wrong, Doris? Is something wrong with Kenny? Is he okay?"

Before Doris had time to answer, Shirley said, "No . . . not to me, please . . ." Tears began a slow cascade down Shirley's smooth, round cheeks, and her shoulder sagged against the doorframe for support.

"Is he dead?"

Doris knew there was no absolute answer to that question yet. "Let's go inside, Sweetie."

Doris had known Shirley for just a little over a year, and she was one of Doris' favorite wives. During that time, she'd found Shirley to be one of the more stable of the twenty or so officer's wives under her protective wing. She liked Shirley's sincerity and her mature personality. In addition, she had learned that Shirley could accomplish any project she gave her with zeal and finesse. Doris had already decided that Shirley would be one of the wives she'd lean on to help the younger wives make it through their first cruise. Doris now doubted whether she'd be able to hold up personally in the present situation, much less support Shirley in her time of need.

Doris wiped the first tear from her own eye and then grabbed Shirley's hand and led her back inside to the couch. At first, Shirley collapsed in Doris' tender embrace, but then mustered the courage to sit upright. The chaplain spoke in a slow, soft, and soothing tone.

"Mrs. Fields, I regret to inform you, your husband has ejected over enemy territory in South Vietnam and is missing in action. I have been asked to serve you as the Navy's representative Casualty Assistance Officer [CACO] in your time of need."

Shirley thought a CACO served only when a pilot was dead. She was flabbergasted. "Is Kenny dead?"

"Mrs. Fields, the Navy doesn't yet know whether he's dead or alive. I'm so sorry."

Then, no one spoke. Doris and the chaplain just looked at her, waiting to see how she accepted the news. Would she break down and sob uncontrollably like most wives? The chaplain had seen that happen often and thought it was a good release of emotion. He'd already learned from too many tragic episodes that a "pilot missing" scenario made it difficult to predict the wife's reaction. He stared at the young pilot's wife. Would someone so petite have the physical and mental strength to handle the news?

Shirley tried to think of her questions as she sobbed softly. Her mind was aflutter, incapable of logical thought.

The chaplain proceeded to brief Shirley as to my current missing-in-action status based on what the Air Force had passed to the Navy. It was short and to the point. He told her my plane had been hit by enemy gunfire in South Vietnam, I had ejected, but hadn't been heard from since ejection.

Shirley had great difficulty absorbing even the small details that were being provided. She heard only that I'd been shot down and my status was "missing." She wished it wasn't true, but her experience with her father's situation in World War II made her think I was probably dead. She found it difficult to be positive at the time.

A small boy's voice came from the bedroom hallway.

"Mommy, who are these people? Why are you crying?" Terry, my five-year-old son, had been awakened by the commotion and was now standing timidly at the end of his bedroom hallway.

Shirley's heart was broken, but the sight of her slim son made her realize she had other responsibilities and had to pull herself together quickly, for the sake of the children. She got up, walked over to Terry, and leaned over to hug him. Shirley noticed at that moment that Terry looked even more like me when he was confused. Gently, she took his hand and led him back down the hallway to his bedroom. On the way, she glanced in at Kim, our daughter, and saw that she was still sleeping soundly and sucking her fingers as usual.

Terry climbed back in bed and again asked what was wrong. Shirley lay on the bed beside him and made an instant decision that she didn't want the kids to know about my status yet. She made up a story that the two visitors were there to just talk about Daddy's work and everything was okay. Terry hadn't really fully awakened so her little lie was accepted, and he fell asleep quickly while curled against his mother's breast.

Shirley's thoughts were jumbled as she lay on the bed trying to gather them. She wondered how she would cope with two kids and a pregnancy if I didn't make it back. It would be so hard, and she was having doubts already about how she'd handle it.

Then, she realized she was wallowing in self-pity at a time when I was in need of mental support and prayer. She felt a little ashamed that her first thought had been of herself. As she lay beside Terry, Shirley invoked her first prayer of the night.

"God, please, please be with Kenny and guide him in his attempt to survive. Let him be rescued, dear God, and give me the strength to endure your will. Amen."

After that, she returned to the family room. She'd thought of a ton of questions and began to rattle them off to Doris and the chaplain. Unfortunately, they knew only whatever information was contained in the initial personnel casualty report and kept deferring their answers until further word was received from the Bureau of Naval Personnel (Bupers). They explained they'd have to wait until further updates came through. After a while, Shirley accepted the finality of their response.

Doris said she'd stay with Shirley until some of the other wives arrived. One of the squadron wives would always be with her to help with the kids as long as necessary. Doris asked Shirley if she had a preference as to which wife stayed with her first. Shirley requested Jenny, Iceman's wife.

Before the chaplain left, he asked if there were any other family members he could notify. Shirley asked him to inform my parents in Holden, West Virginia, but to exercise caution since my Dad had experienced recent heart problems. She would notify her family. The decision was made to wait until morning before notifying anyone, in the hope that good news would have been received by then. The chaplain then asked about our church pastor, and Shirley told him that we attended the Methodist church at the end of the street. The chaplain said he'd inform our pastor about my status and that someone from the base would be back with updates as they came in. Then, he made one final comment.

"Mrs. Fields, before I leave, I'd like to say a prayer, if you don't object."

Doris also believed in a supreme being, God, and had already silently prayed several times, and she held Shirley's hand as the chaplain prayed. After that, he left for the night. Thus began an agonizing thirty-nine-hour wait for Shirley as to my actual fate.

Shirley and Doris conversed for an hour about possible rescue scenarios, my and Shirley's life together, and other small talk. They knew that I'd been on the ground for about fifteen hours, but only knew my status as of the time within a few minutes after my ejection. She and Doris theorized that in those fifteen hours I could've been rescued, but there had been insufficient time for the word to get back to the states. They also discussed that something worse could've happened. I might already be a POW.

During their conversation, Shirley finally disclosed to Doris that she was three months pregnant. It was the first time any of the squadron wives knew of the pregnancy and it was appropriate that the CO's wife be the first to learn. After that disclosure, Doris saw that Shirley was beginning to show the full effects of the day's events. She looked like she could collapse at any moment.

Morning sickness, a long day of caring for the kids, and now bad news— a weaker wife would have broken down by now, thought Doris.

Shirley had been running on adrenalin for the past hour, but now the stress took its toll. Suddenly, she sagged into her corner of the couch and thrust both hands to her face. Doris saw more tears. Shirley was mentally—as well as physically—fatigued and Doris knew she had just hit the "wall."

Doris insisted Shirley go to bed while she stayed awake for any possible follow-up phone calls. She initially resisted, but Doris was so softly persistent that Shirley couldn't say no. Doris had many years of experience as a Navy wife, and her position as the commanding officer's wife gave her an implicit power over the wives of the more junior officers. They loved and respected her, but at the same time they feared for their husband's careers if they butted heads with her.

Worn to a frazzle, Shirley fell into bed and sobbed herself to sleep. After a few solid hours of sleep, she began to toss and turn. She would partially awaken in a daze, recall what had just happened, start crying, and then fall into another fitful sleep—only to awaken again a few minutes later. This went on for several hours before the phone rang.

In a flash, Shirley sat upright. She heard a muffled voice answer softly and strained to hear what was being said. She couldn't, but just the fact the phone had rung in the middle of the night caused a feeling of doom. Quickly, she slid out of the bed and headed toward the family room. Anticipation of bad news made her cry as she weaved her way down the hallway. Doris had taken the call from the CACO and was just hanging up the phone when Shirley reached her side.

"Is he okay? Did they get him out, Doris?"

Doris was also beginning to feel a little frazzled due to the lateness of the night but quickly forgot her own fatigue as she looked at Shirley. Her eyes were puffy from crying and her hair showed the effects of tossing and turning in bed: she looked as if a slight breeze could blow her over at any moment.

"They've talked to Kenny on the ground by radio and he's alive, Shirley. The rescue forces are trying to get him out. That's all the Navy knows right now, but it looks good, Sweetie. They're going to get him out. The CACO said he'd be here around 9 A.M. with all the info he can round up."

As Doris gently guided her back down the narrow hallway to the bedroom, Shirley nearly collapsed and palmed the wall for support. After getting back in bed, she then slept for another couple of hours before the kids awakened her. It was Saturday morning, their normal day for cartoons, but they were reluctant to be in the family room without their mom because a strange woman was in the house. Shirley got up and ushered them into the family room. At that moment, Shirley recalled how I often shared the Saturday ritual with them and wondered if I would have the opportunity to ever do it again.

Meanwhile, Iceman's wife, Jenny, was also up early. On her way to comfort Shirley, she dropped her two kids at the home of the squadron ops officer. Dottie had five kids but still volunteered to babysit Jenny's two while she stayed with Shirley. After arriving at our home, Jenny fixed breakfast for Shirley and the kids as Shirley brought her up to date on my status.

As she listened, Jenny's mind wandered to wives in other squadrons whose husbands had been shot down in Vietnam. Some were already in their third year of waiting for confirmation as to whether their husbands been killed in action or had become POWs. Shirley might also be in for a long, tortuous period of waiting for news, and Jenny didn't know how to comfort her. Both had empty, vague feelings since neither had had any experience coping with such a situation.

Soon, several of the other younger wives arrived and mingled in the kitchen, stunned by the bad news they had received from Doris at daybreak. My shoot-down had come as a terrible shock and a rude awakening to the reality that their husbands were truly now at war. Up to this point, they knew only that we were on our way to the combat zone. Now, it confirmed for all of them that we were flying combat missions. One of the young wives made a succinct comment.

"When I look at Shirley and consider what she's now facing, I realize that she could be any one of us, and we might be in the same situation today, tomorrow, or the next day."

One wife put it best: "We might as well gear up for more of this. Our dashing, young jet jocks are getting shot at every day now, and they aren't as invincible as they often bragged during squadron parties."

The CACO arrived shortly before nine o'clock. Everyone gathered around, hushed, hoping for good news. But it was mostly a formal follow-up to the phone call during the night; nothing new. However, the lack of news actually rejuvenated Shirley, because that meant I was still evading, and she had faith in my ability to survive in the jungle. She was familiar with my backwoods experience so she believed I might actually survive unharmed. At that point, her pessimism ended and optimism soared.

Then, the CACO followed his checklist. First, he asked if Shirley was okay with finances. He briefed her on what to do if she needed money. He also explained how to respond to newspaper reporters when they called, since the story had already made the AP news wire service. She was instructed not to divulge any information about me or the family because it would be used against me during interrogation if I were captured. Shirley sat attentively and asked a few questions as the brief continued. Jenny remained at her side and noticed an occasional tear, but otherwise thought Shirley was handling the situation better than she might if she were in Shirley's shoes.

After the CACO finished, he returned to his office and made a phone call to the naval district where my parents lived. The task to notify my parents was passed down to the commanding officer of the nearest Navy Reserve Center. After several quick fact-finding phone calls to the Pentagon, the CO left his office at 11:30 A.M. Saturday and headed for my parents' home. He drove an official black car with U.S government insignia and spent the next two hours driving to Logan County, West Virginia. As he got close to the town of Logan, the roads were very narrow, winding, mountainous, and full of dump trucks carrying coal to a nearby tipple for processing. Finally, he arrived in the little community of Holden.

My dad, seated in his favorite chair, could see anyone's approach to the front of the house. Dad was a short, small man but very strong-willed and intelligent. He had mined coal for thirty years to put food on the table. His career started in 1936, after he dropped out of the eleventh grade to help his father earn money to support the other five members of the family. He started at the bottom as a coal loader and worked his way to the number-two position as a mine foreman. Now, he was retired because of a career-ending heart attack deep inside the Island Creek Coal Company's Holden Mine just a year earlier. On that fateful day he had been making his rounds as mine foreman and at the time was bent over, inspecting the cut status of a forty-eight-inch-high coal seam. The feeling of a solid blow to his chest made him fall to his knees. Dad tried to walk but found he didn't have the strength to duck-walk back to the head of the cut. The mine rescue team was alerted, and four men carried him out on a stretcher. His coal-mining career ended that day.

From his chair, Dad glanced out the window just as a black car turned onto the dirt road that would bring it uphill, past one house, before arriving at his. He saw an emblem on the side and his heart fluttered. His gut told him bad news was on the way. He watched the car slowly drive up the hill and park, and then the door opened and a man in pristine Navy blues stepped out, a large manila folder in his hand.

Dad steeled himself for the knock on the door, rose, and shouted to my mom. "Lib, I think we're about to get some bad news." My mom rushed in from the kitchen.

"I regret to inform you that your son has been shot down, and as of now is evading the enemy." Over the course of the next several hours, the commander tried to explain the ramifications of that statement to my unworldly mountain father and mother.

Dad received the news in a quiet, reserved manner and listened intently but asked few questions. Inwardly, he knew his son had a good chance at survival because he had grown up in the mountains and played or hunted in them almost daily. My mom was different. She took a fatalistic approach and just knew I was now dead.

Immediately after the commander left, Mom called my younger brother, Doug, who lived five hours away in Cincinnati, Ohio. She informed Doug of the facts and then finished by saying she and Dad were pretty sure I wouldn't be rescued, but would be captured and die in captivity. Mom asked that Doug and his wife come home as Dad wasn't feeling well after the news, and she was afraid he'd suffer another heart attack. About an hour later, the phone rang and Mom ran to it in fear that more bad news was coming. She didn't want my Dad to be the first to hear it.

"Mrs. Fields, this is Mary at the market. I'm calling to let you know that your name has just been drawn as the winner of this week's Money Marathon prize of $200. You can drop by and pick it up anytime. Congratulations, Mrs. Fields."

Two hundred dollars was a lot of money back then, but they found it hard to get very excited about their good fortune in light of their earlier bad fortune. Two hundred dollars was not an even trade.

My brother Doug rushed home, arriving just before dark. He found our parents to be totally convinced I was lost to them, never to be seen again. During the rest of the evening and throughout the next morning, at my Mom's insistence, they had considerable discussion about my funeral, where I should be buried, and how they would help Shirley support the kids now that I was dead.

Around noon, Mom called Shirley for an update. After Shirley told what she knew, Mom began to ramble. She said she and Dad had been briefed on the possibilities I faced. I could've been killed during the ejection, or captured on the ground and imprisoned, or killed by the troops on the ground. Then, Shirley was shocked and dismayed by Mom's next statement: "If Kenny is not rescued, I hope he's killed rather than captured."

Why did my own mother take such an approach? I can only guess. In 1968, it was well known by the general population that captured pilots were being severely tortured as POWs in North Vietnam, and that fact was obviously known even in the backwoods of West Virginia. Mom was not too confident of my rescue, didn't want me to endure that type of treatment, and so wished me death instead of capture. That kind of talk was certainly not good for Shirley's morale. But it was just like my mother to speak exactly what was on her mind.

Several hours after the CACO left my parent's home, he was on the phone to them again. He needed to verify that my dad was physically okay, for he'd made a grievous mistake in the notification process. When he arrived back at his office, he checked his paperwork to ensure he'd fulfilled all of his responsibilities. To his dismay, he discovered his background papers had included a statement about my dad's physical condition and that he was recovering from a heart attack. Higher authority had directed that a doctor accompany the CACO when he notified my parents of my dilemma. He hadn't seen that before he made his visit, and now he realized his mistake.

Did Mr. Fields experience another heart attack due to the bad news? He hurriedly called my dad and found out he was still fine. Dad chuckled about that incident for many years.

Shirley hadn't yet had the strength to call and inform her mother, Jean. She was seated at the kitchen table with several of the squadron wives and having her first cup of coffee when she announced she was in a quandary about how best to notify her mother. She knew it'd be an emotional phone call, and she couldn't convince herself that she was up to that yet. One of the wives volunteered to make the call for her and assured her that was an acceptable way to go. Coincidentally, at the time her friend called, Shirley's mother was also enjoying a visit with her neighbors and they, too, were sitting around a table and drinking coffee.

"Mrs. Garrett, I'm a friend of Shirley. She has received some bad news and is too distraught to talk right now, and asked that I relay a message to you. Shirley and the children are fine, but Kenny has been shot down and is hiding on the ground in Vietnam. They're trying to rescue him now. And—"

Before she could finish, Jean interrupted and said, "Hold on a minute. I can't handle this."

The news hit Jean hard. She had a strong feeling of déjà vu. Her husband had been killed in war, and now Shirley's husband might be facing the same fate. Jean couldn't stomach the thought. She yelled for the husband of her next-door friend.

"Holly, come in here quick and talk to Shirley's friend."

Then, she placed the phone receiver on the table and sank deep into the sofa in disbelief. Tears welled in her eyes as she grasped the pain that this news must be causing her daughter, but Jean didn't have the ability to talk until she got her own emotions under control. As of now, she couldn't think clearly and didn't know what to do or say to her daughter.

Holly walked in promptly. "What's wrong, Jean?"

"Something's wrong with Shirley's Kenny and I don't believe I can talk to her about it right now. You do it for me."

Holly picked up the receiver. "Hello, Shirley. What's the problem?"

The friend then explained why Shirley wasn't on the phone, calmly briefed him on my situation and asked him to inform Shirley's brother and sister. She told him she'd call again if there was any news. Holly asked few questions as he clearly understood the bad news.

Holly then turned to Jean. "I've got all the facts and can explain the situation to you. Do you want to talk to Shirley's friend now?"

"No. Tell her I'll call her back when I'm in better shape, but tell her to tell Shirley I love her."

Shirley watched her friend hang up the phone. She'd listened intently with tears in her eyes as her friend explained everything, and now she was crying. She didn't know why. Maybe she was a little disappointed that her mother hadn't been able to comfort her some. But even as she cried for herself, she knew her father's death had made her mother incapable of response right now. It was just sad that neither her mother nor mine offered her much solace. She stiffened her spine in the chair and decided right then she was the strong one in both families, and she'd have to carry the burden for her mother and mine.

Just before dinner, the doorbell rang and a wife went to answer it. A courier was delivering a telegram from the chief of naval personnel (CNAVPERS) in Washington, D.C. Even though it didn't concern her own husband, the young wife still quivered as she signed for it. She couldn't imagine what it would be like if this pertained to her husband. The wives didn't yet know the exact routine for family notification of death, and several of those standing around thought this might be that. They watched as Shirley tried to open the envelope. Her hands trembled and she felt as if her knees would buckle. She tried, but she couldn't get a finger under the envelope flap. She was scared, getting frustrated, and everyone was watching. Doris could stand it no longer.

"Shirley, why don't you let me read it first, Sweetie?"

Shirley looked up with a fatalalistic expression. Shaking, she handed the envelope to Doris, who first read it silently. It seemed to take Doris an eternity to read the telegram. The others watched for any expression of grief, but finally saw a little smile surface as she looked up.

"It's okay, Shirley. It's basically the Navy officially telling you what we already know. Let me read it to you."

I deeply regret to confirm on behalf of the United States Navy that your husband is missing in action since 6 P.M., 31 May 1968, after he ejected from his aircraft which was hit by hostile fire while on a mission in Southeast Asia. A parachute was observed and voice contact with the downed pilot was reported. Search and rescue efforts are in progress. You may be assured that every effort is being made with personnel and facilities available to locate your husband. Your great anxiety in this situation is understood. When further information is available concerning the results of the search in progress, you will be promptly notified. I join you in the fervent hope for his eventual recovery alive. I wish to assure you of all possible assistance together with the heartfelt sympathy of myself and your husband's shipmates at this time of heartache and uncertainty. If I can assist you, please write or telegram me. My personal representative can be reached by telephone at Oxford 42746. The area in which your husband became missing represents the possibility that he could be held by hostile forces against his will. Accordingly, for his safety in this event, it is suggested that in replying to inquiries from sources outside your immediate family you reveal only his name, rank and serial number and date of birth.

Signed,
Chief of Naval Personnel

"It sounds very positive," Shirley said through a tiny smile. The wives took turns hugging her to celebrate the small bit of good news.

Iceman's wife, Jenny, supported Shirley all day. But soon after preparing dinner, she left to pick up her own two kids. Ruth would now spend the night with Shirley.

Jenny and her kids had a fast-food dinner on the way home, and by then she was pretty stressed out. Her day with Shirley had been very emotional, but she was glad she'd been able to spend the time with her. Jenny felt she got a whole lot closer to Shirley as a friend that day as they had time to talk in detail about their life experiences, how they met their husbands, etc. But she was grateful that she was not in Shirley's shoes.

After getting out of the car, Jenny walked toward the front door and noticed a yellow piece of paper next to the doorknob. Reluctantly, she grabbed it. It was a telegram from the Navy and looked like the one she'd seen at Shirley's house. Her heart sank. *No. It can't be. Is this terrible news about Fred?*

Her first inclination was to avoid the news by not opening the telegram, but she couldn't stand the suspense so she ripped the envelope open and started to read. The paper was shaking so much that the words were out of focus. She looked upward, took a slow, deep breath and again tried to read the words.

Thank God, Fred is okay! Jenny clasped the telegram against her heart. It said Iceman had safely ejected over water but had been rescued with no injuries. As she opened the door and walked in, Freddy Junior began clamoring about the envelope.

"What did the piece of paper say, Mommy?"

"It's okay, guys, it's just the Navy telling us that Daddy is okay."

At least for now, Jenny thought as she turned to lock the door. But she fumbled, her hands shaking and her legs wobbly, just like she'd seen Shirley do. But no one was there for her as they had been for Shirley. She sagged forward, and her shoulder found the door for support. With head bowed, Jenny sobbed. *I don't think Fred or Kenny knew what they were getting into. Can Shirley and I handle the burden of this war, and will our husbands return home safely?*

Chapter 17

LEOPARDS AND TIGERS

While sitting with my back against a tree, I checked my watch. One o'clock . . . I had been on the ground for nineteen hours, the last four in my current position near the monkey tree. Around me, it was very quiet and tranquil, and had been so for the past ninety minutes since the bombing halt around 11:30 A.M. In fact, it was too quiet, and it was beginning to concern me that I hadn't heard any recent troop activity. I wondered about the current position of the troops I had seen earlier in the middle of the field. Had they been killed by the mysterious A-1s, or were they still hovering around? Was everyone except me on lunch break, taking a siesta, or just avoiding the rain? I had no idea what anyone was doing because I hadn't spoken to any of the rescue force since around noon when the Nail pilot tried to pinpoint my position. I initiated my hourly check-in call to get an update.

Crown answered, and his voice now sounded older and tired. First, he reiterated that the weather was still too bad for bombing, and then asked if my status had changed. I briefed him on my new location, and he said he would pass that info along. "Continue to lay low," he said. Lay low—I was amazed at how simple he made that sound.

Meanwhile, Nail 66 had arrived back at NKP around 11:30, totally frustrated. It was nearly one o'clock before he finally answered the last of many questions thrown at him by the senior officers who represented the Nail, Sandy, and Jolly squadrons. Apparently, Seventh Air Force wasn't happy. The commanding general was embarrassed by the inability to rescue one of the Navy's boys and growing tired of the admiral's testy messages. Therefore, the general's staff was applying a lot of heat on the commanders of the Sandy and Jolly squadrons to "get the guy out." They kept asking Nail 66 the same question in a variety of ways, over and over again.

"Why can't we wipe out all the damn AAA gun sites?"

In response, Nail 66 kept repeating that the Nail FAC's needed more CBUs because the enemy gunners were too entrenched. Nail was asked to elaborate.

Emphatically, he made his point. "It's not the fault of the fast-movers," he said. "It's because the damn gunners are jumping into holes or something. I saw Thuds drop retarded bombs time after time, right down the throat of the damn 37s. Each time, before the Thud cleared the target, and before the dust settled, the guns would be scorching his ass again with AAA. We need more CBUs and napalm."

After his debrief, Nail 66 staggered wearily to his room. He was exhausted, sweaty, and mentally stressed out. He needed a nap, but it was nigh impossible. He would fall asleep, only to be awakened a short while later by the same nightmarish dream he had during last night's sleep. An A-7 was tumbling end over end. He woke up screaming, "Eject, Eject." Finally, he gave up and took a shower. Afterward, he and a friend went to the O Club. He thought a few drinks might help him sleep a little better.

After a few beers with lunch, a fellow Nail walked in and told him he wasn't scheduled to fly tomorrow. Instead, he was scheduled for four days of commensurate time off (CTO). He had earned it, but he was still astonished to hear he wouldn't be going back tomorrow if Streetcar 304 wasn't rescued today. Had he angered the senior officers with his outburst about the CBUs? He went to find out.

"The decision is final," he was told. He wouldn't be flying the Streetcar mission again because the senior officers thought he had taken enough risk.

Nail 66 wasn't happy but accepted the fact, and decided he would make his first trip to Bangkok tomorrow. Now, he could get on with some serious drinking since he wouldn't fly again for five days. Back at the O Club, Nail 66 asked his friends to raise their beer bottles for the first of many toasts to Streetcar 304 and Sandy 7.

Within a few minutes Jolly 9 walked in, sweating like a pig. Nail 66 heard him tell some other Jolly pilots he had just rescued Sandy 5, who had now lost his second A-1 on the Streetcar mission. Jolly 9 said the Tchepone area was hotter than shit with AAA, the weather made it worse, and he wasn't looking forward to going back for an afternoon rescue attempt. He had time for a quick lunch while the rescue was on hold for weather, and while they replaced his two fuel drop-tanks. About then, another pilot from the Jolly squadron walked in.

"Hey Dave, your co-pilot just took himself out of the game. He said one rescue a day was enough for him. Yuhas volunteered to take his place, and now the ops officer encourages you to let a replacement RCC take your place. You've completed your tour, so why don't you accept?"

Without hesitation, Jolly 9 gave the same casual answer he had given the previous time he was offered an out. "No, I'll fly it because I'm familiar with the scene."

Jolly 9 then finished lunch, went to the plane line, and verified that new fuel tanks had been installed on his bird. Then, he waited on alert for the scramble horn to sound the next rescue attempt.

Meanwhile, I sat against the tree with my legs bowed up and my pistol resting on my crotch. My situation was looking brighter since the rain had stopped, and the jungle was beginning a fascinating transformation. Just a short time ago everything was soaking wet, but vapors now rose from foliage as it became heated by the hot afternoon sun. Even my flight suit was dry. Mother Nature was sucking moisture for her normal, late afternoon monsoon downpour. The solitude and heat had made me slightly drowsy, so I hadn't been very alert.

Just then, a slight movement to my right stirred my attention. I couldn't believe my eyes. A fully-grown leopard was standing broadside, about ten feet in front of me. I hadn't heard a sound, and the sage-like brush had obscured it during its approach. Slowly, I eased my pistol forward and took aim. Why hadn't the monkeys alerted me to its presence? Were they not afraid of it? Maybe they hadn't heard its approach either. Regardless, its blond, stationary broadside was now directly in front of me, head erect, but facing left to right toward the field. It tilted its nose upward at an angle and sniffed the slight breeze, twice. Had it picked up my scent back along the trail and tracked me to this point, or was this just a coincidental meeting? Would it smell my scent now? I moved my eyes to a tall stem of grass and checked the wind. Lucky me—a favorable breeze was blowing my scent right to left, so the cat couldn't get a whiff of me. About then, it dropped his head, turned away from me, and then walked two steps to a small tree trunk. It then stretched its front paws several feet up the tree, and proceeded to use it as a scratching post. I silently chuckled about my conclusion. He got my scent, and was sharpening his claws for the kill.

While it scratched, I marveled at its body. Its yellowish coat was pristine, and its shoulder muscles were taut. Its head-size, height, length, and weight appeared about the size of a Rottweiler dog. But it looked gentle. I'll be in big trouble if it turns my way after it finishes scratching! If so, what should I do? A pistol shot will certainly alert the bad guys to my location.

I eased my hand upward and slowly removed my six-inch, serrated-blade knife from my survival vest. If the leopard charged me, I would stab at it rather than risk a shot.

For about thirty seconds, it scratched with both front paws just like any old domestic cat would do. It didn't look my way. Then, it lowered its front legs to the ground, sniffed several times, and sauntered off upwind. It kept sniffing the breeze without making any noise, and fortunately never looked back.

As the leopard left, I turned toward the monkeys. They were absolutely motionless, and at least fifteen were sitting erect, facing me. All eyes were riveted on me as if they'd been watching to see how I handled the situation. I glared, and then reprimanded them in a stern voice. "Thanks for the alert, guys. A lot of help you are."

I made a mental note that the leopard had walked in the same direction as my escape heading for my next move, so I needed to watch for it if I changed my hiding spot.

It was about two o'clock, and the sky was pretty much cloudless. It was perfect weather for bombing. So, where was the frapping Air Force? Maybe a new Nail was looking for me in the wrong area. I had been told to stay off the radio except for hourly checks, but I couldn't stand by and let good weather go wasted. I called Crown.

Calmly, I made my case. "It hasn't rained for maybe twenty minutes, and the weather in my area is clear as a bell. In my opinion, it's perfect for a rescue attempt."

He rogered, and said he'd pass it to the Nail FAC.

Shortly thereafter, I heard Nail's prop but nothing on the radio. He made a single, high pass over my area, and then radioed Crown that the weather had indeed cleared. Nail wanted fast-movers, ASAP, for a probable two- to three-hour period of good weather. In a few minutes, Crown replied that a fast-mover force would arrive in about an hour for a Blue Chip–ordered three o'clock rescue attempt. He also told Nail that the gas agent A-1s had been scrambled at Pleiku, but it would take them thirty minutes to get airborne and another hour and fifteen minutes before they arrived overhead, around 4 P.M.

Nail and his wingie had just relieved the two Nails who had earlier relieved Nail 66, so they had yet to try and pinpoint my exact location. Crown cleared the two into the area to positively pinpoint my location, and instructed them to be ready to do a lot of flak suppression when the fighters arrived.

I heard none of the preceding radio talk. Finally, Nail called me and said he was flying into the area. I assumed this meant there might be a quick rescue attempt since the weather was perfect, but first he had to pinpoint me. And, to help, I decided to take a calculated risk and talk more openly on the radio. Our conversation might be picked up by the enemy's radio direction finding equipment, but I pledged to describe my area in more detail than any previous time.

I began to brief Nail. I described the adjacent field, my tree, and its approximate bearing and distance from my plane's crash site. When I saw his plane, I would give him additional vectors.

With that in mind, I thought it would be easy to vector Nail to my exact hiding spot. However, Nail forgot to tell me one very important fact. Unknown to me, two Nail planes would fly into the area: one would fly low to spot me, and the other would remain high to monitor the safety of the low bird. I only expected one.

Soon, I saw a Nail plane pass overhead at about five thousand feet. *He's too high to ever spot my tree,* I thought. But maybe he was scared of the guns, rightfully so. I wouldn't push him to go lower. I told Nail to dip his left wing and sight along it to see the field below. He reported he did, but the plane I was looking at never dipped a wing. "What's wrong with this guy?," I muttered out loud.

I got hacked off. This puke was wasting my battery big time. Scratch the radio directions. I would try my signaling mirror. On Nail's next pass, I described my position, left or right, in relation to the plane's wing. While the pilot supposedly looked my direction, my mirror projected a white, laser-pointer-like beam of light which terminated on the side of his cockpit. Incredibly, he claimed he couldn't spot the beam, but I could see it flashing against the plane. I hit him with the beam several times but he never saw it. Unbelievable! That hurt my pilot pride. It was a clear day, and I should have been able to direct the guy to me. What was wrong with my technique? Or maybe, what was wrong with the Air Force puke?

I was really frustrated. I had to get it done more quickly! The longer I talked, the more chance the enemy had to home in on my radio position. Nail had to await the arrival of the fighters so he was in no hurry. He was calm.

Fearing a return of bad weather, I got desperate. It was again time to suck it up, so I exercised what I thought was my final option. "Nail, I'll take a big risk, and fire a pen flare the next time you fly over!"

I spotted him in a turn toward me, but very high, again. My pen gun was already loaded to use as an extra pistol, so I put my thumb on the little knob of the firing pin and stretched the spring back to the safety detent.

"Turn ten degrees left, Nail, and you'll be heading right toward me."

He didn't turn.

I eased the firing rod out of its safety detent, and then aimed at a spot directly in front of Nail's plane.

"Nail, stand by for a pen flare. Firing *now.*"

The firing pin sprung forward and hit the back of the flare. It sounded like a pistol shot as it zoomed out of my hand. "Flare away, Nail."

Even though it was sunny, the red tracer was brightly visible, and I saw it pass under the nose of the plane. Guess what? Nail said he hadn't seen the flare.

I was flabbergasted. After thirty minutes of trying, I still didn't believe Nail knew my exact location, or even the field next to me. Nail was flustered too, but said he knew my general location well enough to vector a Sandy to me. I doubted that. But Nail didn't tell me a formal rescue attempt wasn't scheduled till 3 P.M.

Sagging against the tree, I closed my eyes in disgust. Today's rescue effort was now in its eighth hour and had steadily gone downhill. My hiding spot had probably been compromised by all the radio talk and the signal flare.

I was certain that the enemy, especially the guys in the middle of the field, had heard and seen my flare, so I sat on pins and needles. When the least little twig popped, my head shot that direction. Should I move out? No. First, I would wait to see if a quick rescue attempt was made at this site. I became totally engrossed in thought as I debated what to do in the event one wasn't forthcoming.

Suddenly, totally out of the blue, I heard a really loud crashing noise behind me. My heart skipped several beats as I quickly spun to my left and rolled to the ground facing the rear quadrant from which I had run that morning. About then, I heard several exclamatory shouts by men seemingly running toward me, and their voices were close enough that they scared the living daylight out of me. I thought a squad of gomers would appear in view at any second. To heighten my fear, the monkeys went bananas, jumping from limb to limb and squealing like . . . like a bunch of monkeys. They were really cutting a shine, obliterating any other noise, but they weren't looking in a specific direction to help me locate the source. In a prone firing position, I cocked my pistol. My eyes scanned rapidly back and forth between the monkeys to my right and the area straight ahead. I stared, slightly downhill, with a good view for about three hundred feet, fully expecting to see enemy troops at any moment.

The scene looked just like one would expect a jungle setting to look. In the background, I could see the large, forested area where I had spent the night. In front of that were several good-sized trees amidst a clearing with lots of foliage and brush, and lots of large leaf fronds capable of masking a human, or animal. I spotted a large tree lying on its side about fifty yards away. Maybe it had been damaged by the bombing and had just now fallen to the ground? The voices seemed to be on the opposite side of the tree from me. Just then, a rifle popped from the right of the fallen tree, and I hunkered tighter against the ground. Had troops fired at me? My pulse raced, and my eyes darted over the scene.

There—I saw some movement. What was that? To the right of the fallen tree trunk, in the midst of the tree's heavy foliage—was that a man moving? Yes, I could see a gomer's head sticking up.

My gun hand trembled slightly as I aimed. I realized I had some time because he was out of pistol range. I peered more closely and watched as his head bobbed among the fallen tree limbs. He stopped and looked my way. Then, he climbed on a limb and looked toward me again. I got a full broadside view of the gomer's body and could see he was bent forward at the waist as if struggling to maintain his balance. But this gomer wasn't clad in black. His body was dark orange with brown hair, and his broad, muscular shoulders moved side to side as he walked the limb. I saw a swishing movement. Then it hit me. Damn it, it was a huge tiger. What a frapping idiot I was. I sighed with relief and watched as it tried to clear itself from the fallen tree. It casually stepped from one limb to another. Suddenly, I heard another rifle shot and the tiger fell to the ground and disappeared in the foliage.

Had it been climbing the tree, and its weight caused it to collapse? Had the gomers rushed toward the crash sound and shot it?

Still not certain of what was happening, I lay on the ground in an anxious, watchful state and monitored the area around the fallen tree for at least five minutes. Where had the tiger and the gomers gone? My queasiness slowly subsided, but I still worried about the voices that rushed the tree. Which way had the gomers gone? Eventually, I rolled over behind my protective tree again and rose to a sitting position. I finally concluded that enemy troops had been nearby when the tree fell. They shouted out in alarm, and then rushed to check out the noise. They probably retreated to their original position after seeing the tree and tiger. I adjusted my sitting position so I could face that area a little more than I had most of the day.

I glanced toward the monkeys. All of them were sitting hushed, all eyes were still fixed toward the fallen tree, and that worried me. The noise had obviously scared them, too. Were they simply concerned about the tiger, or did they sense more danger on the way? My gut said, *Bolt, get away from this area. Move.* But I couldn't make myself do it. I would be exposed if I walked in the daylight. I would wait for a diversion, or darkness, and I wouldn't have to wait long.

Unknown to me, Air Force planners had scheduled a massive wave of bombing to commence at 3 P.M. and continue for two hours, or until all AAA gun sites were silenced. At 5 P.M., if the AAA was suppressed, and Blue Chip had approved use of the gas agent by then, A-1s would saturate the area with gas, and I would be plucked out by Jolly. The Sandys were hoping against hope that Blue Chip would okay the gas agent.

The gas concept for pilot rescue was authorized four months earlier, in February 1968, for specific use in Laos. The planning staff felt my situation was the perfect scenario for its use because the area was sparsely populated by civilians, and the enemy gunners were well entrenched. But, the general was hesitant for some reason, and it may have been because no one could assure him of my exact position. If approval of the gas was not obtained by 5 P.M., the Sandys and Jollys would make a pick-up attempt, but only if *all* guns had been silenced. I wasn't told about any of the preceding for fear the gomers would also hear the plan over the radio.

A first wave of fourteen fighters took off to be in place for the 3 P.M. kickoff. Two A-1s, loaded with gas agent, would arrive in the area around 4 P.M. Two more A-1s with gas capability were placed on alert at Pleiku in case the first two got low on fuel before the final decision was made. Three A-1s, call sign Spad, took off from the base at Danang to augment the Sandys for close air-support during the Jolly pick-up phase. Routinely, the Sandy A-1s would handle the close air-support for the Jollys, but the Sandys had lost several planes and couldn't provide the total of eight A-1s the planners thought necessary. Three rescue Jollys would launch from NKP around 4 P.M., with an ETA of 4:45.

Around 3 P.M., Crown advised me to find some good protective cover because a lot of bombs were about to rain down. "Find a good hole and dig in," he said. I took that call to mean the rescue was finally underway, and I would soon be aboard a Jolly. My spirit soared. No one told me that the Jollys were still sitting on the alert pad at NKP pending destruction of the enemy guns.

At the same time, the two Nail pilots began to brief the first of fourteen fighters to arrive at the scene. Most were F-105s. This was a deliberate move by the ops planners because the area was so hot. Thud's had a much better capability to absorb battle damage and still fight.

Finally, the bombing diversion I had nervously awaited since the tiger incident kicked off. Earlier in the morning, it sounded as if many of the AAA sites had been killed, or maybe the gunners had run low on ammo. Was that really so? The first fighter rolled in and I got my answer. The area around me erupted in AAA fire. Obviously, the enemy gunners were prepared for this moment, and had been fully resupplied with ammo.

Talk about disheartening. But to help kill the guns, I noted the relative position of each firing AAA site, and then passed that info to the Nail. The intensive bombing continued for over an hour, nonstop, and I lost count of the number of active AAA sites. One after another, the fast-movers kept dropping bombs. Valiant, determined aviators with call signs Cobra and Calico, then Panda, Zodiac, and Barracuda, followed by Shako, Methane, and Detroit, then Locust, Buick, Kaiser, Seabird, and Speedo . . . on and on. . . .

Around 4:30, the AAA gunners ceased fire, and I surmised the gunners were dead, out of ammo, or faking it to lure the slow-moving Jollys into a trap.

"Streetcar, this is Nail. I'm coming into the area to see if I draw any fire." Nail made his pass and I heard no gunfire.

Ten minutes later, Sandy 3 transmitted that he was flying into my area to pinpoint my position. Sandy 3? This was the first time I had worked with him. All right, Sandy is coming in for a look, and that means there's a real rescue attempt underway. Maybe this new jock could pull it off.

Sandy asked for a smoke flare. "Negative," I replied, and I didn't bother to tell him why.

Didn't these guys talk to each other? Didn't they all know by now I only had one smoke, and I was saving it for the Jolly? Didn't they know my plight in the weeds? If I popped a smoke, it would probably be seen by hundreds of troops scattered around the large open field I was sitting next to. So, no smoke.

In a few seconds, I felt bad about my callous thoughts. Sandy would be risking his life to fly low and spot me so I had to help him. I knew rifles would be fired at Sandy as soon as he appeared. Maybe I could work with that. Maybe a pen-gun *pop* would blend in with the rifle fire.

"Sandy, this is Streetcar, listen up. No smoke. When I spot you, I'll give you an advisory just before I shoot a pen flare. Do you copy? Over."

He acknowledged and said he was about two minutes out.

I failed to ask, and he didn't tell me the direction he'd be flying. All the Sandy passes I had observed since I ejected had been made on a northerly heading so I assumed this one would be the same direction.

I rose to one knee and stiffened my back to have a good view toward the south, which placed the field off my right shoulder. I placed the pistol on the ground between my legs, held the radio in my left hand, and held the loaded pen gun in my right hand. Enemy rifles began to pop in the distance, but from the north, behind me. For just a few seconds, I heard a slight engine roar and strained to make out the direction from me. But before I could, his engine sound was blocked out by a steady crescendo of enemy fire from directly across the field. A ZPU spit out a long burst amidst the sound of smaller automatic weapons. Sandy must be close! My head was on a swivel.

Suddenly, I heard his engine, but from behind my right shoulder. I spun quickly and saw his plane across the field roaring along its perimeter from my right to left. Sandy was in a shallow dive no more than two hundred feet above the tree line, and, I thought, about to crash. Damn it, damn it, not again. Another Sandy was about to be shot down.

Sandy looked faster and lower than any I'd seen thus far, and at first view, it looked like he was going to fly into the trees in the next few seconds. I heard his guns rattling, and realized he was strafing the

ZPU. At the last possible moment, the plane's nose jerked up, and Sandy leveled off at treetop level. I was looking at a broadside version of a speeding plane then and had little time to react. I yelled into the radio.

"Sandy 3, I'm off your port wing, across the field, and firing a tracer—now." This would be like a shot at a speeding duck. Quickly, without any time to aim, I thrust the pen gun his direction, and fired toward a spot in front of Sandy's plane. A red tracer streaked across the field, but crossed his flight path to the rear. My lead had been insufficient. Immediately, Sandy began a shallow climb, and for a moment I thought he hadn't seen the tracer. However, he sharply dipped his left wing about thirty degrees before he flew out of sight beyond the tree canopy.

"Got a lock on you, Streetcar. I'll be back, so hang in there."

"Shit-hot, Sandy," I retorted. He had seen the tracer after all. *What a gutsy move that was,* I thought.

Sandy 3 had flown past on a southwesterly heading. In a few seconds, in that direction, I heard several large booms, and saw red, flaming balls arcing upward. Sandy told Crown he was picking up fire from three large AAA guns in addition to the smaller fire he had taken on the way in. He also said he had a positive lock on my position, but the three AAA sites had to be taken out before he would bring the Jolly in. Nail was given the job.

Nail had seen the intensity of the AAA, and requested more fighters with CBUs. Crown told him to stand by for a moment as they were picking up a Mayday call. Had Sandy been shot down? After a few seconds, the guys in the back of the plane reported that a Jaguar 858 crew had just declared a Mayday, and a second Crown plane was responding to the call. Crown then got back with Nail and was told that Nail would attempt to knock out the guns, but he still wanted the CBUs. Crown made the request.

During the next ten minutes, I heard nothing on the radio. I looked at my watch. A few minutes before five o'clock, Crown called. "Streetcar, prepare to authenticate."

Ecstasy! It meant they were finally serious about a pick-up attempt. He wanted me to verify that I was really me, and not some enemy impersonator trying to lure the rescue forces into a trap. And he wanted to ensure I didn't have a gun placed to my head, forcing me to trick the Jollys into a trap.

"Streetcar, what's the city with a baseball team nicknamed the Red Legs?"

Whoa. That question wasn't on my authenticator card. Had this guy not received my list? I had listed red as my favorite color, and someone from the Navy must have told the Air Force I was a baseball fan. I panicked, with no answer in mind. *Settle down and think, damn it.* Then, it hit me. For the past fifteen years, most sportscasters had been referring to them by the shortened version.

"Roger, Crown, that would be Cincinnati! My dog's name is Daisy, and my Blood Chit Number is—" Shamefully, I released the transmit button before I gave the number away. I had just committed my most grievous mistake since ejecting.

Crown quickly reprimanded me. "Streetcar, settle down, and only answer the question that I ask, over."

"Roger, Crown, sorry about that. Got a little carried away because I'm anxious to get outta here, over."

Crown showed a lot of compassion that time and kept his reply short. "Hang in there, Streetcar, you're doing great."

I sank back against the tree, thoroughly disgusted at myself. I'd been scared a few times, but this was the first time I had lost my composure, and I was thoroughly disappointed. It wouldn't happen again, I vowed.

Crown then informed Nail there were no more CBUs available in the local arena, and he would have to make do with what he had. Ten fighters were standing by overhead with GP bombs, so Nail smoked the gun sites, and the fast-movers rained bombs again.

I talked to myself. More bombs meant a further delay. *Come on, come on, let's get on with it.* My position surely has been compromised by all the radio talk. I couldn't decide what to do. My gut told me to relocate, but at the same time the authentication indicated a probable pick-up attempt. I didn't want to confuse the issue by moving to a different hiding spot. Time trickled by while I sweated bullets.

Suddenly, I heard a distinctive sound I'd previously heard only in old training movies. In the movie, an enemy soldier carried a portable directional-finding device on his back while he listened with headphones for enemy pilot radio transmissions. Once heard, the enemy soldier could home in, i.e., get a direction to the pilot's position.

A whirling, high-pitched noise was coming from about seventy-five yards downhill in front of me. I cocked my head in that direction.

Yes, a crank was being used to power up a small generator. I would have bet my last dollar that the enemy had been monitoring all the chatter between me, Nail, and Crown and were approaching with a radio directional finder.

The sound was heading right at me. I stood up, in a slight crouch, and stared forward, downhill toward dense jungle foliage, to get a visual fix on the enemy. Words were being exchanged. I looked that direction and saw a khaki-colored cloth cap bobbing along above deep grass, heading my way. Oh shit, regular army. It appeared I had only a minute before the directional-finding radio team got to me. I was boxed in. I had seen troops in the open field to my right, and the base camp was also on that side. Troops had been behind me all morning, and now troops were directly in front of me.

By then, thirty minutes had elapsed since Crown asked me to authenticate, and I hadn't talked to anyone since. The fighters had been actively pounding the three gun sites about a mile away, and it didn't take a rocket scientist to know that the guns were giving them fits. No rescue would take place while the guns were still alive. I had to find a new hiding spot before the guys with the homing equipment got to me, and quickly decided it would be around, and on the other side of them. I needed to get past them so all known danger would be behind me. It was definitely time to run again! I called Nail and told him about my little problem, and asked him to put some bombs fifty yards to my south, ASAP, for a diversion. Hopefully, Nail knew my position, or one way or the other, I was mincemeat.

Shortly, I heard a fighter in a dive and listened to the whine of his engine as he whistled downhill. A small boom sounded as the pilot lit the afterburner for climb-out. His bombs were away and would explode in eight to ten seconds.

The AAA stopped, which meant the gunners were diving in their holes. I took off downhill at full speed toward the tree line, and a little right of where I had last seen the radio guy. *If he spots me, I'll shoot but keep running*, I thought. I sprinted through an open area of knee-high grass and was exposed to anyone looking my way. I looked skyward. "Be with me, God," I quickly uttered.

I needed a bomb to explode directly in front of me so the radio guys would have their heads down when I ran by them, slightly off to the side. And I needed at least a pair of bomb blasts to make my total run-distance possible. The second blast had to be farther from me than the first, or I would be killed.

"Nail, this is Streetcar. I'm on the move, running to a different location. Can't talk now, will advise you later. I say again, Streetcar is running to a different location, out."

I just barely got the last word out before a huge shock wave buffeted me. The first bomb had hit right where I had hoped and exploded in the area where I last saw the radio guy. From the blast force, it appeared to be a 750-pounder, and hopefully it decimated the radio team. They were either dead or cowering from the huge bomb blast, and this was my chance to dash by, unseen. In a microsecond, the third and fourth bombs exploded dead ahead, and farther away. Damn, someone's got my six and is watching out for me big time. "Thank you, God."

It was all so perfect that a short thought occurred. This is so stupid and brazen that no one would expect it, and I might just get away with it.

The enemy gunners started to fire again as the jet climbed out, but I kept running toward the sanctuary of the denser jungle foliage about a hundred yards ahead.

Nail heard my running call and flinched when he heard a bomb explosion in the background. A second blast occurred before I finished talking. It made a big impression, and he knew I was running for my life. I ran maybe two hundred yards from my original spot before I finally reached the tree line.

Once inside, I continued at a slow jog and watched for a good hiding spot. I took a huge risk to continue jogging, but the protective cover wasn't yet quite what I was looking for. Suddenly, a small clearing appeared ahead, and for some reason I had a really bad feeling about crossing it. I stopped, bent over, and sucked air as I scanned ahead for troops and a spot to hide. I seemed rather calm. But I couldn't just keep standing there. *Make a decision, damn it.*

To my right was a really tall, large-diameter tree, and the trunk was hollowed out at the base. I ran to it, knelt down and, unbelievably, it looked like I might fit inside. Quickly, I sat down and scooted back until my entire body was inside the trunk. A perfect fit. The hollowed-out portion faced in the direction of my escape path toward the small clearing, and the solid portion protected my back from the direction I had just run. Once inside, the tree trunk was like a giant security blanket. I felt like I was in hog heaven.

Chapter **18**

VALLEY OF DEATH

At about 5:30 P.M., I hunkered down inside the hollow tree trunk and pulled my knees close to my chest. My entire body was inside and visible to an enemy only if he stood directly in front of me. The top of my head was only an inch or so from the wood, and my shoulders were braced by it on both sides. The opening was such a tight fit that anyone larger than my 5′ 10″ and 140 pounds would not have fit inside. But there were two tactical problems with the position. First, I could see only a few spots of open sky due to the massive tree canopy overhead, so I wouldn't be able to readily spot a Sandy plane. Second, if I moved my head slightly forward, I could then turn and monitor anyone approaching from either side, but I couldn't see anything directly behind me. I vowed that if a bad guy suddenly appeared from the rear and spotted me, I'd shoot him before I determined how many more there were. I would shoot to stay alive.

Nail was still trying to kill the three AAA guns that shot at Sandy 3, so bombs were still sporadically bursting nearby. But I felt safe and knew it would take a direct hit to kill me while inside the large trunk. About that time a Thud, call sign Detroit, pulled off after having dropped two 750-pounders. The pilot felt something strike his plane. Within seconds, his wingie joined on him and verified his leader had taken a hit in the plane's nose area. Detroit flight was through for the day and RTB'ed. Nail told Crown it was hopeless to try and knock out the guns with GP bombs and, for the umpteenth time, a Nail told Crown he needed CBUs. Crown replied that two Sandys were being diverted to the area with some as they spoke. But rather than wait and do nothing, Nail continued to press the attack with the resources he had available.

Ah, shit. Within a minute or so after hiding inside the trunk, I heard loud voices approaching from about fifty yards behind me. *These guys are persistent, I thought.* Had the enemy seen me running to this spot? I strained to listen for their movement direction and, after a few moments, determined that at least two men were walking directly toward me. I was sure they would pass extremely close by the left side of the tree and then appear in front of me. Do I shoot if two guys turn and spot me? I pulled the hammer back on the pistol, bent forward, and twisted slightly left for a quick peek. Damn it. I saw the point gomer before snapping my head back inside the trunk. Rifle, no helmet, dressed in black, followed by others. They were talking loudly, and I considered that a good sign. It might just be a normal patrol and not one hot on my trail. I scooted back tightly against the tree and steadied my pistol on a knee. Were they going to pass in front of my tree? Perhaps not. The voices now seemed to be veering slightly farther left and continued to a position that sounded about twenty feet left of my tree. I couldn't chance another peek. They stopped and stood quietly for thirty seconds or so. I could hear my heart pounding. *Are they looking at my tree?* After the lull, the conversation resumed and the voices started to move again. Their voices projected more noticeably toward me. Panic: *Are they moving toward me? Are my boots completely inside the tree?* Poised on high alert, I anxiously tried to determine their new path. In a few seconds, I decided they were drifting off farther to my left, still talking. *Great, they're going to miss me.* The talking continued until they were out of earshot. How far, I don't know. And I wasn't sure how many men were in the patrol. I exhaled slowly.

After releasing the hammer on the pistol, I extended my sore leg and closed my eyes for a moment of reflection. It was late in the afternoon and the Air Force had yet to make a pick-up attempt today. Just thirty-five minutes ago, Crown made his authentication and I had thought I'd be rescued at any moment. Now, things had gone to pot again because of more vicious AAA and more nearby troops. I was absolutely certain that Jolly would not survive a pick-up attempt with the current amount of AAA and ground troops around me. There might not be any pick up today, and that sucked. A second night on the ground would certainly reduce my chance of survival.

I was sweating and thirsty, even though I'd been sipping water regularly all afternoon. At ejection, I had two eight-ounce plastic bottles of water and still had one full bottle and about a third of the second remaining, so my rationing was going well. I took another sip but it didn't satisfy me. To heck with it—that last patrol made my mouth turn to cotton, so for the first time since hitting the ground, I took several large gulps. While indulging, I noticed the jungle had become eerily quiet again, so I sort of daydreamed about my wife. I wondered how she was coping with my situation. *She's emotionally strong,* I thought, *so she'll be fine.* I recalled our time together in Paris a few years earlier, during my second cruise in A-3s. We stayed in an unheated hotel room to save money—and it was cold. One afternoon we got under the bedcovers for warmth while we lunched on bread and cheese with cheap wine. We bundled, smooched, and held each other tight. . . .

Whoa, out of the blue I saw a slight movement straight ahead, toward the clearing that had caused me to stop and hide in this tree. My body stiffened. Utterly amazed, I saw a gomer pop up about twenty-five yards directly in front of me! Now he was looking in my direction! Sunbeams cast down on him just like floodlights on an actor's stage. He was outfitted in black shirt and black pants but had no weapon, helmet, or cap. His hair was jet black. *Oh, crap, he's a Pathet Lao.* He started making weird movements with his arms, as if punching thin air. I focused on his eyes to see if he was staring at me but couldn't confirm it. *Don't move an eyelash,* I told myself.

I sat immobile and my pistol rested on my right knee as I cocked it again. Abruptly he froze, with one arm drawn back with a fist and the other arm extended, pointing at me. I saw him clearly, so unless I really blended in well with the tree, he most certainly could see me. Was he pointing me out to someone?

I thought, *I've been had, the bad guys who walked by a few minutes ago probably have me surrounded. But this guy has no weapon. No one else is in sight. Is this a brazen guy who's just teasing me and showing they know where I'm hiding?* That made me mad. In frustration, I whispered toward him. "Screw you, gomer. I'll call your bluff."

My next move was stupid, but I was frustrated. Slowly, I extended my arm and elevated the pistol to an eye-level firing position. At that point, I held it steady, aimed right at the gomer's head. He was looking toward my tree but didn't flinch, and I was too far away to clearly see his facial expression. He still held his immobile pose, pointing my direction. Was he not scared of the pistol, or too far away to see it?

He stood fully erect and started to make one move after another as he turned, stabbed his straight arms outward, and alternately raised one leg and then the other. I watched his performance for a minute.

A thought hit me: *Is he just exercising? The guy may be doing some form of Tai Chi exercise and he's too far away to make me out in the tree.* Slowly, I lowered my gun arm.

The scene lasted for about two minutes, and I couldn't come to any conclusion. Perhaps the patrol that walked past a few minutes ago just coincidentally stopped for a break twenty-five yards or so ahead of me, and this guy was exercising. Or, perhaps he was actually standing up to identify my position and I was being used as bait. Crap, I didn't know. One thing was certain: the bad guys were in front of me again. Just as quickly as he appeared, the gomer stooped and disappeared into the foliage.

The gravity of my situation sank in fully. There were so many ground troops around, even if one got close, Jolly would be shot down or I would get shot as I was hoisted up. Right then I made a vow: if not rescued by dark, I would run all night to place more distance between me and this infested area.

My radio had been off for some time, so it was time to check in. Sure enough, Nail was calling. They were going to try a 6 P.M. rescue attempt since the 5 P.M. one had been tanked because of continuous AAA. I spoke in a loud whisper and gave Nail directions to where I'd moved, not really thinking he'd understand. He replied that he got the picture and would shoot a Willy Pete to confirm my location. I told him to fire when ready, but I really didn't expect to see his smoke.

Before long, I heard his prop drone, and in a few seconds heard a whizzing sound as the rocket passed overhead. It zoomed down through the tree canopy at my eleven o'clock, about a hundred yards away. I heard the impact and watched as a puff of phosphorus smoke billowed up just beyond where the gomer had done his exercise routine. This Nail had a lot of savvy. He was damn good. His smoke was "close enough for government work."

"Shit-hot, Nail. Roger your smoke. That's a good pick up zone, out." I then wondered if the single gomer thought he was going to get pounded by bombs as the smoke was practically on top of him. Hopefully, the smoke made him and any buddies run out of the area. Then I waited, waited, and waited some more. I checked my watch. Great, I thought, it's past 6 P.M., and thirty minutes have dragged by since I was promised another rescue attempt. An hour had elapsed since I was asked to authenticate.

Unknown to me, there was no general agreement about the feasibility of a rescue attempt. The Sandys and Jollys had been holding for several hours while the fast-movers tried to knock out the guns. The Sandys were getting low on fuel, rain clouds were approaching, and the enemy gunfire was still such that most of them thought it unwise to try a rescue under current conditions. But higher authority was still trying to make it happen. Out of the blue, the Spads with the Juicy Fruit announced they were at bingo fuel and returning to Pleiku. Now there was no gas agent available at the scene. At that point, most of the Sandys and Jollys thought it was time to go home and return to fight another day.

Sandy 3 radioed Crown. Sandy recommended that the rescue attempt be aborted for two reasons. The weather had gone downhill, and the fast-movers hadn't suppressed the AAA to his satisfaction. Nail was shocked. Who did this Sandy guy think he was?

Crown acknowledged Sandy's transmission. "Stand by, continue to orbit." Then, he passed the recommendation to Blue Chip.

Sandy 3 didn't have the combat pilot image. If you stood face to face with him, he wouldn't look like much of an opponent because he was over six feet tall and skinny, like Popeye. He was well liked because of his quiet, easygoing disposition, and normally he'd be in the background of most conversations, just timidly listening. Sandy 3 normally got the job done but had a reputation of being a conservative pilot who at times could get very jittery. He was showing signs of that nervousness now. He really didn't want to make a second ID pass to pinpoint my position because he had been really hosed during his pass over the field. But that earlier treetop strafing pass along the edge of the field, when I shot the tracer at him, showed me that he had some moxie. However, he became conservative. Too many guns were still hot, and he just knew he'd be killed.

Fifteen minutes later, the three A-1s, call sign Spad, finally arrived late from Danang to support the scheduled rescue attempt. They joined up with Sandy 3's flight of four at an altitude of 12,000 feet, and the seven A-1s flew in a circular orbit around my area as the fighters still pressed their attacks. The Spads had little specific awareness about the mission or my plight prior to takeoff and didn't receive any further briefing now because Sandy 3 really thought the mission would be scrubbed. That was okay with the Spads, as they'd spent the morning trying to find the pilot of Trump 01 who'd been shot down. They had been unsuccessful and Trump 01 was now declared missing in action. Two nights before, these same Spads had also been involved in the twilight rescue of an F-105 pilot who'd been shot down very close to the area I was in. The Spads knew the area could be hot at times. They didn't need a lot of brief; but then, they didn't know I'd been on the ground for twenty-four hours because of really intense AAA. Soon though, they got the picture. Each time the seven-plane gaggle of A-1s flew around the north side of the circle, a 57 took pot shots at them. The Spads pressed Nail to kill it.

Finally, Nail put a flight of Thuds in against it with "retarded" bombs. This meant a little lower release altitude for the Thuds, and more chance of an enemy hit. The A-1 pilots watched in disbelief. Each time a Thud dropped his bombs, it appeared to be a direct hit and each explosion caused a huge cloud of dust. But as the Thud climbed out, tracers and red, flaming balls would come flying out of the maze of smoke and dust. The Sandys and Spads became more frightened each time they saw it happen. How could they survive that kind of enemy firepower when it was so difficult for the fast-mover, workhorse Thud?

Shortly after 6:30 P.M., and about thirty minutes after Sandy 3 recommended they abort the rescue attempt, he still didn't have an answer. The low Jolly, Jolly 9, was now into his tenth hour of stressful combat flight for the day, so he was worn to a frazzle. He, too, thought they'd be sent home for the night at any second. Finally, the answer to Sandy 3's question arrived from Blue Chip. Jolly 9 couldn't believe his ears.

"This is Crown, transmitting to all rescue planes. Blue Chip directs all rescue forces group now for an immediate rescue attempt, regardless of cost. The use of the special agent is not approved at this time. All twelve fighters presently in the vicinity will make one coordinated, simultaneous, massive strike at the guns to be closely followed by the rescue force of seven Sandys and Spads and three Jollys. Nail, you coordinate with Sandy Lead to make it happen. Good luck men, Crown out."

Jolly 9 couldn't decipher much of the transmission due to static caused by bad weather in the area, but he did clearly hear one disturbing sentence: *"Effect rescue immediately, regardless of cost."*

He turned toward his co-pilot. "Yuhas, did you get all that gobbledygook?"

A shake of the head. "No."

"Crown, this is Jolly 9. Say again. I only got part of that message, over."

"Jolly, you are ordered to effect rescue immediately, regardless of cost, out."

Jolly 9 heard it loud and clear that time. He was astonished. His authority was being pre-empted. This was really out of the ballpark for normal rescue ops. The chain of command for rescues was clearly established—and always adhered to. When a pilot went down, the FAC controlled the scene till the Sandy on-scene commander arrived, and then it was the Sandy's call as to when the area was safe to send the Jolly in. Once it was declared safe, the Jolly pilot became the commander of the rescue attempt. If the Jolly pilot deemed it too unsafe past that point, he had the authority to scrub the rescue attempt. The final authority for "go, or no go" on a rescue attempt always belonged to the Jolly pilot. Jolly 9 was infuriated, and shouted over the radio to Crown.

"By whose orders?" Jolly 9 asked. "I'm the RCC. It's my decision, and I'm not ready to make the pick-up, over."

Crown's response was quite firm. "Jolly, the commanding general, Seventh Air Force, personally orders you to make the rescue immediately, regardless of cost, out."

The Seventh Air Force staff was closely monitoring the rescue effort. When Sandy 3's recommendation to terminate for the day wound its way to the staff, the general was out of the building so his staff haggled over their response longer than usual. The duty officer was a "bird" colonel who finally issued the order under the guise of the general himself because he knew how much the general wanted to get the Navy guy out. He didn't think the general would condone a full day of dragging their feet without a single rescue attempt. The colonel had in mind a rescue plan similar to what fighter and attack pilots referred to as a mini-alpha strike.

The term "alpha strike" was used in combat flight operations over North Vietnam and referred to a pre-briefed massive attack by thirty to forty planes against a known, hard target. All planes would roll in against the target at a nearly simultaneous time. A mini-alpha strike was the same, but involved fewer planes. The colonel envisioned a coordinated strike wherein the Jolly would arrive overhead immediately after the fighters had either killed the gun crews or caused them to jump into their protective holes. It may have been a good idea, but the required in-flight briefing by the involved participants while in the midst of persistent AAA fire was nigh impossible.

"Regardless of cost . . ." Jolly 9's emotions went haywire. He had a feeling of doom and knew he and his crew could never survive a rescue attempt under present conditions. Even though he was orbiting some distance away, he was close enough to see the many tracers of the large number of guns still active around me. It would be suicide. Also, Jolly couldn't fathom how he could reach me before it was totally dark. He had heard reports that troops were all around me, so he'd surely take fire from them as he tried to hover. Maneuvering his large, cumbersome helo in near darkness would be crazy. He didn't feel the risks were worth the reward under present conditions. But his co-pilot didn't say a word, and just looked at Jolly 9 as he weighed his decision. It was solely Jolly 9's call and he felt his crew would support him either way; it was still a tough call. It didn't take him long to make his decision. He keyed his intercom button.

"Orders are orders. We're going in. Calhoun, Harding, test your door guns, we're going to need 'em." He advised Sandy 3 that he was ready to try a pick-up.

The pilot of Jolly 9 was a tall, handsome, devout Christian from La Puente, California, who had graduated from the University of La Verne. He, too, had an easygoing, quiet demeanor and carefully considered his words before he spoke, but then spoke with authority. For that he was well respected by his crew. He now had a full year of combat under his belt so he knew what he was doing, and he'd proven that during his previous ten pilot rescues. The most recent one was just this morning when he rescued Sandy 5 after he was shot down. But none of those rescues approached the intensity of this one. Everyone in the squadron knew he was a great pilot, and they also knew he was a man of great religious conviction. When he told Sandy he was ready to try a pick-up, the crew knew instantly that Jolly 9 would either make the pick-up or they'd all die trying.

Twenty-two planes flew around in circles and jockeyed for position while a rescue plan was discussed and analyzed for nearly thirty agonizing minutes. Utter confusion reigned at times. Finally, Sandy 3 and Nail devised a plan, and then briefed the twelve fighters, four Sandys, three Spads, and three Jollys in an attempt to coordinate a simultaneous attack. It was difficult to accomplish while all twenty-two aircraft were trying to avoid flying into each other while continuously avoiding the enemy AAA fire.

Two of the twelve fighters were F-4s with the CBUs Nail had been asking for all afternoon. Nail insisted they be the first two strike planes to roll in, to kill anyone who was close to my position. A plan was developed and then passed to all airborne participants.

The two F-4s, call sign Banyan, would attack first, come in low and drop their CBUs on the area designated by Nail's smoke rocket. CBU bomblets would saturate the area and all enemy troops and gunners within the pattern would hopefully be killed or incapacitated. Immediately following that, the other ten fighters would roll in simultaneously from 12,000 feet and drop their ordnance against any guns that hadn't stopped firing from the effects of the CBU salvo. Two Sandys and the three Spads would arrive over my location at 1,000 feet immediately after the ten fighters salvoed their bombs. On the way in, they would target any other visible guns or troops. Two more Sandys would follow those five at five hundred feet as escort for the three Jollys. Jolly 9, the low Jolly, would fly at twenty feet above the trees and the other two would be a little higher in a one-mile trail position. It was critical that the Jollys arrive over me immediately after the five A-1s did their thing. All seven A-1s would then orbit and provide cover for Jolly 9 as he hovered to pick me up. The other two Jollys would stand off as backups. If the plan went as briefed, all twenty-two planes should be over my position within a minute or so of each other. It sounded like a good plan, but it required lots of coordination—which usually required practice. But Seventh Air Force said, "Do it now."

The plan had one little flaw that could kill me. Several of the pilots, including Jolly 9, voiced concern that they didn't know my exact position. Nail could get them close, but Sandy 3 hadn't yet completed that part of the rescue wherein he pinpointed my location down to the exact clearing and tree. Sandy hadn't done so yet because he thought the enemy AAA was still too hot. Therefore, Nail advised he'd kick off the event by shooting a smoke rocket to identify the pick-up site, and then the first two F-4s would blast the area south of it with CBUs. If the F-4 pilot erred on his aim point, I could become mincemeat.

(Cluster bombs were the best weapon to neutralize enemy AAA gun crews and ground troops for the rescue force. The CBU looked like any other bomb in shape but once dropped, it split open and nearly 600 blue bomblets the size of tennis balls popped into the air and scattered over a half-acre area. Each bomblet contained an explosive charge that, on ground impact, would spew 300 shotgun pellets into the air creating a deadly force of 180,000 projectiles per bomb, not including the shrapnel from the bomblet casing.)

Meanwhile, on the ground, I had heard nothing from anyone for over forty-five minutes. I didn't know if the rescue was on, off, or if I'd been deserted for the day. I was confused but vowed to stay in the tree until nightfall, and then relocate. Finally, out of the blue, Nail made a simple call to me but didn't explain the plan.

"Streetcar 304, this is Nail. Get your smoke ready. We're coming to get you out, over."

Hallelujah! It was about time. Promptly, I removed the smoke flare from my vest and placed it on the ground between my legs, while I held my radio in my left hand and my pistol in my right. I figured there were maybe twenty minutes left before darkness, so I was unsure as to which end of the flare I would activate, night or day. I decided to go with the day end first. The orange smoke should still be visible in the twilight.

Sandy 3 had been orbiting with a flight of seven. He directed two Sandys to rendezvous with the three Jollys and start moving them into position. But belatedly, the Jollys announced to Crown that each would have to refuel before they could take part in the rescue attempt. That caused a great deal of consternation. Now, the entire gaggle of planes had to orbit even longer as they waited on the Jollys. Weather conditions were deteriorating and the clouds were causing an early sunset, so all pilots were getting quite jumpy.

At 7 P.M., Crown received another irate radio call from Blue Chip. "Execute the plan without any further delay." Crown then passed it on to all planes.

Jolly 9 couldn't comprehend that a staff person hundreds of miles away was directing a rescue attempt in the midst of intense enemy gunfire. He might regret it later if he didn't at least make one more plea for sanity. He made a radio call to his immediate superior in the chain of command, call sign King, and advised him that the Sandys didn't yet believe it was safe to attempt a rescue. King immediately directed Jolly 9 to follow Seventh Air Force's orders and attempt a pick-up before darkness. Orders were orders, so Jolly 9 told Sandy 3 he was ready to do it.

At about 7:15 all planes were finally ready, so Nail kicked off with his smoke rocket. I heard it whizzing in and watched it impact near the same clearing area as before, this time about seventy-five yards in front of me. Smoke began to billow upward. Then, Nail asked my relative position to the smoke.

"Don't worry about my position Nail. Count on me being at your smoke for pick-up, but make sure the Jolly knows that troops will probably be nearby. Copy?"

Nail rogered.

I made up my mind I wasn't going to break cover until I heard the Jolly. After all, I could sprint to the smoke area in about ten seconds.

And thus far I had yet to talk to the Sandy who should be calling me any second now because he would want to pinpoint my position by flying over several times. I theorized it would be several minutes before I ever saw a Sandy or Jolly.

Wrong assumption, 304. Suddenly, I heard a much louder roar of jet engines than at any time since hitting the ground, and I could tell there were a lot of fast-movers heading my way, but I couldn't spot them. I peered toward the sound of a diving jet.

Surprisingly, I hadn't heard any large guns firing, but then an automatic rifle fired at the diving jet. The sound was really close by. Bullets were spewing out at a rapid rate of fire and a burping sound was reverberating among the trees. Stunned, I stared in the direction of the rifle fire, unable to believe how close it seemed. Where was the guy? The rifle fire seemed to be high above me.

I saw an F-4 through one small opening of trees and it was in a shallow bomb dive, flying right to left in front of me. Just then, a second burst of gunfire erupted and it seemed to come from a tree about twenty degrees off to my right and fifty yards away. I quickly scanned up the tree trunk, limb by limb, just like I was squirrel hunting. Then, about a hundred feet up, I saw a slight movement.

At first, I didn't believe my eyes. A gomer in black clothing was standing on a good-sized limb, with one shoulder against the tree trunk. He had an AK-47 strapped to his arm and, as I watched, he fired several quick, short bursts at the Phantom. I was staring right at the gomer and wondered how in the world I hadn't seen him earlier, since I'd been panning that direction for nearly an hour. *That's his duty station—he must've been in that tree all day long,* I thought.

My eyes swiveled back to the F-4. I was flabbergasted. The pilot was pressing his run and appeared to be only seconds from impacting the treetops. *Pull out, pull out,* I pleaded. As if hearing me, the jet's nose started to rise sharply. The pilot must have had target fixation, I thought. The jet appeared to be frozen in flight.

Just then, the gomer fired another short burst at the jet's broadside. I felt an urge to do something. Quickly, I raised my pistol and took aim at the guy. *Can I kill him from this distance with a .38 pistol?* Before I uttered "no," mini-explosions from the F-4's first bomb resounded about a hundred yards away, and that quickly diverted my attention. "Aw, crap," I uttered. I realized that the Phantom driver had dropped a CBU. Numerous bomblets were falling through the trees and making *ping* sounds as they bounced off tree limbs on the way down, but most were exploding dead center in the smoke that was still drifting skyward from Nail's smoke rocket. That secured the pick-up zone, but it's a good thing I stayed inside the tree trunk because the explosions were walking toward me.

I looked back at the gomer in the tree. He knew what was happening. He had a mighty bear hug around the trunk for protection as bomblets exploded around us. After the explosions ceased, he straightened up and began to reload his weapon.

What should I do? Should I try to kill the guy and risk having my location disclosed by the shot? Would the enemy even recognize a pistol shot as coming from me versus one of their own? Would it be wise to duel with an AK-47 at this range? The answers to the three questions were no, no, and no. The best thing I could do was stay hidden and take a shot only when the target was very close and absolutely required, to avoid capture.

Another jet was now diving in but I couldn't pick him up in my view. I heard the pilot add power and commence his climb, and shortly thereafter I heard more CBU bomblets exploding off to the right of the guy in the tree. Lots more. From the explosive pattern, I could tell the bomblets would walk through the bad guy's tree and then continue on to me. I scooted back tightly against the trunk and pulled my legs as close against my chest as possible to deflect any shrapnel or pellets to the chest. Hundreds of exploding bomblets resonated as they hit trees or ground on their rapid path toward me. What about the gunner? I looked, and he was holding on to the tree for dear life as explosions now rocked his tree. I could hear bomblets hitting tree limbs above me.

I saw something fly by. Suddenly, there was a blinding flash of light and monstrous boom directly in front of me about twenty feet or so away. Death appeared to be rushing toward me! Without thinking, I lurched backward to avoid killer shrapnel, and my head cracked hard against the tree trunk. It happened so fast I thought I was a goner. There was no way I should have survived because of the proximity, but I wasn't even injured.

I wasn't out of danger yet. Just then, I heard the pinging sound again and realized there was a second bomb, this one even closer. Bomblets were raining down on top of me and the gomer, hitting the trees and bouncing in all directions, then exploding. I heard a ping maybe forty feet to my right as one bounced off a limb. I stretched forward and looked that way. It pinged again as it hit a second limb, and a couple of seconds later I saw an object flash downward in front of me and impact with a thud near my feet. I looked down and a bomblet was lying within inches of my right foot. *This ends the game for me,* I thought. My first thought was to grab it and throw it, but I froze. I stared unbelievably at the round, baseball-sized hunk of blue metal.

I had held dummy bomblets during weapons training classes, and knew they weighed about three times the weight of a baseball, so they were practically a grenade. Was this one on a time delay and due to explode at any second? Should I pick it up and hurl it away before it exploded and killed me? Then, I realized any time delay would have occurred during the time it was bouncing from the tree impact or as it lay at my feet, and it was most probably a dud. My foot was no more than six inches from it.

Should I gently move it, or leave it alone? Should I pick it up and save it for use as a grenade? I didn't know enough about the frapping thing and decided to leave it alone.

After I regained my composure, I glanced back to check the status of the gunner in the tree. He was gone. I scanned the trunk to see if he was climbing down but saw no action. Had he been hit by an explosion? Was he lying at the base of the tree? I couldn't tell from my position. I never saw him again and never heard any more fire from that tree. God does indeed work in mysterious ways.

At 7:15 P.M., the designated kick-off time, the other ten fighters were in and off their targets in less than a minute, and the valley reverberated with the sound of multiple secondary explosions. It became quickly evident that the remainder of the rescue force would not arrive anywhere close to their scheduled time because of miscalculations in speed and distance. Sandy 3 had his gaggle of five A-1s at 12,000 feet in a daisy chain when the group started in. They were hustling to make up lost time because of a late start, but Sandy 3 was still three minutes from Nail's smoke when the F-4s dropped their CBUs. Now, the AAA gunners would have time to re-group before Sandy 3 arrived with his five A-1s. Sandy 3 increased throttle to gain speed.

The two Sandys who went to escort the Jollys had even worse timing problems. The Jollys were in an orbit so far away that it was physically impossible for the helo to fly fast enough to be overhead my position by 7:15, and in fact, they could arrive as much as five minutes later than the fighters. The two Sandys took up a weave position five hundred feet in front of the Jollys and started toward the smoke.

Jolly 9 flew at twenty feet above the treetops, followed by the other two back-up Jollys a mile or so behind. Based on Sandy 3's recommendation, Jolly 9 had chosen to fly a route that would bring him in from the safer area to the south. In the last few miles, he would fly north up a ravine, crest a ridge, and then fly downhill to my location.

In no time, the entire operation started to crumble. Sandy 3's gaggle was a considerable distance from the Jolly group, so Jolly 9 went to maximum power to catch up, but knew he couldn't stay at that setting forever. He would overheat.

When they were three minutes out from Nail's smoke, Sandy 3's gaggle began to receive intensive enemy ground fire and the five planes began shooting rockets at anything that moved or fired. As the flight descended through 5,000 feet, Sandy 3 and his wingie were now outrunning the three Spad flight members. The number three Spad plane heard Sandy 3 make what sounded to be a frantic transmission.

"Sandy 3 is taking intense 37 fire, so I'm aborting, out." Sandy 3 and his wingman turned to the south and left the area, followed in the distance by the three Spads. None of the five made it to Nail's smoke.

At about the same time, one of the backup Jollys suddenly developed an overheated, critical-stage transmission temperature. Jolly 9 then directed the third Jolly to ride shotgun over the second one, while he continued on the Streetcar mission. At that point, my rescue force consisted of two Sandys and one Jolly.

The Jolly with the problem decided the transmission would fail and cause a crash if he didn't take immediate action, so he set it down in a nearby field. Once on the ground, he kept the engine running but reduced power to cool the transmission. After two minutes, the right door gunner suddenly screamed that enemy troops were running out of the woods on his side. Immediately, the pilot lifted off and staggered another two to three miles before the temp again reached critical, and he headed for a second safe landing zone directly ahead. On the way, he flew over troops running within a half mile of the site, so Jolly made an urgent plea for air support. The Jolly then landed safely, but the crew knew they didn't have much time. Now, there were seven Americans on the ground, or in the water, as a result of my shoot down.

Sandy 3 heard Jolly's panic call but said he was at bingo fuel and needed to RTB, so he directed the three Spads to return and provide covering support for the downed Jolly.

Jolly 9 never heard Sandy 3's abort nor RTB call, and pressed onward at his maximum speed of 100 knots, skimming across the treetops. His two Sandy escorts had been weaving across his flight path at 220 knots to provide covering fire. But then, they, too, began to outrun him. A ridgeline lay directly ahead of Jolly 9 and the two Sandys were nowhere in sight. Apparently, they had already crested the ridge, so Jolly 9 had no Sandy protection or Jolly back-up. He was totally alone.

As Jolly 9 neared the top of the ridge, he carefully scanned the terrain. Suddenly, he screamed into the intercom, "Look out, big trouble on the left side."

A gun crew was frantically removing a camouflage tarp from what appeared to be a ZPU. The gun barrel began spitting fire as rounds flew out even before the gun completed its swivel toward the helo. Jolly 9 banked right to avoid the gun by flying to the other side of a thirty- to fifty-foot-deep gully. Immediately, the co-pilot screamed that a gun was firing from that direction also, so Jolly 9 rolled back left and saw that yet another gun site was now hot on that side. Three guns were now aimed at him and he was nearing the ZPU he had first sighted. He rolled the helo in a sharp, left bank as he flew directly overhead of the gun. For a brief moment, the FE door gunner was looking right down the throat of the gun barrel, so he emptied an entire belt of M-60 ammo, killing the entire gunner crew.

Jolly luckily made it up the ravine, but slowed to a crawl when he finally reached the top. He took a quick look at what lay in his flight path down in the valley and it scared the hell out of him. It looked like a Fourth of July celebration. The valley was dimly lit because the setting sun was partially blocked by the high karst to the west, but Jolly caught a faint glittering from the river below. The dark, foreboding ground had circles of white muzzle flashes and the pinkish-blue sky was lined with criss-crossing, speedy red tracers intermingled with flaming red balls. By chance, he saw his two Sandy escorts about a half-mile straight ahead, but well below him in the valley and nearly obliterated by flak. Finality hit him: "This is where I buy the farm." To Jolly 9, it looked like his personal valley of death.

After the F-4s dropped their CBUs, several minutes passed while I sat inside the tree trunk anxiously waiting for Sandys or Jollys to appear. After what seemed like forever, I heard the roar of approaching planes mixed between bursts of enemy AAA. It was the same bass roar I'd heard each time before when the Sandys got close. A-1s were diving toward me. Their mini-guns were rattling and spewing out bullets, and I heard cracking and popping as the rounds impacted ground and trees near Nail's smoke.

I quickly scooted out of the trunk and rose to a knee as I watched for a Sandy to appear. In a flash, I saw one A-1, and then a second in trail, diving through the treetops above the clearing where Nail had placed his smoke. As I watched in awe, they pressed their gun runs to as low as 150 feet. Man, I hope the 20 mike-mike wiped out the gomers in the clearing. The two Sandys barely pulled up in time to avoid the treetops, banked to the right, and climbed for higher altitude. They were in view for one brief moment, then gone. Less than a hundred yards away, I noticed how dim the sky was behind them and I realized for the first time it was nearly dark.

I pressed my transmit button. "Way to go, Sandys. Streetcar saw that shit-hot run." I expected an acknowledgment, but got none.

Meanwhile, Jolly 9 was about to leave the ridgeline, but hesitated. He recalled a magnificent Fourth of July fireworks show he'd once attended, and this was the first time he'd seen a show that rivaled that one. During the earlier show, the viewers were each given a candle and match as they entered the arena. After dark, upon a signal, all those present lit their candles. Intermittent flashes occurred as the matches were struck, soon replaced by a blooming glow from the candles. Jolly 9 thought the valley ahead looked that same way now.

It didn't take him long to decide to turn around. He announced to the Sandys who had just flown over me that the enemy fire was too hot, and he was taking it out to try a different route in. He executed a sharp bank and flew back down a ravine, but one that was a ridgeline over from the initial one. After a few miles, Jolly went into an orbit to regain his composure and wait for the Sandys to join on him.

While waiting, Jolly 9 questioned Crown again about the feasibility of another rescue attempt. After all, Sandy 3 and his wingman had gone home, and the three Spads were hustling to the overheated back-up Jolly. Jolly 9 was emphatically told again, in no uncertain terms, to pursue his rescue attempt of Streetcar 304 with the two Sandy escorts.

About that time, the three Spad A-1s arrived in the nick of time overhead the second Jolly, which was still cooling down in the middle of a clearing. The Spads strafed the approaching troops until they withdrew, while the third Jolly landed and uploaded the crew of the second Jolly. Within minutes, Blue Chip gave permission for the third Jolly to RTB. "Abandon the second helo," he said.

Meanwhile, I was still on one knee at the tree, and no one was talking to me. I'd already halfway decided this attempt was like earlier ones, and wasn't going to be pulled off. I would give them a few more minutes before running to a different hiding spot.

Jolly 9 retreated for twenty miles and then circled to re-enter the hot zone from a different direction. About ten miles out, he started to pick up ground fire again and the intensity rose to the point he considered disobeying direct orders. But he pressed on. It was down to him and two Sandys, and Jolly 9 couldn't shake a gut feeling. If he entered the valley, he'd be blown out of the sky.

Just then, Crown broadcast a prodigious statement. "Blue Chip has ordered a termination of the day's SAR effort, and all planes are to return to base." I didn't hear the call.

Jolly 9 did, though, and he immediately banked and turned to scat toward the south. A terrible feeling of guilt surged within him because this was the first time he'd personally left a downed pilot to fend for himself overnight. But, it wasn't that uncommon. Darkness was close and the Jolly helos weren't equipped to handle a night rescue, nor one under inclement weather. He really hated to leave me because I might be captured or killed during the night; but, there came a time when the RCC had to consider the lives of the three other men in his crew. Jolly 9 was fleeing in a right turn when tracers zoomed by from guns to his rear. *Thank God,* he thought. *Fortunately, Blue Chip came to his senses before I got closer to those guns.*

The third Jolly, now with the back-up crew aboard, also heard the termination order. The RCC had already taken up a heading for NKP and was just now finally unwinding from his traumatic rescue of the back-up Jolly. The RCC thought he was sufficiently away from danger. But, as he scanned the ground ahead, he saw a guy stuff a round into a mortar gun barrel. "Mortar gun on the left," he screamed into the intercom. Before the door gunner could spot it, the mortar round zoomed out of the barrel at the Jolly. It barely missed. The bad guys were firing everything they had.

Thirty minutes had elapsed since the first F-4 kicked off with his CBUs, and I had yet to see a Jolly or receive an update. As if reading my mind, Crown called and his voice inflection was different. It was slow and methodical sounding.

"Streetcar 304, this is Crown. The SAR effort is terminated for the night. We'll be back again in the morning. Copy?"

Then, there was nothing. That was it. Not even a "good night, sleep tight." Crown sounded as if he was just bidding me a nightly farewell before he left the office.

"Roger, Streetcar copies Crown, out."

I had no idea just how hairy it had been for the rescue force, but right then, I was devastated. I was hacked off. I felt betrayed. Slowly, I rose and forced my stiff back erect. I put the smoke flare and radio in my vest. After that, I stared up at the spot in the sky some three hundred feet ahead where the Sandys had strafed earlier, and spoke out loud to vent my anger.

"Piss on you, Crown. I'm tired of waiting on your guys, so I'm going to save myself, even if I have to walk all the way to South Vietnam."

I'd had it up to my eyeballs.

Chapter 19

THE BAD GUYS
CHASE ME

Blue Chip had abruptly terminated the second day's rescue attempt. After that, I swiftly turned my radio off and stuffed it in my vest as I had no intention of talking to anyone until morning. It was about 7:45 P.M., and the sun had nearly faded below the tree canopy, so it was twilight inside the jungle. I could wait fifteen more minutes and it would be dark. But, I was afraid the enemy would rush in and capture me now, before dark, if this had been a trap. Without trepidation, I took a step to run.

Right away, I stumbled and nearly fell. My legs had fallen asleep inside the cramped tree trunk and my right leg and lower back, which took the brunt of the seat pan on ejection, had stiffened badly and ached. I twisted my ankles up and down several times to wake my legs, and I also twisted my torso to loosen my back. Then, I gutted through the pain and began to run pellmell on a straight line to the wooded area across the clearing. If the gomers there weren't dead, maybe I could catch them by surprise and be past before they realized what I was doing.

Fortunately, the terrain between me and my goal was initially slightly downhill and only consisted of light brush between widely spaced trees. I arrived at the right edge of the clearing and wasn't yet winded, and I was two-thirds of the way to my goal. At that point, I was running through a sagelike grass that reached up to my knees, just like it had when the gomer stood and pointed at me earlier. My head was on a swivel as I scanned for him. I began to breathe hard because now I was running uphill to get to the densest portion of the wooded ridgeline. I was in full stride and fifty feet from the woods when I reached a position where I got my first good view of the entire clearing. I looked back at it over my left shoulder while running, as though I was about to catch a football thrown from there. I looked slightly downhill at the middle of the clearing, which was illuminated by the setting sun. It made the sage-like grass glisten golden-yellow. The top of the grass was rippling in a slight breeze in the forefront of a dark green background of jungle foliage. Suddenly, I saw movement.

Oh, crap. About a hundred feet away, a lone man in black clothes rose up, looked my way, shouted, and then excitedly pointed at me. (I swear he looked just like the exercise guy.) I turned to check in front for cover, but hadn't yet made the woods. I looked back toward the gomer and saw other black forms rising and shouldering their rifles. They must have been lying in the grass. Hell, how did they survive the bombs and guns? They had either intended to bed down there for the night, not knowing my position, or they had me staked out to make sure they didn't lose their trap bait. Either way, they saw me running.

I turned around and focused on the woods, forty feet away. My only chance was to get there quickly and find a good hiding spot before they arrived, but I braced for a rifle shot in the back at any moment.

In a few seconds, I made it safely to the tree line's security blanket and then paused. I turned for a quick look at my opponents. *Way to go, Streetcar, now you've done it.* Ten or so guys were running single file toward me in hot pursuit.

I busted into the trees and ran for about twenty-five feet up the hill. *Whoa,* I thought, *if I'm going up the hill when they hit the woods, they'll surely see me from below.* I took a right and ran for another twenty feet before seeing a hollowed depression directly ahead. I was running full speed so I did my best baseball slide and placed myself in a full laid-out position facing the direction from which I had just run. Then, I frantically began to claw, rake, and pull leaves over my body in an attempt to cover all but my head and right hand, which held the pistol. I was now glad I'd earlier wiped black dirt over my hands and face. After covering myself, I then turned to see where they were. It was almost dark but looking back, I could clearly see the point where I'd entered the woods.

At that very moment, the first guy of a single-file formation entered the tree line about eighty feet further away from where I'd entered. Then I noticed he had a helmet. That meant he was probably more trained and adept at this game. He carried his rifle in a ready position and walked slowly and cautiously. Why wasn't he running? Then it dawned on me that he was listening for my footstep noise. I counted nine more bodies as they followed, single file, behind their leader. *Come on, nightfall. Fall down over me. Please, get dark before they get close.*

I clawed at the ground to deepen my hole. I wasn't shaking, nor quivering, nor were my teeth chattering. My mind was under control and my muscles seemed relaxed. My breathing was even and I could even hear my smooth exhalations. I held my breath for just a moment to relax even more. Why wasn't I afraid? Once more, I had to prove I was better at this hide-and-seek game than they were.

During the next several minutes, I marveled as I watched them slowly take a step, stop, take another step, stop. . . . They moved as one up the hill and fortunately veered a little left, which kept them fifty feet away from me. They were extremely patient. One step, listen, another step, listen. . . . As they inched slowly along, I quietly readjusted my position to keep my pistol pointed at the leader. It must have taken them five minutes to walk up the hill to a point where they were now maybe fifty feet above me. At that point, they spread out in a single line about thirty feet along the ridge. The leader was maybe ten feet to my right and fifty feet up the hill and staring downhill. From right to left, the next guy was facing uphill and the next was turned to face downhill, and so on down the formation line.

This group was well disciplined. Each member of the platoon stood very erect but nearly motionless as they moved only their heads, as if listening and looking for me. They obviously didn't know my hiding spot, but were waiting for me to move. They'd placed themselves in an ideal range for my .38 pistol and it would be like shooting cans off a log if I wanted to chance it. Obviously, they must have been trained that American pilots wouldn't engage in gun battles, and I wouldn't get off more than two shots before receiving automatic rifle fire in return if I surprised them by shooting.

The scenario was tense and baffling. For fifteen excruciating minutes, it was difficult to understand the enemy's intention. It was as if they knew I hadn't continued to run away and that I was hiding close by. They were waiting for me to bolt, but they didn't try any of the tactics that had been used the evening before. They didn't call out "Hey, G.I. Joe, give up, come on out." They didn't fire any warning shots. It was mystifying, and I spent the time trying to discern their intent.

During those fifteen minutes, none of the troops made a sound or moved a muscle—other than their moving heads and searching eyes. They were completely stationary, as if they'd turned to stone. A single Marine with an automatic rifle could've taken them all out easily.

I knew this was a well-trained unit and the least movement or noise from me meant certain capture. My mind raced. *What do I do if they see me and start approaching?* I had a six-shot pistol and there were ten of them. Do I start a running gun battle, or do I just surrender and become a POW? I personally had a better chance of survival in a running shoot-out than as a POW. I feared POW status more than dueling it out here, right now. But neither option sounded good.

I needed help. Silently I prayed, "Hurry, God, drop your blanket over daylight."

Seconds went by like minutes, and I still was indecisive about firing the pistol. It was a tough decision. What if they simply announced they were going to take me captive and asked me to give myself up? I couldn't make up my frapping mind, but it was getting darker as I weighed my options.

Darkness settled and slowly enveloped the black-clad men, and it became harder to distinguish body parts. I had a better chance now. Maybe one shot would make them run for cover since they were in the open? No, this was a seasoned Pathet Lao combat unit and I decided they wouldn't run. If I killed one, the others would be really hacked off and rip me apart. That's what we had heard these guys did to pilots. They were vicious.

It got so dark, the forms were about to disappear from view. I was amazed they still hadn't moved. But neither had I. *They must not know where I am or else they'd capture me before I become lost in the darkness.* Their tactic was confusing. Were they waiting for darkness to surround me, and then make their move to capture me?

Now it was completely dark. I couldn't see sky, or trees, or even my hand. I tried, but couldn't see the pistol at the end of my arm. How could I aim if I fired? Suddenly it dawned on me that I could no longer see any body part other than their faces. I'd been staring intently at their eyes to see if any focused toward me, and I'd failed to notice the rest of their bodies were no longer visible. I blinked to refocus and was surprised to see that each of their faces was glowing in the dark. That was the only reason I could still make them out. Had they applied some type of phosphorescent substance to make their faces glow so they could see each other in the dark? I could still make out each guy's position, but only by the glowing face. That meant they probably couldn't see me, and now I had the advantage.

Abruptly, with no preceding thunder or drizzle, it began to rain. In just a matter of seconds, it increased to a torrential downpour. The water beads pelted the tree canopy and foliage with such ferocity that it drowned out any other sound. The rain was coming down in sheets, splattering my eyes with such force that it was difficult to keep my eyelids open. My view of the glowing faces was now totally obscured. God saved my butt again.

I didn't think twice before I was on my feet and frantically running to the right. I felt no pain, so I must have been really scared, though I didn't sense it. It was my intent to place as much distance as possible between me and the bad guys before the rain stopped. I ran at full speed, unable to see anything, and blindly bounced off trees and tore through brush. Several times I ran smack dab into a tree with such force that the blow knocked me down, but each time I got up and ran full speed again. I lost all sense of time and distance and had no idea if the enemy even knew I had bolted. I had to push forward as long as the rain made me invisible.

Soon, though, my lack of sleep and food over the past thirty-eight hours began to catch up with me. My strength was sapped and I got tired. In fact, I was exhausted and starting to stumble. About then, I ran smack dab into a really large tree trunk. I hit it hard with my forehead, bounced backward, and fell on my butt. I scooted forward and probed with my hands until I found the tree again. Its diameter was huge. At that moment, the rain stopped, just as quickly as it had started.

Instantly, the jungle was startlingly quiet and that made me feel vulnerable again. I knew I couldn't risk noise by continuing to run. I deftly scooted around to the other side of the tree to use it as a shield against any enemy coming from the direction I had just run. I rose to one knee and realized I was sucking air and exhausted. I turned my head slightly to listen for foot noise behind me. Were the gomers hot on my trail? It was quiet, but since the rain had stopped, I knew the bad guys would now be looking for my tracks in the wet soil. I was sure they would have no fear of using flashlights. I scanned, but couldn't see any shining my way. Maybe I'd placed some cushion distance between us. I needed to put even more distance between us before dawn, particularly since I couldn't see if I had any protective cover around me other than the tree. I was wiped out from running and stress, so I sat down and leaned back against the tree trunk. *I'll stay here for just two minutes,* I vowed.

It was pitch-black and I felt secure. To be safe, I twisted my body and looked back from where I'd run. My heart skipped several beats. About a hundred yards away, I saw the glow of what appeared to be a single, bobbing flashlight. I watched for maybe twenty seconds and then it was gone. Had the person turned it off, or had he changed direction so I could no longer see its beam? I watched intently for another minute but never saw it again.

I allowed my weight to sag against the tree. "Two more minutes and I'm out of here," I muttered. Instantly, though, a horde of ferocious mosquitoes attacked. I seemed to be engulfed by hundreds. Where had they been the night before when I'd seen none? The little bloodsuckers were having a field day around my ears and nose, and I couldn't rest for swatting them. It seemed with each passing moment that more were feasting on me and trying to crawl up my nostrils and into my ears. It got so bad that I finally reached down, grabbed some mud, and crammed it into my ears and nose.

I leaned back against the tree again and raised my hands to rest on my bent knees. For crying out loud—my hands glowed in the dark. I looked at my boots and saw that the soles were also glowing. Then it dawned on me that the local dirt must contain some type of fluorescent material. I remembered how I'd deliberately spread dirt over my face and head the night before. Had that dirt also contained the fluorescence, or was it just this area's dirt? Was my face glowing in the dark now? Was my face glowing while I watched the glowing faces of the ten bad guys?

I removed a water bottle, poured some in one hand, and wiped my face. I did that several times until my hands and, hopefully, my face no longer glowed. But I left the mud in my ear canals and nostrils as the mosquitoes were really attacking in force. Next, they swarmed my eyes. I couldn't keep them out, so I closed my eyelids and cupped my left hand over them as a shield.

After a minute or so of bug torture, I wondered about the time. I was determined to stay awake for now a second night, and after a short rest place more distance between myself and the gomers and bugs. I looked at my small, round-faced combat watch and the dial had just enough luminescence to allow me to see it was 8:45. Eight hours or so until morning and the return of the rescue forces. Could I make it through another night? And what was the status of Sandy 7? Was he still alive for a second night?

While I changed location three times during the day, Sandy 7 spent all day strapped in his tree. Last night, he'd been excited for morning to arrive so the bad guys could pack up and leave. They didn't, but nothing adverse or spectacular occurred throughout the day unless you count the stress that occurred when bad guys constantly weaved back and forth near the base of his tree. Because of that, he was barely able to shift his weight on the limb most of the day. His rear end was sore already. But at twilight, he really needed the protective blanket that only darkness could provide because it felt like his bladder was about to explode. He'd been holding it all day and he really, really needed to take a leak. However, he was afraid to try as it would require too much maneuvering on the limb to aim his spray, and one of the troops below just might see the mist. So he sat in agony, awaiting darkness.

Just before sunset, Sandy 7 watched hundreds of soldiers drift back into camp in small groups, all within the space of thirty minutes. It appeared to be a unionized quitting time for the Pathet Lao. The scene scared him, but at the same time it intrigued him. He watched as the soldiers socialized with each other and seemed to recount the day's events. Most of them didn't appear too happy, and most looked tired and weary. *Weird,* he thought, *there appear to be no sentries around the camp.* Soon it was chow time, but Sandy had no desire to partake. Hunger and thirst were not his problem. His bladder was about to pop.

Around 8:30 P.M., most of the base camp was peacefully sitting or lying near their campfires. Without warning, a gully washer of a rain hit the area. Multiple fires were snuffed out immediately and the gomers ran to their small, thatched lean-to. Sandy 7 was high in the tree in the midst of a loud, driving rain, enveloped by total darkness—such that he couldn't see the ground and couldn't hear himself talk. The rain was pelting the tree canopy above and the jungle foliage below with such force that all other sound was obliterated. No one could see or hear anything, so he indulged himself in the most satisfying act of the day. He slit his torso harness with his knife and took a long, long leak in the rain. After that, he felt like a new man.

Sandy 7's thoughts meandered to Streetcar 304 and he wondered if I had been rescued. About twenty minutes earlier, he'd heard a long series of booms in the distance that sounded to him like an all-out effort to suppress guns just prior to a pick-up by a Jolly. He wouldn't know for sure until morning, though. If he heard more bombing then, he'd know Streetcar was still evading on the ground. And, in the morning, he'd find out if the soldiers in the camp below would pack up and break camp so he could call Crown. Sandy 7 let his head sag against the tree trunk for the umpteenth time that day, closed his eyes, and visualized the ocean tide rolling in at the basin of the Columbia River. Would he get to see that ever again?

It was 8:45 P.M. and I was on a planned two-minute rest break. My head settled back against the massive, wet tree trunk and I listened to my smooth and easy breathing. I was calm. Should I eat some more Charms for energy? No, that would require a flashlight. Instead, I pulled the Redman bag out of my side pocket and stuffed a new wad in my cheek. Its sugar and nicotine would do till morning.

The mosquitoes were driving me crazy and I was ready to try anything. So, I spit some tobacco juice in my hands and rubbed it around, hoping the bugs didn't like the smell. I spit again and rubbed it over my neck and ears, hoping its pungent odor would repel them. Then, I closed my eyes and waited to hear if the steady drone and buzz abated any. *Zit, zit, zit, zit.* The sound was like a lullaby, and within seconds I was asleep in a virtual lion's den.

While I slept, Jolly 9 landed at NKP around 9 P.M., after ten-plus hours of stressful combat flight in one day. He was furious about the way the last rescue attempt was managed and he didn't intend to take it lying down. After landing, he stormed into the TUOC and angrily demanded to know why his RCC authority was usurped by 7AF.

The answer was simple. The Seventh Fleet staff had expressed concern that a Navy pilot had been on the ground in a known location for two days and hadn't yet been rescued by the U.S. Air Force. "Was Seventh Air Force sure they didn't require Navy assistance?"

The general took that as an affront to the quality of his fighter command and issued an order to his staff. "Get the Navy guy out of there at any cost." While the general was out, his aide sent the "rescue at all costs" directive because it looked like the day would end without a single pick-up attempt. Supposedly, when the general returned, he immediately countermanded the aide's order.

Jolly 9 was reassured that the Jolly pilot retained the final decision about when it was safe to send a Jolly in for pick-up. Tomorrow, though, when they went back again to get Streetcar, he personally wouldn't have to worry about that. Jolly 9 was scheduled to be only the back-up, so the new low Jolly would be faced with the safety decision.

Tempers flared among other participants as well, and some were beginning to question the tactics used thus far. The higher-ups thought the rescue force should've been able to roar in with overwhelming fighter support, easily knock out the guns, and then pluck the Navy guy out. The Sandys and Nails countered that they weren't getting the necessary support to make it happen. They vehemently confronted their seniors about the paucity of CBUs. "We need more CBUs, get as many as you can round up. Give Nail the necessary CBUs and napalm to wipe out the damn AAA."

The Sandy pilots, in particular, were becoming very outspoken and adamant that any attempt to rescue the survivors meant certain death for the Sandy and Jolly pilots. The Sandys believed the enemy had already captured Sandy 7, and were using me as bait to lure the Sandys and Jollys into a trap. They were already conjecturing among themselves whether it was wise to attempt further rescue of me in light of the probable trap. "Is one pilot worth the loss of additional men and planes when one of our own has probably lost his life and five more have come close?"

Nevertheless, Air Force staffers began to plan for tomorrow's rescue attempt. About 9 P.M., 7AF continued the no-bomb line on a five-mile radius around mine and Sandy 7's position for our personal protection. That meant no planes from any service could drop any ordnance inside that area, unless they were part of the rescue effort.

That created a second problem for the 7AF staff. Air Force Intelligence had been trying for several months to find the remnants of a division estimated at ten thousand troops which had withdrawn from the Khe Sanh area following the Tet Offensive. Many of the enemy had been located and killed during their withdrawal, but many more were known to be lurking in the jungle, recouping and resupplying. During the attempt to rescue me, the Air Force began to realize they might have found that retreating division. 7AF wanted to decimate it and was eager to unleash their B-52s in a massive Arc Light strike to totally destroy the division. The only thing preventing that was me. I was in the midst of the division, alive and talking on my radio. It would be very bad press to send the B-52s in to kill the troops but also kill a Navy pilot with friendly fire. The general wanted me out *now*, before the North Vietnamese Army (NVA) troops had time to disperse. It really annoyed the Sandy and Jolly pilots that the general's "no cost too great" approach to save a Navy guy might mean the death of some Air Force pilots.

The Seventh Air Force staff realized things weren't going well, so they considered other options. "What about using a Bright Light team?" one member suggested. Special Ops had four- to five-man ground teams trained to assist in the rescue of downed pilots. The team could be inserted by helo close to the pilot, then hike and locate him, and provide perimeter protection during a helo rescue.

That option would not have surprised me. Prior to the first combat day, all my fellow squadron pilots and I had been required to have a picture taken in our flight suit with both side and frontal views, for use by a Bright Light team for ID purpose. Unknown to me, one of those teams was now given a copy of my picture and inserted by helo at a safe drop-off point some distance from me. It was presently trying to make it to my position, but there was no estimate how long it would take.

Finally, late at night, an operational plan for the third-day rescue attempt was sent out to appropriate units. One Nail pilot would take off to arrive overhead of the scene at sunrise to confirm if Sandy 7 and I were still alive, and if so, to also verify the weather was suitable for launching the fast-movers. If both of those items were a go, then two more Nail planes would take off to relieve the first one and to coordinate the final destruction of enemy gun sites. Initially, twenty-six fighters were tasked to support the two Nail planes; more would be on alert to scramble as needed. Additionally, two gas agent A-1 Spads would orbit near my location, awaiting permission to use their agent; and two additional Spads with Juicy Fruit would be on ready-alert at NKP. Eight Sandys and three Jollys would complete the force.

Most of the same Sandy and Jolly pilots who had been on today's mission were again tasked to fly tomorrow. That was surprising to several, and frightening for all—and rightfully so. One Sandy pilot was really reluctant to fly the mission and wanted to ensure that higher authority was aware of the gravity of the enemy gunfire that had been thrown at them in the past twenty-six hours.

At 10 P.M., a phone call was made by the Sandy pilot who was scheduled to fly the dangerous low Sandy plane for tomorrow's rescue attempt. He asked that his comments be officially entered as a recommendation against sending rescue forces in tomorrow under current conditions, and that his comments be passed all the way to Blue Chip.

He didn't mince words. "Unless the area around the survivor is completely sanitized [all gun sites destroyed] one-hundred-fold better than today, any Jolly sent into the area will be shot down. I estimate many guns have yet to be seen and the enemy is just waiting for the slow-movers to show up. I estimate extremely heavy gun positions within ten to twenty meters of the survivor. The survivor is in an open area fifty to seventy-five meters long, running north and south with defenses along the entire western edge. I feel it's a trap and the enemy could take the survivor at any time."

This may have been a fairly accurate assessment about the AAA and possible trap. But, it does reflect that the Sandy didn't know I'd twice moved since my position near the monkey tree by the open field.

Sandy's recommendation was received and considered, but tomorrow's rescue plan was not changed. After that little hassle, the planners now moved their attention to the downed helo that was abandoned after its transmission overheated. At 12:30 A.M., another helo took off and inserted some friendly troops at the downed helo site about twenty miles from me. The troops set up a defensive perimeter around the downed helo so that another helo crew could be inserted in the morning to assess its air-worthiness, and if possible, fly the helo back to base. (The next day, a helo with a crane flew in, plucked the overheated helo, and carried it back to NKP.)

Meanwhile, I sat with my back against my tree in a deep sleep. Startled by something, I awoke in a daze during total darkness with my chin resting against my chest and my right hand with pistol resting on my drawn-back right leg. I was groggy, didn't know what had awakened me, and didn't have any situational awareness. I had no idea how long I had slept. I made a feeble attempt to raise my head, but even as I did, my eyes were closing and I was falling off to sleep again. Just then, I felt a hand firmly touch my right shoulder. Half-awake, I stiffened in panic and raised my head. I turned to look at my shoulder but couldn't see it. My eyes were open but my eyelids were swollen from the mosquito bites. I looked through small slits but saw nothing, simply total darkness. Was I dreaming? I was in a sleep stupor.

Unbelievably, in a couple of seconds I began to drift off to sleep again. The hand returned to my shoulder. It shook me slightly. I struggled to be more alert. I turned my head to look at my right shoulder again, and just then the hand forcefully pushed me sideward and off balance. I put my left hand to the ground and steeled myself to return upright against the tree, now fully awake. *What the heck is going on here*, I thought. Someone was disturbing my sleep but I couldn't comprehend who, or why.

Abruptly, I felt the hand on my shoulder again. It was large, warm, and calloused. I turned toward it. Holy Cow, a face, no more than a foot away from mine, was glowing. Slowly, as I stared face-to-face, I inched the pistol toward what I perceived would be its midsection. I cocked the hammer, ready to shoot. Out of the corner of my eye, I saw movement to the left. More glowing faces, at eye level: one was to my left, and two were directly in front of me, all three about eight feet away. *I've been captured, I'm dead meat,* I thought. Why hadn't they grabbed me and tied me up?

I'd fallen asleep sitting on my butt with my knees raised and my pistol in my right hand. I was still in that same position when I scanned the faces and weighed whether this was a dream or reality. It was no dream. I was actually awake and a warm, muscular hand was pressing my shoulder. Now the hand firmly patted my shoulder!

At first glance, three of the forms were kneeling or resting on one knee in front of me, and the fourth was hunched over my right shoulder. I stared to see their bodies or weapons, but could see only their faces. I watched the forms in front begin to close in and move rapidly side to side, as though they were trying to see both sides of my face. They were very excited and making weird sounds. It was like they were intrigued by me and excitedly pointing out my differences to each other. I shifted my eyes to the right and the glowing, round face was still no more than a foot away from mine.

I was totally mystified. Damn it. The bad guys with the fluorescent shit on their faces had found me and now they were standing right in front of me. I'd lost the game and now I was a POW for sure. But how come they hadn't tied me up as I slept? What were they waiting for? How come they hadn't grabbed me yet, and why hadn't they taken my pistol? Maybe they couldn't see it in the dark?

Crap. I had another decision to make about firing the pistol. Could I kill all four before they got off a shot?

I leaned back against the tree and stared at them for a minute or so as I tried to decide about taking a shot. They became stationary and stared right back at me. My vision slowly improved, and I finally saw the forms were short and their arms and legs were thin. Their faces appeared much larger than normal in proportion to the rest of their bodies. Small torsos also. . . . I still had my pistol pointed toward the body of the one off my right shoulder while I waited for their next move. What were they waiting on? Then, I saw what looked like rifles pointed at me by the two in front!

Then, the realization hit me like a sledgehammer. *I'll be deader than a doornail if I fire the first shot.* One stupid mistake of falling asleep had now cost me big time. I'd been captured! Any moment now, I would most likely be tied up.

In total frustration, I spit out my Redman and let my head settle against the tree with one thought. I was mentally stressed out, physically exhausted, and about to be bound. While the damn gomers make up their mind, I might as well rest. So, I closed my eyelids while my mind wandered. I thought about my wife. I had let her down.

Sorry, Shirley. I evaded well for over twenty-eight hours, but one little screw-up counters ten attaboys. I was depressed about her plight during my probable years as a POW. In a matter of a few seconds though, I fell asleep again.

Chapter **20**

NAIL 69 ENTERS
THE GAME

At midnight, Lt. Walt Moser retired to his stateroom on board USS *America*. He was dead tired after sixteen hours as SDO because the squadron's second day of combat had been just about as bad as the first. But, as was his custom, he wouldn't sleep until he summarized the day in his personal diary. He wrote:

> 1 June 1968. Today was a frustrating day all around. It began with very bad weather, and many hops [sorties] were canceled due to heavy cloud cover over the beach. No FACs were available either because we think they were all working on the rescue of 304. Worst part of the day though was Kenny. At 0630, we heard that voice contact was reestablished with him, and then the FAC called in the rescue forces and they started hosing the area down with GP bombs, CBUs, and rockets. Another Sandy was shot down. I think the pilot was rescued, but that was never confirmed. This was the third Sandy shot down we believe. The forces withdrew for a while. Another effort was made, but they too had to pull back due to ground fire. In that exchange, some type of helo went down, but the crew was rescued. Toward dusk, a last rescue effort was made by eight Sandys, eight F-105s, and some F-4s. Also, a C-130 and many other support aircraft were involved. Two or three helos were also brought in. Still, no luck with Kenny. . . . The FAC told him to dig deep, and they'd be back in the morning. We're still wishing the best for him. Everyone is saying prayers

before hitting the sack tonight. Iceman returned by COD a few hours ago. He told us what happened, and it certainly was a wild story. He also briefed us on what he knew about Kenny's shoot down. Iceman was pretty shook up. In fact, he almost turned in his wings. We all talked to him, and I think he feels better now that he's back aboard ship.

Lieutenant Moser then hit his bunk and tried to sleep. Tomorrow, he was scheduled for his second combat hop, and he was a little scared. He uttered a short prayer on my behalf, and his own.

While most people slept, Nail 69 was in Bangkok getting a massage from a lovely, dark-haired Thai girl. He was just about to doze off when the head masseuse entered the room with a message: Call your hotel immediately. There, a message from his squadron directed him to return immediately to base for a special mission.

Once back at his base, Nail 69 received a preliminary brief: A Navy pilot had been shot down near Tchepone, was evading for a second night, and was likely being used as a decoy. The enemy AAA was so intense that the Nails had been unable to kill all the guns so the Jollys could get to the survivor. Tomorrow, they were counting on him to get the job done.

Who was this Air Force ace-in-the-hole? Nail 69 was a cavalier, twenty-seven-year-old bachelor Yankee who had attended the University of Colorado on a ROTC scholarship. While there, he was on the football team. During the previous three years, he'd flown 225 combat missions in the F-4, many of them over North Vietnam. After back-to-back F-4 tours, and a short break back in the states, he'd boldly requested orders to the war again. This time he was assigned as an O-2 FAC because he'd already had his allotted fighter tour. In mid 1968, the Air Force had more fighter pilots than cockpits in Vietnam.

Nail 69 now had 120 missions under his belt as a Nail FAC and was sort of like Sandy 7. He had come to think of himself as fearless and invincible, even though he had experienced more than his share of thrills. He'd been shot down twice in F-4s over North Vietnam, and while performing as a FAC, had successfully crash-landed an O-2 after taking a AAA hit along the busy Route 9 highway.

Following the first F-4 shoot down, he had made it safely out to sea and was rescued without injury or incident. His second ejection was over enemy territory, and his chute hung up in a tree where it dangled precariously from 5 P.M. one day until he was rescued at 7 A.M. the next morning.

Obviously, Nail 69 understood what it took to kill a AAA site from a fast-mover's standpoint, and he understood what it felt like to be downed in enemy territory waiting to be rescued. He had proven he was heroic. So, higher-ups assumed he might hang it out a little more to kill the guns around me. In addition, some fellow pilots said he had one of the best sets of eyes in the Air Force, and that enabled him to spot AAA sites better than most.

Nail 69 offered what the ops planners were looking for. He had fast-mover experience. He'd been a survivor. He was cocky, heroic, and brazen enough to get the Streetcar 304 guy out, dead or alive. But he'd never flown as the low Nail FAC in a search and rescue mission. Nevertheless, he got the job.

Nail 66 was unhappy at the move. He wouldn't be going back the third day, after he'd worked with Streetcar 304 for nearly five hours the first day and another five hours the second. He had been working with Streetcar when he was shot down, and he felt like it was his duty to ensure he was rescued. Now, he couldn't fathom sitting it out on the sidelines while a new quarterback replaced him. Nail thought it rotten and unfair, but no amount of discussion could change it. The third-day mission belonged to that damn hotdog, Nail 69.

Jolly 9 had flown ten hours of combat-support time on day two, and he was ragged tired but had no appetite. The heat and subsequent sweat had him on the verge of dehydration, and he found he couldn't get enough to drink. That evening, he and several members of his squadron sat around drinking beers while they discussed the task of rescuing me. Every pilot in the room agreed that I was being used as bait to lure the slower Jollys and their four-man crews into a trap. The general consensus was that they needed a different tactic or they'd lose a couple of Jolly crews the next day. It was now common knowledge that I had reported gunners with AK-47s in the treetops. Jolly 9 was concerned that at first light, the enemy would haul larger machine guns to the treetops, and then the Jollys would be ripped to shreds when they hovered over me.

After a laborious and heated discussion, the Jolly pilots agreed I needed to move to a new spot, out of range of the AAA sites, but they didn't want to suggest it. The pilots agreed I was taking a tremendous chance each time I broke cover because of the large number of troops around me, and thought I'd done more than my part already by moving four times. Plus, they assumed I must be dead tired. No, they wouldn't ask me to move again, but each person in the room silently and fervently hoped that I would take the initiative and run like hell during the night to a better pickup area. Jolly 9 silently prayed, asking God to help me get out of the valley of death before sunrise.

At one point, one of the Jollys brought up the use of the gas agent. After discussion, a proposed plan was agreed upon. The area around me should be heavily bombed, and then the gas agent should be released. Ten minutes later, after the enemy was hopefully incapacitated, the Jolly would land, and the crew would walk around to locate and rescue me. There was only one possible glitch. The gas would tend to settle to the ground, and therefore the treetop gunners would most likely not be affected. CBUs could be used to handle that problem if they were fused to explode at treetop height.

Jolly 9 participated in the discussion and thought the plan was dumb shit, but couldn't sway the opinion of the more senior officers. He was only a mere captain, and the "big boys" were involved now. The senior officers wouldn't be flying the mission, but were now heavily involved and calling the shots, and they strongly recommended that Blue Chip approve the use of gas.

Jolly 9 then returned to the alert hut, where he expected to grab a little shuteye before a scheduled 3:30 A.M. brief. He huddled with his waiting crew and briefed them on the plan as it now stood. Afterward, his three crewmen said they had a group question: Why do we have to go back? They were in there twice today, rescued one pilot already, and several times almost got shot down themselves. They also reminded him that per squadron procedures, he didn't even have to fly on the mission since he was due to rotate back to the states. They encouraged Jolly 9 to remove the crew from the game.

Jolly 9 told them that it was his feeling that if anyone has to enter that valley again, it should be his crew. "We were the only Jolly to make it far enough to get a peek at the valley, and I feel we have a better chance than someone who is totally unfamiliar with the scene. I can't ask another pilot to take over for me, and couldn't live with myself if one did and was killed because he was unfamiliar with the situation."

Jolly 9's crew remained dubious. He then pointed out that they were only scheduled to be the back up high Jolly. But, if the primary low bird was shot down, they'd still have to enter the hot zone to rescue that crew, so they might as well go in first. No vote was taken. Jolly 9 sent his co-pilot to the ops officer with a recommendation that Jolly 9's crew be assigned the low Jolly instead of the high one. That request was flatly denied.

Later, Jolly 9's roommate came by the alert hut. He had heard that tomorrow's mission was going to be a rough one. Jolly 9 grinned. "I've heard something to that effect," he said.

His roommate then bet him a nickel he wouldn't come back alive. Jolly got about three hours of sleep before his brief.

Nail 69 entered the briefing room at NKP at 3:30 A.M. He was overwhelmed by the amount of "brass." Normally, there might be four or five fellow pilots and the briefer. Today, there were so many eagles and silver-leaf insignia on the shoulders and collars of those gathered that the room could have taken off and flown.

The briefing officer first stated that it was imperative they rescue the Navy pilot today, so we can bomb the hell out of the area with B-52s before the enemy disperses. He began a description of my and Sandy 7's location, as he knew it. I was located at map coordinates Xray Delta 243390, due northwest of a sharp bend in the nearby river. The briefing officer took his pointer and placed it on the map.

"Fly north along the river till you see the large bend. It sticks out like a large tit and points directly at Streetcar 304, about five hundred meters from the shoreline. And we think Sandy 7 is in the karst about one click northwest of Streetcar, if he's still alive."

Next, the briefer meticulously pointed out a Sandy pilot's confirmation of about thirty AAA gun sites within a five-mile radius of my and Sandy 7's locations. One of the Sandy pilots placed an X on his map at each spot where the larger 37s and 57s had been observed. Once finished, his map had five X's just to the north of my position, four on the west side, and another six to the east across the river, along the karst. In addition, an unknown number of the even more deadly ZPUs and smaller guns were hidden beneath the tree canopy. And, the briefer said, hundreds of enemy troops had been spotted on the ground in the vicinity near me.

The brief continued. Nail 56 would take off as a single in time to be over me by sunrise around 5:50 A.M. Nail 56 had been involved in the mission the previous day, had talked to me, and knew my approximate position. Nail 69 and his wingman would be on alert, pending Nail

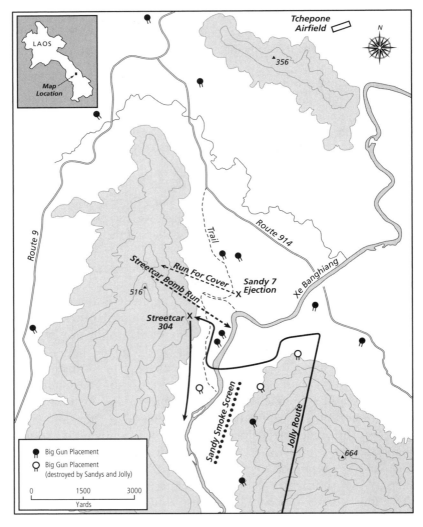

Tchepone area, depicting target and Jolly flight path for pick-up/egress of Streetcar 304. (Map by Christopher Robinson)

56's verification the weather was good enough for gun suppression by the fast-movers. If the weather was adequate, Nail 69 and wingman would take off to be over my position by 7 A.M. to relieve Nail 56. Nail 69 was briefed he'd initially have thirty fast-movers for gun suppression, twenty-two of them F-4s, and eight F-105s. More fighters would be loaded and on ready-alert, awaiting Nail's call.

The overall airborne command and control of all forces would fall to the Crown bird. Its pilot would take off from another base around 5:30 and be in position to in-flight refuel the three Jollys who would take off from NKP at 5:45. Planning dictated that the Jollys and Crown bird complete the refueling so the Jollys could be ready to fight by 7 A.M. A second Crown bird would orbit nearby for backup refueling support, to keep the fighters on station in case the weather turned sour.

Sandy 9 was designated at the last moment to be the low Sandy, replacing the nervous pilot who was originally scheduled to lead. That pilot was the one who, during the night, had voiced concern up the chain of command about a possible trap scenario and how it would be suicide for the Jollys, and maybe for the Sandys, too. He would still fly the mission, but not as the low Sandy.

It was not coincidental that Sandy 9 was chosen to lead. He was short in stature, but long in experience. He had piloted F-86s in the Korean War, and prior to this current A-1 tour he had been an instructor pilot in T-33s and T-37s for seven years. He was known for his maturity and fearlessness under fire. But, most importantly, he had shown time and again during tense and difficult Sandy missions that he possessed an innate tactical ability to find the best route for the Jollys to avoid AAA fire. He never bragged, and was uncharacteristically low-keyed and reserved for a fighter pilot. Today, his skill and mettle would be given a fierce test, and Sandy 9 knew from experience that luck would play a hand.

Sandy 9 would take off from Udorn AFB at 5:30 A.M., leading three other A-1s. He and his wingie would rendezvous with the three Jollys from NKP while the other section flew on to NKP and joined four more Sandys on runway alert. Sandy 9 would then escort the Jollys to the holding point twenty miles or so from my position, and fly protective cover while they refueled. The six alert Sandys would take off once Sandy 9 decreed it looked like the guns were sufficiently suppressed for the Sandys to attempt rescue. Once scrambled, a total of eight Sandys would be involved in the rescue.

Two A-1 Spads were loaded with Juicy Fruit and on alert at NKP. Two more would be on alert at Pleiku. Blue Chip would make the final decision as to the use of gas dependent upon wind conditions at the scene. Nail 69 had never worked with the gas agent, and its possible use made a big impression on him. *This mission might get real hairy,* he thought.

The briefing officer finally summarized the rescue plan. One Crown HC-130 would serve as airborne command and control and refueling tanker, but would be backed-up by a second Crown bird just in case the tasking became too monumental for one. Two Nail FACs would be overhead to positively pinpoint my location and suppress any enemy gunfire before calling in the Sandys. Nail 69's wingman would be there for communication support. Thirty fast-mover fighters would scramble, eight every thirty minutes, then fly to an orbit point to await Nail 69's call. His Nail wingman would provide the initial briefs as the fighters checked in, and he'd then release them two at a time to Nail 69 as needed. Nail 69 would then mark the location of enemy guns so the two fighters could kill them. More fast-movers would be on runway alert at various bases. Eight Sandys, each loaded for bear, would be used on the mission, along with three Jollys. (The Jolly pilots were in unanimous accord that the low lead Jolly would most probably be shot down, so they had requested that three Jollys be used on this mission.) The three Jollys and two gas Spads would eventually take up station in an initial holding pattern about twenty miles to the southwest of my position, and wait while Nail 69 suppressed the enemy gunfire. Once the AAA was neutralized, two Jollys would proceed to a kickoff point about eight miles due south of my position, while the third Jolly remained twenty miles out with the two gas Spads.

For the final rescue, Sandy 9's six planes would escort one Jolly in for the pick-up, while the second Jolly remained eight miles away for backup under the protection of two Sandys. The low Jolly would ingress along the back (east) side of the karst, across the river from my position, since the six guns along that route would be aimed toward the west where I was. Four of the six Sandys would lay down a smoke screen along the west side of the karst so the gunners wouldn't be able to see across the river toward my position. The low Jolly would have the backside of the 2,100-foot-high mountain karst to shield him as he passed the first batch of guns, but once past the karst and due east of my position, the terrain dropped off into a valley. After passing the karst, the Jolly would head due west toward my position, cross the river, and immediately veer south a couple of miles as a diversion to avoid the guns to the north. He would then turn back north to make the final dash for me. After pickup, the Jolly would retire to the south.

Just one caveat: Blue Chip could change the entire scenario at any moment if he authorized use of the gas agent.

Nail 69 had never heard such an elaborate, detailed brief. Initially, he wasn't the least bit scared about this mission, but as the brief dragged on and on, he understood why the Navy guy was still on the ground. The area was hot, in fact scorching hot. The AAA wasn't just your one or two sites, here and there variety. These bad boys were well dispersed along the karst so their range and aim was greatly enhanced. Plus, they were positioned so the Navy guy was bore-sighted. Any plane entering the area would be seen by a multitude of guns, so Nail 69 now understood why the rescue planes were being eaten alive.

Nail 69's pencil slid out of his fingers as he tried to write a note. He noticed his palms were sweating. He glanced around the ready room at the other pilots. It was readily apparent as to which ones had been involved in the Streetcar mission the previous day. They were the pilots who looked solemn and ashen. By their faces, one could tell they hadn't slept. Their flight suits were green with big splotches of white because they'd sweated so much on day two that the moisture had penetrated through the material, dried, and left salt residue on the outside. He looked at his. Moisture was now soaking through the outer layer. Could he handle this mounting fear, and could he muster the strength to fly low enough to pull off this rescue?

Several of the players, Jolly 9, Sandy 3, and Sandy 8 specifically, had been involved on both days, and they doubted whether they'd survive a third day in the same hostile area. All three felt they were stretching their luck and might not make it back alive. Many of Jolly 9's fellow squadron mates felt he was pushing his luck and that no matter how good a pilot, today would be the day he'd run out of luck. After all, his roommate—of all people—had made a bet.

Jolly 9 only had a few days remaining on his one-year tour the day I was shot down, and the squadron didn't want to schedule him for any more hazardous missions. The squadron ops officer basically considered Jolly 9's tour over and didn't want to see him killed with only a couple of days remaining before he was sent home. However, the squadron was short of RCCs, so on day one, Jolly 9 had been tasked to commence alert duty at 6 P.M. for the next forty-eight hours. His luck was good that day. I was shot down about fifteen minutes before he actually took over the alert position, so the crew he was to relieve scrambled before he assumed the alert, and Jolly 9 didn't fly that day.

After Sandy 7 and I were shot down on day one, the squadron ops officer offered to replace Jolly 9 with another pilot for the day two alert since it looked like the mission would get hairy. Jolly 9 declined the offer; he didn't want the death of another pilot on his hands if one was killed after having replaced him.

During the morning on day two, Jolly 9 was scrambled. During that mission he rescued Sandy 5 from the tree, and his helo miraculously avoided enemy gunfire damage. Jolly 9 earned compensatory time off for rescuing Sandy 5, but again he declined. However, his co-pilot accepted the offer to back out as he thought one rescue a day was enough for him, and a new co-pilot was assigned.

During the afternoon on day two, Jolly 9 was the primary low Jolly for the aborted rescue attempt just prior to nightfall, and during that attempt he'd received heavy enemy gunfire. So Jolly 9, who the squadron was trying hard to protect, had now flown more hours than any other pilot in the squadron in support of the Streetcar mission and was scheduled again today. If all went well, he would only be a backup Jolly today.

On day one, Sandy 8 was the wingman of Sandy 7, who was shot down. On day two, he was the wingman of Sandy 5, who was shot down in the morning and rescued from the tree by Jolly 9. After Sandy 8 returned from watching Sandy 5 shot down, he spent the afternoon in the TUOC. He closely monitored the radio transmissions during the abortive twilight rescue attempt since he had a feeling he'd be going back for a third time if I wasn't rescued then. Once he learned he was again on the flight schedule for day three, he questioned the decision to keep him in the fight. His gut said that today was his turn to get shot down. He asked if it was prudent to send him back again since both his leaders had been shot down in the past two days. Maybe he was a jinx, and no one would feel comfortable flying with him. He was unceremoniously told to suit up, regardless of any jinx.

Once Sandy 8 found out he'd be going back to hell for a third time, he again wrote another "farewell" letter to his wife—his second in two days. He was totally stressed out, a mental mess, and sure he'd be shot down. In the letter, he told his wife about the details of the hazardous mission and that he felt he might not make it back. Once he finished, he placed the letter inside his metal locker and then placed his wedding band on top of the letter; he thought it a nice gesture in case he didn't return from this flight. He was sure his good luck had run out, and he'd only been flying combat for three weeks! Today he would fly wing on Sandy 3, who had led the aborted rescue attempt just the night before.

Sandy 3 had mixed emotions and didn't yet know how he would respond if the AAA got as hot today as during last night's aborted attempt. During the brief, Sandy 8 noticed that Sandy 3 was extremely nervous, and it was very evident that Sandy 3 didn't want to go back a second time. That gave Sandy 8 a really morbid feeling.

Fear. Nail 69 could see it in the other pilot's eyes and hear it in their voices. This was a mission that no one wanted to fly. Pilot after pilot told him in no uncertain terms that he better knock the shit out of the enemy guns before he called in the Sandys and Jollys. Nail 69 left the ready room with a heavy load on his shoulders. He had to produce, he had to be at his best, or pilots were going to die today, and many of the survivors would blame him. Would he fold under the pressure? He never had before. . . .

Chapter 21

MORNING, DAY THREE

After the hand-on-my-shoulder event, I stupidly, but unintentionally, slept most of my second night on the ground until I was rudely awakened by a lone man, dressed in black, with no helmet. He was about ten feet in front of me, staring at me, and holding a rifle. In slow motion, he began to shoulder it toward a firing position, and I realized I had to run before he killed me. I rose, but stood petrified as the rifle had reached a firing position and was now aimed at me, point blank. My eyes focused on the man's finger and it began to slowly squeeze the trigger. Frantically, I tried to run but my legs were tied. I couldn't escape. Was I being executed? A white flash occurred at the end of the rifle barrel, and I heard the shot echo. The bullet was on the way.

At that moment, the sound of the shot awoke me from my bad dream. I was startled, in between dream and reality. Had I heard a real shot, or was it the dream? I was still seated against the tree trunk, and it appeared I hadn't moved during the night. My legs were still bent at the knees, and amazingly I still had a death lock on my pistol, but it was quivering. Then, it dawned on me that I could see my hands. What time was it? I glanced at my watch. It was nearly 6 A.M. Damn it, I had just slept about nine hours in the midst of enemy troops.

Suddenly, I recalled the events right before I fell asleep. I remembered my encounter with the ten glowing gomers stalking me, and my panic-run during the rain. Where had they gone? Then I recalled awakening to a hand on my shoulder, the four human forms, and their glowing faces. Instantly, I felt fear. Obviously, I hadn't been captured by them, but where were they now? And, who—or what—were they?

I rubbed my eyes to clear the sleep effect. Just then, a sound occurred a few feet above me. I looked up and saw a monkey jump from one limb to another. He looked down at me, threw a small object, and made a loud noise. Several others were also jumping around. Had the monkeys hit me with something and that awakened me? Or was it the dream rifle shot, or even an actual rifle shot?

By then, I was fully awake and unable to believe that I was still sitting against the tree in daylight. What the crap was I thinking to fall asleep while being chased by ten bad guys? I should have been able to stay awake for two nights in a row.

Sunrise was just beginning to brighten the sky above the tall tree canopy, but at ground level, it was still quite murky. A gray, foggy mist hovered around me and made the scene a little surreal. I could see for a couple of hundred feet, which meant that my chasers would also be able to see the same amount of distance. Terror struck: my heart began to race, and adrenalin surged through my body. It felt as though I was visible to the entire world. I wasn't hidden, and it appeared it would take a good run to get to suitable terrain for cover. I quickly scanned for a more secure spot. To the left, the terrain went uphill. To the right, it continued to drop off. Neither direction offered any heavy foliage.

Turning, I scanned my rear quadrant for the troops from the night before. After several minutes, I concluded no one was in sight. I still didn't want to get up, though, for fear of being spotted but commanded myself to rise. Once up, I'd never felt so stiff in all my life, but I didn't have time to loosen up. I took off at a jog in the opposite direction from my encounter with the ten-man platoon the evening before. I didn't have much time to hide before daylight enveloped the woods, so I trotted at a pace that allowed me to move quickly but still watch for any sign of the enemy. My eyes peered behind tree trunks for their eyes. It would take some luck to make it—unseen—to the edge of the woods.

Out of breath, I stopped my run next to a large tree for camouflage. I stood erect and tightly against the trunk, checking my rear. *Cool it, Streetcar. You've made it this far, so don't blow it by panicking. Settle down, look behind you for signs of anyone following you. Listen for their foot noise.*

I held my breath to settle down, then scanned the rear area again and listened closely for another thirty seconds. No one was in view. I craned around the tree to check my next pathway. Good to go. But before I did, I crammed a wad of Redman in my mouth for quick energy. Everything would be okay now, so I broke into a trot.

About two hundred yards ahead, the edge of the woods basked in full sunlight. That became my target spot. Slits of sunbeams were also streaking through the tree canopy, so the protective morning mist had lifted until it was now ten feet above the ground. I was really exposed, so I ran faster. I noticed an odd effect: without a conscious thought, my head was swiveling rapidly, side to side, of its own volition, to search for signs of any enemy movement. It was almost an uncontrollable movement, like my teeth-chattering episode.

Finally, I reached the edge of the woods and knelt in a protective crouch as I surveyed the area before me. A sizable clearing lay ahead, and it bristled in full daylight. Just perfect for someone to see me if I were to walk through it. I needed to make a quick decision.

I was on a ridgeline that continued level through the clearing for about 175 feet before it narrowed down considerably and dropped off sharply on the far side. To my left and right, the ridgeline dropped off immediately. To the right would take me back toward the base camp, and to the left would take me toward the river. Left or right didn't feel right. The clearing would provide immediate cover, so I scanned it carefully.

An area about 100 × 175 feet had once been cleared of large trees, and now there was significant new jungle growth about ten feet high. There was a tree in the middle about thirty feet tall, so it stood out like a sore thumb. The tree would serve as a good locator for Nail, and I'd be on top of a ridge that should be easily visible from the air. It was a good place to hide and a good place for helo pick-up. I decided to make the area near the tree my next hiding spot.

But, to get to the tree, I'd need to cross about thirty feet of open space before reaching thick vegetation. This time, I'd be more cautious crossing a clearing. For several minutes, I scanned the area in front of me to ensure no one was lurking, while also watching for the platoon from my rear.

Just then, I heard the faint sound of a plane and surmised that Nail was in the area checking the weather. I gave him a fifteen-second beeper to let him know I was still alive.

The time was around 6:30 A.M. when Nail gave the weather report: "It's clear, except for a morning fog in the valley near the survivor's position. Visibility is six miles, but there's a stratus layer of clouds at 6,500 feet to the west. The weather is currently too bad for flak suppression, but I estimate it'll lift in the next thirty minutes. I've been unable to make voice contact with either Streetcar 304 or Sandy 7, but did pick up a beeper from one of them." His orders after that were to remain over the area and attempt further contact with the two survivors until Nail 69 arrived to relieve him.

I listened to the sound of Nail's plane for a few seconds before cautiously duck-walking maybe seventy-five feet through short vegetation to the middle of the clearing. I stopped about twenty feet from the tree. The shrubs were over my head, about ten to twelve feet tall, and would provide decent cover if I stood. When I sat down, the shorter vegetation was very dense and provided excellent camouflage. I knelt and surveyed my situation. The clearing was large enough for a Jolly pick-up, and I was shielded such that no one would see me unless they were a few feet away. I would be able to pick up any enemy troops exiting the woods around me before they could see me in the ground cover. All I had to do now was await the arrival of jets, and then I'd turn my radio on and make morning contact with Nail. Until then, I saved my battery.

Secure in my hiding spot, I lay down on my back and absorbed the warmth of the morning sun. It felt soothing and dried my wet clothes. I stretched out to ease my aching back and leg and scanned the sky. It looked like it was going to be a wondrous day.

I was thirsty, and my bladder ached. The heavy rain from the previous night had deposited pools of water in the large, curled leaves of the elephant plants, so I crawled to one and pulled it down toward my open mouth. Water flowed with such volume that I choked. Before draining a second leaf, I had my water bottle ready. Then, I drank as much as I wanted from a third leaf before it dawned on me that there might be some bacteria in the water that would make me sick. Too late now. But I did tell myself not to drink the bottle containing the leaf water until I had exhausted the other bottle, which contained the ship water.

Most rescue planes were airborne before 6 A.M. The Crown bird and Sandy 9 and 10 took off from different bases and then rendezvoused with the three Jollys who lifted off at NKP. Six more Sandys, plus the two gas Spads, remained on alert at NKP. Shortly afterward, Nail 69 and his wingman took off from NKP and headed directly for my position.

During their one-hour flight to the Rooster Tail, the three Jollys practiced flying with their gas masks tightened around their face. After that, they refueled from the Crown plane so they'd have maximum time to orbit and await Nail 69's call for a pick-up. After completion of refueling, the Jollys went into an orbit at twelve thousand feet, with Sandy 9 and his wingman serving as protective air cover.

Shortly afterward, the low Jolly announced he had a transmission leak that required him to return to base. He was in no immediate danger, but declared his plane unfit for the mission and headed back to exchange his helo for another. Upon hearing that, the TUOC scrambled the alert Jolly to replace the returning helo, but it wouldn't arrive for fifty minutes. Now, the second Jolly was promoted to low Jolly, and the one to attempt a pick-up today. Guess who?

Jolly 9 was again in the hot seat for the second time in a twelve-hour period after he thought he was just going to be the back-up Jolly today. He didn't feel comfortable being low Jolly again and felt fate was about to deal him a brutal deathblow. He knew no one would criticize him if he passed the low lead to the third Jolly, but he also knew in his heart that Streetcar 304 had a better chance at survival if he made the rescue attempt. Without hesitation, Jolly 9 stepped up to the plate.

Jolly 9 was a deeply religious and devout Christian with total faith in God. He couldn't let another pilot down, so he resigned himself to the fate God would deal him. He'd do his best to rescue Streetcar, or die trying. Jolly 9 said a quick prayer and then left his fate, and that of his crew, in God's hands.

Meanwhile, I'd finished drinking and refilling my water bottle. The sun fully illuminated the clearing now, and I could readily see several hundred feet in all directions. I knelt and tried to meticulously scan each tree, shrub, and brush pile for any nearby sign of enemy activity. Over the next several minutes, I saw none.

I looked up at the sky and watched as a small, white, puffy cumulus cloud floated into the area. Were more on the way? Would the bad weather hold off till I was rescued? I wondered how many enemy troops had been killed because of my situation, and complimented myself for still being alive. But, heck, I'd almost forgotten about Sandy 7. Had he made it through the night?

I hadn't yet tried to contact him this morning, so in a whisper, I called Sandy 7. Nothing. I tried again, this time a little louder. Again, nothing. I decided to risk it and talk in a loud voice. With authority, I again called for him to come up on the radio. No answer. The thought of Sandy 7's fate was uncomfortable for me. If he'd been captured, he most likely was being physically abused right now, and that was not a pleasant thought for someone who thought it was his fault. I felt like dog shit.

About 7 A.M., I heard a loud chopping sound on the far side of the clearing. Each time the ax blade hit wood, its sound echoed, making it difficult to accurately judge the distance but it appeared to be only seventy-five yards away and slightly downhill. Troops were again nearby, and I suspected it might be the ten-man platoon from the night before.

In a matter of minutes, I heard a different but also distinctive sound from the valley in the opposite direction. A motorboat of some type had just started its engine. I looked down the hill and strained to see the river, but a morning fog obliterated my view of the valley floor. However, I was pleasantly surprised to see that I was indeed on a high ridge, about six to seven hundred feet above the valley.

The boat engine's roar echoed up from the valley and gave me a good indication of the distance to the river. It was a half click or less away, and that was good to know. Quickly, I took a compass bearing on the sound. A heading of 155 degrees would take me to the river, so if I didn't get rescued today, I could try and make it there tonight. I listened as the boat got underway and headed down river, and my mind meandered. I had destroyed a barge with my first-run bombs, and hopefully most of its contents, and had at least diminished the amount of supplies being shuttled down river. But was that worth the life of Sandy 7?

Sandy 7's day got off to a bad start. A soft, warm, morning sunbeam had made it through a small opening in the treetop crown and was shining directly on Sandy 7's face while he dozed, strapped to the tree. It dried his face from the previous night's rain and then its heat made small beads of sweat form and trickle down his forehead. One bead trickled into the cavity of an eye, and the salt sting woke Sandy. Immediately, his body lurched forward in fright when he realized he'd dozed off. If not for the tie-down line, he would've fallen out of the tree. He looked straight down. Had the enemy seen the piece of bark he had dislodged from the tree?

No one was running toward his tree. But this morning's scene was different from the day before. Sandy rubbed the sleep from his eyes and looked again. He was ecstatic. It appeared the enemy soldiers were packing up in preparation for breaking camp. It was hard to contain his excitement as he visualized how he'd soon be calling Crown.

During the next thirty minutes, most of the camp packed up and left en masse. A few stragglers remained, and Sandy began a game of counting down the number remaining in his view. First thirty, then twenty, then only five to go. . . .

From his view above, Sandy watched with dismay as the last five men approached and loitered at the base of his tree. They were all dressed in khaki uniforms. *Just my luck,* he thought, *North Vietnamese army regulars.* But soon it appeared they, too, were leaving, when each of them grabbed a backpack, shouldered a rifle, and began to walk away. At the very last moment, some idle talk occurred, and one of the older soldiers sauntered over to Sandy's tree. He sat down, removed an AK-47 from his shoulder, and lay flat on the ground with his head resting against the base of the tree. Deftly, he rolled a cigarette, lit it, and took several puffs as he faced straight ahead while talking to another soldier. Sandy 7 stared down at his face for what seemed an eternity. The small cigarette was nearly gone, and Sandy thought the ordeal was about over when, all of a sudden, the bad guy rolled his eyes up the tree trunk as if he'd heard something. Maybe a bird, as Sandy hadn't moved an inch. Sandy could see the man's eyes clearly now. Could he see Sandy's eyes? Yes! Sandy recoiled back against the tree trunk in fear as the gomer leapt to his feet while raising the AK-47 to a chest-high firing position. Sandy was staring directly down the gun barrel as he first saw white flashes and heard the loud burst of exploding bullets. They struck the tree trunk just above Sandy's head, and he flinched and tried to move, but couldn't because he was tied down. For a split second he thought he was a goner. Then he felt a hot searing pain along the side of his right cheek. He touched the area and found it bloody. A bullet had just grazed him. Miraculously, the AK-47 jammed at that moment, and Sandy watched as the gomer tried to clear the jam. A bullet tumbled out, and the rifle was again being raised. *He's going to kill me!*

Suddenly, shouting troops ran toward the tree from all directions, and the gomer who'd fired was restrained. Sandy saw at least six rifles pointing up at him, so he did, for him, the absolute unthinkable. Never in his wildest dreams did he think he ever would: he threw up his arms in a surrender pose. Immediately, arms beckoned, no, directed him to climb down the tree. Thoroughly pissed at himself, he unfastened his tie-down and started down. Somehow, he got down from his perch without falling, but winced when his broken foot hit the ground. He was grabbed and held by two soldiers while a third removed his survival vest and searched his pockets. The smaller soldiers appeared intimidated by his six-foot, four-inch height and nervously talked to each other as he was restrained. Then they led him away from the tree. At first it felt like he wouldn't be able to walk on the broken ankle, but he was firmly pushed from behind with the pointy end of a rifle, so he hobbled quickly.

They took him to the main camp a couple hundred feet away, and Sandy was surprised at the amount of equipment and men still there. First, they tied his legs together so he couldn't run, and then they tied his arms behind his back. After that, he was allowed to sit on a log while the senior officers conferred off to the side. He found it very disconcerting when they gestured toward him and wondered if they were discussing imprisonment or instant death by firing squad.

One of his guards was smoking so Sandy motioned to indicate he wanted a smoke, and amazingly one was skillfully rolled tightly and placed in his mouth. With that, another soldier who spoke some English walked closer, and he and Sandy began to talk. During a short conversation, Sandy was willingly told that these soldiers were part of a North Vietnamese army division that had withdrawn from Khe Sanh. The soldier further stated, "Our division was cut to pieces by the American war planes, and we retreated here to regroup and re-supply before moving out again for the South."

Sandy 7 slowly inhaled the last of the little cigarette just before he saw the ranking officers headed toward him. At that moment, Sandy 7 heard the sound of a small plane and wondered if Nail was coming back to just look for him, or for Streetcar, too. *I hope the Navy guy got rescued so this damn mission was worth something,* he thought. Then he steeled himself for the unknown.

Around 7:30 A.M., the sound of a plane's engine jarred me into looking up. Damn it, the weather had gone downhill a little. The cloud base was only four to five thousand feet above me and the stratus layer had darkened, but I saw Nail's O-2 plane several miles to the east. It was at a lower altitude than any O-2 I'd seen since I got shot down. After Nail 66 left yesterday, most of his replacement Nails had cautiously flown over me around five or six thousand feet, but this one was below the cloud base, and no higher than 2,500 feet. I then heard the sound of another prop at a higher altitude, above the clouds.

I feared my last radio battery might be near depletion so I decided to wait until the Nail expanded his search pattern and flew directly overhead before I made my first morning contact with him. I knew he'd be antsy to confirm my status, but I'd make him wait. It wouldn't hurt to let the Air Force sweat a little before letting them know I'd survived the night. For the next twenty minutes or so, I didn't make a peep as Nail droned back and forth to the east and south of me, out of my radio's range.

During that time, it was quiet around me. In fact, it was too quiet, and I heard neither bird sounds nor animal screams. Soon, though, I heard a noise off to my left, down the hill, but not one associated with normal jungle sounds. The noise was getting closer.

At first the sound was almost a knock, but it changed to metal banging against metal. I heard the knock again, followed by a rattling combination of knock and metal clanging. Okay, it hit me: water bottles were clanging against each other, and two men were talking back and forth. *Crap, here they come again. I didn't escape them after all.* Two men, maybe more, were closing on me from the south about fifty feet away. Quickly, I considered my options. Retreating to the rear didn't thrill me, as that was where I'd evaded the bad guys the night before. I couldn't risk moving straight ahead, as that was where the earlier chopping had occurred. I had no way of knowing which direction the gomers would take after they passed me. Moving to my right would again put me closer to the enemy gun sites and base camp. Before I decided, the voices were nearly on top of me.

There was no time to run. I pounced on the ground in a stretched out firing position toward the voices and adjusted my arms to steady my pistol. *Don't twitch a muscle!* My pistol hand was quivering, so I anchored my elbow and used the other hand to steady my aim while I cocked the hammer. I sighted down the length of the three-inch barrel toward the closest voice. *Aw, crap!* I saw a dirt trail about eighteen inches wide that I hadn't seen until now, and the gomers were walking on it. It was less than ten feet away, with dense foliage between it and my position, but since I could clearly see it, that meant anyone who stopped there and looked my way might see me.

The gomer out front was talking non-stop. I stared toward the voice. Then, I saw a body from the waist down. A black-clad Pathet Lao walked into view about thirty degrees left of my gun aim-line. I was eye-level with his ankles, could see his black rubber sandals, and looked up at the side of his face. He was beaming, as if in a chuckle, and he seemed full of vim and vigor. He wasn't wearing his helmet and had a rifle slung over his right shoulder. Both arms were stretched out to his sides and bent at the elbow, and his hands steadied a single pole that lay across the back of his neck and rested on his shoulders. From each end of the pole, a water bottle dangled and sloshed. As he closed within ten feet, I anxiously watched to see if his eyes rolled my way. If they did, and if he dropped his bottles, I would shoot and ask questions later. But at the closest point his head dropped slightly as the guy behind him picked up the conversation, and he didn't glance my way. Just like that, he was out of sight, and I was temporarily out of danger. How many more?

A few seconds passed before the next gomer appeared, and everything about him was identical to the first. They looked like twins. Same age, same height, same type rifle, and he also walked by without turning his head toward me.

I realized I'd been holding my breath and could no longer do so. I exhaled quietly and then slowly sucked a deep breath. Is that all of them? I lay motionless and listened for several minutes as the two trudged off to my right toward the chopping noise. Slowly, their voices melded in with the sound of the wind rustling the trees, and they were gone, out of sight, out of voice range. After a long sigh of relief, I sat upright. At that point, I couldn't contain my bladder any longer. All the excitement had gotten to me, so I relieved myself on the spot. I rolled to my side, unzipped my trouser fly, and let it flow. Quickly, I covered the liquid with dirt.

I was frustrated. What else can happen? Why don't they send some special ops teams to take care of these guys? What kind of frapping war are we fighting where the enemy walks brazenly in the open, talking freely and openly re-supplying at will, with no fear of being engaged, except by aviators?

Chapter 22

FAST-MOVERS HAMMER
THE GUNS

For about twenty minutes after the two gomers walked by, I listened to the sporadic, faint sound of Nail 69's small plane. He was executing a box search in an attempt to contact me. He started at the river, and slowly expanded his search to the west, but was too far away for my weak radio battery so I didn't even have it on. Finally, in the distance, I saw the white underbelly of an O-2 plane at about 2,500 feet against the backdrop of a gray-colored cumulus cloud. Nail was very low, but I heard no guns firing. A trick—the gunners were waiting for the Jollys? Or, maybe they had had enough? Which way was it? Were the enemy gunners out of ammo, and out of the fight, or were they simply sucking the Jollys into a trap? The O-2 droned by, left to right, about two miles away, and then disappeared. I couldn't tell if he continued straight ahead or was in a turn, but I'd waited long enough. It was time to get the ball rolling so I called Nail. Crown answered instead.

"Roger, Streetcar. Good morning, this is Crown. We thought we'd lost you there for a while since Nail couldn't raise you. What's your status, and have you heard from Sandy 7? Over."

"Roger, Crown. I'm shit hot, and just saw a Nail fly past. I've had no contact with Sandy 7 since five minutes after he went down, over."

"Roger, Streetcar. We're ready to start today's process of getting you out. Are you still in the same position? Over."

"Negative, Crown. I think I'm about three hundred meters in the direction of Las Vegas from my position last night. It appears to be a much better area for pick-up since I'm on higher ground. But, be cautious Crown. Bad guys are all around. Ten chased me last night, two walked by a few minutes ago, and I hear several voices a hundred yards west. During the rescue attempt last night, I saw enemy troops in the treetops, and they fired AK-47s at planes as they pulled off the target, over."

"Roger, Streetcar. Sit tight and I'll get back to you, out." Crown then notified everyone of my status, and my brief about the treetop gunners.

Immediately, Blue Chip scrambled two flights of fighters, call signs Honda and Cobalt. Four more Sandys scrambled to join Sandy 9's two at the Jolly holding pattern. Every eight minutes, more fighters would take off to be in position for their turn at the AAA sites. Two more Sandys remained on runway alert at NKP to scramble when the rescue attempt was imminent.

About then, Sandy 9 called Crown from about twenty miles away from me, where he was protecting the Jollys. Sandy stated it would be impossible to see a single gomer high in a tree, and the Jollys would be shot down. "Fast-movers won't hack it against treetop gunners. I recommend we use the gas immediately," Sandy 9 urged.

Crown concurred with Sandy 9 and passed the recommendation to Blue Chip, who responded immediately. "Negative on the use of CS for now. Use the fast-movers to knock out the AAA, and then have the Jollys pick up the survivor." The staff weenies made it sound so easy. Blue Chip was more prudent today, though. The two Spads with Juicy Fruit on alert at NKP were scrambled to rendezvous with the Jollys, but were not granted final clearance to spray.

"Streetcar 304, this is Crown. Are you familiar with an airborne, released agent that will temporarily put you out of action? Over."

"Crown, Streetcar. I'm familiar with the agent and have no objection to its use. Whatever it takes to get me out, over."

"Roger, Streetcar. Before use, we'll positively locate you first so we can make a quick rescue, over."

"Whatever," I answered.

It really surprised me that they considered the use of a gas agent. Our Spook had recently briefed us on its basics so I was somewhat familiar. It was new to the combat zone, and there was no known use of it during a rescue of any Navy pilot, so the Spook couldn't tell us much more. I didn't know all of the specifics, but did know that it wouldn't kill me. (I found out later it makes you feel like you want to die for a thirty-minute period.)

Meanwhile, the weather condition appeared shaky. It was still sunny directly overhead, but some nearby puffy, grayish cumulus clouds worried me. They seemed to be drifting toward me. Unknown to me, Sandy 9's section and the Jollys were orbiting in and out of light rain and clouds twenty miles away. They thought the rain was headed my way, so the additional Sandys and Spads that had scrambled minutes earlier were directed to expedite before the mission was scrubbed for weather.

After Crown and I talked, Nail 69 knew I was still alive, and my approximate new position, so he started to execute his plan for creating a safe pathway for the Jollys. He meticulously selected the specific AAA sites that he needed to take out to clear the path. Then he asked for two fast-movers to start knocking out his selected targets. Crown told him to hold off a minute. The additional four Sandys and two Spads had just arrived from NKP, and Crown told them to hold with and protect the two Jollys. Sandy 9 was then given an order; "Fly over Streetcar 304 and confirm his precise location before the fighters start bombing and kill him by mistake."

At 8 A.M., Sandy 9 was still leery that I was being used as bait for a trap, so he insisted that Crown have me authenticate before he and his wingman flew into the area.

"Streetcar, this is Crown. Give me the name of your dog, over." Quickly, I keyed the mike. "Daisy, like Daisy Mae, over."

"Stand by, 304." His transmission was so weak I feared my final battery had just about shot its wad, so I turned the radio off for about ten minutes till I heard the sound of an A-1's engine.

Quickly, I turned the radio on and pressed RECEIVE. Sure 'nuff, Sandy 9 was calling me for specific landmarks around my area. I described the ridgeline I was on, and the specific tree that was nearby. During the next fifteen minutes, he made several passes near my vicinity, and I heard his plane several times, but only saw him once, a mile away. Each time he got closer, I heard lots of AAA booming to the north and northeast of my position so I advised him of that. Sandy 9 said he knew where I was, but I doubted that. I turned my radio off again because Sandy seemed to have trouble hearing me, and it was difficult to hear him. I would be in a hell of a mess if my last battery went completely dead.

Sandy 9 departed the area, and informed Crown that I was a good distance south of the ground fire of yesterday and was in a much better position for rescue. "Lay in some fighters with ordnance and see what happens, Crown."

Nail 69 was told, "Have at 'em."

I lay on the ground, and listened for the sound of enemy activity. I'd been on the radio with Crown and Sandy far more than I felt comfortable, and still had the enemy radio directional finder from yesterday in the back of my mind. I could still hear a chopping noise and several voices a hundred yards across the clearing, but they weren't getting closer. Shortly, I heard the mild drone of an O-2's engine, and deduced Nail would soon fly over me for the first time today. I waited till he was maybe a mile away, and then turned the radio on.

"Sandy, this is Nail 69. Are you sure you talked to him right around this area? He's not answering."

I broke in before Sandy could answer. "Nail, this is Streetcar, over."

"Ahh, Roger, Streetcar 304, this is Nail 69er. You scared me there for a minute. I thought we might have waited too long. It's my turn to try and get you out, and I'll begin by wiping out most of the AAA, but first, I have to pinpoint your exact position, over."

The new guy's voice inflection was drawn out, but sounded so positive that I thought he didn't have a clue about what was in store for him today. More clouds were popping up like corn overhead so I couldn't waste time with chitchat because of the weak battery and declining weather. I took the initiative.

"Understand, Nail 69. To expedite spotting me, I'm going to give you a short count for an ADF steer to my position. Get ready." Then, I paused before counting. "One, two, three, four, five; five, four, three, two, one, over."

"Roger, Streetcar, got it. I'm turning toward you now. Be advised, it sounds as if your battery is weak. Your short count was breaking up. Change your battery, over."

"Negative, Nail. I'm on my last battery so you best hurry, out."

I heard Nail's engine increase in rpm, and it also sounded like he went into a shallow dive. In about thirty seconds, I looked toward the engine sound and saw the plane at about 2,500 feet over the tall trees to the east where I'd spent the night.

"I've got you in sight, Nail. Drop your right wing to confirm, over."

"Dipping now, Streetcar."

"Roger, Nail. I've got you. Look off your starboard wing-tip about sixty degrees down for a small clearing on a ridgeline with a tree sticking up in the middle, over."

"Roger, Streetcar. Talk to me in Air Force terms, over."

"Off your right wing, check for a tree in the middle of a clearing on a ridgeline, over."

"Roger, Streetcar. I think I have the ridge but I'm too high to see a lone tree. Wait one till I take it out and drop down about a thousand feet and then I'll be back."

As he flew past, I heard him reduce power and start a descending turn. But, his heading would place him near the river and well within range of the multiple guns along the karst opposite the river. I had doubts about whether he would make it back if he descended too close to the karst.

Nail 69 looked back continually over his left shoulder as he flew toward the river, intent on not losing sight of my ridgeline. Suddenly, from his higher position, his wingman's voice crackled over the air. "Watch out, 69, you're really getting hosed."

Nail 69's head snapped for a frontal view. Tracers were soaring past his plane's nose. "Dumb shit," he screamed. Rapidly, he added full power and commenced a right hand turn. Then, he glanced at his altimeter. "You stupid clown," he shouted in frustration. Unknowingly, he had allowed his plane to descend to 1,000 feet, and he prayed that the guns would miss him.

The guns fired for another thirty seconds and then, for some strange reason, stopped their fire even though he was still in range. As Nail flew back toward me, he noticed that the weather had started to worsen, and the cloud bases were between 4,000 and 5,000 feet. He realized he didn't have much time before another weather abort. After leveling at 2,500 feet, he asked that I hit him with my signal mirror when I had a visual. In a few seconds, my mirror cast a beam on his cockpit side door.

"Streetcar, piece of cake—got you, buddy. I see your position, but I'm going to keep flying this heading until out of sight to confuse the enemy, and then I'll turn and fly over you once more to confirm the exact tree, out."

Damn, it felt good to be talking to a Nail again, but for the umpteenth time I was talking to a new Nail pilot, and one who hadn't been in our fight yet. However, he was flying low and really hanging it out below a scattered cloud layer. This new guy, Nail 69, was either very stupid or very brave.

During the past thirty-seven hours, I first worked with Nail 66, and he returned again the morning of day two. I knew him well and liked the way he worked. Following that, I worked with Nails 35 and 13, followed by 56 and 24, followed by 58 and 15 and 28 at the end of day two, I think. It was a little difficult to keep them all straight. Nail 56 had been the first in the area in the morning, but now Nail 69 was overhead and his wingman might be 58, but I wasn't sure. I needed a scorecard to keep up with all the Nails and Sandys.

"Streetcar, Nail 69 is inbound toward your position. I know the ridgeline you're on, but I need to know the exact tree you're next to because I'm going to put the bombs very close today. Give me a smoke when you see me, over."

Utter B.S.; here we go again. Another pilot wants to see a smoke. I wondered if this guy would ask for a smoke if he was bumping into as many bad guys as I had seen.

"Nail, no smoke till I see the Jolly inbound, can't risk it with troops nearby, and I can't be on the radio for any length of time because of enemy homing equipment. I'll give you a signal mirror if you want it, over."

"Roger, Streetcar, we'll try it your way." Ah, his voice inflection just changed. Nail 69 sounded a little hacked off, but I didn't give a rat's ass. He had just entered the fight, and didn't even have a little picture yet of the amount of enemy gunfire and troops in the area. Once he got the big picture, I was sure he'd understand my logic.

I heard him approaching again, and looked to the southeast over the tall trees. His plane sounded close but wasn't visible. Its white fuselage was camouflaged against the white clouds that were rolling in from that direction. When I finally spotted him, it looked as if he had descended to fifteen hundred feet.

All right, this guy did have big balls. I listened for the gunfire to start blasting at him, but none did. I waited until he was nearly overhead, and then told him I was just off his right tip. "Stand by, Nail. Hack, hack, hack." Quickly, I hit him with the mirror beam again.

"Streetcar, I've got the tree positively located, so stand fast while we wipe out the AAA. I've got enough fast-movers to bomb all day if need be, so dig yourself a deep hole. The bombs are going to be really, really close today, dude."

"Copy, Nail."

Did he really see the tree? No frapping way! This guy was shooting me a bunch of bull. To his credit, though, he was the first to fly low enough to ID a tree, so I had only one thought. *Show me your stuff, big guy.*

Nail 69 had a lot of concern about the increasing cloud layers and descending ceiling. It would greatly affect bomb accuracy, and the last thing he wanted to do was to kill me with friendly fire. The fast-movers would have to be carefully positioned atop the clouds, dive through them blindly, and bust out around 4,500 feet. After bomb release, they would bottom out between 500 and 1,000 feet. Not many pilots could do that accurately, but Nail took that into consideration. He would only allow the seasoned flight leaders to bomb when the runs got closer to me. Still, being a betting man, Nail gave me a fifty-fifty chance of surviving his bomb blitz. (Years later, I heard a rumor that Nail 69 had been told to get me out, dead or alive. He only chuckles when I try to pin him down.)

Crown's watch indicated 8:25. He heard Nail say he was ready to lay in some bombs, so he requested the last two Sandys to scramble from NKP. Sandy 9 and 10 would provide high cover for Nail 69, while four more Sandys and two Spads orbited with the Jollys. There were eight Sandys airborne, and the third, replacement Jolly had just arrived in holding with the other two.

Nail 69 hadn't been in the area on either of the two previous days so he had yet to see any of the big guns, but he had a plan. He would lay in some GP bombs on the karst across the river and the first AAA gun to fire would receive CBUs from the next plane to attack. Then, Nail would slowly walk more CBUs on a path toward Streetcar to wipe out all AAA sites along the way. The plan was simple. Lay down a circular ring of CBUs around Streetcar to kill all gun crews and troops within two miles of him. Cobalt, Honda, and Tomcat flights began to finally kick ass.

The first explosions I heard were distant, and I thought that Nail had really, really shot me a line of bull. He had the wrong location for my position. But, over the next half hour, I listened as the sound of explosions got closer and closer.

Unknown to me, a Raven FAC, flying an OV-10, was orbiting around the site some twenty-five miles away where the Jolly had landed with an emergency the night before. He was sent to determine the feasibility of another helo hoisting the downed Jolly back to base if the enemy hadn't destroyed it.

For an hour, I lay on my side listening to bombs and secondary explosions. At that point, I began to notice little opposition and heard only a sporadic, solitary crack of rifle fire in answer to a diving jet. It appeared to me that the enemy was devastated. Nail 69 agreed and told Crown that it shouldn't be much longer before the Jollys could be brought in. Nail said he had a definite visual on my position within two meters at map location Xray Delta 241388, and he asked Crown to advise the Sandys of same.

Nail 69 called and casually asked how things were going. It sounded like he just wanted to be sure I was still around. I tried to be cool.

"Oh, it's going okay, I guess. How much longer?"

He replied he was walking the bombs toward me—which I knew from the sound—and I would know when it was nearly time for the pick-up because the bombs would get really close.

"By the way 304, are you familiar with a gas agent?"

"Yes, Crown briefed me," I replied.

"Don't worry," he said. "I won't let them use it unless I can actually see you on the ground."

Almost coincidentally with that, I got my first glimpse of a fast-mover in its bomb run about a half-mile away. While watching it, I realized the sky was a solid overcast now. As a fast-mover pilot, I understood the complexity of what was happening. Because of the weather, it would be very easy for a fighter to fly into the ground by mistake, get shot down, or kill me.

All of a sudden, I heard a jet whistling down the chute, and it was the first one today to sound like it was coming right at me. I looked up just as a Thud popped out of the clouds, dipped his wing quickly about ten degrees, and then leveled again for several seconds. He pulled up sharply, and I saw bombs eject from the plane. I watched as he continued to mush toward the ground even though his nose was above the horizon. The Thud seemed to be in slow motion as he bottomed out about five hundred feet above the ground. *Boom* went the afterburner, and all I could see was the ass-end of the Thud as it finally started to climb.

All of a sudden, an automatic weapon opened up, no more than seventy-five feet away in the tree line off my left shoulder. My head jerked that direction. Because of a similar encounter the evening before, I already knew to scan the tree trunk to spot the gunner. For just a few brief seconds, I saw him bracing an AK-47 while sitting on a limb on the opposite side of the tree. As I watched, he fired another, longer burst. I turned to check the Thud, and it appeared to be hanging in mid-air. I cringed. It was still climbing, and well within range when the gunner fired for the third time. My teeth clenched—I'd had enough.

Without hesitation, I rose to one knee and aimed my pistol toward the tree gunner. At that moment he moved slightly and the tree trunk blocked my view. Try as I might, I couldn't see him. For fully a minute, I watched for any movement or noise. Nothing. The gunner sat completely immobile and obscured on the far side of the tree. Had he seen me when I rose? I stretched out in a prone position toward the tree, resting on my elbows, pistol aimed. I had to kill the gunner before the Jollys arrived, or we would both be dead meat.

As the Thud pilot climbed out, he felt a slight thud somewhere in the airframe. One of the Sandy pilots heard him advise his wingman he'd been hit and needed visual verification of damage. The wingie determined that his leader had taken a round right through one wing, but it was negligible damage. At that moment, many of the Sandy pilots cringed in fear. If the fast-movers couldn't avoid the enemy fire, what chance did their slower, Korean War–vintage A-1s have?

"Nail 69, this is Streetcar. It appears the enemy AAA gunfire has been suppressed. But, I just saw another gomer fire an AK-47 at the last Thud from a nearby treetop along the north side of the ridge. I say again, enemy troops are in the northern tree line, so make damn sure the Jollys know this, over."

Nail 69 rogered and very casually said he had only one more troublesome 57 to take out and then he'd deal with the tree gunner. Nail said the 57 was a little north of me, and the bombs might get close, but I shouldn't worry. He knew my exact location. Ringo flight attacked next and drew some 37 fire. The ground again rumbled, and I heard booms reverberating from the valley beyond the ridge.

By that time I was really impressed with Nail 69, even though I could tell he was a typical cocky, smooth-talking Air Force puke. He had a slow, methodical manner, with no apparent excitement in his voice. And he was forthright. But I still liked him, and maybe I was no different except for being Navy. Maybe I sounded the same way to him. Maybe none of the Air Force guys liked me from the tone of my voice. Screw 'em, they still had to rescue me, even if they didn't like the way I talked.

Around 9 A.M., they had yet to kill—or even subdue—the fire from the northern 57 gun, and everyone was getting antsy about the weather. After a Tomcat flight socked the 57 site one more time, Crown asked the Sandys to give him an evaluation. Sandy 9 had been closely observing the situation and knew that most guns right around me had been knocked out. But he wanted it completely sterile.

"Crown, it looks like we've hurt 'em bad, so we may be able to work around the hot 57, but Nail has to clear the treetops of all gunners around the survivor. Have him keep pounding while I move the Jollys to a closer initial point (IP) position."

Jolly 9 and his wingman then broke orbit, escorted by four Sandys. From twenty miles away, they flew through a heavy rainstorm under a cloud base as low as 200 to 800 feet in order to reach an IP orbit just eight miles south of me. Once there, the visibility below the clouds was excellent. The third Jolly remained in the original holding pattern, protected by the gas Spads.

Within a few minutes, though, Blue Chip impatiently stepped in again and passed another direct order to Crown: "Commence rescue attempt immediately. Put the F-105s in first, followed by the Sandys with smoke, and then the Jollys."

Sandy 9 couldn't believe his ears! He was livid and infuriated at the gall of Blue Chip. Staff officers, hundreds of miles away in Saigon, were giving orders as if they were on-scene commanders. Sandy's temples nearly exploded in rage. . . .

Chapter **23**

JOLLY TO THE RESCUE

ommence rescue immediately . . . Nail 69, like Sandy 9, thought
the order from Blue Chip was ill timed. Nail was only a captain,
but today rank had no privilege, and he wasn't about to let anyone's death be on his shoulders. He transmitted in a loud, firm voice.

"This is Nail 69. Negative on that, we're not going in yet. I've got a
visual on Streetcar, and there's still one hot gun site to the north. We
need to knock it out before risking the Jollys."

No one rebutted Nail, so he continued to pound the 57. But more
and more gun sites started to open up in the north quadrant and that
could have meant a deadly delay. Sandy 9 made a circular pass around
the entire area and verified that the only remaining big threat was in
that quadrant.

"Nail, I can bring the rescue formation in from the south and
avoid most of the fire," Sandy reported. Nail 69 agreed, but he would
first neutralize the treetop gunner near me.

The next few minutes of action were something to behold, as Nail
walked bombs closer and closer to my position. Trees shattered and
fell, animals screamed, the ground rumbled beneath me. It was quite
obvious that a rescue attempt was imminent, and I really got pumped
up. Since I hadn't yet spotted the treetop gunner, I assumed he had left
the tree. So, in my exuberance, I sat up and watched the Air Force
blast a path through the jungle. I was in a great spot for pick-up, and
it should occur any minute. I vowed to sit right where I was until
it happened.

Abruptly, though, my confidence was utterly shattered. I heard a
number of voices off my left shoulder in the tree line where I'd seen
the tree gunner, less than a hundred feet away. My head snapped

toward the sound. Staring through the brush, I got a glimpse of two, maybe three, black-clad men darting along the tree line. Instantly, I sank down and hugged the ground. Damn it, the Pathet Lao squad from the night before had found me again. From their frenzy, I immediately recognized that troops were now taking up defensive positions near me. They were excitedly talking back and forth so they too must have expected a Jolly any minute. In a whisper, I called Nail 69.

"Nail, this is Streetcar. Enemy troops are about seventy-five feet away in the same tree line on the west side of the ridge where the treetop gunner is located, over."

"Streetcar, they're next on the agenda. We'll be hitting them with CBUs on the first pass and then 20 mike-mike, so it may get hairy. You're in harm's way, so dig a deep hole, and keep your ass down, out."

CBUs within a hundred feet? My heart really began to thump. Nail 69 knew this was an iffy bomb run, and I knew it, too. Bombing accuracy was seriously degraded by the weather conditions, and the Air Force jocks were probably no better than I. A normal, good circular error probability (CEP) with general-purpose bombs was about seventy-five feet in 1968. The pilot could make a great run, but a little thing like a bent bomb fin might still make the bomb err by seventy-five feet or even more.

Frantically, I bounced to my knees. Hopefully, I had time to dig a small hole. As I rapidly scooped dirt with both hands, I uttered a short prayer out loud. "God, let this next jock be the most accurate Top Gun in his squadron, for one run."

Nail 69 had the same thought. Before clearing him hot, Nail verified the F-4 pilot who was to roll in next was not a junior wingman, nor nugget. He was the flight leader, very experienced, and this final bomb run would complete his one hundredth mission. Unknown to me, Crown then told Sandy 9 that his slow-movers were cleared for action after two more fighter bomb runs. Nail also advised Sandy through Crown that four Thuds would be blasting AAA sites to the north of Streetcar as a diversion while the Sandys and Jollys rushed in for the pickup.

Holy cow, less than a minute after Nail's CBU advisory, a Willy Pete rocket whistled in and impacted about mid-length along the tree line where the enemy squad was positioned. That meant a fast-mover was on the perch, and I hadn't yet dug deeper than two inches. My only hope was to watch for the jet to bust out of the clouds and make sure he was on the right heading before bomb release. I was on both knees, with the radio mike within an inch of my mouth, my right thumb in a ready position on the transmit button in case I needed to talk fast. Did I have enough battery juice?

I cocked my head just slightly to better hear an inbound jet. Within seconds I heard the engine whining as the jet screamed down the tube toward me. I stared toward the sound but saw only puffy, gray clouds over the far edge of the clearing.

Quickly, I turned to the left to check Nail's smoke, and it was billowing straight up through the trees and not toward me. That was good. I looked back at the clouds. Just then, a Phantom's nose ripped the clouds apart, allowing the pilot to see the ground. Shit-hot, his line-up was perfect. Within two seconds, though, he made a heading correction. His left wing dropped. Damn it, why did he do that? The F-4's pointy nose was aimed right at me instead of the smoke. Holy cow, he was going to bomb me instead of the tree line. I had only another second or two before bombs away! In a panic, I put a death grip on the transmit button and screamed.

"F-4, this is Streetcar. You're lined up left and heading toward me. Abort your run. Abort, abort, abort."

For just a moment, it appeared I had reacted in time as the Phantom's nose rose upward. But suddenly, I saw space between the plane's wing and a black object. The jet was climbing, but a bomb was falling directly at me. *Oh, shit, clear the pattern, I've got to run and get outside the bomb's burst path.* In one quick bound, I was up on my feet and running. Thoroughly disgusted, I screamed out loud in total frustration. "Is the whole frapping world in cahoots to kill me?" I said it loud enough that the gomers must have heard me, but I no longer cared. I was ticked off and felt like lashing out at everyone. I didn't care because it no longer mattered. It didn't matter because the gomers and I were about to die unless I could get my ass at least seventy-five feet from the projected center of the burst pattern. I was on my toes and running to the right as I stared at the falling bomb over my left shoulder.

Everything momentarily seemed in slow motion. The black bomb stood out clearly against the white backdrop of the lightly colored clouds. I saw the bomb's conical shape, saw its nose start to rise, and then it snapped open and looked like a half-open clam shell. The top half panel went sailing backward. Oh no, a frapping CBU. In a flash, hundreds of baseball-sized bomblets sprang outward like a circular fireworks burst pattern. The sky darkened, and the bomblets hurtled through the air directly at me. My brain was in afterburner. *Hurry, run out of the pattern to the side!*

Maybe it was because of my injury, but I never felt so slow in all my life. My legs felt like lead. I ran harder toward my and Nail's tree, needing to reach the other side before the bomblets reached me.

About five seconds after the pod opened, I heard multiple explosions in the woods off my left shoulder. I didn't have to look; all hell was about to break loose. In a split second, the explosions passed through the woods and now, in quick succession, were speeding across the clearing toward me. Within three seconds, I sensed the explosions were nearly on top of me and I wouldn't make it out of the blast pattern. *Dive to the tree trunk for protection.* So, with all I had, I dived the final six feet.

The explosions raced past me as I sailed in midair toward the tree, stretched out fully but slightly rolling. I felt a concussion blow to my belly, and then a stabbing pain hit me several times in quick succession. I landed on my side with a burning pain in several spots on my body and knew immediately that I had taken shrapnel damage.

I lay flat on the ground with my nose buried in the loamy soil and listened to the final few seconds of explosions. Then I heard the thunderous roar of the F-4 as he climbed past about five hundred feet overhead. After rolling over to my side, I saw him in a sixty-degree climb, and I was genuinely happy he'd made it safely through his run. Just as I spotted him, the pilot rapidly banked forty-five degrees left, and I imagined he was looking back to check his BDA. *Good-bye, you turkey, thanks for all you've done.* (In retrospect, I owe my life to that heroic turkey.)

Amazingly, the radio and pistol were still tightly clutched in my hands even though my right hand was covered in blood. Immediately, my thoughts returned to the Pathet Lao squad in the tree line. I rolled, rose until both knees were planted on the ground, and turned to scan the tree line. Nothing was moving, but a haunting sound echoed from there. Someone was groaning in agony. For several seconds I listened warily, thinking it might be a trick, but then other men began to moan and wail. One seemed to desperately cry out for help. Was it a trick? At first I felt compassion, but my attitude quickly changed. I felt no remorse and hoped the bomb had mortally wounded the entire squad as payback for Sandy 7.

I felt dizzy so I sat down and lowered my head to rest on my knees. My body felt very warm from the side of my left thigh all the way across to the right buttock. I looked down and saw that my pants were dark red. Only a minute or so had passed since being hit, but my fatigue pants were already soaked with blood around my groin. Blood had also seeped through the right pant leg just below the knee. The amount, and speed, of blood that had soaked through in such a short time scared me. I could bleed to death before help arrived.

Then, a severe throbbing pain surged from my right foot, as if part of my foot might be missing. It hurt like heck so I leaned forward and twisted to inspect the bottom of the boot, expecting a portion to be missing, but couldn't do so because of groin pain. I leaned back and took a deep breath. *At least I'm alive for the moment.* I humbly looked skyward. "God, thanks for saving my butt."

Everything seemed tranquil. The sun was shining, and my mind seemed to be thought-free for the first time in several days. For a minute I just sat there, stunned. Then I started to look around again. The tree was about six feet away, so my dive had been short. Circular holes, about five feet in diameter and perfectly symmetrical, were in the dirt all around me with only twelve to eighteen inches of undisturbed soil between holes. Each hole had a scooped-out depth of about ten inches in the center. I sat between holes, completely surrounded by them, and I couldn't comprehend why I wasn't toast, killed by the shrapnel. I didn't move while I gathered my thoughts. After looking again at my bloody torso, I was shell-shocked. Was I going to die right here? Then I heard the moaning from the woods again. There was less than before. Other men were dying.

"Streetcar 304, this is Nail 69. Did you see that last CBU and did it neutralize the treetop gunners, over?" I looked up at the sky and put the radio very close to my lips.

"Nail, what the hell? I told the Phantom driver to abort his run, but he dropped the damn CBU right on top of me. I took a hit, so if you want to get me out alive, you better make it fast, or I'm going to bleed to death. Streetcar out."

"Streetcar, get your smoke ready. The Jolly is coming to get you, over."

"Right, Nail, I've heard that before."

Nail's initial response took me by surprise. That's it? That's all they were waiting on? All I had to do was tell them I'm injured and they send the Jolly in? If I had known that, I could have lied much earlier. But now, when and if the Jolly arrives, I might not be able to stand up due to the bomb injury. *Damn it, they can just hoist me up from where I'm now sitting!*

Nail's magic words about Jolly lifted me from my stupor. I grabbed my smoke flare and pen gun flare from the survival vest. I felt the nipples on the night end of the six-inch smoke flare, turned it around so that the day end was up, and then snapped the pop tab up slightly to a ready position. I was still seated and vowed to remain so until I heard the Jolly or Sandy engines because I wasn't sure all the enemy troops on my perimeter had been fully taken out. A disturbing thought kept recurring. *What if some of the gomers on the perimeter survived the CBU attack and are just waiting for the Jolly to enter a hover over my position so they can blast it out of the sky?* If I was in the open at that time, they also would probably shoot me. I needed to stay on my toes.

Jolly 9 had been observing the fast-mover bomb smoke from his position at the IP eight miles away, so he had a fairly good idea of the direction to my position. Following one ripple of CBU explosions, Jolly 9 heard me say I was hit. *Oh boy,* he thought. *This really rips it! What should I do?* The AAA was still active, and Sandy 9 hadn't yet assured him it was safe to enter the fray. Jolly 9 also knew he wouldn't be able to cope mentally if he lost me without going in once for a rescue attempt. It didn't take Jolly 9 more than a few seconds to make up his mind. If he didn't try now, he might as well just go home and write me off. He said one more short prayer out loud so his crew could hear.

"Lord, provide your protection for this crew today. Amen."

Then, he transmitted in a firm, positive tone to Sandy 9. "Jolly 9 can see the survivor's location and is going for the pickup. Sandy 9, pack 'em tight around me."

Sandy 9 didn't hesitate. "All Sandys, push 'em up and set 'em up." He pushed his power lever forward, set his mixture to rich, and armed his weapons.

Out of the blue, an anonymous Sandy pilot made a conciliatory transmission. "You don't have to go, Jolly."

"Jolly 9 is a positive go for pickup. All Sandys, join on me at the eight-mile IP."

Six Sandys had been pre-briefed to hurriedly form a protective cocoon around Jolly 9 on his call. Two more would remain at the eight-mile IP with the second backup Jolly, and the third Jolly would orbit at twenty miles with the two Spads.

Sandy 3 and his wingman, Sandy 8, were then in a very loose trail position behind Sandy 9's flight of four. After Sandy 9 increased speed, Sandy 3 dilly-dallied. Sandy 8 noticed that he and his leader, Sandy 3, were dropping farther behind the other four planes. After a few moments, Sandy 8 suggested that Sandy 3 should push it up to catch up. Sandy 3 only shook his head. Was there a problem? Sandy 8 then made a second advisory call and got the same response. At that point, Sandy 8 didn't know what the problem was, but he sharply broke away from his leader, added max power, and raced to join Sandy 9's flight of four. Sandy 3 lagged behind the group. Only five Sandys— pilots Campbell, Foster, Vaugn, Kuhlman, and Marrett—would protect Jolly 9 on his rescue attempt.

While watching the fast-mover bombing, Sandy 9 had meticu- lously plotted the enemy gun sites and smartly selected a route to my position that would keep Jolly 9 clear of them. Sandy 9 and his wing- man would lead Jolly 9 north, along the east side of the river, to swing around the heavily defended karst on its blind easterly side. At the same time, the three other Sandys would lay down a smoke screen along the west side of the same karst to neutralize the gunners on that side who were firing across the river toward my direction. Once Jolly 9 reached the northern edge of the karst, he would turn west to cross the river under cover of the Sandy smoke screen. Once across the river at a point one and a half clicks south of my position, Jolly would make his final dash due north, first through the valley of death, and then the final dash of a half-click up a ravine to the top of my ridge.

Jolly 9 looked back at his door gunners, "What's our motto?"

Back came the response, "That others might live."

"Okay. It's time, boys, let's go get him."

Jolly commenced a descent to twenty feet above the ground and headed north toward the karst. He set max power, and soon his air- speed maxed out at ninety-nine knots. Oh, how he wished for more speed. The five Sandys flew around him in a protective Luftberry Weave pattern, between 200 and 500 hundred feet at 220 knots air- speed. They weaved back and forth in front of Jolly's helo so one A-1 was in front at all times in case an enemy gun fired at Jolly. The gaggle was only eight miles from my position. In normal ops, that would take them about five minutes to reach me, but Sandy 9's circular route would take longer.

At that point, Sandy 9 called me with some smart advice. He instructed me to pop the night end of my smoke flare on his first call for smoke, and then pop the day end when I had Jolly in sight. Great idea—I hadn't thought of that. His procedure would give me two flares to work with, so I pushed the tab back down on the flare's day end and raised the one on the nippled night end.

Not long after Jolly left the IP, Crown finally received a transmission from Blue Chip authorizing the use of the gas agent, if all else failed. For now, Crown wouldn't clutter the airwaves with that info.

The gaggle was still six miles away when they picked up their first enemy automatic weapons' fire. From that point, the Sandys began to fight their way in, one enemy gun after another. Just then, another anonymous Sandy voice made a transmission, this time to me. He sounded blunt, callous, and spoke in a stern voice. It caught me totally off guard.

"Streetcar, unless your position is one hundred percent better than yesterday, you're going to have a dead Jolly crew on your hands today."

At first I was stunned, unable to reply. The threat implied I wasn't doing anything right. My pride was wounded, along with my body. I was furious.

"My position is excellent and much better than yesterday," I retorted. "If it's not good enough for you guys, I'll find a better one."

Later on, I was told by someone in passing that one of the radiomen in the back of the Crown plane keyed the intercom at that moment. "Streetcar must still be okay because he's giving Sandy hell."

For five minutes, Jolly 9 flew in and out of clouds. When clouds were in his flight path, Jolly 9 flew at two hundred feet and used them as protection. When he was out of the clouds, he flew at twenty feet above the ground. When they got close to the karst, three Sandys accelerated ahead and laid down the smokescreen along the west side while Sandy 9 and his wingman protected Jolly along the east side.

Ten excruciating minutes passed after Nail told me the Jolly was on the way, and I had yet to see or hear a single plane. Even Nail was nowhere in sight. I was still bleeding and felt like I'd been duped again. The gomers had finally ceased groaning, but I still didn't know if they were dead or faking it.

Jolly 9 finally made it to the northern edge of the karst, and smartly turned left toward the river, and me. The three Sandys rejoined with Jolly 9 at that point. Sandy 9 and his wingman broke away, accelerated, and flew directly toward my position with the intent to suppress some of the perimeter enemy fire before the rest of the gaggle arrived. As Sandy 9 crossed the river, he looked to the north where the fiercest guns were located and saw the Thud's diversionary bombs exploding and sending up large dirt clouds. He called me.

"Pop your night end now, Streetcar."

Hallelujah. I couldn't see his plane, but I popped the tab and the flare ignited in a dazzling white, sparkly spray. I waved it a few times before Sandy 9 said he saw the flare and had a lock on me. Then, I became concerned that the enemy would also see it, so I carefully placed it on the ground, backed twenty feet away, and assumed a kneeling, defensive posture.

Meanwhile, Jolly 9 sensed the crew getting very tight about the danger level. They kept mumbling about a trap and being blasted out of the sky as soon as they got close to me. Jolly 9 needed to relax them so they wouldn't choke, or panic when the shit hit the fan. He knew their M-60s would come into play before it was all over, and he needed them to be accurate. Jolly 9 was planning to pickle his drop tanks after he crossed the river so he came up with a game plan to do it just a little early and relax the crew at the same time. A small sandbar lay directly ahead of his flight path. He announced with bravado that he'd buy the entire crew a steak dinner if Yuhas could pickle the tanks so they landed on the sandbar. In the midst of a war, a bet was on. The door gunners roared in approval after the tanks tumbled but hit the sand bar. Bull's eye. Jolly 9 then snorted. "I'm now out four steak dinners." His crew laughed.

After crossing the river into Jolly 9's perceived valley of death, the enemy fire really intensified so the three A-1s swarmed around him like a bunch of gnats, slapping at anything that moved or looked suspicious. Enemy tracers rose up from a site dead ahead, and one Sandy after another shot rockets in retaliation. *Can I survive for two more clicks,* Jolly thought?

After spotting my flare, Sandy 9 flew toward it with the intent of strafing the treetops around my position. On the way, he encountered a ZPU. In the midst of a retaliatory rocket run, he felt a thud.

"Sandy 9 has been hit. Check me for damage."

His wingie broke off his attack and spotted Sandy 9 in a left-hand turn. The wingie rolled into a forty-five-degree bank to the left and commenced a rapid sliding rendezvous. He slid into a right wing-tip formation position in seconds. Once there, he inspected the right side of the leader's plane, eased off a little power and slid left under his leader's belly, added some power and settled into formation off the left wing.

"Boss, it looks like you took several hits in the belly, but I don't see any hits to flight controls, and I saw no fluid leaks other than the normal oil trail."

"Uh, Roger, all instruments are normal, so let's get back in the fight."

Jolly 9 could see the jungle tree canopy on a rising slope just ahead. If he could survive till then, he wouldn't be as visible to enemy gunners. He estimated he was two minutes from my position so he made his first call to me.

"Streetcar 304, this is Jolly 9. Pop your smoke now, over." No joy. Again, Jolly called. Again, no response from me. Sandy 9 tried once more. He screamed for me to pop my smoke. No joy—had Streetcar passed out, or died?

For nearly fifteen minutes after the CBU, I waited in a kneeling position fully expecting bad guys to enter the clearing at any moment. The moaning had ceased in the tree line, but I still didn't know if it was a trick. Badly wounded, I vowed I would not be taken prisoner in that condition.

Out of the blue, a loud reverberation sounded from the valley floor below, and the sound echoed like thunder up the ravine toward me. My heart began to thump wildly. I faced that direction, stared down the ravine above the top of the tall jungle foliage and strained to spot the Jolly. I could hear his rotor blades whopping but couldn't see any planes, so brazenly, I rose to my feet. I needed my flare, now.

After shuffling twenty feet to the fizzling flare, I grabbed it, ready to pop the day end as soon as I saw the Jolly. Just then, I had a bad thought. *Check your six, Fields!* I turned toward where I had last seen the treetop gunner and then scanned farther left to where I had last heard moans. Nothing. I turned back to the left and stared again down the ridge. Still no planes in sight, but there was a humongous amount of plane noise. Sandys? I walked forward about five steps and stopped on the foot trail for a better view. Beautiful! I could see over the tops of all trees and had a full view of the valley floor. But though I heard lots of engine noise, I still couldn't see any planes.

Out of the corner of my left eye, I saw some motion so I glanced upward. Holy Toledo . . . Nail 69 was passing left to right at about 1,000 feet. I had a full broadside view of the plane. This was the closest any Nail had been to my position during the fight, and my first thought was that he just wanted to watch my pickup. But what a gutsy move, I thought. I could see him in the cockpit so I held my left hand up and waved it a couple of times as I transmitted a casual, "Hello there, Nail 69." Nail dipped a wing. As he flew past, he saw our tree, but didn't see me standing twenty feet away and waving.

Nail had also become concerned about the length of time it was taking the Jolly to reach me and wanted to assure that all was going well. Crown told Nail the Sandys should be arriving any second, but Nail didn't have them in sight either. Nail wanted to verify I was still alive since my radio range had degraded significantly.

"Streetcar, this is Nail. Crown says the Jolly is about a mile out, and he's screaming for your smoke. I don't see him. Do you have a visual?"

"Negative."

"Pop your day smoke Streetcar."

"Negative, not until I see the helo." I slightly raised the day smoke end tab a little more.

Nail 69 was disgusted with my reluctance to pop my final smoke so he decided to smoke my position for Jolly. He had only one Willy Pete left. I saw him make a very sharp turn toward me, dip the plane's nose, and suddenly a rocket was literally screaming straight at me. I watched its path and tried to decide which way to run.

At the last possible moment, the rocket wobbled a little, which fortunately caused it to whoosh past me about thirty feet above my head. I quickly turned and watched as it impacted very close to the base of the tree where the treetop gunner had been. Great shot! A large, white, puffy, dense smoke cloud totally obliterated a long section of the trees. Shit hot—Sandy could use the smoke to find me and it would also shield me from the treetop gunner if he was still there.

Reverberations from the helo's blades were getting so loud that surely I should have been able to see Jolly before now. I turned around and looked down the ravine, toward the whopping noise. I was seven hundred feet higher than the valley floor and should be able to see him. I focused on an area just above the treetops, as that was where I expected Jolly to be, but I still saw nothing. Then, there they were, turning and diving like a big gaggle of hawks.

Damn, how'd I miss that many planes? Now I understood why I was a bomber instead of fighter pilot. My scan had been fixed at treetop level, and I had missed the five Sandys flying at two- to three hundred feet above them. The gaggle was just exiting the valley about one and a half clicks from me, and just beginning to fly over the jungle treetops where the ravine began. At that distance, they looked like a bunch of gnats darting about. I moved forward a few more feet for a better view and stood tall as I stared downhill at the unfolding scene. I should be able to pick Jolly up at any moment. But though I could see the Sandys, I couldn't spot the Jolly. Don't waste the smoke just yet!

Standing erect on the pinnacle of a ridge, amidst a clearing, fully exposed me to any enemy within a hundred feet. A bullet could strike me at any moment, but I dismissed the feeling. I had to chance it and get this Jolly vectored to me without delay before the enemy perceived what was happening. As if on cue, I again heard moans, louder this time, so I turned. It was easy to pinpoint their position as no more than 125 feet away. Loud voices were now mixed among the moans. Had more troops arrived? I was concerned. At any moment, the ten bad guys from last night might burst out of the tree line. My head stayed on a swivel as I scanned back and forth between the Sandys and the moans.

For fifteen seconds or so I couldn't see any forward motion toward me by the Sandys. They appeared to be stagnated over one position, and I assumed they had trouble with a particular enemy gun. But now, the gaggle was again relentlessly weaving toward me. I looked back at the tree line briefly. When I scanned back to the Sandys, the plane in front rolled out of a hard forty-five-degree turn, leveled his wings, and immediately shot a rocket in the direction of the river. Now, a different A-1 was leading the pack. That pilot pushed his control stick about ten degrees nose down, also fired a rocket, and followed with a sharp banking pull-up to the left. The sky seemed full of A-1s, all in the same small box, at the same time. They were turning, firing, and turning again in such a tight group that they all appeared within feet of each other. How were they avoiding mid-air collisions?

The next scene was just like a damn John Wayne movie, and every detail of that image is etched in my memory forever. I'm looking down the ravine to watch the Sandys at about a twenty-degree slope over the top of a dense, dark green tree canopy. In the background, I see the lighter-colored valley floor through a slight haze. The sun is beating down on me, but one small, obtrusive cloud is blocking the sun from illuminating the Sandy planes. The sky near them is a smoky, cloudy gray and their planes appear very dark and sinister. Flashes of their mini-guns stand out like lighting. After several seconds, the patchy cloud moves just enough to allow the sun to soak the A-1s in glory. I could clearly see the slow-mover brutes now.

My radio made a crackling noise, and I assumed one of the Sandys had depressed the wrong button. A mike button was keyed, but I couldn't hear a voice, but did hear engine noise in the background. Then, a voice weakly penetrated the static.

"Streetcar 304, this is Jolly 9. I say again, can you copy? Over."

"Streetcar copies, the Sandys are heading right for me. Keep it coming."

But Jolly didn't hear me. My battery was almost kaput.

The sun was spotlighting the five Sandys as though they were on a stage. The rescue armada was now fully illuminated for all to see, but to either side it was still dark and gloomy looking. Jolly's whopping noise now seemed so close I began to think he must be in the next ravine where I couldn't see him. I scanned frantically.

Abruptly, from his valley of death, up popped the Jolly! One millisecond he wasn't in view, and in the next I saw him rapidly rise straight up like he was on an elevator. The Jolly Green was about a mile away. He leveled off in the protected center of the A-1 gaggle, about fifty feet above the treetops, with his nose pointed right at me. The timing could never be duplicated for an air show. It was magical. Indescribable! I was ecstatic and couldn't believe what I'd just witnessed. Then, to cap it off, a sunbeam spotlighted Jolly 9. I grinned. What a beautiful picture, what a feeling. I couldn't contain my emotions. Flaunting any enemy who might be watching, I pumped my right fist triumphantly into the air and shouted down the valley at the top of my lungs.

"Shit hot! Way to go team! That maneuver was way better than any frapping movie I've ever seen."

Then I realized my mistake. I was standing in the open and shouting. Tentatively, I turned to scan the trees behind me, fully expecting to see troops with rifles walking my way. None were, but for some stupid reason, I taunted the wounded enemy. I stood erect, raised my arm toward the area of groans and moans, pointed a finger, and spoke in a commanding voice.

"Show your faces now, gomers, and you're dead meat. If you come out into the clearing, the Sandys will eat you alive."

Finally, I had seen Jolly and thirty-nine hours of pent-up frustration was vented, and I felt like a man. A stupid one, but a man!

It was time to react so I popped the day end of the flare. Smoke billowed out reddish orange in color, and I began to wave it, first in front of my body, then over my head. Within seconds, I was shrouded in the smoke, but the plume was only about ten feet diameter. Weak flare! Jolly was heading right for me so he must have seen it. I looked back at the flare and it was still spewing. In another fifteen seconds, its smoke began to drift low along the ground due to a cross wind, and it appeared to be about ready to peter out. My damn flare was old, just like the radio batteries.

I looked down the ravine. Jolly was about a quarter mile away so I carefully laid the simmering flare on the ground in front of me. Just a little smoke was rising, so I reached in my trouser pocket for the pre-loaded pen flare gun. About then, I heard a radio call. "Where's the day smoke?"

"Jolly, Streetcar is firing a pencil flare tracer at you, now."

I aimed downhill at Jolly and shot, reloaded, and fired another at him. Big mistake!

Suddenly, a Sandy flew diagonally across the nose of Jolly 9, and I thought they would collide in midair. But the Sandy turned sharply and ended up in front of Jolly, heading right for me. He thought an enemy gunner had fired the tracers! Not aware he hadn't heard my advisory call, I thought he was just looking for targets, so I pumped my arm into the air and shouted. "Give 'em hell, Sandy." Then, his wings leveled and I was looking directly at his A-1's big, ugly nose. A flash occurred under a wing, followed by a little smoke puff. A trail of smoke dropped several feet and leveled off. In a split second, I realized Sandy had just fired a rocket, and the plume of smoke was on a ten-degree dive slope and coming right at my face.

Watch the rocket to determine which way you need to run. At a distance, it appeared slow. As it got closer, the closure speed accelerated but I could still predict its probable impact point. Suddenly, it began to twirl, and it nose began to dip up and down erratically. *Shit, it's out of control!* When it was a few hundred feet away, I heard it hissing. At the very last second I determined it would pass over my head, but not by much. No need to run. I dropped to a knee and heard a *whoosh* as the rocket passed maybe ten feet over my head. I dove to the ground for protection and watched as it exploded maybe fifty feet away near the edge of the tree line. A helluva shot if he was going for the tree gunners, but pee poor if he was shooting at me. *Keep it coming, Sandy. Don't take any ordnance home today. Blast the hell out of anything that moves,* I thought. I grinned, jumped back to my feet, and turned toward Jolly. He was about two-thirds up the ravine and still tracking directly toward me, but my smoke flare was nearly depleted. I began to call out heading advisories.

"Keep it coming, I'm right on your nose. Turn port a couple of degrees, you're drifting starboard." But Jolly 9 got only half of my words because of my weak battery.

Jolly was maybe two hundred yards out when another Sandy dived in front, again aimed at me. I had a really bad feeling. I heard a short burp, followed by a small gray puff under Sandy's wing. I froze! Before I could say the words "20 mike-mike," Sandy's mini-gun rounds began smacking the ground about ten feet forward but twenty feet to my right. Their explosions caused small, individual dirt clouds as the rounds splattered through the clearing, raced by me, and splintered wood in the tree line behind me. I was still erect, frozen in my tracks. It happened so fast I didn't move. Quickly, I turned back toward Sandy, who was still bearing in on me. I knelt to the ground and placed the radio up to my mouth. Before I had time to shout out, another burp occurred, but this time the first rounds whacked the trees behind me. Having pressed a gun run before myself, I knew I had just survived two squeezes of the gun trigger. He pressed, released, and fired again. Thank God his aim was a little left of me.

I ran to stand beside my smoke flare, which now looked like a small campfire with little smoke. When Jolly got to a position about one hundred feet in front of me, I pressed the transmit switch. "Jolly, stop. Hover, hover, hover."

Jolly 9's rotor blade noise blocked out any reply, but the helo lurched up a little and slowed to crawl speed. I was off his port side and could easily see Jolly 9 in his cockpit about fifty feet above me but he was staring dead ahead toward the dangerous tree line. The door gunner was scanning over my head toward where I'd heard the moans, but wouldn't look down. How could they both miss my smoke? I yelled at Jolly a second time. "Look down. I'm off your port about forty-five degrees. Stop. Hover."

No reply! The helo was slowly sliding forward and beginning to drift farther away. It dawned on me that Jolly 9 was staring down at the locator tree and allowing the helo to slide further right so he could keep the tree in view. I was only about twenty feet from it, but he was fixed on the tree and never looked in my direction. I began to wave my arms.

"Nail 69, this is Jolly 9. I just flew by the tree but saw no one or any smoke. Where is he?"

"Jolly, he should be within fifteen feet of the tree."

"Roger, Nail. We'll continue looking, but right now we're a sitting duck."

Jolly 9 frantically and repeatedly asked his crew for status. They responded that the foliage was so heavy that none of them could see me, or my smoke. Jolly 9 was agitated and also scared because his three crewmembers had been looking for over a minute now.

This is a trap, he thought. *Streetcar is not here, and I'm going to get us all killed. But, maybe he's too injured to talk? Should I put my PJ on the ground to look for him?*

As the helo started to ease forward more, I yelled loudly into the mike. "Jolly, come port, I'm off your port side! I'm off your port side. Stop! Hover! Ease it back to port." *For heaven's sake, Jolly!*

No response, but Jolly heard part of the words. He heard "port," but in the heat of battle, he couldn't recall which way it was. He stopped his forward motion just short of the tree line about a hundred feet from me, where the treetop gunner had been and eased ninety degrees to the starboard in a hover about sixty feet above the ground and just below the treetops. At that point, I was looking at his starboard broadside and could easily see the PJ manning his gun. Finally, he looked my way. I waved both arms over my head.

The co-pilot calmly kept asking the door gunners if they had me yet, and the answer was repeatedly, "No." Tree limbs were less than twenty feet from the tips of the rotor blades, and he was concerned whether Jolly 9 could hover steady enough to avoid impact.

Nail 69 made several cautionary calls that panicked the entire crew: "Jolly, don't forget. There are guys in the treetops with AK-47s."

The co-pilot and door gunners couldn't make themselves look at the ground to locate me as they were more concerned with scanning for treetop gunners. I tried repeatedly to catch their attention by waving, but they didn't look down. The door gunner looked real antsy as he swung his M-60 back and forth. The rotor noise was deafening, but I tried the radio one more time.

"Jolly 9, I'm at your five o'clock, about a hundred feet. Ease it to starboard, and you should see me below." No response! My eyes were glued on the door gunner, who fired his gun every few seconds, but he still didn't look down. Even when he did, the downwash ripped up dirt around me, and the air swirled with light debris, hindering his view of me.

Since leaving the valley, Jolly 9 had heard some of my transmissions, but most of what he had heard was broken static, gobbledygook. But he had heard enough to warrant continued hovering. Seconds went by like minutes, and a minute seemed to be a quarter of an hour. It was pure hell to hover while he listened to firing M-60s, and he didn't know how long he'd be able to gut this one out.

I was in a panic also. *If I don't do something quickly, Jolly is going to get shot down.* I looked down at my waist. My gut and thighs were covered in blood. Can my legs run? Jolly made the decision for me.

At that moment, Jolly 9 made the first really clear transmission I'd heard since he started up the ravine. He spoke firmly and his words came out very slowly.

"Streetcar, if you don't show yourself in ten seconds, we're out of here."

Jolly 9 regretted the transmission as soon as he made it. *How foolish it must have sounded to Streetcar 304, especially if he was badly wounded and couldn't stand up.*

But I understood and sympathized with him. He wasn't going to wait for me all day and get killed so he was breaking his hover in ten seconds. My reaction was immediate. I screamed on the radio this time.

"Hold your hover, Jolly, I'm running to you. Don't break hover, I'm coming."

Jolly 9 was flabbergasted at the clarity. For the first time, it seemed like Streetcar suddenly had an amplified microphone in his radio. He reacted immediately and began his normal hoist routine.

He looked down, found one specific bush to focus on, and intently maintained his altitude and position over it. As he worked hard to keep the helo motionless, he knew this was now the most perilous part of the rescue. An enemy gunner could knock him out of the sky even with a pistol. He was sweating and scared and really concentrating on the bush when suddenly, out of the corner of his eye, a brilliant white light swirled in and enveloped his helo. Its brilliance was such that he thought it would blind him if he raised his head and looked at it. He could see the bush and nothing else, not even his co-pilot an arm's length away. None of his crew made a comment on the light even though he could hear Yuhas talking to both door gunners.

Jolly 9 felt God's presence. A protective light shield was around his helo, and he was certain the Shekinah Glory of God was protecting him at his moment of greatest peril. The light would shield his helo from all danger while he was inside the protective bubble. Jolly 9's fear subsided. He would hover until I appeared, and the light would protect him regardless of time, or danger.

I panicked, though. Jolly 9 was going to leave me if I didn't get to his helo ASAP. Without thought of pain, I started to run fast and yelled again into the radio. "Streetcar is running to the Jolly. Streetcar is on the run."

At first, I dashed along a line parallel with the hovering Jolly since my path was seriously impeded by the ten-foot-tall, densely clumped, and sometimes impenetrable vegetation. I couldn't get to Jolly! On the verge of hyperventilation, I still ran at full speed, but my legs were dead. I struggled to keep them moving. My eyes were glued on the door gunner for any sign of recognition while I wildly shoved the undergrowth away with both arms. I felt the sting of briars as they bit into my cotton fatigues and slowed me down. The same thorns lashed my face, but I didn't have time to circumvent them. After sixty feet, I changed direction and ran directly toward the helo. A thick mat of vines blocked my path so I tried to bust through them, but became entangled. I was trapped in foliage towering over my head. I stopped struggling and looked up. The door gunner was directly in front of me about fifty feet away and sixty feet up, but he was still concentrating on the treetops. Standing erect, I waved my arms but got no response.

Should I fire the pistol or a flare to get his attention? No. I'd try the radio one more time. I keyed the mike and shouted. "Streetcar is right below you off your right side. Tell the door gunner to look down."

Immediately, the gunner's head snapped down toward me. With both hands on his M-60, he rapidly swiveled it until the barrel was pointed right at me. *He's going to shoot me! Does he recognize me as a friendly? Should I dive to the ground?* I froze, afraid the least movement would cause him to fire.

The PJ door gunner looked down the barrel and straightaway saw a small human head in the midst of heavy foliage. He screamed over the intercom. "I see a guy on the ground waving a pistol." His finger tightened against the trigger of the M-60 as he processed "friend or foe." The white head stood out like a floral bloom because it was so much lighter colored than the uniform below it or the surrounding green vegetation. The head was slightly balding, with what appeared to be a flat-top hair cut with some reddish hair along the side. Then the gunner recognized the head was attached to a guy wearing green pants and a green shirt with the collar turned up about his neck. His face was partially blackened but still glowed in the morning sunlight. His hands were covered with gloves, and one hand was holding an object next to his mouth. It appeared the individual was talking to someone. A pistol was in the other hand but wasn't aimed at him. It was being waved in an up and down motion as if the guy was signaling for something to happen. Finally, after a few frightening seconds for me, the gunner made his decision. A wide grin spread across his face, and his left hand left his gun and pressed his radio mike to his lips.

"PJ to pilot, I see Streetcar. He's standing and looks okay. Slide fifty feet to the right. I'm dropping the penetrator."

While I watched, the helo inched slowly toward me. *Damn it, come on Jolly, speed it up!* I saw the door gunner reach out with his right hand to steady the hoist cable as the penetrator began its descent. Suddenly, the helo's closure rate increased dramatically, and the penetrator rapidly swung toward me. I was caught off guard by Jolly's quick slide, and both hands were filled with radio and pistol. At first I thought the penetrator would cold-cock me, but it hit the ground when it was about five feet away, bounced once, and swung away before I could grab it. *Ah, shit!* Quickly, I crammed my radio in my vest but kept the pistol in my right hand just as the penetrator again swung toward me. It hit the ground a few feet short for a second time, but bobbed up. That time, I grabbed it and wrapped my arms around it.

I'd been trained to snap a fitting to the penetrator to secure myself so I wouldn't fall off, or be pulled off as I was hoisted through brush or trees. But I wasn't about to take any more time to try and snap anything in place. I hugged it mightily, then looked up at the gunner and gave him a thumbs-up. Immediately, I was yanked up through the foliage.

Fear swelled. *Will the gomers shoot me now if they think they're about to lose their bait?* I tucked my head tightly against the metal tube and watched for them as the penetrator spun slightly in a rapid climb. No one rushed out from the tree line. *We killed at least ten of them,* I thought. Oops! Something just fell out of my survival vest. I looked down and saw my faithful radio tumbling to the ground. Damn it, that one item had been more valuable to me than a handful of gold.

My heart was beating a mile a minute. As I approached the side door, the gunner pushed the cable to swing me outward and then back through the open door. It didn't work, and I bounced off the side of the helo. He quickly grabbed the cable again and gave a much harder push. I swung out again, and this time I flew back through the door with such speed that I hit the floor hard, lost my death-grip on the penetrator, and rolled across the floor toward the other side door. Only the FE/door gunner's leg on that side stopped me from tumbling out.

I looked up and the door gunner gave me a quick, sheepish smile. Then he turned back to his M-60. The PJ was at my back, grabbed me by the shoulders, and helped me to a sitting position. His face broke out in an unforgettable broad smile as he gave me a solid pat on the back. Then he, too, returned to a crouched firing position over his M-60, and both of them started to scan the trees.

I sat immobile for about a minute as I counted my blessings. I had survived. I had beaten the bloody bastards at their own game. It felt good to simply relax, not having realized while on the ground how tightly wound I was. Suddenly, though, I felt drained. All my sap was gone. I felt humble.

"Thank you, Lord," I mumbled. Then, I looked out the left side door and saw how close the trees were. Scary close! We were below the tops and still in a hover. That was confusing. The longer we hovered, the more chance of getting shot down, again!

Chapter 24

CELEBRATION AT NKP

After a minute on the helo, I turned to admire the hero who had risked his life to save mine. The cockpit was elevated so I looked up. Jolly 9 was staring straight ahead, focused on his instruments, while he waited for the Sandys to form around us. He was busy, but I couldn't wait to thank him. I shouted, "Way to go, Jolly 9!" He didn't turn but the co-pilot did, with a quizzical look and a thumbs-up. I returned the signal to indicate I was okay and then tried to push up. I couldn't, because I was entangled in brush that had tried to hold me back as I rode the penetrator. The PJ noticed my dilemma, reached over, ripped off a large clump, and tossed it out the door. As I stood up, Jolly 9 turned toward me for a brief moment, but with his visor down. I couldn't tell what he looked like. But I mouthed, "Thank you," just before the co-pilot sternly told me to move to the back, away from the open side doors. He didn't have to tell me twice. I shuffled to a cot along the left side and sat down just as the helo began to move forward.

Jolly 9 had hovered precariously for over four minutes as he waited for his crew to spot me. Miraculously, he and his crew were still alive, but now it was time to make like a bandit and get the hell out of there. He knew it wasn't over yet. He'd have to fly maybe twelve miles before he'd be out of immediate danger.

"Jolly 9 has Streetcar on board. I repeat, Jolly 9 has Streetcar and is leaving the area. Let's move out, Sandys."

I wasn't out of danger, yet, but we did finally break hover. Jolly 9 pulled full power up on the collective, the rotor blades changed their pitch, and the helo began rising. About fifty feet above the tree canopy, he lowered the nose slightly and began to move forward and pick up more airspeed at treetop level. In a matter of seconds gunfire tracers were spitting past, and he maneuvered to avoid them, killing what little forward speed he had gained. His bird strained to climb quickly enough to crest the next ridge.

Damn, I'm going to be shot down again, I thought. Every few seconds I would see the outline of an A-1 as it sped by the side door in an attack mode while I sat pensively on the hard, rigid cot. And, minute by minute, I seemed weaker. I looked at the PJ, hoping he could check my wounds, but he was busy firing his gun. I began to feel worse so I took the Redman out of my mouth and threw the wasted plug out the side door. I felt light-headed.

Quickly, I did a self-diagnosis. One of my gloves was saturated in blood and had a rip where a bomb fragment had torn it, but the hand didn't hurt much. The entire frontal area around my groin was soaked in blood, and that area of my green fatigues now looked like the split-open insides of a watermelon. But I didn't seem to have much pain there either. My back ached, and it was uncomfortable in the seated position so I leaned forward to ease the pain. I felt my lower back, and the clothing there was also moist with blood. The most pain was coming from my right foot. A searing, burning pain. *Was my foot still in place?* Fearing the worst, I tried to check it but couldn't. I was sure part of the foot had been mangled. I looked toward the PJ again for help and suddenly felt woozy. I started to position my head between my legs but felt myself blacking out. I fell back on the cot just as I did. The PJ saw me fall backward and rushed to my side.

Jolly 9 continued to fly up the hill. He dreaded cresting it, as he knew the large 37s and 57s might fire at him from across the river on the karst. Near the top, Jolly 9 saw a circular, white light flashing on the ground ahead of him. It flashed, stopped, and then flashed again. He hit the intercom.

"Triple A site at eleven o'clock." Jolly just knew he was about to buy the farm.

A tracer whizzed up and passed between the spinning rotor blades. Amazingly, it didn't impact them. Aghast, Jolly stared as the enemy gun crew furiously cranked the gun barrel down from its elevated position. But even as they did, shells were exploding and spitting out the barrel, and it looked like a twinkling spotlight shining at the helo. It all happened in a flash, and there was no time for his customary prayer.

Jolly 9 jerked his flight control for a hard bank to the right. Immediately, the co-pilot screamed, "Watch out on the right!" Jolly looked that way and saw that he was about to chew up one of the Sandys with his massive rotor blade.

Sandy 9 had been at the right rear quarter of Jolly 9 when the first tracer soared past the helo. He pointed his plane's big nose toward the enemy gun and was preparing to fire when Jolly turned sharply into him. Before Sandy had time to react, Jolly turned away first. Sandy 9 continued his attack and fired several rockets right down the nose of the gun site. Direct hit! The flashing light was gone, replaced by a dust cloud and flying debris. Whoops. Sandy 9 had pressed his attack too low, flew through the debris, and barely pulled out safely, just avoiding the ground.

Jolly 9 couldn't avoid the debris either. As he sped by the smoking gun, Jolly's heart slowly resumed its beat. A cocoon of light had encircled his helo during his hover over me, and he had attributed it to the glory of God. This time, he praised his earthly angel, Sandy 9. Jolly took a long, deep breath as he smoothly crested the hill, and then flew south without further incidence.

A biting odor in my nose woke me up. I looked up, and the PJ put the spent ammonia capsule in my hand. "Take another whiff," he said. Then he pointed at my groin. He had stuffed a lot of bandage material inside my trousers, and some of it was now sticking out above my web belt. Looks like a frapping diaper, I thought.

The PJ was built like a muscular, twenty-year-old football tight end, and looked the epitome of a warrior. Again, he flashed me a huge smile just like the one I saw from the ground when he first recognized me in the weeds. I took another sniff from the capsule and tried to match his smile, but knew there was no way I could ever do that. His grins were too special.

He knelt beside me and pulled two small, airline-size bottles of bourbon from his pocket. I had trouble opening one because of my injured hand, so the PJ took the bottle and promptly proceeded to drink half before he handed it back. I took a small swig and the burning liquid made me lurch and nearly jump up. The PJ laughed. I offered him another drink just to be nice, and damn if he didn't take the bottle and chug-a-lug it. Then he opened the other bottle and handed it back to me. *Air Force medicine tastes great*, I thought.

Movement on the port side made me turn that way and I saw that the FE was watching our little celebratory scene. It was a Kodak moment: he was at his gun station, on one knee, with his right hand still on his M-60 trigger. Smoke was still pouring from the barrel.

Through his side door, I could see the treetops flashing by against a blue sky. He was shorter than the PJ, more portly, and his flight suit was spotted with sweat. His smile was more subtle and full of relief, I thought.

I raised the bottle to offer it to him as an expression of my gratitude. He waved his hand to indicate "no," and I read his lips. "No thanks, you need it more." So I performed my first-ever celebratory chug-a-lug.

After my puny display of manhood, the PJ asked me if I was okay. I told him my foot may have taken bomb damage so he removed my right boot. I watched intently for any ghastly expression, but he rose, smiled again, and then totally confused me by informing me there was no injury to the foot. That was hard to believe since it was giving me so much pain. "Okay then, put the boot back on," I directed. Immediately the PJ's grin disappeared, and I knew I had just stepped on my lizard big time. Coolly, he handed the boot back to me.

"You put it back on," he said. I was a pilot who still had two hands, and he was a crusty PJ and not about to put any officer's boot on.

I put my own damn boot back on as he excitedly told me about the recent encounter with the AAA site. I could tell it was a hairy time and regretted I hadn't seen it unfold and conclude. He told me I was one lucky dude.

"Lie back and enjoy the ride home," he said.

I think I was asleep before my head hit the cot.

When Jolly 9 rescued me, my position was 120 degrees and 103 miles from NKP, so it would be at least an hour before we arrived at the base. But soon I was rousted by the PJ. Jolly 9 thought that I, as a pilot, would like to see a Jolly refuel in flight from a HC-130. Not really, not right now, but I sat up, still in a slight stupor.

From the cot, I could see the pilot and co-pilot in an elevated position in the cockpit. I felt a burning desire to again make eye contact with the guy who had just saved my butt. However, when Jolly 9 turned his head toward me, his dark sun visor was still down. I motioned for him to raise it. After a quick scan out front, he complied and then turned toward me again. His strong-looking face had a wry grin on it as we looked in each other's eyes for the first time. I jabbed my clenched right fist at him, popped a thumb up, and mouthed the words "Shit hot." He shot a similar gesture back, lowered his visor, and went back to work. I stared at him and admired the man. He was a real, live, frapping hero, and I wanted to shake his hand, give him a bear hug, and buy him a drink. He was the guy I wanted to compare war stories with, but right now was not the time, nor the place.

Feeling weak, I sort of scooted to the front of the cot and watched the pilot's refueling technique. It was a slower-speed version of what I did in the A-7, but there was one huge difference. The pilot of the Jolly and the one in the HC-130 had to be concerned about the huge rotor blades of the HH-3. Any slight screw-up by Jolly 9 could result in those choppers slicing into the HC-130. I knew this, and wondered just how proficient Jolly 9 was in this procedure. It was like being in a car when someone else is racing. I wasn't as comfortable watching the Jolly pilot execute the maneuver as when I did it myself. He was smooth with the controls and inserted the helo's refueling probe into the basket on the first attempt. It was impressive, and just another sign that Jolly 9 was an outstanding pilot. I gave the PJ a thumbs-up and sank back onto the cot for the rest of the ride home. In no time, I was fast asleep.

We landed at NKP one hour and four minutes after I was hoisted into the helo, and a few minutes more than thirty-nine hours after I was shot down. The PJ roused me again, and though I felt drained, I started to stand. I wanted to disembark like a man, but the PJ emphatically said, "No." He and the FE then picked up my cot, which turned out to be a litter, and carried me off the helo.

The saga of Streetcar 304 required 189 combat sorties and was one of the largest rescues of the Vietnam War, but it was finally over. I was free and would return to fight the same enemy again. However, Sandy 7 was captured and bound in leg chains as a prisoner of war. Why him, and not me? Many years have passed, and I still don't have that answer, but Sandy 7 and I agree that God does indeed work in mysterious ways.

But God didn't do it by himself. Many angelic men heroically risked their lives to save mine. I thank them for their action, and I thank God for providing them with the courage and skill to do so. May God shine his grace down upon my heroes forevermore.

EPILOGUE

Back aboard USS *America*, many of my squadron buddies had been in CIC most of the morning monitoring my rescue. They had listened intently to the mounting suspense as the fast-movers inched their bombs closer to my position. As A-7 pilots, they understood the danger of bombing within seventy-five feet of my location. "Are the Air Force pilots that much better than us?" one of them asked.

Then, they heard a Crown transmission. "Streetcar sounds as cool as a cucumber even with bombs exploding around him."

One of my squadron's prima donnas retorted, "He's from West Virginia. If anyone can get out of the jungle alive, it'll be him."

They cringed when they heard I was hit by a CBU. Collectively, they thought, *Kenny's dead,* because they clearly understood the kill potential of a CBU bomb pattern.

Within minutes, though, they heard Crown's call that Jolly 9 had me on board. To quote Lieutenant Moser: "Pandemonium broke out. Pilots pounded on the backs of fellow pilots in sheer joy. Tears began to flow in many of their eyes. Almost immediately, the ship's captain announced to the entire 5,000-plus man crew, 'Lieutenant Fields has been successfully rescued and is now on his way to an Air Force base.' You could hear a simultaneous shout from deep in the bowels of the ship as the crew celebrated the news."

Meanwhile, at NKP, a large contingent of base personnel greeted us with raucous applause when we exited the Jolly. While being littered to a waiting ambulance, several "Bird Colonels" smiled down at me before I was whisked away without a chance to shake anyone's hand. Once inside, I promptly fell asleep again.

Sandy 9 landed at NKP immediately after Jolly 9. Both had been in the cockpit for over five hours of harrowing combat time. After mingling with many compatriots who congratulated him on his remarkable save, Sandy 9 sauntered in true fighter pilot style to the parked Jolly. Sandy 9 wanted to see the Navy pilot who had caused so much hell in his life and that of his fellow Sandy pilots. I had already been littered away, so he asked that the pilot of Jolly 9 be pointed out.

He was directed toward a tall, good-looking, angular, and sloping pilot who was sagging against his helo. In the past day and half, Jolly 9 had flown nearly seventeen hours of the last twenty-nine, so he was physically beat. Sandy 9 stuck out his hand and stated that he was the Sandy pilot whom Jolly 9 had nearly sliced apart, and the one who rocketed and killed the 23mm gun that fired at Jolly.

"Those were my last rockets, and I'd already expended my 20 mike-mike, so you're one lucky dude."

"We had a little help from God," Jolly replied with a huge grin. Jolly 9 grabbed Sandy's hand and bear-hugged him. "You're one helluva of a shot, Sandy 9. Those rockets saved my crew, and we'll never be able to repay you."

For payback, Sandy 9 only wanted to inspect the damage Jolly's bird had taken. He was shocked when told the helo didn't have a single hole from enemy gunfire.

"This can't be the bird you were flying today—impossible!" Sandy 9 exclaimed. "I was never below 220 knots airspeed during the entire mission, and you were less than a hundred knots most of the time. You hovered over Streetcar for nearly five minutes with bullets flying all over the place, and you want me to believe you've got no bullet holes. Are you shooting me a load of B.S. about this being your bird?"

Jolly 9 laughed as he followed Sandy 9 to his A-1. After inspecting it, Jolly described it as looking like Swiss cheese. It was full of holes.

Soon afterward, Jolly 9's roommate walked up and made good on their side bet. Jolly 9 got his nickel and made a silent vow. He would keep it in his pocket as a good luck charm for the rest of his life.

In typical tradition, the Sandy pilots then migrated to their Sandy Box, where several were drunker than skunks before lunch. The Sandy pilots had a reputation for bravery under fire, but many non-squadron pilots believed that courage came from the Sandy Box. Why else would anyone in this day and age pilot a single-engine, propeller-driven plane at 220 knots and a hundred feet above the trees, in the face of daunting enemy AAA gun sites? Just to save a Navy pilot?

I don't recall the ambulance ride, or being off-loaded at the small ten-bed dispensary at NKP, but several minutes later something touched me, and I awoke with a frightened jolt. I was lying on a hard, rigid, but cool surface. My mind was in a fog, and I was still in an escape mode. I heard voices, but couldn't comprehend the words or see the speaker. A bright light, which I assumed to be the sun, was spotlighted on my face. I heard the distinctive sound of a hard object hitting a piece of light-weight metal. Then I saw a khaki-colored uniform centered directly above me. Holy cow, had I been captured?

The voice spoke again, this time more clearly. "How're you doing, Lieutenant Fields?"

The speaker changed his position slightly and stepped out of the bright light. Standing before me was a young naval officer in a khaki uniform with a pair of silver bars on one collar and a flight surgeon's insignia on the other. Suddenly, it all came back. I was at NKP, but it was an Air Force base. Why is a Navy flight surgeon attending me? The doc moved to his left a little, and at that moment I noticed that, yes, he was in a naval uniform, but he had medical gloves on. In one hand he held a scalpel, and in the other some forceps. The scalpel probe had probably stirred me awake. But wait a minute, what the heck was this guy cutting on?

"Who are you, Doc, and what's going on?"

He laughed and asked how much booze the PJ had given me, because he hadn't given me any sedative.

"Sedative? For what?"

"We're in the NKP Dispensary. You've got a bunch of CBU pellets in you, and I'm digging them out. Sort of like surgery. Most of them aren't real deep, so let me know if you feel too much pain."

Then, his hand probed, and I felt a minor sting. His hand reappeared and dropped a small object. When it landed, I heard a *clink*.

Ah, the sound I heard earlier was just a CBU pellet landing in a metal bowl. I took a deep breath and tried to relax. Out of the corner of my eye, I saw an Air Force guy in uniform walk into the room. I couldn't see his rank but guessed he was a senior officer from his tone and presence, and that he had barged in to interrupt my "surgery."

"Doc, how's he doing? Is he okay? Everyone outside wants to know."

"He's okay, but really lucky. He's lost some blood but the damage was flesh-only, and no vital organs or arteries were hit. He took about a dozen hits from the CBU, but he'll be fine."

"Thanks, Doc. I'll let everyone know." Then he looked down at me. "You take it easy, young man. You put on one helluva show out there."

I really needed that pat on the back. Now, I felt totally relaxed for the first time in three days. In fact, I was content to let the doc cut on me as he pleased and didn't even care enough to watch. I was just happy to be alive. Nothing else mattered right then. I thought of nothing, but simply absorbed the feeling of life versus death. Yes, it was one helluva show, and now it was over. Just as my eyes closed, another voice stopped me.

"Streetcar 304, man, am I glad we got you outta there." A pilot with a round and slightly rosy face was standing over me across the table from the doc and grinning very happily.

I looked into his face but had no idea who he was. Where had I heard those words, "outta there," lately? Then it hit me.

"Hello, Nail 66, nice to finally meet you. Thanks a lot for all you did for me. By the way, where did my second-run bombs hit? Did I get 'em?"

Nail laughed and apologized. "Streetcar, I was way too busy watching your bird tumble to see any bombs." He told me he was on the way to Bangkok and would see me in a few days. "We'll lift a few drinks together. I owe you one, Streetcar. You hang tight till I get back."

I began to fade again and closed my eyes to escape the bright light. My back was aching, my right foot throbbed with pain, and I couldn't find a position on the metal table that would provide any relief. Just before I dozed off, the doc spoke. "Here's another one," followed by one more *clink*.

While some pilots and aircrews toasted their success, other pilots were still at work. The war was still going on. I hadn't won it single-handedly. More pilots would be shot down today, and fresh Sandys and Jollys were already standing alert, ready to scramble when it happened. But I was out of the war, for now, after only one mission—make that three-quarters of a mission.

Nail 69 remained over the rescue area for another hour or so after everyone else RTB'ed and diligently searched for Sandy 7. At one time, he saw what appeared to be a pencil gun flare fly upward toward his plane. Nail flew over that area several times and called on the radio, but no one answered or appeared in the open near where the flare was fired. He wanted to investigate further, but for some reason his fuel depleted faster than normal so he bingoed to NKP. After landing, he climbed out of the plane and a lone maintenance tech met him. Nail 69 had missed the hero's welcome party. The Airman approached and pointed out a leaking fuel line, and upon further inspection, the two of them discovered that a bullet had caused the damage. Nail 69 was very lucky, as well as being very good.

Nail then sauntered over to the TUOC, expecting to be asked a million questions about Sandy 7, and how many guns Nail 69 had killed, etc. But the Ops Center was practically empty. He was told most of the pilots had already debriefed the mission and had gone to the Sandy Box to celebrate. Nail was then debriefed in a very low-key manner, and afterward he went to the O' Club for a solitary lunch.

In response to Nail 69's sighting of the pencil flare, several Sandys and a fresh Nail scrambled back to the scene. They trolled until dark for any signal or radio call from Sandy 7. None was received so after their return, the Sandy 7 rescue mission was officially closed around 4 P.M.

Nail 69 heard the news and reflected on it for three hours. What if he was in the shoes of Sandy 7 and had shot the pencil flare as his only means of communicating with the Nails? He couldn't bear the thought so he went back to the TUOC and contested the decision to close the Sandy 7 mission. Finally, he convinced the powers-that-be to re-open the mission. Nail 69 would take off at daylight.

Late in the afternoon of my rescue, Seventh Naval Fleet sent a message to Seventh Air Force, with the following words of praise. "For three days, Seventh Fleet units have followed the extraordinary professional efforts and heroism of the SAR units involved in the rescue of Streetcar 304. I sincerely believe that such demonstrated concern for human life is one of the major differences between U.S. forces and our enemy. It is a distinct pleasure to fight for and with such men as the Jolly Greens, the Sandys, the Nails, the Spads, the Crowns, the Tomcats, and all the other many fighter pilots who made this SAR effort successful in the face of almost insurmountable odds. Please extend my personal appreciation to all units involved for their heroic efforts in the rescue of Streetcar 304."

Near dark, the Air Force threw water in the face of the enemy. A helo flew to the site where the Jolly had landed the night before with the overheated transmission, attached cables to it and ferried it back to NKP. The wounded Jolly Green Giant would live to fight another day.

It was around 11 A.M. when the doc removed the last pellets and fragments from my body. I was still asleep when they finished and didn't wake up when they wheeled me to a single room in the back of the dispensary where I continued to sleep, undisturbed and without dreams or nightmares. I awoke around 8 P.M. with a jolt, bleary-eyed and leery of my surroundings. I was lying in a small bed, in a very small room with a single overhead lightbulb. Through an open doorway, I saw a totally dark, black hole. Where was I? Then I remembered. I looked around the room and saw how stark it was. I was in a hospital-type bed, and its head was cranked up at about a thirty-degree slope. The only other piece of furniture was a bedside table, and I looked there for water but found none. I did notice a small metal pan and inside were fourteen souvenir CBU pellets.

I was wide awake by then and thought about my wife and kids. Undoubtedly they'd been notified of my rescue by now. I hoped Shirley wasn't too distraught, and I vowed to call her as soon as I found a phone. She would want to know what injuries I had incurred. I looked down at my groin area, but a single white sheet covered me. After lifting it, I saw no clothes, only a hospital gown and, under it, lots of bandages. A chilling thought occurred. It's time to verify all my parts are still in place.

My upper torso appeared unscathed. There was obvious damage to the right hand, and it was wrapped extensively in bandages. Looking good so far! I used my left hand to move my gown to an open position. "Hells bells," I sputtered. My groin area was bright red where my blood had seeped through the bandages. There was one bandaged entry wound on the outer left thigh, one bandage on the inside of that thigh, heavy dried blood around the penis area, another bandage on the inside of the right thigh, and a large bandage on my right buttock. There were several smaller bandages on both legs. Cautiously, I raised each leg and concluded the muscles and bone were undamaged. But a constant, searing pain was still radiating down my right leg and culminated in the ball of my right foot. I checked the condition of my back since it felt very stiff. There was a small bandage near the lower lumbar region, but I could bend forward without much pain. Most of the damage was from my waist down.

Finally, I stared at the blood-saturated area of my groin. I lifted some of the bandage and found my "little guy" shriveled up, encrusted with blood. "Ah, shit," I exclaimed. "He's dead." It looked like the poor guy had gone into hiding in a little cocoon of blood and skin. With my left hand I gingerly rolled the skin back, becoming very concerned about my manhood when the thick, crusted blood began peeling off in pieces. I pulled some more and recoiled in disbelief. A CBU pellet rolled out from under the skin.

"Holy crap—this is just unbelievable. How did a pellet get here?" I picked it up and placed it in the bedside pan along with the others—this one was truly a gem. With trepidation, I bent over and looked more closely at "his" head. *There, right there, is where I took the hit,* I thought. I could see two small, white, scarred spots where the hot pellet had landed. I fell back against the pillow and imagined what must have happened. First, it was hard to believe that a CBU pellet had penetrated my clothing, but at such low force that it didn't penetrate the skin. But it had still been red-hot at impact and had left a burn scar. Second, it was also hard to fathom that I had been placed in a hospital room with a bandage applied over an area before it had been thoroughly cleaned. What kind of frapping hospital was this? It reminded me of *M*A*S*H.* I was now madder than at any time since I was shot down. This was an affront to my rank and my status as a combat pilot, so I yelled out.

"Corpsman, hey, anyone out there?"

In a few seconds, a young Air Force corpsman walked in from the dark space and casually asked how I was doing. He was so timid, I softened my approach.

"Find the Navy doc and tell him I found a pellet that he missed. Tell him it was rolled up inside the skin of my penis and left a burn scar. And tell him there's blood all over the area because it wasn't cleaned before someone applied a bandage."

The corpsman sheepishly smiled and left. On his way out, I hit him with one more bullet.

"Damn it, this isn't a laughing matter."

Within a few minutes, he returned with a metal bowl of water, and inside was a washcloth and a small bar of soap. He handed it to me and said that the doctor had laughed when told about my injured penis and then ordered that I be given the bowl so I could clean myself. The doctor would see me in the morning.

"You gotta be kidding me. Is there a phone I can use to call my wife?"

Nicely, he told me I could make a call from the MARS hut. It was a military-affiliated radio system that could link me to a phone in the states. "However," he said, "you can't do it until you're cleared to get out of bed. The doctor made it clear: no walking for now."

The corpsman left to reheat my dinner while I cleaned myself. I began to have doubts about my earlier praise for my Air Force compatriots. Did the Air Force have any respect for Navy pilots?

Thousands of miles away in Florida, Shirley had just spent a long, ago-nizing twenty-four-hour period awaiting news of my fate. She cried at times, often in the solitude of our bedroom, but she generally main-tained her composure and carried on in her image of a professional military wife. She talked to the many other wives there for support, told stories of our courtship, and showed pictures of our times together as a family. She impressed them with her fortitude. She seemed strong and in control. They watched Shirley and thought they could soon be in the same boat, and that scared them. How would they handle the same situation? This was no longer a game wherein their husbands bragged about their training exploits and what shit-hot pilots they were. They now knew this was a real war. Their husbands could make one little miscue, or just be unlucky, and they would be the next to suffer Shirley's fate.

Their day had been spent waiting for the phone to ring with good news, or the doorbell to ring, followed by bad news. There were no updates. Shirley knew only that I was evading and the Air Force was trying to rescue me. Other than that, it was wait and see.

The second day dragged on, and around 8 P.M. the on-duty wives were relieved by one who came to spend the night with Shirley. After the kids went to bed, Shirley and her friend stayed up late hoping for a call. At 12:30 A.M., the other wife finally convinced Shirley to go to bed and conserve her strength while she stayed up to take any phone calls. Shirley made her promise to wake her immediately if one came.

About the time I was having my first dinner in the dispensary, news of my rescue finally funneled back to Florida. At the first ring of the phone, Shirley sprang from the bed. Her friend answered the phone, but Shirley was at her side in a flash. Then, the phone was handed to her. A voice spoke calmly at the other end.

"Mrs. Fields, I'm happy to inform you that your husband has been rescued, and he's been taken to a base in Thailand. He has some injuries but is okay. That's all we know right now, but I'm sure he'll be calling you." Shirley clasped the phone against her breast, slowly inhaled a deep breath, and then turned toward her friend.

Tears trickled down Shirley's face, cascading through the crease of a smile. "He's okay. They picked him up, injured, but okay."

Shirley then collapsed forward into her friend's arms, and they hugged in joy. Her ordeal was over. Her prayers had been answered. She still didn't know yet if I was badly injured but decided she could handle that until I called. *As Kenny says, "A piece of cake,"* she thought.

Shirley decided to wait until morning to notify the rest of the family. She wanted our kids and parents to sleep while she regained her composure and strength. Shirley's friend suggested they break out a bottle to celebrate, and they spent the rest of the evening sipping wine and telling "hubby" stories.

As they talked, the younger wife told Shirley how she planned to cope with a war that she couldn't support. "I'm thrilled that Kenny is okay, but now I'm going to put the past three days out of my mind forever, as if it never happened. I'm not going to think that it could happen to my husband, and I'm not going to worry about him all the time."

Unfortunately, though, that was not the case. The ordeal caused such mental anguish that later on she wrote a "Dear John" letter to her husband. In that letter, she explained that she couldn't handle the war and wanted a divorce, which she later got. Soon thereafter, we heard she might have joined a hippy commune.

During breakfast, two other wives arrived, and they were ecstatic and relieved to hear the good news, so they called the other squadron wives to share the joy. Then Shirley called my parents and her mother. After that, Shirley felt the need to attend the morning church service. The other two wives thought that was a great idea and asked to go with her. Edna, a neighbor down the street, offered to watch the kids.

The three of them were seated in church, and after a few songs the pastor, who knew me and my plight, started his morning prayer. He got to a point where he was asking God to watch over me and keep me safe till rescued. One of the wives was sitting next to the aisle and motioned to a nearby usher. She whispered that I had been rescued, and he went to the pulpit in the midst of the pastor's prayer and informed him of my rescue. The pastor continued to pray and thanked God for my safety.

On 2 June 1968, during a major-network prime-time news program, a recap was given of that day's action in Vietnam. (I have been unable to verify this directly from CBS News, but several shipmates aboard *America*, whose names I have no record of, told me that their parents personally heard it on their televisions.) On the "CBS Evening News with Walter Cronkite," Cronkite ended his program with, "Today, in Vietnam, the Air Force announced they rescued a Navy pilot thirty-nine hours after he was shot down and after 189 sorties were flown in the largest rescue effort of the war thus far." Then, as was his custom during the war, he finished with, "And that's the way it was today in Vietnam."

At 11 P.M. that night, Shirley was in a deep sleep. The past few days had taken their toll, but her routine had returned to normal, and she was now alone with the kids. She still had no idea whether my injuries were serious. Suddenly, she was awakened by the doorbell.

Oh no, has Kenny died? Half asleep, she ran to the door. A messenger was there with another telegram from the chief of naval personnel. Trembling, she closed the door and tore open the envelope. "I am pleased to inform you that your husband, Lt. Kenny Wayne Fields, has been recovered alive as a result of search and rescue operations and has been returned to military control." Shirley was relieved but disappointed that it didn't spell out my injuries.

Meanwhile, back at NKP, it was daylight on the fourth day. Nail 69 and two Sandys flew back to the area where Sandy 7 went in and conducted a more extensive search pattern over a five-square-mile area. The weather was crappy, and they again found no indication that Sandy 7 was still in the area. By nightfall of the fifth day, Nail 69 was back in Bangkok finishing up his massage. Hopefully, he would run across Nail 66 there, and the two of them could tip a few beers and decide who had come closest to killing me.

Over the next four days, an extensive search continued for Sandy 7, but nothing was found so the search was again officially closed. Immediately after that, the no-bomb-line that had been placed around him and me was canceled, and an Arc Light B-52 mission then clobbered the area around the enemy base camp where Sandy and I had spent two nights, about one mile apart.

During the ensuing two weeks, Sandy 8 talked to every participant for clues and diligently spent a little extra time at the end of every mission to search for his leader, Sandy 7. Finally, even Sandy 8 wrote him off.

My stay at NKP lasted fourteen days. During the afternoon of the second day, I was debriefed by Air Force air intelligence. The Spook was interested only in my escape and evasion activities and had no interest in the location of enemy gun sites, base camp, or troops. Weird, huh? However, he confirmed that a B-52 strike had already blasted the area and should have taken them all out. Sandy 7's and my shoot-downs may have precipitated the death of thousands of enemy soldiers—if they had not yet left the area.

The flight surgeon also paid a visit that afternoon, and after a cursory exam said I was in good condition. Several fragments had gone three- to four-inches deep, but all were clean wounds and would close over in a couple of weeks. His only explanation for the continued pain in my right foot was that it was probably nerves and would go away with relaxation. He only laughed and blamed the corpsman when I quizzed him about why I was patched up before the dried blood was removed.

Jolly 9 and his co-pilot came by after dinner. "Hello, Streetcar, we're the Jolly Greens who pulled you out of the jungle. How're you doing?"

I wanted desperately to jump out of bed and hug them, but couldn't. I tried verbally to express my gratitude, but it felt inadequate. I wished I were better at such matters. Nevertheless, I shook their hands and told them they were my heroes because I alone knew just how much enemy fire they had braved to rescue me. I also told them I would be forever in their debt, and I hoped they would get the medals they deserved.

They graciously accepted my compliment, and then Jolly 9 spoke. "You did everything right and maintained your cool, or we would never have gotten you out." His comment made me feel the best I'd felt since getting shot down.

Then, Jolly 9 presented me with a souvenir cigarette lighter with a Jolly emblem on the side, and also three of his calling cards. The first said, "We bring 'em back alive." The second said, "Good for one free ride on a Jolly Green Giant." And the third said, "Need a pick-me-up? Contact Crown, Sandy & Jolly Green on 243.0 emergency guard channel." We had a good time rehashing the saga and then the Jollys were gone, and I hoped I never needed their services again.

Over the next few days, I had other visitors. The Crown mission commander came in and lifted my spirits tremendously since I wasn't completely sure yet how the other folks had perceived my actions on the ground. I had done my best, but that might not be good enough to live with for the rest of my life. Crown's nice words gave me great consolation.

"Streetcar, you were the coolest one on the radio of the entire rescue, and that added a calming effect to a really hectic, frantic situation. I don't believe you would have made it back without that coolness under fire and threat of capture."

In a few days, the prospective commanding officer of the Sandy squadron paid a visit and sauntered in like a true fighter pilot. He said he hadn't flown the mission, but that the Sandys who had flown told him they were scared shitless because it was so dangerous, and it was the general consensus of most that it was too big a risk to attempt rescue under the circumstance. According to him, I owed my life to the commanding general, Seventh Air Force. If not for the general's persistence, I would have been left on the ground to fend for myself until I hiked to a safer area. He was proud of his Sandys and said they went beyond the call of normal duty to get me out.

I wholeheartedly agreed with him, raved about the Sandy's performance, and told him I would name my next child "Sandy." Then he got to the main thrust of his visit, which was to get my details on Sandy 7, which I recounted willingly. Years later, I learned that my Sandy visitor (Col. William Jones) earned the Medal of Honor for his courageous actions during a Sandy combat mission.

A day or so later, Nail 66 bounded into the room with a big smile on his round face and grabbed my bandaged hand like I was a long-lost buddy. He appeared genuinely happy to see me, and I, too, felt a close kinship to the FAC who worked me on my first mission. He kept repeating how sorry he was that we got sucked in, and said it was his fault entirely, which I disputed. He followed that up with some kudos about my bombing accuracy and our great BDA. There was one problem, though. He was still having nightly dreams wherein my tumbling plane awoke him, in a sweat, and his R & R hadn't helped in that regard. But, he had another idea that might. He wanted me to go to the Officers' Club with him. I was on antibiotics, had no clothes, and hadn't been cleared by the flight surgeon to walk yet, so we agreed to delay and do it in three days.

Sure enough, on the appointed day at 8:30 P.M., Nail again bounded into the room. "Let's go," he said, and then proceeded to help me out of bed. We sneaked out the back door without telling anyone, and Nail ushered me to our private jeep. Nail said I shouldn't ask how he got it as we roared off to the O Club. When we walked inside, none of the pilots seemed to notice I had a hospital gown on because 95 percent were drunk as skunks. "Streetcar" was well known, everyone wanted to buy me a drink, and before long I was also drunk. Everyone said the Navy guy couldn't hold his booze, which I couldn't, maybe because I was still on medication. Several of the rescue pilots had tried to kill me during the rescue, and now Nail and his buddies were making one last attempt. I have no memory of the ride back to the dispensary!

That night, I slept fitfully and awoke, sweating like a pig. I'd experienced awful nightmares during most of the night, and I couldn't understand what was happening. Had the booze caused it, or was it because I had recounted my evasion story to most of the pilots in the bar? I was still pondering the situation, and still sweating, when the flight surgeon rolled in around 10 A.M. I described my symptoms. In his medical opinion, I was suffering from post-traumatic stress. *Hogwash*, I thought. I had slept soundly for several nights before now.

"Try not to think about it or discuss your combat experience for a few days to allow yourself to unwind. Then you should be okay," he said. Then he made a point to tell me again that I shouldn't walk until he cleared me. Did he know about the O Club trip?

During the O Club visit, one of the pilots had explained how I could call my wife from the MARS hut just outside the dispensary. After lunch, I slipped out the back door again, found the station, and explained my situation to the operator. In no time, he had me on the phone with my wife. The connection was poor and we lost the signal after a couple of minutes, but that was enough to make both of us feel good. Just the sound of Shirley's voice lifted my soul.

Over the next few nights, my sweats and nightmares worsened to the point I could hardly get any sleep, but the doc still insisted it was due to stress, or maybe a virus. I asked if I might have malaria, but for some reason he didn't think so. On the fourteenth day, the doc finally released me to duty, but I hadn't had any communication with anyone in the Navy about transportation to USS *America*.

I went to the lone Navy squadron based at NKP to inquire about a ride to Danang, and fortunately met a squadron navigator who was a former training classmate. He requisitioned new fatigues and boots for me and scheduled a meeting with his commanding officer. I requested that one of his planes ferry me to Danang so I could ride the carrier-on-board delivery (COD) plane back to my ship, but he thought it would be too dangerous for one of his slow P2-V planes to traverse the high-threat area between Danang and NKP. My request was denied, but I couldn't blame him. I agreed. It was too dangerous because his two-engine prop planes only cruised at a measly 160 knots, yet their mission was to drop electronic monitoring devices along the Ho Chi Minh Trail. Only a few weeks before, one had been shot down, and the crew of nine had been forced to bail out over enemy territory. I wasn't overly enthused about riding the slow-mover myself, but it seemed to be my only option. The CO promised to send a message to the ship that I needed a ride home. I left the squadron in a quandary.

Fortunately, that afternoon a squadron buddy, Lieutenant Brown, had to divert to Danang to off-load some hung bombs before returning to *America*. While there, he found a landline phone and called me. It was great to hear his voice, and he seemed really thrilled about my escape. For the first time, though, I was told that my wingie, Iceman, had ejected shortly after I was shot down. That news destroyed me. I knew then that my first combat mission would forever be considered by many to have been a total failure. Before hanging up, my buddy promised he would personally relay to Skipper my request for a ride back to *America*. Skipper then informed CAG, who made it happen. Later that evening, the P-2 squadron CO was ordered to fly me to Danang the next day. On my last night in Thailand, my navigator friend took me into the little town of Nakhon Phanom for a sightseeing tour and buffalo steak dinner.

Late on the afternoon of the fifteenth day, I was welcomed back aboard USS *America* by a rousing, cheering group of shipmates on the flight deck. It felt good to be back, but things went downhill from there.

After dinner that evening, Skipper asked me to sit beside him in the Ready Room during the nightly movie. Before it started, he surprised me with a statement and question. There was a Navy instruction that directed that if a pilot's name was divulged to the enemy by flight gear left on the ground, the pilot would not be required to fly further combat missions against the same enemy. Skipper asked if I wanted him to invoke that Instruction on my behalf.

Without any misgivings, I answered, "No, Sir."

"Okay, then," Skipper said. "Let's watch the movie and talk tomorrow about getting you back in the saddle as soon as the flight surgeon gives you an 'up' chit."

It was nice to know Skipper still wanted me to fly as one of his boys, but I wondered if my wife would concur with my decision. Many years later, she provided the answer in a Veterans' Day card: "Kenny, Thank you for serving our country so honorably for twenty-two years. Some of it was very difficult but I would not want you to change any of it. I love you, Shirley."

That love was not shared by everyone. The next day, without any advance notice, CAG directed Skipper and me to accompany him to the admiral's quarters aboard *America*. I had no idea what to expect, but once we were in the admiral's presence, CAG shocked me when he told the admiral I had screwed up by violating his airwing policy of "one bomb run only" when AAA was present. CAG wanted the admiral's concurrence to put me before a Speedy Board (pilot's disposition hearing) to determine if my wings should be taken away. I just about fell out of my seat.

Calmly, the admiral then asked me to describe my first and second runs, which I did in an honest and precise manner. Afterward, without hesitation, he announced his decision. "CAG, I would have flown the mission just like Lieutenant Fields did, and I commend him for his action." He turned back to me and said, "Welcome back, Kenny."

Then he turned and asked, "Will there be anything else, CAG?"

The answer was, "No, Sir."

As we walked back to the Ready Room, CAG mumbled about a lot of displeasure with Skipper and me.

But my spirits elevated over the next few days. One after another, a countless number of shipmates gave me press clippings their parents had sent from their hometown newspapers about my mission, and many said their moms and dads sent their wishes for a speedy recovery. That support from home motivated me to try and get back in the cockpit as soon as possible.

A few days later, I was asked to brief the air-wing flight crews about my encounter in Laos. During that brief, unknown to the other pilots, I developed my most severe chills to date and started physically shaking. I'm sure some of the pilots thought I was just nervous as I recounted my story. After the brief, I was admitted to sick bay. The flight surgeon sat at the end of my bed and rummaged through his medical book as he listened to my symptoms. He concluded I most probably had malaria.

After only a few days aboard ship, I rode the COD to Subic Bay with orders to check into the hospital. Malaria was confirmed, and after two days of treatment, my chills and sweats went away. On the third day, however, the room started to spin, and I suspected some type of overdose and demanded a review of my medicine. Sure enough, I had been overdosed, and after the dosage was reduced I returned to normal. However, my foot still hurt like hell, so a few days later I was transferred to Clark AFB to see a specialist.

A surgeon decided to do exploratory surgery on my buttock where I had taken some CBU damage. Once inside, he found four more CBU pellets and discovered that shrapnel had damaged the sciatic nerve, and that was causing my foot pain. He inserted some type of packing around the area of the damaged nerve and it alleviated most of the pain. Oddly, during my recovery period, the surgeon tried his best to convince me I had taken enough risk, and he thought I should take Skipper's offer to go home instead of returning to combat. I again refused to abort, so the surgeon offered me orders for R&R in Hawaii before I returned to the ship. I accepted, and coordinated to have Shirley meet me there.

Amazingly, she was able to pull it off on short notice, and two days later I met her plane in Honolulu. By then I had dropped from my normal 145 down to 119 pounds, so she was shocked, but happy to see me. She, though, had gained weight because she was then about five month's pregnant. We had a wonderful three days together.

Our reunion was just as I had imagined while in the jungle. I met Shirley's plane in paradise. As she walked down the ramp and saw me, her cute face glowed, and I knew before she said the words that I was her love, and she, mine. I enfolded her in my arms and her body radiated energy within me—energy that I had been sorely missing since my rescue. At that moment I truly realized we had been made for each other by God and that we would be together and love each other for the rest of our lives. During our three days of frolicking, Shirley never once tried to talk me out of returning to combat. She only asked, "Do you have to go back?" I answered, "Yes." I couldn't forgo combat on a sour note.

Good times and warm, fuzzy feelings didn't last long. On my return flight to Clark AFB, I had a recurrence of malaria, so I returned to the hospital, where I was treated with a different medicine. During that stay, my bed bumped across the room one day because of a small earthquake, and that confirmed for me that my first combat cruise was indeed jinxed. Eventually I made it back to the ship, where the bad news continued.

The flight surgeon discovered my back had not been X-rayed after the ejection, and after doing so, he found I had a compressed fracture of the lower vertebrae caused by the seat pan striking my butt during the ejection. That meant I couldn't return to flight duty until he determined me fit. That meant administrative duties only for me, and I painfully watched as my fellow squadron pilots accumulated about seventy-five missions each while I was grounded. My morale was very, very low during that time, as even some of my squadron mates questioned why I hadn't jumped at the chance to go home.

Finally, four months after my shoot-down, I put a fresh bag of Redman in my survival vest and flew my second combat mission. It was over North Vietnam as the wingie of my gung-ho squadron ops officer. To ensure I hadn't lost my stick skills, or my confidence, he had me fly in tight combat cruise formation as we did acrobatics over North Vietnam for about five minutes. He found me capable, so we proceeded to our target where we promptly got hosed by a couple of 37s, but the fire was nothing like I had encountered on my first mission. However, during the mission debrief, my ops officer said the enemy AAA had been the heaviest he had seen in his seventy-five missions. I laughed, and told him there were places with a lot more out there. A few minutes later, I was told my plane captain had discovered that I had taken an unknown enemy round in my plane's nose radome, which required its replacement. Two missions, two planes hit! Was I jinxed, or what? But I flew another thirty-one missions during that combat cruise without further incident. However, it was not uncommon for me to hear after many of those missions that the flight had experienced more AAA than the pilots had seen prior to flying with me. It seemed I was a magnet for AAA. Finally it ended, and the ship left the line and set sail for the continental United States (CONUS).

Because of my wife's due date, I was allowed to fly home on the "magic carpet" commercial jet with other air wing pilots instead of riding the ship back. We landed in San Francisco for a layover, and I accompanied a buddy to get a haircut in the airport barbershop. While there, four customers in the shop made continuous slanderous remarks about our uniforms and Vietnam service. That was a helluva welcome home for us, and I was ready to fight again right there, in the barbershop, but my buddy urged caution.

I arrived home just days before our third child, Todd, was born. I wanted to name him Sandy, but Shirley didn't feel that we should do that since it would constantly remind her of the war. Now, I wish I had insisted, or at least given him that nickname, or maybe "Jolly."

A year passed quickly, and once again, my squadron deployed to Yankee Station. That time, we pilots carried 9mm pistols versus the .38 snub-nose, and had new batteries for our survival radios. On my first mission of that cruise, a strange twist of fate occurred.

I was the section leader of a four-plane flight. We checked in with Cricket and were given the bearing and distance from Danang for rendezvous with a Nail FAC. I didn't even have to check the map—the numbers are stamped in my brain. Unbelievably, it was the same target area at Tchepone as when I was shot down on my first mission a year earlier. I had ninety miles to think about the possible ramifications of the coincidence.

As we arrived overhead the Nail, the visibility was CAVU so I could see the actual area where I had evaded one year earlier. Was someone trying to tell me something? My flight leader announced that he and his wingman would make two bomb runs each before my section was cleared in. Crap. As an experienced combat pilot, I knew his section would wake up the gunners and make my section sitting ducks. Sure enough, AAA soared up at the two planes during all four individual runs and I had to watch, knowing the gunners would be zeroed in and just waiting for my section. Fortunately, the flight leader recognized the intensity of fire and his mistake. After his last run, he instructed my section to only make one run each, and I concurred whole-heartedly.

The Nail gave me a target smoke near the river, and I told my wingie to roll in tight behind me. After we dropped our bombs and cleared the target, Nail reported that one plane's bombs were on target, but the other plane's bombs had been long, off target. My wingie's bombs had hit the smoke, but my bombs, which Nail thought were long, hit right where I aimed. I placed them dead center in the midst of pots and pans in the base camp I had walked around a year earlier. It was payback time.

During that second combat cruise, I flew another 108 missions, mostly over North Vietnam, for a total of 139 in my two combat deployments. Each of the last 138 missions was a piece of cake compared to my first. Coincidently, my shoot-down occurred on 31 May 1968, and my last mission was exactly two years later, on 31 May 1970. Our bombs that day caused four secondary explosions, and it was a great way to end my combat duty.

I'm Streetcar 304, Lt. Kenny Wayne Fields, USNR. After so much fun, I stayed in the Navy and retired after twenty-two years of service, 3,350 flight hours (mostly in single-engine jets), and 475 aircraft carrier landings. Shirley and I developed and managed the Burke Racquet & Swim Club in the Fairfax, Virginia, area and we remain silent partners. Afterward, we owned and operated three electronics retail stores, but are now retired and live modestly in North Carolina.

Iceman, Lt. Fred Lentz, USN, returned to duty aboard USS *America* just a day after his ejection. Weeks later, it was determined his plane had flamed out due to incorrect switch settings through no fault of his own. The A-7 "Pilot Pocket Checklist" for emergency procedures was changed to reflect a new procedure for management of fuel switches during in-flight refueling of the A-7.

Iceman initially considered turning in his pilot wings, but was convinced by fellow pilots that day one had just been a fluke. He continued to fly combat missions during the next three weeks, but then things turned sour again. He launched from the ship with eight 500-pound mines. At one mile ahead of the ship and five hundred feet above the water, he made a quick transmission to the air boss.

"Streetcar 308 has heavy smoke in the cockpit, and the plane is shaking, over."

The air boss replied, "Say again, Streetcar."

Just then, Iceman heard a loud boom, and the engine seized. His jet was powerless. Without hesitation, he ejected, landed safely in the water, and was plucked from the sea without injury before he had a chance to get in his raft. CAG met him on the flight deck and said Iceman was making a habit of ejections.

Though he ejected twice in three weeks, Iceman continued to fight in a gutsy and meritorious manner. He bravely completed our first combat cruise and returned again with me a year later to complete our second combat deployment together. After our first disastrous mission, he flew an additional 187 combat missions.

Iceman eventually retired from the Navy after twenty-five years, 4,420 flight hours (many as a test pilot in fifty different types of aircraft), an amazing total of 720 aircraft carrier landings, and an additional 666 aircraft carrier "touch and goes" as a test pilot. After retirement from the Navy, he worked for fifteen years as a civilian test and evaluation engineer with the Naval Weapons Center, rising to the position of chief test engineer wherein he approved over five hundred flight test plans. He is now retired and lives in Victor, Montana, and his ex-wife, Jenny, lives in San Diego, California. I believe it's fortunate for all Americans that Iceman didn't follow through on his threat to give up his Wings of Gold.

Skipper, Cdr. Jack Jones, USN, continued to serve honorably and eventually retired from the Navy. He had flown valiantly during the Korean War, and during our time with him in Vietnam none of us ever saw him back off from any target, no matter the danger. He was fearless. He was also one of the nicest guys you could ever meet. But he never received another promotion. He wasn't promoted to captain, and that fact still weighs on me as I sometimes think his support of me may have been the unjust cause. He is now deceased. His wife Doris lives part of the year in Colorado Springs and the remainder in Surprise, Arizona.

Spider, Lt.Cdr. Ken Webb, USN, logged fifty-two combat missions in the A-4E prior to my shoot-down and completed another ninety-nine in the A-7 afterward. During that time, he participated in the rescue of six pilots including one mission that was so harrowing the Navy rescue helicopter pilot received the Medal of Honor. I believe the Navy was extremely callous and selfish in regard to Spider's brave effort to buy me time after I first hit the ground. He deserved a medal for heroism because he certainly saved me from capture. But none was awarded. Spider stayed in the Navy and retired after twenty-seven years, 3,750 flight hours, and 563 aircraft carrier landings. After that, he was president of a construction company and then director of asset management for the U.S. Treasury seized-property program. He is now retired and lives in Bellevue, Washington.

Nail 66, Capt. Jon McMurtry, USAF, was sleep-deprived and haunted by nightmares of my plane tumbling end over end for more than a month after the shoot-down, but he continued to fly another 226 combat missions before the end of his tour. After that, he reported to duty at the USAF Academy where the legendary fighter pilot Gen. Robin Olds presented Nail 66 with a Silver Star for bravery during my rescue. Nail 66 retired from military service after twenty-eight years, 6,252 flight hours, and 250 combat missions. After that, he worked with a company that specialized in the design and manufacture of aviation training equipment, and later in various positions as a safety specialist. He and his wife, Jane, now reside in Tampa, Florida.

Nail 69, Capt. Pete Lappin, USAF, continued to fly combat missions for another eight months and also received the Silver Star for his truly heroic efforts during my rescue. After seven years of military service and 5,610 total pilot hours (of which 2,510 were combat), he left the military and became an airline pilot. Following a seventeen-year period with Continental Airlines, he became a stockbroker and now works and lives in Las Vegas, Nevada, with his wife, Becky. He's now my financial advisor.

Sandy 3, Maj. Mel Bunn, USAF, safely completed the remainder of his one-year tour and received the Silver Star for his effort to rescue me. Later, in 1970, he participated in the highly courageous surprise raid on the Son Tay POW camp in North Vietnam. Unfortunately, the prisoners had been recently moved, but the raid inside North Vietnam caused a consolidation of prison camps and is thought to have greatly improved the conditions of all POWs then held by North Vietnam. Mel retired from the Air Force after twenty-seven dedicated years. For years, he worked in the real estate business in Florida, but has since passed away. Mel's wife, June, lives in Ft. Walton Beach, Florida.

Sandy 5, Maj. Bill Palank, USAF, retired from the Air Force after twenty-six years, 8,500 flight hours, and 1,940 combat hours. For my mission, he received a Silver Star, his second. He's now in his eighties and still flies his own refurbished SNJ-6 plane in Fair Oaks, California. I send him a Christmas card each year to wish him well, although we have never met face to face.

Sandy 8, Capt. George Marrett, USAF, did in fact make it back alive without any of his "in the event of my death" letters being mailed to his wife, Jan. He received a Distinguished Flying Cross (DFC) for his bravery and airmanship during my rescue effort and completed another 185 combat missions before the end of his tour. Then, he said "sayonara" to the Air Force. Upon his return to the states, he accepted a test pilot position with the Hughes Aircraft Company, where he was involved for twenty years with the testing of many of today's modern weapons. After that, he became a highly successful book author, having written *Cheating Death, Howard Hughes: Aviator,* and *Testing Death.* In between books, he pilots his own 1945 Stinson L-5E to air shows around the West Coast from his home in Atascadero, California. Recently, he was inducted into the Nebraska Aviation Hall of Fame.

Sandy 9, Maj. Tom Campbell, USAF, was the on-scene commander during my final rescue, and his effort was so heroic that his unit recommended him for the Medal of Honor. It was downgraded to the Air Force Cross, but is the second-highest award possible for bravery under fire. After that, he flew another hundred combat missions during which he was further commended with a Silver Star and two DFCs. Sandy 9 told me that fifteen of the twenty-four squadron pilots he began his one-year tour with were either killed or injured badly enough to warrant a free ride home. Such was the life of a Sandy pilot in 1968 over Laos. But he continued to serve in the Air Force and retired after twenty-two years and 4,300 flight hours. Before final retirement, he was the general manager of a machine manufacturing plant and now lives with his wife, Ada, in Henegor, Alabama. Each time we talk, he begins by saying, "Streetcar, you're the luckiest man alive."

Jolly 9, Capt. Dave Richardson, USAF, accomplished his heroic rescue of me during his 107th and final combat mission. Only twice in those missions did he encounter the shielding light that protected him on my rescue. For his bravery under fire, he was awarded the Silver Star. His Air Force career spanned twenty-four years and 3,000-plus flight hours. After the Air Force, he taught eighth-grade math for thirteen years, and now he and his wife, Kaye, operate an online travel agency at kay.worldventures.com in Abilene, Kansas. Jolly 9 has carried his lucky nickel now for thirty-seven years.

Sandy 7, Capt. Ed Leonard, USAF, participated in the successful rescues of seventeen pilots. His attempt to rescue me on day one was his 257th and final combat mission, and for his bravery he was awarded his third Silver Star. Now, I would like to provide a summary of his POW experience, much of it in his own words.

Following capture, he was force-marched on his broken foot for a week through bombed-out jungle during daylight. Nights during the first week were normally spent in caves. One afternoon he was herded into a cave, and at dusk he was put on a truck and strapped face-down to the bed. Periodically during the drive that night, the truck would stop on the edge of a village, where he was offloaded with his arms bound behind his back, then he was pulled by a noose about his neck through the village.

In each village, he walked through a gauntlet of angry villagers who had been whipped to frenzy by a small band of political organizers. The villagers were armed with clubs, jabbing sticks, and rocks. Once he made it to the other side of the village, he would be placed back on the truck until the scene was repeated at the next village. At dawn, the truck would park several hundred yards from the road under the camouflage of trees and then commence the same routine again at dark.

After several weeks of that, he was offloaded at the edge of a broad valley and marched several miles across rice paddies to a jungled rise. Under a tree canopy, Sandy was placed in his own private bamboo cage. Other cages were nearby and contained various POWs, including U.S. Army infantrymen and chopper pilots, a captured television crew, a military store (BX) clerk from Saigon, a German female nurse, and a U.S. Agency for International Development (AID) pig expert.

During the second evening in that camp, he was led down a trail past a large rice paddy with a small stream nearby where he was told to bathe. As he was about to wade in, the head of a Marine captain surfaced. He introduced himself as the senior ranking officer of the camp, and queried Sandy 7 as to his date of rank. Upon hearing that Sandy 7 outranked him, the Marine captain made a prodigious statement.

"Now, you're the senior ranking officer, you poor son-of-a-bitch."

Sandy then learned he had command of eighty-six infantrymen, Special Forces, civilians, and Marines.

After several weeks of self-pity and believing he was a dead man, he finally grasped what he had to do. He would serve his fellow POWs to the best of his ability, even if it meant physical pain. *After all, he thought, what can they do to me? I'm most probably going to die anyway.*

After several months the camp occupants were moved to an old French military post sixteen miles southwest of Hanoi. The POWs called it "Farnsworth," after an old Red Skelton routine. Sandy 7 spent the next several years there, doing his best to lead and enhance secret communications among prisoners.

When let outside his cell, he did his best to act as if on parade—head up, shoulders square—because the lives of his POWs depended on his action. Physical torture and brutality became so commonplace it was routine, and he was engaged in battle twenty-four hours a day. His rules of battle were simple: Keep faith with your country, keep faith with your fellow prisoners, and resist the enemy to the utmost of your ability.

Ed's plight was magnified as senior ranking officer. Whenever a prisoner was caught trying to communicate, that individual and the senior ranking officer had their attitudes corrected with pain, sleep deprivation, and dehydration. Stretching and twisting body joints seemed to be the favorite way to get a prisoner to change his attitude. After two prisoners escaped from another camp, Ed and three others were tortured for six weeks until they were broken into subhuman residue. At that moment, Ed was overcome with a sense of complete failure, shame, and towering guilt. Finally his ropes were removed, the beatings stopped, food and water were restored, and sleep was allowed. Six months later, he was finally able to struggle to his feet without help.

However, he soon rebounded and regained his ability to resist further. But boredom weighed upon him, too. For example, one day a POW's voice came from a solitary cell across the compound.

"My goodness, October 3rd, 1970, already. Where does the time go?"

From another cell came a simple reply, "It's 1971 already."

In late 1970, after an unsuccessful American raid on the empty Son Tay POW camp in North Vietnam, all of the POW camps in the countryside were relocated within Hanoi, and Ed's group ended up at one called Plantation Gardens. Soon thereafter, Ed took several POWs to task in front of the guards for not following the code of conduct. He was chained to a wall. When he came to later that night, he had excruciating pain from the waist up and could feel nothing below the waist. His action caused morale to improve in the camp, and the POW resistance stiffened even more.

Finally, in 1972, after five years as a POW, Ed was released along with the other POWs. His teeth had been knocked out, his neck had been cut, and both shoulders and both hips were screwed up. He weighed only 123 pounds, having lost nearly 80 while a POW. A comical side point of his POW days was a letter for him, delivered to his father's address, notifying Ed that he had been drafted (while he was a POW).

During the Vietnam War, fifty-four A-7 pilots were shot down during combat. I was one of twenty-six who were rescued. Twenty of those shot down died from the combat action or while a POW. I'm a survivor, thanks to Sandy 7 and the others.

In 1998 Sandy 8 coordinated a reunion of pilots involved in my rescue. We had met several times in the past thirty years, so I picked him up at the airport on my way to the motel. After checking in, I couldn't wait for our first scheduled group meeting to finally meet Sandy 7 for the first time, and instead went to his room.

At his door, I paused in trepidation. I felt nervous because it suddenly dawned on me that I hadn't thought about what I was going to say upon meeting Sandy 7. How do I express my gratitude to a man who tried to save me, but instead spent over five years in a tortuous prison, and I've yet to thank him personally? I had thirty years to think about it and still didn't know the right words, but I knocked. A lovely lady opened the door.

"Hi, I'm Streetcar 304." In a flash, she broke out in a smile, hugged me, and thanked me for saving her husband's life. I was caught off guard, but followed her through the door and saw Sandy 7 for the first time, standing erect but leaning on a cane. My heart sank as I walked toward him with my hand out.

"Hey Sandy 7, I'm Streetcar 304, and I'm sorry it took me so long to say thank you, buddy."

He smiled broadly, ignored my hand, and gave me a gigantic bearhug, which I returned mightily. Then he quickly moved to brace himself against a chair in order to stand and talk. He, too, reiterated that I had saved his life, because if not for his capture, he would have haphazardly killed himself on some other mission because he had gotten so aggressive. I thought he was just saying that to make me feel better and break the ice, but he's a huge man in more ways than one.

As we talked, I learned that Sandy's current wife was the reason he was in a hurry to make the MAC flight to the Philippines on the day of my rescue. Suzanne was waiting in a friend's empty apartment at Clark AFB for him, as he was being shot down. She diligently waited, terribly worried because he hadn't shown up at the appointed time. Two days afterward, a mutual Army nurse friend called her and asked if she had read that day's *Stars and Stripes* newspaper. It told the story of my shoot-down, rescue, and, to her dismay, the shoot-down of Ed. That evening she sat on the porch during a wild Philippine storm. Bolts of lighting flashed across the sky and thunder roared as rain and tears ran down her face. She sat there for hours, crying and wondering why her love had been snatched away. Years later, after Ed had been released from prison, the two of them finally found each other again and now live happily in Illwaco, Washington.

Later that day, I finally met Nail 66 again and, for the first time, Nail 69, Sandy 3, Sandy 9, and Sandy 5's wingie, Capt. Gene McCormack. During the two days together, we relived the rescue over and over and listened to each other's versions. Several years later, Jolly 9 joined us for a reunion, and about that same time I talked by phone with Sandy 5 for the first time. Now, we all keep tabs on each other through e-mail, phone, cards, or reunions. A brotherhood has been formed.

Sandy 7 retired from the Air Force after twenty-four years, during which he logged 8,000 hours of flight, 2,500 of which contained a lot of freaky combat time. After that, he graduated from law school, was a defense attorney, a prosecutor, and finally mayor of Illwaco, Washington. During that time, he has had shoulder and hip replacement surgery, but still smiles.

Now is the time for my final reflection on this saga. I joined the Navy fully expecting to fight a war if our civilian leaders deemed it necessary, and not just fly for the fun and pay and then back off when the situation got hairy. My heritage influenced me to fight a war as trained. I got sucked in on my first mission, but it could have occurred just as easily on my 138th. I don't regret my actions that day and am proud of the fact I fought, faltered, but returned to fight. I did, however, carry for thirty years the stigma placed on me by some Navy prima donnas who said that my shoot-down was a personal mistake. The reunion with the Air Force pilots in 1998—those who were actually in the arena with me and fully understood the precarious situation—finally alleviated most of the stigma.

I do regret that Sandy 7's life was changed by the events, but we both agree we wouldn't change our actions if given a second chance. I also regret that several of the pilots involved in the mission waged the war over and over in nightmares for years thereafter. But we all agree that even though things could have gone a little better or been done a little differently, we're proud of how we supported each other and the war effort.

Thirty-seven years have passed and not a day goes by that I don't think of 31 May 1968. All it takes to start the memories is the engine sound of a small plane overhead, a distant roll of thunder on a sunny day, or a nearby thumping helicopter. My wife says my legs run sometimes during sleep, and I sometimes wake up abruptly in a sweat. But 99 percent of my war memories are proud ones, not traumatic, nor unnerving. I got to see real live heroes in action. Not movie heroes, not sports heroes, but the real-deal ones. They are now my friends, and we share a lot in common. The enemy tried its best to blow us out of the sky, to intimidate the hell out of us, and in one case to tear us apart limb by limb. But all of us continued to fly another mission and fight another day to win a frapping war that we all knew was poorly supported back home.

I've read some articles stating that during the Vietnam "Conflict," an unsubstantiated 58,169 Americans were killed and 304,000 wounded, out of a total of 2.59 million who served. Most did so with courage and honor and left countless stories of heroic actions. I prefer to dwell on that courage rather than on the fact that not everyone had the will or audacity to win a war that many thought unwarranted. And I truly hope that heroism was the main theme that came across in this story. Sure, mistakes were made, but most were countered with true heroism. I hope this story inspires you to think twice about the word "hero." Use it only for the real ones!

In my prayer on day one, I told God I'd try to live a better life if I were rescued. My thought was similar to Psalms 50, verse 15: "And call upon me in the day of trouble. I will deliver thee, and thou shalt glorify me."

After rescue, I vowed a renewed dedication to God, country, and family. I can honestly state that I tried diligently, but often failed. I haven't always glorified God. I've served my country well and have done a halfway decent job with the family, but have shorted God at times. Only in recent years have I come to think more and more that God had a hand in my rescue for a purpose, for some type of life change. But why me? After thirty-seven years of waiting, that purpose has not been disclosed, or if it has, I've missed it. The question of purpose swells inside me at times to the point I want to scream and demand an answer. "What am I to do?" Often, I believe I missed the opportunity he gave me, perhaps by an untimely word from my mouth, and at other times I think it's still in my future. But maybe my God-given purpose was just to write this book in a feeble attempt to glorify him and to remind you who the real heroes are.

ABOUT THE AUTHOR

Kenny Fields is a coal miner's son, and proud to be so. He was born in Lex, West Virginia—a small mining community that bears the name of his great-grandfather. He was schooled in the southern mountain area of West Virginia, but during a four-year span while living in Kentucky, he attended a one-room school that used a traditional potbellied stove for heat. During his freshman year he attended Lockland High School in Ohio and played on the state-champion baseball team. Afterward, he was a three-sport athlete at Big Creek High School in West Virginia, which his schoolmate Homer Hickam wrote about in his best seller, *Rocket Boys*. Kenny graduated from Lincoln Memorial University where he married one of the school cheerleaders and played second base on the Railsplitter baseball team.

During twenty-two years in the Navy, Kenny compiled 3,350 flight hours, 139 combat missions, and 475 carrier landings. He was a bombardier/navigator in the A-3B, piloted A-7A and A-4C attack jets, and was a jet flight instructor in T-2s and TA-4s. After retiring from the Navy, he became a business entrepreneur and "piloted" the start-up of two small corporate ventures. He and his wife, Shirley, live in Mooresville, North Carolina.

Kenny believes his mountain heritage and athletic past provided the unique survival skills to evade the enemy after being shot down in Laos. . . .